HISTORICAL DICTIONARIES OF RELIGIONS,
PHILOSOPHIES, AND MOVEMENTS
Edited by Jon Woronoff

To the memory of my paternal grandmother
Jessie Docherty (*née* Hill)
Born: Forfar, Scotland, September, 29 1874
Died: St. Andrews, Scotland, November, 20 1918
Domestic servant and victim of tuberculosis

Historical Dictionary of Organized Labor

Historical Dictionaries of Religions, Philosophies, and Movements, No. 10

James C. Docherty

The Scarecrow Press, Inc.
Lanham, Md., & London
1996

SCARECROW PRESS, INC.

Published in the United States of America
by Scarecrow Press, Inc.
4720 Boston Way
Lanham, Maryland 20706

4 Pleydell Gardens, Folkestone
Kent CT20 2DN, England

British Cataloguing-in-Publication Information Available

Library of Congress Cataloging-in-Publication Data

Docherty, J. C.
    Historical dictionary of organized labor / James C. Docherty.
        p. cm. — (Historical dictionaries of religions, philosophies, and
movements ; no. 10)
    Includes bibliographical references.
    ISBN 0–8108–3181–3 (cloth : alk. paper)
    1. Labor movement—History—Encyclopedias. 2. Trade-unions—
History—Encyclopedias. I. Title. II. Series.
HD4839.D58   1996
331.88'03—dc20   96–11417
                                                                CIP

⊖™ The paper used in this publication meets the minimum requirements of
American National Standard for Information Sciences—Permanence of
Paper for Printed Library Materials, ANSI Z39.48–1984.
Manufactured in the United States of America.

CONTENTS

EDITOR'S FOREWORD

This is a trying time for organized labor. Many old-established labor unions are losing members, while young ones in the Third World are having trouble striking root. The old threat of Communism on the left has receded, but the growing penchant for untrammelled free enterprise around the world entails other perils. In general, labor unions and labor parties are less popular than before, and fewer persons (union members or the general public) are swayed by labor causes. While this can-and should-be seen as a failure, it is partially one born of success. It is only because the unions have been so successful in improving working conditions, reducing working hours, and providing better health and old-age coverage that they can be neglected in the luckier countries.

To know how much has been achieved by organized labor in the advanced countries, it is sufficient to consider the not-too-distant past, which is amply portrayed in this book. On the other hand, the situation in many developing countries remains harsh and worrisome. There is still much to be done; and, of the bodies committed to progress there, the unions are among the most important. What the tasks are is also described herein. The many entries on significant persons, places, and events, those on specific unions and countries, and others of a more general nature give us an excellent view of the past and present and some notion of the future. Additional background is provided in the introduction and chronology, while the statistical appendix includes an original contribution to our knowledge of the growth of unionism. Further information on all these subjects can be found in the bibliography. The author of this *Historical Dictionary of Organized Labor*, James C. Docherty, knows the field well from both the academic and current policy angles. He carried out the first scholarly investigation of the early years of organized labor in the railroads of southeastern Australia for his master's thesis and examined the social and urban impact of heavy industry on Newcastle for his doctoral thesis at the Australian National University.

Jon Woronoff
Series Editor

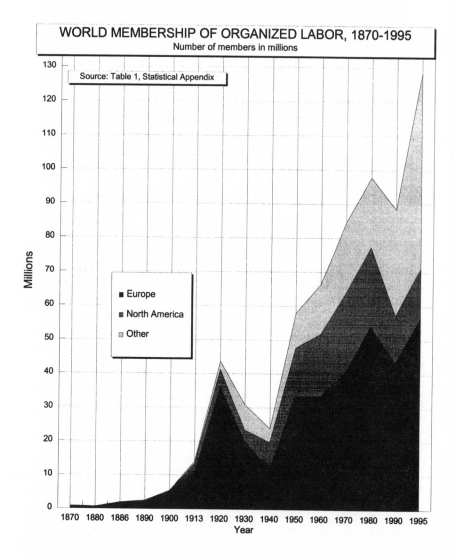

WORLD MEMBERSHIP OF ORGANIZED LABOR, 1870-1995
Number of members in millions

Source: Table 1, Statistical Appendix

■ Europe
■ North America
▨ Other

Millions

Year

PREFACE

This dictionary is an introduction and invitation to the historical study of organized labor. It is about what organized labor has done or tried to do rather than what it ought to have been. It is about a mass movement with many enemies. Some see organized labor as a barrier to the operation of a free-market economy and therefore harmful to economic growth; others consider it to be the vanguard of radical economic and social change. Too few consider organized labor in its own terms.

Despite appearances, this work is *not* an encyclopaedia, even though it contains much information which has not been conveniently made available in one work before. I underscore this now before reviewers take me to task over the omission of items they consider vital. I know only too well that to do full justice to the topic, a number of volumes would be needed.

That said, the dictionary conforms to the guidelines laid down by Scarecrow Press for this new series on *Religions, Philosophies, and Movements*. It provides 277 entries on individual countries, international as well as national labor organizations, major labor unions, leaders, ideas, political parties, and other aspects of organized labor such as changes in the composition of its membership. The entries are biased towards institutions because they tend to survive and so provide a framework for the interplay of individuals and ideas. They are also a useful way of capturing the unsuccessful as well as the successful part of the historical process. The entries are my selection from what is available and make no claim to be a representative sample. They reflect my judgments about what is important in a work of this scale. Others are welcome to disagree and no doubt will. Country entries cover all members of the Organization for Economic Co-operation and Development. All sixteen current international trade secretariats have their own entries as do all the principal international labor bodies both past and present.

My first aim in this dictionary is to make the subject as accessible as possible. Many of the works on organized labor frequently make implicit assumptions about the level of knowledge of their readers which may be difficult for beginners. Those unfamiliar with the topic might consider reading the entries on the United Kingdom, France, Germany, Italy, the United States, and Japan, as well as the

Introduction. The glossary of terms, chronology, statistical appendix, and the bibliography are designed to complement the entries and to act as signposts for finding out more about the subjects I have neglected in the body of the dictionary. I mention this as some of the information the Dictionary contains might be regarded as elementary by specialist readers. Nevertheless, I would like to think that even experts might find the work of interest.

My second aim is to show the variety of labor studies. Economists, political scientists, sociologists, and lawyers have long been well represented in this field, often long before historians showed any interest. These disciplines have much to offer historians either by asking new questions about the subject or developing improved frameworks for analysis. Similarly, industrial relations, although a comparatively recent arrival to the academic disciplines, has much to offer by its synthetic approach even though the focus of its study is usually on the present rather than the past. The dictionary also includes more information on Australia than is customary in such works, because I believe that organized labor in Australia deserves to be better known by scholars in the United States and Europe. My third aim is to encourage a greater international outlook on the topic than is apparent in most works on organized labor.

Apart from the limitations of space-which means that there was no alternative to be often brutally brief about important subjects-I found the scale of this work daunting. I take solace in the knowledge that no one individual knows all there is to know about organized labor but am grimly aware that its sheer scale means that the possibilities for errors and misleading statements are enormous; where these occur I take full responsibility. For research assistance, it is my pleasure to thank the International Confederation of Free Trade Unions, Professor Michael Quinlan (University of New South Wales), Tim Wardrop (Australian Bureau of Statistics), Raj Jadeja (Noel Butlin Archives Centre at the Australian National University), Louise Corcoran (British Department of Employment), Stephen Woodland (British Department of Trade and Industry), and Linda Walkden (Co-operative Wholesale Society, Manchester), and the authors of all the works I have used.

JAMES C. DOCHERTY
LYONS, A.C.T.
AUSTRALIA

June 1996

ACRONYMS

AAM	Amalgamated Association of Miners (United Kingdom: 1869-75)
AATUF	All-African Trade Union Federation (1961-73)
ACTU	Australian Council of Trade Unions (1927)
ACWA	Amalgamated Clothing Workers of America (1914)
AEU	Amalgamated Engineering Union (United Kingdom: 1920)
AFL-CIO	American Federation of Labor-Congress of Industrial Organizations (1955)
ALF	Australian Labour Federation (1889-1914)
ALP	Australian Labor Party (1891)
ALU	American Labor Union (1898-1905)
AMA	Amalgamated Miners' Association (Australia: 1874)
AMWU	Amalgamated Metal Workers' Union (Australia: 1973)
ASCJ	Amalgamated Society of Carpenters and Joiners (United Kingdom: 1860)
ASE	Amalgamated Society of Engineers (United Kingdom: 1851-1920)
AWU	Australian Workers' Union (1894)

CCOO	*Confederación Sindical de Comisiones Obreras* (Union Confederation of Workers' Commissions) (Spain: 1960s)
CEC	*Confédération Européenne des Cadres* (European Confederation of Managers) (1993)
CESI	*Confédération Européenne des Syndicats Indépendants* (Confederation of Independent European Trade Unions) (1990)
CGIL	*Confederazione Generale Italiana del Lavoro* (General Confederation of Italian Labor) (1944)
CGL	*Confederazione Generale di Lavoro* (General Confederation of Labor) (Italy: 1906-24)
CGT	*Confédération Générale du Travail* (France: 1895); *Central Geral dos Trabalhadores* (Brazil: 1986); *Confederación General del Trabajo* (Argentina: 1930); *Confédération Générale du Travail-Force Ouvriere* (General Confederation of Labor-Workers' Strength) (France: 1948)
CIO	Congress of Industrial Organizations (United States: 1933-55)
CIT	*Confederación Interamericana de Trabajadores* (Interamerican Confederation of Workers: 1948-51)
CITUB	Confederation of Independent Trade Unions of Bulgaria (1944)
CNLU	Colored National Labor Union (United States: 1869)
CNSLR	*Confederatia Nationala a Sindicatelator Libere din România* (National Free Trade Union Confederation of Romania) (1990)

COHSE	Confederation of Health Service Employees (United Kingdom: 1946-93)
CPUSTAL	*Congreso Permanente de Unidad Sindical de Los Trabajadores de America Latina* (Permanent Congress of Trade Union Unity of Latin American Workers) (1964)
CROM	*Confederación Regional Obrera Mexicana* (Confederation of Mexican Wage Earners) (1918)
ČS-KOS	*Česka a Slovenská Konfederace odborových* (Czech and Slovak Confederation of Trade Unions) (1989)
CSEU	Confederation of Shipbuilding and Engineering Unions (United Kingdom: 1891)
CTAL	*Confederación de Trabajadores de America Latina* (Confederation of Latin American Workers) (1938-62)
CTM	*Confederación de Trabajadores de Mexico* (Confederation of Mexican Workers) (1936)
CUT	*Central Unica de Trabajadores* (Chile: 1953-73); *Central Unitaria de Trabajadores* (Chile: 1988)
CWU	Communications Workers' Union of America (1945)
DAF	*Deutsche Arbeitsfront* (German Labor Front) (1933-45)
DGB	*Deutscher Gewerkschaftbund* (German Trade Union Federation) (1947)
DMV	*Deutscher Metallarbeiter-Verband* (German Metal Workers' Union) (1891-1933)
ETUC	European Trade Union Confederation (1973)

EUROCADRES Council of European Professional and Managerial Staff (1993)

FICSA   Federation of International Civil Servants' Assocations (1952)

FIOM   *Federazione Italiana Operai Metallurgici* (Italian Union of Metal Workers: 1901-24; 1944 to date)

FMWU   Federated Miscellaneous Workers' Union (Australia: 1915-92)

FOTALU   Federation of Organized Trades and Labor Unions of the United States and Canada (1881-86)

GFTU   General Federation of Trade Unions (United Kingom: 1899)

GMWU   General and Municipal Workers' Union (United Kingdom: 1924)

GNCTU   Grand National Consolidated Trades Union (United Kingdom: 1834)

IBT   International Brotherhood of Teamsters, Chauffeurs, Warehousemen, and Helpers of America (1903)

ICATU   International Confederation of Arab Trade Unions (1956)

ICFTU   International Confederation of Free Trade Unions (1949)

IFBWW   International Federation of Building and Woodworkers (1934)

IFCCPTE   International Federation of Commercial, Clerical, Professional, and Technical Employees (1921)

IFCEGW	International Federation of Chemical, Energy, and General Workers (1964)
IFCTU	International Federation of Christian Trade Unions (1920)
IFFTU	International Federation of Free Teachers' Unions (1928)
IFJ	International Federation of Journalists (1952)
IFPAW	International Federation of Plantation, Agricultural, and Allied Workers (1960)
IFTU	International Federation of Trade Unions (1901-45)
IFWPAU	International Federation of Workers in Public Administration and Utilities
IG Metall	*Industriegewerkschaft Metall* (Metal Workers' Industrial Union) (Germany: 1950)
IGF	International Graphical Federation (1949)
ILGWU	International Ladies' Garment Workers' Union (United States: 1900)
ILO	International Labour Organisation (1919)
ILU	International Labor Union (United States: 1878-c.1887)
IMF	International Metalworkers' Federation (1904)
ISAMMETU	International Secretariat for Arts, Mass Media, and Entertainment Trade Unions (1965)
ITGLWF	International Textile, Garment, and Leather Workers' Federation (1970)

ITU	International Typographical Union (United States: 1869)
ITWF	International Transport Workers' Federation (1898)
IUFAWA	International Union of Food and Allied Workers' Associations (1920)
IWMA	International Workingmen's Association (1864-76)
IWW	Industrial Workers of the World (United States: 1905)
LIGA	Democratic League of Independent Trade Unions (Hungary: 1989)
LSI	Labor and Socialist International (1923-39)
LO	*Landsorganisationen i Sverge* (Labor Union Federation of Sweden) (1898); *Landsorganisasjonen i Norge* (the Labor Union Federation of Norway) (1899)
MAGB	Miners' Association of Great Britain and Ireland (1842-47)
MIF	Miners' International Federation (1890)
MNU	Miners' National Union (United Kingdom: 1863-98)
MSzOSz	*Magyar Szakszervezetek Országos Szövetsége Tagszervezeteinek Címlistája* (National Confederation of Hungarian Trade Unions) (1990)
MWF	Mineworkers' Federation of Great Britain (1890-1945)
NALGO	National and Local Government Officers' Association (United Kingdom: 1946)

NAUL	National Amalgamated Union of Labour (United Kingdom: 1889-1924)
NAUTPL	National Association of United Trades for the Protection of Labour (United Kingdom: 1845-67)
NEA	National Educational Association (United States: 1857)
NLU	National Labor Union (United States: 1866)
NTU	National Trades Union (United States: 1833)
NUPE	National Union of Public Employees (United Kingdom: 1928)
OATUU	Organization of African Trade Union Unity (1973)
OBU	One Big Union
OECD	Organization for Economic Cooperation and Development
OPZZ	*Ogolnópolskie Porozumienie Zwiazków Zawodowych* (All-Poland Alliance of Labor Unions) (1984)
ORIT	*Organización Regional Interamericana de Trabajadores* (1951)
PAFL	Pan-American Federation of Labor (1918-40)
PSI	Public Services International (1935)
PTTI	Postal, Telegraph, and Telephone International (1920)
PTUC	Pacific Trade Union Community (1980)
SAF	*Svenska Arbetsgivaresöforreningen* (Swedish Employers' Confederation) (1902)

SAK	*Suomen Ammattiliittojen Keskusjärjestö* (Central Organization of Finnish Trade Unions) (1930)
SGB	*Schweizerischer Gewerkschaftsbund* (Swiss Labor Union Confederation) (1880)
SZOT	*Magyar Szakszervezetek Országos Tanácsá* (Central Council of Hungarian Trade Unions) (1948)
TGWU	Transport and General Workers' Union (United Kingdom: 1922)
TUC	Trades Union Congress (United Kingdom: 1868)
UADW	Universal Alliance of Diamond Workers (1905)
UAW	United Automobile Workers [full title: United Automobile, Aerospace, and Agricultural Implement Workers of America, International Union] (1935)
UGT	*Unión General de Trabajadores* (General Union of Workers) (Spain: 1888)
UMWA	United Mine Workers of America (1890)
USWA	United Steelworkers of America (1942)
WCL	World Confederation of Labor (1968)
WFTU	World Federation of Trade Unions (1945)
WLU	Western Labor Union (United States: 1898)
WU	Workers' Union (United Kingdom: 1898-1929)
ZAG	*Zentralarbeitsgemeinschaft* (Central Labor Association) (Germany: 1918-29)

INTRODUCTION

This dictionary could in some ways be seen as a study of failure. Since 1980, organized labor in most Western countries has faced falling membership, continued defeats by employers and a general loss of direction and power. Never before has there been so much questioning about the need for labor unions and their prospects for survival. Against this gloomy contemporary background, it seems especially important to take stock of the history of organized labor, to see where it came from and where it has been.

There are a number of reasons why the study of organized labor should be given more notice by the academic community rather than regarded as just another speciality. For all the research of the last thirty years, there is still a tendency to treat organized labor as a marginal topic in the general and economic histories of most countries. As a rule, organized labor has tried to make the world a fairer place. Even though it typically has only ever covered a minority of employees in most countries, its effects on their political, economic, and social systems have been generally positive. The historical record shows that when organized labor is repressed, the whole society suffers and is made less just. This introduction presents a general view of the development and growth of organized labor as a historical movement in a global perspective, explores some of the characteristics of organized labor and offers some observations on the crisis it has experienced in many countries since 1980.

LABOR IN HISTORY

The beginnings of organized labor

Labor unions are usually defined as voluntary organizations of employees created to defend or improve the pay and conditions of their members through bargaining with their employers. As institutions, labor unions have existed only in the last 200 years, that is with the advent of the Industrial Revolution, but in fact organized labor has existed throughout history. It is simply that in a documentary record dominated by the powerful, labor, unless it caused trouble, was hardly mentioned.

Bargaining between rulers and the ruled has always occurred to some degree. Often this bargaining took the form of petitions by labor

1

to their rulers complaining about some matter in the hope of redress. In 1152 B.C. the Egyptian pharaoh's tomb makers struck work over the failure of their rulers to supply them with grain; it was history's first recorded labor dispute. The Old Testament records that during the Israelites' Egyptian bondage, their foremen complained to the pharaoh about the lack of straw they needed to make their quota of bricks. The Old Testament also records the pharaoh's haughty dismissal of their complaints (Exodus 5:6-23).

Rulers from ancient times saw any unauthorized gatherings or organizations as a threat to social order. This can be shown by two examples from the Roman Empire. In about A.D. 54 there was a disturbance among the silversmiths of Ephesus over the threat to the trade in cult objects for the worship of Diana caused by the preaching of St. Paul. A local official pointed out that the gathering was illegal and could lead to the use of force by the Romans (Acts, 19: 23-40). A second example occurred in about A.D. 110 when Pliny the Younger, the governor of the troubled province of Bithynia, requested permission from the emperor Trajan to allow a fire brigade of 150 members to be organized. Trajan denied the request on the grounds that the brigade might become a focus for political opposition as had happened elsewhere in Asia Minor.

With most of the labor performed by tied labor forces or slaves, there was little scope for the formation of a large body of free individuals who earned their living by their labor in the societies of classical Greece and Rome. Indeed the concept of "labor" as a general function in these societies scarcely existed. Both the Greek and Latin words for work ($\check{\epsilon}\rho\gamma o\nu$ and *labor*) were associated with unremitting toil, compulsion, and slavery. The purpose of the government was to maintain the social and economic order. The Roman emperor Diocletian's well-known edict of maximum prices of A.D. 301 laid down maximum wages as well.

Despite government policy, some groups did engage in rudimentary forms of collective bargaining. Evidence for this comes from the early Byzantine Empire. In A.D. 544 one of the "new" laws of the emperor Justinian I forbade sailors and laborers from demanding or accepting pay increases on penalty of having to pay the treasury three times the amount at issue.

Although distant in time, these precedents showed the attitudes of the rulers towards their subjects which were held until fairly recently in recorded history. In the absence of political bargaining, most groups often had to resort to rebellion to make their presence felt. Usually they had no agenda for social reform although the Mazdakite movement in sixth century A.D. Persia with its curiously modern call for redistribution of wealth was an exception.

During the Middle Ages in Western Europe religion could also be an outlet for those seeking social change as shown by the activities of revolutionary millenarians. It is interesting to note it was the radical wing of organized labor which was to continue the millenarian tradition through its imagery of a bright and shining tomorrow (*see* Iconography). Organized labor emerged very slowly from the economic and urban population growth of Western Europe from about A.D. 1200. The money economy began to assume greater importance as signalled by the revival of regular gold coin production at Florence and Genoa in 1252. Although the broad pattern of economic and social development across Western Europe differed widely, some common elements were present. Of particular significance was the rise of a wage-earning group in the population whose existence is documented in Portugal as early as 1253. Wage earners, especially its skilled members, were the founders of the first labor unions.

The birth of organized labor in England

Among the Western nations, the experience of England can claim special importance because it was there that many of the institutions and much of the lexicon of organized labor had their origins. From about A.D. 1100, guilds or societies of masters and journeymen were the main agents of economic regulation. They could fix the price of their products, had responsibility for maintaining their quality, and controlled entry into their trade through an apprenticeship system. The guilds could also set the wages of journeymen. The word "wages" was known to be in use in England by about 1330.

Journeymen were men who, having served an apprenticeship and become qualified in their trade, were employed by a master. Once qualified, they could find themselves in an awkward position in the medieval labor force: they were conscious of being in a socially superior position compared to peasants but could suffer from changes in price levels through being tied to the money economy of the towns. At the same time, opportunities for advancement to a master could be limited or non-existent.

These conditions gave rise to persistent attempts by journeymen in many trades to organize themselves for higher pay from as early as

1381 when the Corporation of the City of London forbade congregations or alliances among the trades. In 1383 some journeymen saddlers of London were accused of having formed "covins" (a term of conspiratorial suggestion first recorded in 1330) to raise their pay. With the decline of the guilds after 1500, the English parliament started to make laws covering a wider range of economic regulation.In 1548 parliament passed a general law prohibiting combinations among artisans and laborers. This law, the Bill of Conspiracies of Victuallers and Craftsmen, was signficant for introducing the concept of combinations as conspiracies into English law. Other laws passed in the 1550s were designed to preserve the economic order: they applied to the textile industry (one of the first industries to employ large concentrations of employees) and restricted how many looms a person could own and outlawed gig-mills. In 1562 the Statute of Artificers gave justices of the peace the power to set the wages of artisans and laborers and provided penalties for breach of contract by employers and employees. The statute also laid down that a seven-year apprenticeship was required for a man to become a journeyman.

England's economic growth, and particularly its rate of technological change from 1700, made the intent of the sixteenth century labor laws increasingly difficult to apply to an increasingly dynamic economy with its fluctuating levels of real wages. It was also an economy with a growing manufacturing labor force. In 1980 P. H. Linhert used samples from burial registers to gauge occupation change in England before 1800. His revised estimates, although admittedly tentative, suggest that the importance of commercial and industrial occupations in the pre-1800 economy had been underestimated. Lindert estimated that between 1700 and 1801-03, the number of males employed in manufacturing doubled from 155,000 to 324,000, a modest rate by later standards but impressive for the time. These developments also provided unintended fertile soil for the germination of labor unions. Despite the anti-union laws, journeymen and others continued to form secret labor unions and, from at least 1717, to conduct strikes, a term which had acquired its modern meaning as early as 1763. By 1769 settling labor disputes (q.v.) had become an important part of the duties of justices of the peace.

In his 1980 study, C. R. Dobson documented 383 labor disputes in Britain between 1717 and 1800, which covered more than 30 trades; of these, most occurred among woolcombers, weavers, and wool spinners (64), seamen and ships' carpenters (37), tailors and staymakers (27), bricklayers, carpenters and building laborers (19), and coal miners (18). Disputes over wages and hours accounted for 71 percent of disputes; 9 percent were over the employment of apprentices or other persons; and 6 percent were over innovation and machinery. The evidence assembled by Dobson is important for showing that even *before* the start of the Industrial Revolution, labor disputes and labor organizations were established, if unwelcome features of British society. The evidence also showed that the groups who took part in disputes were similar to those who were to play a prominent role in later periods-weavers, coal miners, and building workers-and that the issues that concerned them most were wages and hours. In this period, labor unions had no legal standing but they were clearly a presence even if shadowy as institutions.

It was no accident that 56 percent of all the disputes between 1717 and 1800 which were identified by Dobson were over wages. Real wages fluctuated considerably from year to year in the eighteenth century making it all too easy for the living standards of groups of employees to fall behind the cost of living. Falls in the standard of living were most conducive to increased activity by organized labor especially during the 1790s when England's wars with France caused real wages to fall by 42 percent and led to some successful strikes for higher pay by London journeymen. Parliament responded to the labor unrest by the Combination Acts (q.v.) of 1799 and 1800 which, it has been argued, were largely wartime security measures aimed primarily at labor disputes rather than labor unions as such.

The next twenty-five years were difficult ones for organized labor. The Industrial Revolution gathered pace and with it came a host of technological changes which benefited some groups in the labor force and destroyed the livelihood of others. The legal suppression of strikes encouraged illegal outlets, such as the organized destruction of machines in the woollen industry by the Luddites between 1811 and 1813 (*see* Machine Breaking). Parliament and organized labor differed fundamentally on economic policy. Organized labor wished to preserve the pre-industrial economic order with its extensive regulations. Parliament was determined to move towards a free enterprise economy with minimal government regulation. The triumph of the new economic order based on manufacturing was symbolized by the repeal of the wages clause of the Statute of Artificers (1562) in 1813 and the apprenticeship clause in 1814. There was opposition to both actions. One petition presented to parliament opposing the repeal of the apprenticeship clauses was signed by 30,517 journeymen (13,000 in London and 17,517 outside it), an action which gave some indication of the extent of organized labor at the time.

Organized labor and social protest were closely allied. Much of the social protest of the period was economic in origin and intent. Two well-known examples were the planned march to London by some Manchester weavers (the "Blanketeers") of 1817 who were dispersed by the government after the arrest of their leaders and the "Peterloo" Massacre at Manchester when a militia charge killed eleven people in a crowd which had gathered for a political demonstration for parliamentary reform in 1819.

Although the Combination Acts were repealed in 1824, they were replaced by new legislation in 1825 which effectively prohibited strikes. Despite this, labor unions continued to survive. Francis Place (q.v.) estimated that in this period there were about 100,000 journeymen in London, all potential candidates for union membership. The word "union" itself seems to have come into use at this time in its modern sense in the shipping and shipbuilding industries. By 1834, the term "employee" had also come into use.

During the first half of the nineteenth century, two élites were evident among the artisans who comprised organized labor in England: an older élite of carpenters, tailors, potters, and curriers and a new élite in ironworking, engineering, and the new manufacturing industries. Other occupations, most notably that of handloom weaver, were destroyed by mechanization of their trade. New unions began to emerge: journeymen steam engine makers (1826), carpenters (1827), a national union of coal miners in 1842 which claimed 70,000 members for a time, carpenters and joiners (1860), and, most famous of all, the Amalgamated Society of Engineers (1851).

According to the first directory of British labor unions published in 1861, there were 290 trades with unions in London alone, nearly all of them in manufacturing or construction. How many members of labor unions there were in England before 1860 is not known with precision but the available evidence suggests it was small and the numbers varied wildly according to the state of the economy. The Grand National Consolidated Trades Union (q.v.) in 1834 is thought to have had only about 16,000 members. Even well known unions had relatively small memberships. Both the Amalgamated Society of Engineers (q.v.) and the Friendly Society of Operative Stonemasons had only 5,000 members each in 1850-51. These and other figures suggest that total membership for Britain in the early 1850s may have only been about 50,000. It would have had more than twice this level but for the collapse of the Miners' Association of Great Britain and Ireland in 1848 (q.v.). There was significant growth in the membership of skilled unions in the 1860s. The Amalgamated Engineers grew from 21,000 members in 1860 to 35,000 by 1870, the Ironfounders from 8,000 to 9,000 and the newly formed Amalgamated Society of Carpenters and Joiners (q.v.) from 618 to 10,200. At the 1869 meeting of the Trades Union Congress (q.v.) there were forty unions represented claiming a total membership of 250,000.

The example of England

Outside of Britain before 1835, labor unions seem to have existed only in France (q.v.), the United States, Canada (q.v.) and New South Wales, Australia (q.v.). After the French Revolution in 1789, journeymen carpenters in Paris formed a union which aroused complaints by employers; the union was suppressed by the law *Le Chaplier* (1791), which was also applied to employers' organizations (q.v.). Strikes were forbidden by the Penal Code of 1810. In North America, the idea of labor unions was imported from England by journeymen immigrants. A British register of American emigrants maintained between 1773 and 1776 showed that of the 6,190 emigrants whose occupations were known, 49 percent were artisans, mechanics or craftsmen. The first American union was the Federal Society of Journeymen Cordwainers (or shoemakers) in Philadelphia; formed in 1794, the society lasted until 1806. In Canada, unions in the building industry made their presence felt at Saint John, New Brunswick, as early as 1812 when they tried to exclude American immigrants to maintain the shortage of skilled labor. In Australia, at least two unions were formed by 1835: one among Sydney shipwrights (1829) and the other among cabinetmakers (1833).

In this period, governments often made little distinction between social unrest and calls for greater democracy and labor unions. The spirit of the age was shown by a revolt by silk workers in Lyons, France, in 1834 after the government attempted to suppress labor unions. Yet, despite the harshness of its laws, the environment in England was, in practice, much freer than elsewhere in Europe. For example, in 1825 the British government repealed a law which had prohibited the emigration of artisans to continental Europe, legislation which had been in English statutes since 1718. If they could survive the severe economic fluctuations of the period and the social consequences of technological change brought by industrialization, labor unions could succeed.

European visitors to England in the 1860s were impressed by its labor unions. In 1862 a deputation of French labor leaders was allowed by Napoleon III to visit the London Exhibition. They returned with a high opinion of English working conditions and unions and asked to be granted freedom of association and the right to strike, freedoms which were not really available under English law. In 1869, the Comte de Paris (Louis Philippe d'Orleans), published a sympathetic study *The Trade Unions of England*, which was translated into English; it had previously been reprinted six times in French and a German translation was prepared as well. In 1868 Max Hirsch, a German mechanical engineer, toured England and was much influenced by what he saw of the skilled unions, particularly their attempts to settle disputes amicably, and by their independence from political parties. On his return he organized a new group of liberal unions known as Hirsch-Duncker trade associations (q.v.) which were based on these ideas. Similarly, the constitution of the Trade Union Congress provided the model for the American Federation of Organized Trades and Labor Unions of the United States and Canada, the forerunner of the American Federation of Labor (q.v.). In Australia, New Zealand, and Canada, British immigration reinforced Britain as the model for organized labor throughout most of the nineteenth century.

It was no accident that England, as the first industrial nation in the world, should have been the birthplace of organized labor. In European, if not American, terms it was a land of liberty as underscored by the Second Reform Act of 1867, which gave the vote to the better-off urban working class, that is, to most of the union members of the time. This early accommodation of labor by the political system, expressed through its alliance with the Liberal Party, marked England off from the rest of Europe and held back the formation of a purely labor party. In other parts of Europe, the political wing of labor was often stronger than its industrial wing.

There were other important differences between the history of British organized labor and that of many other parts of the world. First, British society was divided primarily by social class rather than religion, race, or ethnicity, a fact which eased recruiting. Second, as the center of a global empire up to 1939, British unions were freed from the need to participate in any struggle for national independence. Third, they operated in an advanced and relatively wealthy society, even though the distribution of that wealth was highly uneven.

The role of the state

The spread of the Industrial Revolution, population growth and rising literacy during the nineteenth century gave rise to the well-studied phenomenon of the "rise of the working class." Crude repression, the traditional method used by governments to maintain control, continued in many countries such as Russia, but from about the 1860s onwards the need for skilled workers gradually made this option less acceptable. What was needed was a way of encouraging working class demands and protests into acceptable constitutional channels. By a process of trial and error, organized labor gradually became accepted by a number of governments as one way of achieving this goal. In various ways, often unintentional, the form of organized labor was influenced by the state. This can be shown by the responses of governments to the growth of organized labor in a number of countries.

In Britain, the supportive response of the British government to the moderate trade unionism of the 1860s and 1870s (as indicated also by the Trade Union Act of 1871) contrasted with its hostility to the radicalism of Chartism (q.v.) in the 1840s. It was this moderation which earned the labor unions the scorn of Marx and Engels (*see* "Labor Aristocracy"). The growth of unions, especially moderate ones, seems to have been implicitly encouraged by governments in a number of European countries with the object of reducing support for socialism (q.v.). In France, the government legalized labor unions in 1884 and provided financial assistance to the *Bourses du Travail* (the coordinating centers for local unions) provided they remained out of the control of extremists. This was in the starkest contrast to the state's violent suppression of the unemployed during the "June Days" in 1848 and the bloodshed of the Paris Commune in 1871. In Germany, the labor unions operated in a legal twilight but operated nevertheless if they avoided politics; as well, Bismarck attempted to undercut the threat of socialism not just by banning the Social Democratic Party (1878) but also by a number of social reforms such as sickness insurance (1883). In this sense, organized labor far from operating in a political void, was the target of manipulation by the political culture.

Even benign actions by the state affected organized labor. For example, the introduction of compulsory conciliation and arbitration (q.v.) procedures in Australia and New Zealand assisted the growth of unions by easing the process of gaining recognition from employers for bargaining but also encouraged unduly large numbers of unions.

The spread of the Industrial Revolution from about 1870 and the economic and social changes it brought challenged the social order. Industrial and urban growth fed the growth of organized labor and raised awkward questions about the distribution of wealth, political reform and, ultimately, what form future society should take. Radical political creeds arose to offer answers-anarchism, socialism, syndicalism, and Marxist-Leninism (qq.v.)-creeds which continued to stimulate and divide organized labor throughout most of the twentieth century and made them a continuous object of attention by the state.

During World War I, governments needed the active cooperation of organized labor to maintain the high level of armaments production to fight the war. In the United Kingdom, France, Germany, and the United States, organized labor enjoyed a degree of acceptance by the state which it had not previously enjoyed. In the United Kingdom, France, and the United States, organized labor was courted by the highest levels of government and coopted into the war effort.

The economic difficulties of the 1920s and 1930s brought new pressures to bear on the relations between the state and organized labor which were resolved by widely differing methods. In France (1936), formal accommodations between government, employers, and unions were agreed to, which had long-lasting results for organized labor. In Norway (1935), Switzerland (1937), and Sweden (1938), employers and organized labor came to understandings which had the support of their governments.

Fascism was the other response to the economic problems of the interwar years. With its emphasis on centralized control justified on the grounds of maintaining national unity, fascism was hostile to any independent source of political power. As such, organized labor was a leading victim of fascist repression. German labor leaders were among the first inmates of Dachau concentration camp. In Italy (1924), Germany (1933), and Japan (1940), organized labor was incorporated into the apparatus of totalitarian government, examples which were copied by Brazil (1931), Greece (1931), Portugal (1933), and Yugoslavia (1935). That said, fascist policies had an enduring impact on organized labor. In Italy, the fascist legacy to organized labor consisted of: the legal recognition of unions, a unitary labor organization, compulsory financial contributions, and legally binding collective agreements. In Germany, the forcible organization of labor into national industry groups was a powerful precedent for the simplified labor union structure of the post-1945 era.

During the Cold War, democratic governments intervened in the affairs of organized labor, overtly and covertly, throughout the world to resist communist influence. In these ways organized labor has been shaped by the actions of governments.

The growth of organized labor

The growth of organized labor is one of the unsung success stories of modern world history. In 1870 there were about 790,000 members of labor unions in the world; in 1970 there were about 84 million, that is an increase of a hundred fold. As these figures exclude communist and other authoritarian countries where unions are not allowed to bargain freely, they are all the more impressive. Few other world movements have grown so much without the use of direction from above or force.

In about 1870 most union members lived in Britain (289,000) or the United States (300,000). France had about 120,000 members and Germany and the Austrio-Hungarian Empire had about 81,000 between them. Labor unions also existed in Australia and Canada, but their membership seems to have been tiny, probably no more than 10,000 in total. Union growth after 1870 was neither steady nor sure. The original base of recruitment, the skilled trades, was expanded to include employees in mass employment such as the railroads (q.v.), laborers, and the less skilled and finally, from 1890 onwards, groups like women (q.v.) and white-collar (q.v.) employees. Even so, the rise in world union members was heavily dependent upon the condition of the trade cycle and upon events peculiar to countries with large memberships. For instance, in the United States, union membership reached its pre-1900 peak in the mid-1880s with about a million members-or 53 percent of the world total-but then fell to 869,000 by 1900. This collapse was brought about by internal conflict over what form organized labor should take, in particular, the fight between the American Federation of Labor (q.v.) and the Knights of Labor (q.v.). In contrast, union membership in Britain advanced from 581,000 in the mid-1880s to 2 million by 1900.

The twentieth century opened with a blossoming of organized labor. Between 1900 and 1905 labor unions appeared in Japan (although they were quickly suppressed) and among indigenous workers in Africa (Lagos, Nigeria), the Philippines, and in the Dutch East Indies (Indonesia). Union membership grew also in southern and eastern Europe until, by 1913, there were 14.1 million union members in the world, a remarkable development compared to fifty years before even if organized labor remained a largely European movement. Of the 14.1 million union members in 1913, 10.7 million or 76 percent were in Europe; of the remaining 3.4 million, 2.8 million were in North America. This meant that unionism was essentially European in structure and outlook. Although the International Federation of Trade Unions (q.v.) tried to build up a truly international membership, in practice it remained a largely European organization during its life from 1901 to 1945.

Less obvious, but more serious, was the relatively small proportion of employees enrolled by organized labor in most countries. In 1913, only Australia (31 percent) had more than 20 percent of its employees in labor unions. Within Europe, the highest levels of union enrolment of employees was in Germany (18 percent), Netherlands (17 percent) and Britain (16 percent). With 9 percent of its employees in labor unions in 1913, the United States was comparable with Sweden and Norway (each with 8 percent). Not only did organized labor embrace a small minority of employees, its membership was heavily concentrated in mining, manufacturing, construction, and transportation. Further, the vast majority of union members were males in blue-collar occupations.

Between 1913 and 1920, there was a veritable explosion in world union membership based on high inflation, falling real wages, and the recruitment of large numbers of white-collar workers such as teachers. It was a period of wartime dislocation and political revolution. By 1920 organized labor could claim 43.6 million members worldwide, an increase of 209 percent on its 1913 level. Of the gain of 29.5 million, 7.5 million occurred in Germany, 4.2 million in Britain, 2.2 million in the United States, 3 million in Italy, 1.3 million in Czechoslovakia and 741,000 in Austria. For the first time too, organized labor emerged in India (q.v.) and Japan (q.v.).

The year 1920 was a high point in the strength of organized labor with about half of the employees in Germany, Austria, and Britain belonging to unions, a reflection of their governments' need to enlist the support of organized labor to fight World War I. Labor's new importance was officially recognized by the formation of the

International Labour Organisation (q.v.) in 1919. After 1920, the fortunes of organized labor fell considerably. By 1930, it could claim only 30.9 million members worldwide, a net loss of 12.8 million members. The economic crisis of the 1920s and the revived hostility of the employers cost labor dearly. Those countries where organized labor had grown the most in the period from 1913 to 1920 were those which suffered the largest losses after 1920: Germany and Britain lost 7.1 million between them and the United States 1.7 million. In all, European unions lost 16.2 million members in the 1920s and North America lost 2 million. These losses were only partly offset by membership gains in Latin America, Asia and Australasia of 5.1 million.

With the rise of fascism and the onset of the Depression, the growth of organized labor ceased. In Italy, the unions' declining labor membership enabled their suppression by Mussolini in 1924. In 1933 the free unions of Germany with their 5.6 million members were snuffed out and many of their leaders arrested and imprisoned. In both Italy and Germany, the fascist government suppressed labor movements which were already in decline. The remaining independent labor unions of Japan were suppressed in 1940. Ironically, it was the 1930s which saw a rebirth of American labor unions whose membership during the decade rose from 3.2 to 7.9 million between 1930 and 1940, even though this important growth period only restored the proportion of employees organized by unions to about where it had been in 1920. The other main areas of labor union membership growth were in Britain and Scandinavia.

After World War II, organized labor became embroiled in Cold War politics. In 1945 the former international body of organized labor, the International Federation of Trade Unions, dissolved itself and was replaced by the World Federation of Trade Unions (q.v.) which was the first truly global organization of labor unions. It lasted in this form until 1949 when the non-communist countries withdrew and set up their own international body, the International Confederation of Free Trade Unions (q.v.) whose membership rose from 48 million at its formation to 125 million by 1995. Meanwhile, the World Federation of Trade Unions continued as an organization based in Prague.

What happened to these international labor bodies was probably unavoidable given the international climate of the times, but what was more significant and encouraging was the strong revival of organized labor in Germany, Italy, and Japan. By 1950 these three countries had a total labor union membership of 18.5 million or nearly a third of the world's membership.   The United States also continued to have a growing labor union membership: from 7.9 million in 1940 to 13.4 million in 1950.

The thirty years from 1950 to the late 1970s marked another high point in the history of organized labor. The industries where organized labor was traditionally strong, such as manufacturing and other areas of mass employment, grew to meet the demands of postwar economies. Labor also enjoyed a far more sympathetic political environment, particularly in Western European democracies where social democratic/socialist or labor parties (q.v.) governed or were major political players.

Yet even in the time of their greatest strength, the structural problems which have always bedevilled organized labor remained. Since the 1960s much of the growth in the labor force has been in the service sector, that is those industries other than agriculture, mining, and manufacturing, industries where many women and white-collar workers worked, groups which organized labor either neglected or found difficult to recruit.

Two broad observations may be made about the course of the history of organized labor between 1870 and 1980.   First, union membership has grown mightily, if unevenly, from lowly beginnings in hostile political and legal environments to a position of strength where governments had to take account of its views.   This growth was achieved by democratic means.   Unlike communism, organized labor has come from below rather than being imposed from above. Second, through its political struggles, organized labor has helped change society for the better by fighting for improved working conditions and greater sharing of the gains of economic growth. These successes need to be remembered in any assessment of the history of organized labor. It is also vital to appreciate the many internal difficulties faced by organized labor which are the subject of the next section.

THE NATURE OF ORGANIZED LABOR

The divisions of organized labor

So far, it has been convenient to view organized labor as a single entity to show how it developed and spread as a world movement. But organized labor has never been a single entity, and its divisions are as important as its similarities both within and between countries.

Organized labor has always reflected faithfully its country of origin in all important respects.

The most widespread division in the history of organized labor has been that between the skilled and the less skilled. As has already been mentioned, the strongest labor unions developed among groups of skilled men, and it was these groups which were largely responsible for its survival before the 1880s. Skilled men, of course, had many advantages over the less skilled; they could command higher pay, were harder to replace, and so had more bargaining power with an employer. Further, they had already made a substantial investment of time and effort in their employment through the apprenticeship system. As a result, it was all too easy for the skilled to look down or fear the less skilled, let alone to make common cause with them. At the same time, the less skilled presented a potential threat to skilled men especially when technological change reduced the skills need for a job and opened the way for the lesser skilled to be trained to replace them.

This problem has been a critical issue for organized labor throughout much of its history. It came to the forefront spectacularly with the Knights of Labor in the United States in the 1880s; the Knights were the first labor organization in the world to recruit the unskilled as well as the skilled. The problem gave rise to debate about how organized labor should be organized, by industry or by occupation. An industry-based union implied that all within that industry could be eligible to be recruited into a union whereas unions based on craft or skilled occupations implied that many employees within the industry would be left out. As labor unions emerged among the traditionally less skilled, new problems arose. The American Federation of Labor, for example, the body which only accepted affiliates organized along craft lines also included unions of unskilled employees even in the late nineteenth century. With union growth came the problem of *which* unions had the right to recruit *which* employees. With no clear answer in many cases, there was often much conflict between unions about who had recruitment rights. As a result, national labor federations often had to adjudicate in inter-union disputes.

The second divide in organized labor was between manual and white-collar workers and the distinctions of social class this implied. In late-nineteenth century Germany, it was called the *Kragenlinie* or collar line. Although white-collar unionism began to emerge in a number of countries in the 1900s, it was generally moderate in character and aloof from manual union organizations and their concerns until after 1945 (*see* White Collar Unionism).

As well as these sources of division, organized labor has been and is divided by religion. Before World War II, organized labor in Western Europe (apart from Britain) was divided by religion, specifically into Catholic and non-Catholic movements with the non-Catholic unions largely being socialist in outlook. Since 1945, with the exception of Germany and Austria, this division has persisted in continental Europe despite efforts to unify the movements in France, Belgium, the Netherlands, and Switzerland.

Politics has been a fourth source of division in organized labor. Before 1920, the dominant form of political division was between socialists (of varying degrees) and non-socialists. After 1920 communism (q.v.) became an important and sometimes dominant element in labor union politics. More generally, the persistent political division in labor unions was the relative distinction between those of right-wing and those of left-wing views. Race and ethnicity (q.v.) has, and is, a fifth source of division in organized labor. In some countries, notably South Africa (q.v.), it has assumed huge proportions.

The reality of organized labor

Given the divisions within organized labor and the other formidable obstacles it has had to face, it is surprising that it has survived and grown at all. The key to its success may be found in its continual concern with the practical and attainable rather than the theoretical or ideal. Although the history of organized labor is punctuated by widespread and often short-lived social eruptions, to survive as organizations, labor unions have to become recognized, to make rules and agreements governing how work is be performed and paid and to seek change in an incremental rather than revolutionary fashion. This is the discipline of reality, of having to deal with the world as it is rather than how it ought to be, as advocated by political or social theorists. This is not to say that organized labor has not been often profoundly influenced by ideas but it typically assesses those ideas in terms of their practicality.

Whether they admit it or not, labor unions are political beings. By definition, they represent a potential challenge to the existing distribution of power, goods, and services in society which accounts for their repression by government throughout much of history. They might be won over by government but that implicit challenge is always present. Their participation in the political process can take many forms such as lobbying governments or simply by providing career stepping stones for upwardly mobile middle-class aspirants as has happened through labor parties in counties such as Britain and Australia or in a number of African nations since the 1960s.

Unions are also primarily defensive in character. Typically, they work to preserve and protect the pay and conditions of members. Strikes are a generally last resort of unions and occur when other measures have failed. Periods of inflation are especially productive of labor disputes because they upset the distribution of real wages across and within the employed labor force. This was particularly evident in most countries between 1915 and 1920. Similarly, in periods of rising prosperity, unions seek to gain what they see as their share through strikes for improved pay and conditions (*see* Labor Disputes).

Union membership size, although important, is no guide in itself to bargaining strength with employers. Some numerically large unions representing relatively poorly paid employees may have little bargaining power while others, particularly those in key industries such as transportation and communications, may have a lot. Even so, few unions are so powerful in their own right as to be able to bargain effectively on a large scale (for example, with governments). Organized labor learned long ago to cooperate through national bodies (*see* Trades Union Congress).

None of this is to say that labor unions are ideal organizations. Like any institution they can become corrupt if their leaders pursue their own or some other body's interests to the neglect of their members. Where this has occurred, such as in the celebrated case of the Teamsters (q.v.) in the United States in the 1950s and 1960s, it receives widespread attention but, by and large, these are exceptions. Despite all the dire predictions to the contrary, unions continue to go about their work and have remained democratic institutions. This is not to say that all members participate in their activities all of the time; usually union activities are confined to the committed few, but unions do offer the possibility for all to participate if they choose to do so (*see* Industrial Sociology). As Germany and Austria since 1945 show, organized labor can also be a powerful force for promoting and sustaining democracy.

LABOR SINCE 1980

Since 1980 organized labor in most of the Western world has been on the defensive. This has come about for a variety of reasons and in a variety of ways. The topic which has received the most publicity and pessimistic academic study has been the "crisis of labor," that is the decline of union membership and power in Western countries, particularly in the United States and the United Kingdom. The recession of 1981-82 greatly reduced employment in industries where organized labor had traditionally been strong, such as coal mining, steel, and manufacturing as a whole. General economic problems enabled organized labor to be blamed by conservative governments in the United States and the United Kingdom as barriers to economic efficiency. By the early 1990s the proportion of employees in unions in both the United States and the United Kingdom had fallen to levels of the late 1930s.

Ironically, household surveys in Australia, Canada, the United Kingdom, and the United States show that in the 1980s union members were a relatively privileged part of the workforce. They tended to have higher incomes, higher levels of benefits, and were more likely to work for government or larger enterprises than non-union members. Earnings data for Australia and the United States show that employees who are union members earn more than non-union members although the differential is far higher in the United States. In 1995 full-time male employees in Australia who were union members had a median income which was eight percent more than non-union member compared to 21 percent in the United States. For females, these differences were even greater. Australian full-time female employees who were union members had a median income which was 10 percent above those of non-union employees in 1994 compared to 27 percent in the United States (*see* Appendix 3, Table 15). It has been suggested that this large differential in earnings has been one of the reasons for the steep fall in the proportion of employees who belong to unions in the United States (*see* Union Wage Differential). In 1995 only 14.9 percent of United States employees were union members.

The fortunes of organized labor mirror those of the economy and the structure of employment. The harsher economic conditions since 1980 have brought about management changes which have greatly altered working conditions and opportunities for advancement. The widespread use of computers has revolutionized much office work and has been instrumental in reducing employment in industries such as banking. Part-time employment has also grown, partly through choice, but more often than not through necessity as real incomes have fallen.

When other excuses were lacking, authoritarian governments in

Third World countries have fought unions as impediments to economic growth. In 1984 the International Confederation of Free Trade Unions began to conduct annual surveys of violations of trade union rights in the world. Their reports make for harrowing reading; they document the murder, torture, and imprisonment of union leaders and the denial of official recognition of labor unions which are not controlled by the government.

Needless to say that those countries with the worst record of human rights also have appalling records of the violation of trade union rights. The Middle East usually attracts significant attention in this regard. In 1993 the United States government has shown greater interest in promoting trade union rights in the Third World, such as Indonesia, by the threat of withdrawal of trade privileges.

Another strand in the history of world labor since 1980 and one that is something of a counter to the picture of decay has been the revival of free trade unions in the former Soviet Union and in Eastern Europe in countries such as Poland and Hungary. In 1995 nine percent of the membership of the International Confederation of Free Trade Unions lived in Eastern Europe. It is too early to know how strong this revival will be, but there is much potential for substantial union growth.

In all this, it must be remembered that labor unions came into existence because they were wanted. As economies industrialized, so the stress on society grew. The upsetting of power relationships and the redistribution of wealth which came in the wake of industrialization brought friction. Everything that has happened to organized labor since 1980,- membership decline, defeats in major strikes, a feeling that it is no longer needed, the threat of technological change, has all happened before. In 1932, for example, on the eve of an upsurge in union growth of over 4 million in the United States, an expert questioned if organized labor had a future. The one thing that seems constant in the history of organized labor is the temptation for employers and conservative governments to take advantage of its weakness to by attacking unions, a policy which can revive them.

Finally, organized labor is essentially about economic democracy, and how governments treat labor unions is usually a fair indication of the real level of democracy in their society. True, organized labor can cause disruption through strikes, but the economic cost pales before the cost of industrial accidents, high labor turnover, and the lower productivity of sullen employees. Properly consulted, unions can be a force for higher productivity and economic achievement through reducing labor turnover and making for more contented employees. Industrial society has many built-in conflicts which create the demand for unions. Organized labor can, and has been frequently suppressed, but unless the mainsprings of its grievances can be satisfied, it will not go away.

There is nothing new in the unions' quest for a more just world. In Greek mythology, Plutos was the god of wealth. To punish mankind, Zeus, the ruler of the gods, blinded Plutos so that he would distribute wealth without regard to merit. In his last extant play the ancient Greek playwright Aristophanes considered what would happen if Plutos was cured of his blindness; in the play the cured god distributes his benefits only to the deserving. The play was of course a comedy, but the dream of a fairer world lived on.

THE DICTIONARY

ACCORD   (*See* Union-Government Agreements)

ALLIANCE FOR LABOR ACTION   The Alliance for Labor Action was the name of a campaign initiated by Walter Reuther (q.v.), the president of the United Automobile Workers (q.v.), in alliance with the Teamsters (q.v.), to recruit new union members among white-collar employees and in service industries in 1968. The Alliance was formed outside of the American Federation of Labor-Congress of Industrial Organizations (AFL-CIO) (q.v.), from which the Automobile Workers had disaffiliated (July 1968) and from which the Teamsters had been expelled (1957). Based in Altanta, Georgia, the Alliance's campaign had poor results, partly because of hostility from the AFL-CIO which regarded the Alliance as a rival organization. After Reuther's death in an airplane crash in 1970, the Alliance lost momentum and was disbanded in December 1971. (*See also* Walter Reuther, Teamsters)

AMALGAMATED ASSOCIATION OF MINERS (AAM)   The AAM was a labor union of British coal miners formed as a breakaway union from the Miners' National Union (q.v.) in 1869 in protest over its conservative policies. The AAM was prepared to go on strike to achieve better wages and conditions for its membership which grew from 12,000 in 1870 to 71,200 in 1873. The AAM proved unable to accumulate enough funds to support large-scale and local strikes, and this, plus the economic downturn after 1873, sent it into bankruptcy in 1875. (*See also* Miners' National Union)

AMALGAMATED ENGINEERING UNION (AEU)   Britain's AEU was formed from the amalgamation of the Amalgamated Society of Engineers (ASE) (q.v.) and several other smaller unions on July, 1 1920. For most of its history, the ASE had only admitted skilled engineering employees, that is, men who had completed an apprenticeship; but in 1926 it began to admit lesser skilled workers mainly because of the effects of technological change and also to counter competition from unions such as the Workers' Union (q.v.). By 1939 it had 390,900 members compared to 168,000 in 1933. World War II boosted the demand for engineering workers. In 1942 women were admitted to the ranks of the AEU for the first time; by

1943 they made up 139,000 of its 825,000 members. In 1943 too, the AEU became Britain's second largest union, a position it retained for most of the postwar period. It continued to grow with the economy and also through amalgamation (q.v.) with other unions, notably with the 72,900 strong Amalgamated Union of Foundry Workers (formed in 1946) in January 1968. Between 1962 and 1979 the membership of the AEU rose from 982,200 to a peak of 1,483,400. In 1971 the Technical, Administrative, and Supervisory Section (TASS) joined the AEU which renamed itself the Amalgamated Union of Engineering Workers; in 1988 the TASS left to join the Association of Scientific, Technical, and Managerial Staffs to form the Manufacturing, Science and Finance Union and the AEU reverted to its former title. During 1991 the AEU and the other members of the Confederation of Shipbuilding and Engineering Unions (q.v.) won a campaign which reduced the working week from 39 to 37.5 hours for many of its members. On May 1, 1992 the AEU merged with the Electrical, Telecommunications, and Plumbing Union to become the Amalgamated Engineering and Electrical Union. Between 1986 and 1994 the membership of the AEU fell from 858,000 to 781,000. (*See also* Amalgamated Society of Engineers, *IG Metall*)

AMALGAMATED METAL WORKERS' UNION (AMWU) The AMWU has been one of the strongest labor unions in Australia (q.v.). It began as the New South Wales branch of the English-based Amalgamated Society of Engineers (q.v.) in 1852 with twenty-seven members. From 1920 to 1973 it was called the Amalgamated Engineering Union and the AMWU from 1973 to 1990. Its members were skilled metal workers, and it was one of the few unions to offer members sickness, accident, unemployment, and strike payments. From 1915 it began to admit lesser skilled metal workers into its ranks. Between 1920 and 1969 its membership rose from 16,000 to 149,300. In 1968 it formally severed its links with its British parent union.

After 1945 the AMWU was one of the leading unions in gaining higher pay and better conditions for its members though labor disputes (q.v.). From 1972 it grew by amalgamation (q.v.) with other unions, namely the Association of Drafting, Supervisory, and Technical Employees (1990), and the Vehicle Builders Employees' Federation (originally formed in 1912) in 1993. In February 1995 it merged with the Printing and Kindred Industries Union (formed in 1916) and was renamed the Australian Manufacturing Workers' Union to claim a membership of 211,000. (*See also* Amalgamated Society of Engineers, Australia)

AMALGAMATED SOCIETY OF CARPENTERS AND JOINERS

(ASCJ) A British, and international union, the ASCJ was formed in London in June 1860 with 618 members following a strike in 1859-60 to win the nine hour day. The employers responded with a lock-out and a demand that the strikers sign "The Document" (q.v.). The strong financial support given by the other unions, particularly the Amalgamated Society of Engineers (q.v.), caused the employers to withdraw their demand. Membership of the ASCJ rose to 10,178 by 1870 and to 17,764 by 1880, making it one of the most powerful craft unions. The ASCJ was also an international union; it established branches in Ireland (1866), United States (1867), Scotland (1871), Canada (1872), New Zealand (1875), Australia (Sydney, 1875; Adelaide, 1878; and Melbourne, 1879), and South Africa (1881). In Australia, the New South Wales branch of the ASCJ claimed 33,000 members in 1890. In the United States the ASCJ provided a model for the formation of the Brotherhood of Carpenters and Joiners in Chicago in 1881 by Peter J. McGuire. The Brotherhood proved to be far more successful than the ASCJ in recruiting members. In 1923 the Canadian branches of the ASCJ were closed and merged with the American Brotherhood. In 1911 the English ASCJ merged with the Associated Carpenters and Joiners' Society of Scotland (founded in 1861). Further amalgamations followed that transformed the original craft union into an industrial union which eventually gave rise to the Union of Construction and Allied Technical Trades in 1971. In Australia, the ASCJ retained its separate identity until 1992. (*See also* Amalgamated Society of Engineers)

AMALGAMATED SOCIETY OF ENGINEERS (ASE)

Since 1851 engineering unions have played a central role in the history of organized labor in Britain. The first continuous labor organization in the engineering industry was the Journeymen Steam Engine, Machine Makers, and Millwrights' Friendly Society formed in Manchester in 1826 and known as "Old Mechanics." The ASE was largely formed from the merger of "Old Mechanics" and the Smiths' Benevolent Sick and Burial Society in 1851. Membership began at 5,000 and reached 11,000 by the end of 1851. The formation of the Amalgamated Society of Engineers (ASE) in 1851 was hailed as a pivotal event in the history of organized labor by Beatrice and Sidney James Webb (q.v.) as marking the first of "model" unions with well-developed organizations, high contribution fees, and sickness, unemployment, superannuation and funeral benefits. The ASE was the target of a nationwide lock-out by employers in 1852. Defeated, some left Britain to form a branch of the ASE in New South Wales, Australia, in 1852. In 1851 the ASE founded its first branch in Ireland; it also set up branches in Canada (1853), the United States (1861), New Zealand (1864), and South Africa (1891). With the creation of these branches, the ASE became an international as well as British union, an example later followed by the Amalgamated Society of Carpenters and Joiners (q.v.).

In 1897-98 the ASE suffered an important defeat by a lock-out organized by the engineering employers, an event which led it to become a prime mover in the formation of the General Federation of Trade Unions (q.v.) in 1899. During the lock-out over 28,000 pounds were given by European unions (half came from German unions) and overseas branches of the ASE. Faced with intense competition from American unions, the ASE closed down its American branches in 1920, whereas in Australia, the ASE went on to become one of the major unions as the Amalgamated Metal Workers' Union (q.v.). In 1913 the ASE had 17,000 members (or about 10 percent of its total membership) in nine countries outside of Britain. In Britain, the membership of the ASE grew from 100,000 in 1910 to 174,300 in 1914.

As a result of the demand for munitions during World War I, membership reached 298,800 in 1918. In 1916, George Nicoll Barnes (1859-1940), a former secretary of the ASE, joined Lloyd George's wartime government as minister for pensions. From 1905 the ASE supported the creation of a single union for the engineering industry and in 1918 persuaded seventeen unions in the industry to conduct ballots for amalgamation; nine of these bodies agreed to amalgamate to form the Amalgamated Engineering Union. In 1920 the ASE had 423,000 members. (*See also* Amalgamated Engineering Union, *Federazione Italiana Operai Metallurgici, Deutscher Metallarbeiter-Verband,* Workers' Union)

AMALGAMATION Amalgamation, that is, the merging of a labor body with one or more other labor bodies, has been an important feature of the history of organized labor in most countries. In Britain and in countries where organized labor had British roots (United States, Canada, Australia and New Zealand), there were by the late nineteenth century relatively large numbers of unions organized by occupation or craft. As these unions tried to recruit new members, they soon came into conflict with other unions, and one of the functions of national labor federations was often to adjudicate in jurisdictional (or demarcation) disputes between unions. One solution to this problem was amalgamation, which had the added advantage of better-funded union administrations. A number of large unions have grown by amalgamation, notably the British Transport and General Workers' Union (q.v.) and the Australian Federated Miscellaneous Workers' Union (q.v.).

Amalgamation has accounted for much of the general fall in the number of unions in English-speaking countries. In Australia (q.v.), the number of unions fell from 573 in 1911 to 142 in 1995. In the United Kingdom (q.v.), the peak number of unions was reached in 1920 when there were 1,384 unions; by 1994 there were only 243 unions. In New Zealand (q.v.), the number of unions was greatest in 1937 at 499, but by 1973 this figure had dropped to 309 and between 1985 and 1994 from 259 to 78. Because of its longer tradition of industrial unions, the decline in the number of unions in Germany has been comparatively low. In the United States of America (q.v.), the number of unions affiliated with the AFL-CIO (q.v.) was only 78 in 1994 compared to 139 in 1955. Since the recession of the early 1980s, there has been continual economic pressure on unions to maintain their strength through amalgamation. (*See also* UNISON)

AMERICAN FEDERATION OF LABOR (AFL) The AFL was the leading federation of American organized labor from the early 1890s. The AFL grew out of the Federation of Organized Trades and Labor Unions of the United States and Canada (FOOTALU), which was formed in Pittsburgh in 1881. Modelled closely on the British Trades Union Congress (TUC) (q.v.), it represented 50,000 members and gave autonomy to affiliated unions. FOOTALU faced strong competition for members from the Knights of Labor (q.v.). Inter-union fighting prompted Samuel Gompers (q.v.) to lead a campaign by craft unions which resulted in the setting up of the AFL in Columbus, Ohio, on December 8, 1886. The AFL was based on craft unions not unions based on industries. This led to jurisdictional or demarcation disputes between member unions over which organizations had the right to recruit certain members, particularly in coal mining which the United Mine Workers of America (q.v.) declared as its preserve in the "Scranton Declaration" in 1901. During World War I, the AFL became the recognized spokesman of American organized labor, and it had the support of the National War Labor Board. By 1920 the AFL represented 4 million employees, but this gain rapidly fell away in the face of a sustained offensive by employers for the "open shop." The Depression reduced the AFL to only 2.1 million members by 1933. The membership was disproportionately concentrated in coal mining, railroads, and construction. Gompers, the AFL president since its formation (with one short break in 1894), died in 1924 and was succeeded by William Green (1873-1952) who was president until his death.

Reflecting its craft union roots, the AFL was always a conservative organization and dissatisfaction with its neglect of mass production workers enabled John L. Lewis (q.v.), the president of the United Mine Workers' Union, to set up a rival to the AFL based on industrial unions, the Committee of Industrial Organizations in 1935 which officially became the Congress of Industrial Organizations (CIO) (q.v.) in 1938. In 1937 the AFL had 3.4 million members compared to 3.7 in the CIO, and in 1938 all CIO member bodies of the AFL were expelled in the United States and in Canada (qq.v). Competition for members with the CIO, compounded by its less conservative policies, ensured that rivalry continued with the AFL into the late 1940s. In 1952 George Meany was elected president of the AFL and a formal merger with the CIO occurred in December 1955. (*See also* Congress of Industrial Organizations, Samuel Gompers)

AMERICAN FEDERATION OF LABOR-CONGRESS OF INDUSTRIAL ORGANIZATIONS (AFL-CIO) The AFL-CIO was formed by the merger of the two rival national labor federations in the United States (q.v.) in December 1955. The Taft-Hartley Act (q.v.) of 1947 and the worsening political climate for organized labor encouraged the two bodies to consider joining forces. Providentially too, the deaths of the presidents of both bodies in 1952 (William Green of the American Federation of Labor and Philip Murray (q.v.) of the Congress of Industrial Organizations), long bitter rivals, made the path to unity far easier. George Meany (q.v.) who replaced Green as AFL president worked hard to achieve unity as did his counterpart in the CIO, Walter Reuther (q.v.). Meany became president of the

AFL-CIO, a post he held until 1979. In 1957 the AFL-CIO expelled the Teamsters' Union (q.v.) and the Laundry Workers and the Bakers' Union for corruption.

Although officially non-political, the AFL-CIO has always been closely associated with the Democratic Party. In its international dealing in labor affairs, the AFL-CIO has followed conservative policies. Since the early 1980s the AFL-CIO has petitioned the United States government to exclude China, Malaysia, and Thailand (qq.v.) from the generalized system of preferences for their abuses of human rights and labor union freedom. In 1979 Lane Kirkland (q.v.) succeeded Meany as AFL-CIO president and held the post until 1995. In 1973 the AFL-CIO had 114 affiliated unions with a total membership of 13.4 million; in 1991 it had 89 affiliated unions with a total membership of 13.9 million. (*See also* American Federation of Labor, Congress of Industrial Organizations, Joseph Lane Kirkland, George Meany)

AMERICAN LABOR PARTY The American Labor Party was a socially progressive political party formed in New York State by representatives of the CIO (q.v.) and over 200 labor unions in 1936. One of its founders was David Dubinsky (q.v.), the president of the International Ladies' Garment Workers' Union (q.v.). In 1944 many of the party's supporters withdrew because of communist infiltration. The party attracted 509,000 votes in the 1948 federal election when it opposed Harry Truman and backed the Progressive Party candidate, Henry A. Wallace. The party had little effect after 1948 and was disbanded in 1956. (*See also* Congress of Industrial Organizations, David Dubinsky)

AMERICAN LABOR UNION (ALU) The American Labor Union (ALU) was a short-lived radical organization formed by the Western Federation of Miners in 1898 as the Western Labor Union (WLU) to supplement the eastern-dominated American Federation of Labor (AFL) (q.v.). A socialist organization, the ALU attempted to recruit employees ignored by the AFL, that is the lesser skilled, women, and immigrants. The WLU was fiercely opposed by the AFL and changed its name to the ALU in 1902 to compete directly with the AFL as advocated by Eugene V. Debs (q.v.). The ALU also advocated unions based on industries rather than craft occupations, which was the basis of the AFL. Despite its wider recruiting ambitions (it claimed 100,000 members), the basis of the ALU was the Western Federation of Miners. The ALU was one of the parent organizations of the Industrial Workers of the World (q.v.) which continued its main aims after 1905 after which time the ALU ceased to exist. (*See also* American Federation of Labor, Industrial Workers of the World)

ANARCHISM The term anarchism was derived from an ancient Greek word meaning without government. As a political philosophy, it owed much to Pierre-Joseph Proudhon (1809-1865) who regarded the state as a negative element in society which should be abolished. Mikail Alexandrovich Bakunin (1814-1876), an extremist Russian political thinker, propagandist and activist, absorbed Proudhon's ideas and was one of the leading anarchists of the nineteenth century. Anarchism, as envisaged by Bakunin, sought the overthrow of the state by a general strike and its replacement by democratically run cooperative groups covering the whole economy. It attracted support from certain intellectuals and in rural areas where the local political and economic system was repressive and ignored demands for reform. It drew much support from Spain and Italy (qq.v) where it formed a strand of political thinking with syndicalism. Anarchists held international conferences in Europe in 1873, 1874, 1876, and 1877. They were excluded from conferences of the Second International Workingmen's Association (q.v.) from 1896. In Spain the anarchists formed their own federation, the *Confederación Nacional del Trabajo*, and anarchists remained important until their destruction during the Spanish Civil War (1936-39). Immigration (q.v.) also spread anarchist ideas to Latin America; in 1919 the anarchists attempted to form a federation covering the whole of Latin America.

The violence often associated with anarchists made them enemies of organized labor in most other countries, particularly among socialists who sought constitutional means to achieve their ends. In May 1886, for example, a bomb blast at a meeting called by anarchists in Haymarket Square in Chicago over the killing of four strikers led to the deaths of a policeman and seven others. The Haymarket incident, which led to the hanging of four anarchists, is often regarded as having turned popular opinion in the United States against organized labor in general. (*See also* Argentina, Chile, Spain, Syndicalism)

ANARCHO-SYNDICALISM (*See* Anarchism, Syndicalism)

ARBITRATION (*See* Conciliation and Arbitration)

ARGENTINA Argentina has one of the oldest labor movements in Latin America; in 1857 printers formed a mutual benefit society which they made into a union in 1877. Like North America and Australasia, the population of Argentina was built on immigration; in the case of Argentina, the bulk of the immigrants up to the 1960s came from Italy (q.v.) and Spain (q.v.). Despite its early beginning, union membership was low in the nineteenth century. In 1908 a government survey estimated that there were only 23,400 union members in Buenos Aires and even by 1920, national membership had only reached 68,000. Despite these low membership figures, Argentina experienced a general strike in 1907 in which 93,000 took part. By 1930 when the *Confederación General del Trabajo* (CGT), the General Confederation of Labor, was formed, the number of union members had grown to 280,000. Other rival labor federations were formed by socialists, anarchists, and syndicalists. From 1943 the CGT became an active participant in politics through Colonel Perón. In the turmoil which followed Perón's removal in 1955, the CGT was disbanded and forced underground but re-emerged in 1963.

Thereafter, political rather than industrial concerns dominated Argentinian labor as governments both military and democratic attempted to deal with the country's severe economic problems; these policies produced factional divisions within the CGT. The legal status of the CGT was restored in 1986 following intervention by the International Labour Organisation (q.v.). In 1990 there were claimed to be about 2.5 million members of unions in Argentina. (*See also* Brazil, Chile, Immigration)

AUSTRALIA The first labor unions in Australia arose among shipwrights in 1829 but it was not until after the gold rushes in the 1850s that organized labor became more important. Before the 1880s most unions were formed by employees in a limited range of occupations, but in the 1880s there was an upsurge of "new" unionism, which embraced a wider range of occupations. By 1890 there were about 150,000 union members covering about 17 percent of all employees. Between 1878 and 1900 the seven colonies which made up Australia-there was no national government until 1901-passed laws that recognized labor unions. In 1879 the labor unions held their first inter-colonial congress in Sydney; subsequent congresses were held in 1884, 1886, 1888, 1889, 1891, and 1898. Between August and December 1890, 50,000 workers took part in the great Maritime Strike (q.v.) over freedom of contract; the strikers suffered defeat. Between July and September 1894, the unions suffered a second major setback as a result of the wool shearers' strike in Queensland. The depression of the early 1890s, which was aggravated by a severe drought retarded economic growth and caused union membership to fall to 97,000 (or about 8 percent of employees) in 1901.

The unions also used politics to improve their position. Following the introduction of public payment of a salary to members of parliament in New South Wales in 1889, the Sydney Trades and Labour Council resolved to support labor candidates, a decision which resulted in the election of 35 labor members to parliament at the 1891 election, an event which marked the birth of what later was called the Australian Labor Party (q.v.). Assisted by the introduction of compulsory conciliation and arbitration as a means of settling labor disputes-a system which eased the process for unions to collectively bargain with employers by granting them legal recognition -union membership rose to 498,000 or 31 percent of employees in 1913, the highest density level of any country at the time. As in other countries, white-collar unions began to organize during the 1900s, but most union members continued to be predominantly male blue-collar employees. With the establishment of the Federated Miscellaneous Workers' Union (q.v.) in 1915, the structure of organized labor remained relatively unchanged until the late 1980s. Australian labor unions have been a mixture of large and small organizations since the 1890s. Between 1913 and 1995 the proportion of unions with less than 1,000 members fell from 80 to 49 percent and the number of unions fell from 432 to 142.

Since 1913 union membership rose and fell according to the state of the economy and the distribution of employment by industry. Unionism was strongest among blue-collar workers and skilled tradesmen. It was weakest among casual employees and white-collar workers. As a proportion of employees, unions reached their height in Australia in 1953 when 63 percent of employees were members. Between 1970 and 1995 the structure of union membership in Australia was changed by three trends. First, the proportion of women members rose from 24 to 40 percent. Second, the number employed in the public sector increased from 23 to 42 percent. Third, the proportion of union members who were members of unions with less than 10,000 members fell from 15 to 6 percent. From 1987 to 1996 the Australian Council of Trade Unions (q.v.) and the federal government have encouraged the amalgamation (q.v.) of unions. In August 1995 an official household survey found that there were 2,251,800 union members which represented 33 percent of employees. As in the previous surveys conducted from 1982, the largest divide in union penetration was between the public and private sectors. In 1995 56 percent of public sector employees were union members compared to 25 percent in the private sector. (*See also* Australian Council of Trade Unions, Australian Workers' Union, Federated Miscellaneous Workers' Union, Robert James Lee Hawke, William Morris Hughes, Maritime Strike)

AUSTRALIAN COUNCIL OF TRADE UNIONS (ACTU) The ACTU is the national body representing Australian labor unions. The idea of a single body representing Australian labor unions was first suggested by W.G. Spence (q.v.) at the 1884 Inter-colonial Trade Union Congress, but it failed to attract support although subsequent congresses considered ways of federating the various peak labor bodies in the various colonies. The creation of a national government in 1901 and a federal system of conciliation and arbitration (q.v.) in 1905 created a new incentive to form a national body. But despite further national congresses in 1902, 1907, 1913 and 1916, it was not until the national conference of 1921 that the first steps were taken to form a peak national labor body and even then two further conferences were needed (in 1922 and 1925) before the ACTU was formed in Melbourne, Victoria, in 1927. In addition, until the late 1950s the powers of the ACTU were limited with real power continuing to reside with the State trades and labor councils. It was not until 1943 that it created its first salaried position, and it was only in 1949 that it had its first full-time president, Albert E. Monk, who held the post until 1969. The growing importance of national wage cases and the convenience for national governments of dealing with a single labor body further strengthened the ACTU. In 1968 the then largest labor union, the Australian Workers' Union (q.v.), affiliated with the ACTU. In 1980 the Australian Council of Salaried and Professional Associations joined the ACTU as did the other major white-collar body, the Council of Australian Government Employees in 1981. By 1981 all significant unions and union groupings had become affiliated with the ACTU, that is, it represented about 2.5 million employees.

The ACTU has been at its greatest influence when the ALP was the national government from March 1983 to March 1996. At the March 1983 national election, the ALP won office and the former ACTU president from 1970 to 1980, R. ("Bob") J. L. Hawke (q.v.), became prime minister. A former ACTU advocate, Ralph Willis (1938-), became minister for industrial relations. At the national election in March 1990, another ACTU president, Simon Findlay Crean (1949-), was elected to parliament and was made a minister. Although the ACTU remains based in Melbourne, most large labor unions have their headquarters in Sydney. Between 1986 and 1993 the number of unions affiliated with the ACTU fell from 162 to ninety-four, largely in response to a campaign led by the ACTU for the amalgamation (q.v.) of unions. (*See also* Australian Labour Federation, Australian Labor Party, Union-Government Agreements)

AUSTRALIAN LABOR PARTY (ALP)   The ALP is one of the oldest and most successful continuous political parties based on organized labor in the world. It had its beginnings in a decision of the Sydney Trades and Labor Council in January 1890 to support candidates in the 1891 election following the introduction of state payment of the salaries of members of parliament in 1889. Support for a direct role in politics by organized labor was boosted by its defeat in the Maritime Strike of 1890 (q.v.). Labor unions have continued to provide the basis of the ALP ever since. It represented the culmination of efforts to elect working-class representatives to parliament, which began in the late 1870s. It drew part of its inspiration from the British Liberal Party, the main political outlet for the organized English working- class in the nineteenth century. By the mid-1900s the ALP had been set up in all the states. Its features of a platform of policies and disciplined voting by its elected members began a new era in Australian politics. In time the non-Labor parties also adopted platforms of policies and more disciplined voting by their elected members. Though usually represented by its opponents as a "left-wing" party, the ALP was from its beginnings a moderate social democratic party though it did contain some radical groups. There have been two major splits in the ALP. The first was in 1916-17 over military conscription and the second occurred in 1955 over attitudes to communism. The ALP formed national governments in 1908-9, 1910-13, 1914-15, 1929-32, 1941-49, 1972-74, and 1983-96, but its longest terms of government success have been in the states. Notable ALP prime ministers have been William Morris Hughes (q.v.), James H. Scullin (1929-32), John Curtin (1941-45), Ben Chifley (1945-49), Gough Whitlam (1972-74) and Robert ("Bob") J. L. Hawke (q.v.). At the national elections on March 2, 1996, the ALP gained 39 percent of the vote for the House of Representatives and 36 percent for the Senate. Despite commanding the most votes of any single Australian political party, the ALP in the postwar period has the smallest membership of any of the three major political parties. In 1954 the ALP had about 83,000 members (compared to 390,000 in 1939) but, after the 1955 split, this fell to about 45,000; by 1975 membership had climbed to 90,000 but between 1982 and 1995 it fell from 55,000 to 35,000. (*See also* Australia, Australian Council of Trade Unions, Robert James Lee Hawke, William Morris Hughes, Social Democratic/Socialist/Labor Parties)

AUSTRALIAN LABOUR FEDERATION (ALF) The ALF was an attempt to federate Australia's labor unions. It was formed in 1889 in Brisbane, Queensland, and claimed 15,000 members by 1890. Its platform included legislation for the eight-hour working day, a minimum wage, the direct representation of labor in parliament, and the promotion of cooperative societies. Apart from New South Wales in the late 1890s and Western Australia, the ALF did not attract support outside Queensland. The Queensland part of the AFL was dissolved in 1914 when its main supporter, the Amalgamated Workers' Union (q.v.), merged with the Australian Workers' Union. (*See also* Australian Workers' Union)

AUSTRALIAN WORKERS' UNION (AWU) From the 1900s to 1969 the AWU was the largest labor union in AustraliaIt began as a sheep shearers' union in Ballarat, Victoria, in 1886. In 1887 this union amalgamated with two shearers' unions in New South Wales (also formed in 1886) to form the Amalgamated Shearers' Union. In Queensland, the shearers' union and the laborers' union (formed in 1888) merged to form the Amalgamated Workers' Union of Queensland (1891); this body became the basis of the AWU in Queensland when it amalgamated with it in 1914. In 1894 the AWU was founded in Sydney, New South Wales, with the amalgamation of shearers' and laborers' unions under the leadership of William Guthrie Spence (q.v.) with a claimed membership of 30,000. The membership of the AWU was open to all employees. The AWU expanded by amalgamation (q.v.) with other unions, first with the rural laborers' union in 1894 and then with unions of semi-skilled workers in rural, general laboring. and mining occupations between 1912 and 1917. By 1914, the AWU had 70,000 members.

The AWU has been a powerful but conservative force in the labor movement and in the Australian Labor Party (q.v.), particularly in Queensland and New South Wales. In the 1950s the AWU had about 200,000 members. Structural changes in industries and occupations, as well as internal disputes, have reduced the AWU membership since 1970 from 160,000 to 115,500 by 1990. In November 1993 the AWU amalgamated with the Federation of Industrial Manufacturing and Engineering Employees (FIMEE), formerly the Federated Ironworkers' Association (formed in 1911) and was officially renamed the AWU-FIME Amalgamated Union. (*See also* Australian Labour Federation)

AUSTRIA   Labor unions were legally tolerated within the present borders of Austria in 1870; the unions claimed 46,600 members by 1892 and 119,000 by 1900. Union growth was hampered not just by political and religious divisions in Austrian society but also by the large proportion of the labor force employed in agriculture. In 1920 41 percent of the labor force were employed in agriculture, a proportion which had only dropped to 32 percent by 1934. Even so, as in other Western European countries, union membership grew substantially after 1913 from 263,000 to a million by 1920 when it reached 51 percent of employees, a level comparable with Germany. To a large extent the union growth that occurred just after World War I was the result of legislative change. The newly created Austrian Republic, following the German example, sought to tie organized labor into the new political order by laws in 1919-20 which set up chambers of labor (modelled on the chambers of commerce) within the works' council law of 1919; these laws set up an ordered industrial relations system with compulsory union membership. By 1930 union membership had declined to 38 percent of employees in response to the economic dislocation of the 1920s and the Depression. Unions were also caught up in the turmoil of Austrian politics. After a short civil war in 1934, the socialist unions along with the Social Democratic Party were repressed and placed under the control of a labor federation run by the Catholic unions. After the annexation of

Austria by Germany in 1938, all Austrian organized labor was incorporated into the *Deutsche Arbeitsfront* (q.v.).

The end of World War II saw the immediate rebirth of free organized labor in Austria. Wartime imprisonment of all labor leaders by the Nazis encouraged the Catholics, socialists, and communists to bury their differences and form the *Österreichischer Gewerkschaftsbund* (Austrian Federation of Labor Unions) in April 1945. Comprised of fifteen industrial unions, the *Österreichischer Gewerkschaftsbund* has worked with government to promote economic growth and a stable democratic government. The laws of 1919-20 which set up works' councils were the basis of the "social partnership" which became characteristic of the corporatist approach to organized labor followed by Austria throughout the post-1945 period. In 1994 there were 1.6 million union members in Austria covering about 49 percent of employees. (*See also* Germany)

B

BALTIC STATES Until they gained their independence in 1918, all the Baltic States, that is Estonia, Latvia and Lithuania, were part of the Russian Empire. The new political freedom permitted the emergence of organized labor. In 1921 the labor federation of Latvia joined the International Federation of Trade Unions (IFTU) (q.v.) and remained a member until 1933. Labor federations also existed in Lithuania by 1926 and in Estonia by 1927. In 1923 Estonia claimed 30,000 union members and Latvia, 23,660. In Lithuania, a military government took power; the number of union members fell from 18,500 in 1927 to 1,200 by 1932. The Lithuanian labor federation had the shortest membership of the IFTU of any Baltic State, from 1926 to 1927. In Estonia, the number of union members reached 50,000 by 1932, and the national labor federation retained its membership of the IFTU until 1939. In 1940 an independent labor movement ceased to exist in the Baltic States after their forcible incorporation into the Soviet Union.

The first independent labor union in the post-1940 period in the Baltic States was formed in Lithuania in 1988. In 1989 the communist labor federation of Estonia joined the independence movement. During March 1990 all three Baltic States declared their independence from the Soviet Union. In Latvia, an independent labor movement arose after the country's gaining of political independence although there has been conflict over the ownership of the property of the former communist labor federation. In Estonia, two visiting Swedish union officials were murdered after they had made contact with the independent labor movement. In Lithuania, an independent workers' union was formed in 1989 and claimed 150,000 members by 1992. In 1991 the Lithuanian government nationalized the property of the communist labor federation. In 1994 Estonia was the only Baltic State which was represented in the International Confederation of Free Trade Unions (q.v.). (*See also* Poland)

"BATTLE OF THE OVERPASS" The "battle of the overpass" was the name given to a violent incident on May, 26 1937 on an overpass to the Ford Motor Company between CIO (q.v.) organizers and Ford's private police force. The organizers, who included Walter Reuther (q.v.) and Richard Frankensteen, had planned to hand out leaflets to Ford employees. Ford refused to recognize unions and ordered the organizers to go. In the fight which followed, Reuther and Frankensteen were beaten up by Ford's police. The incident was the subject of some famous photographs in the *Detroit News* and typified the violence of United States industrial relations in the 1930s. (*See also* Walter Philip Reuther)

BECK, DAVID (1894-1993) Beck was one of the main figures in the International Brotherhood of Teamsters, Chauffeurs, Warehousemen, and Helpers of America (q.v.) from the mid-1930s to the mid-1950s. Born in Stockton, California, he joined the union in 1914 and, after service in World War I, was elected to his first position within the union in 1923. He became a full-time organizer for the union in 1927 for the Northwest. In 1940 he became an international vice president. In 1949 he was the fraternal delegate of the American Federation of Labor to the British Trades Union Congress (qq.v.). In 1952 he was elected international president of the Teamsters. He supported Eisenhower's campaigns in the 1950s and became a vice president of the AFL-CIO (q.v.) between 1953 and 1957. In 1957 he was accused of corruption and embezzlement of union funds by Senator McClellan and expelled from the AFL-CIO. Beck served a thirty month jail term between 1962 and 1965 for federal income tax evasion. He later became a millionaire from real-estate dealings in Seattle, Washington. (*See also* Teamsters)

BELGIUM   The first Belgian unions were organized by spinners and weavers in the cotton industry in 1857, but organized labor was weak and divided by religion and ethnicity. Nevertheless, this did not mean the absence of working-class discontent; in April 1893 about 200,000 employees took part in a national strike. Catholic and socialist labor unions emerged in the 1880s, but even their combined efforts at recruitment yielded poor results. By 1900 there were only 42,000 union members or 3 percent of all employees. Only 10 percent of employees were unionized by 1913 but, in common with other Western European countries, union growth was substantial to 1920 when there were 920,000 union members or 45 percent of employees, a level not exceeded until 1950. Since 1960 the Catholic labor federation (*Confédération des Syndicats Chrétiens*, formed in 1909) and the socialist labor federation (*Fédération Générale du Travail de Belgique*) formed in 1937 from a labor body set up in 1898) have developed a closer working relationship to strengthen their bargaining position with employers. In the late 1980s about 53 percent of Belgian employees were members of labor unions. (*See also* Catholicism)

BELLAMY, EDWARD (1850-1898)   Born in Massachusetts, Bellamy became an influential journalist who popularized utopian socialism. His book *Looking Backward* (1888) attracted a large working-class readership in North America, Britain, and Australasia. In this book, Bellamy examined the industrial society of his day (in 1887) from the perspective of a technologically advanced and enlightened society over a century later in 2000. (*See also* Henry George, Tom Mann)

BEVIN, ERNEST (1881-1951)   Bevin was one of the greatest leaders ever to emerge from the ranks of British organized labor in the twentieth century. Born into a poor rural environment in Somerset, he held a number of lowly jobs until finding work as a van driver in 1901. His formal education was very limited. Like other labor leaders of his generation, he was a Methodist. He gained some further education from the Quaker Adult School and joined the Socialist Party in Bristol where he became a speaker and an organizer. In 1908 he became active in the Right to Work movement for the unemployed. During the strike by dockers (longshoremen) at Avonmouth, he organized the dock carters as part of the Dock, Wharf, Riverside, and General Workers' Union so they could not be used as strike-breakers. In 1911 Bevin became a full-time official of the Dockers' Union. An outstanding negotiator, Bevin became one of the Union's three national organizers in 1913. He realized that strong, centralized authority was as vital for unions as rank-and-file support.

In 1915-16 he was the fraternal delegate of the Trades Union Congress to the American Federation of Labor (qq.v.), a trip which gave him an international outlook on the world of organized labor. In 1920 his brilliant advocacy for the dock workers before the Industrial Court won him national recognition as did his leadership of the Council of Action's campaign to boycott the supply of military equipment to Poland (q.v.) for use against the Russian revolutionaries. In 1921 Bevin was the pivotal figure in the amalgamation (q.v.) of fourteen unions to create a new mass union, the Transport and General Workers' Union (TGWU) (q.v.), which by the late 1930s had grown to be the largest union in Britain and, for a brief time, the largest in the world.

In 1925 Bevin became a member of the general council of the Trades Union Congress (TUC), a position he held until 1940; in 1937 he was chairman of the TUC. During the 1930s Bevin successfully fought communist influence within the TGWU. In 1937-38 he conducted a tour of the British Commonwealth and was able to bring about improved labor relations. In 1940 he was made minister for labor, a position responsible for organizing Britain's labor force during World War II. Bevin's last official position was foreign secretary from 1945 to just before his death. (*See also* Arthur Deakin, Trades Union Congress, Transport and General Workers' Union, Waterfront)

BÖCKLER, HANS (1875-1951) Hans Böckler was one of the leading architects of the revived post-1945 German labor movement. The son of a coachman,he qualified as gold and silver smith and joined the *Deutscher Metallarbeiter-Verband* (q.v.) (German Engineering Union) and the Social Democratic Party in 1894. After being wounded in 1916, he left the army to become an official of the Engineering Union. In 1927 he became the Düsseldorf area chairman of the General German Trade Union Federation and was elected to the Reichstag in 1928. In 1944 Böckler managed to avoid capture by the Nazis for his part in the July Plot to kill Hitler.

After the Nazis' defeat, the Allies adopted different policies on the revival of the labor unions. The British policy, following the Potsdam Agreement which encouraged organized labor, was to allow the revival to come gradually from the local level first and to be carefully supervised whereas leaders like Böckler preferred to organize centralized democratic unions quickly using the organizational framework of the former Nazi *Deutsche Arbeitsfront* (q.v.). Böckler and other leaders were advised on the future structure of organized labor by a delegation from the British Trades Union Congress (q.v.) in 1945. The individual independent labor unions which had been approved set up the *Deutscher Gewerkschaftbund* (q.v.) (German Trade Union Federation) in the British zone on April, 22-25 1947 with Böckler as its head. Realizing the need for the labor movement to be better informed, Böckler was the prime mover in 1946 in creating the Institute for Economic Science to give the unions expert advice for their policies and positions. Also, in 1946 Böckler, in an address to the first labor conference in the British zone, made clear his support for the unions to be represented on the managing and supervisory boards of companies. In October 1949 the federations of German labor unions in the British, American and French zones of occupation were merged into the present *Deutscher Gewerkschaftbund* and Böckler was elected chairman by 397 out of 474 votes, a position he held until his death. (*See also Deutscher Gewerkschaftsbund, Mitbestimmung*)

BRAZIL The first labor unions were formed in Brazil in the 1900s but, as in other countries founded by Portugal or Spain, organized labor developed along the political and religious divisions of the mother country as were shown by the formation of Catholic, socialist, anarchist, and communist unions. Although Brazil claimed 270,000 union members by 1930, these divisions allowed the government of Getúlio Vargas to force all unions to become officially registered in 1931, a move which Vargas used to outlaw the communist and anarchist unions. Vargas, who ran the government until 1945, used the example of fascist Italy to build a corporatist state in which unions were controlled by government nominees or supporters and received their finances from compulsory contributions by all employees regardless of whether they were union members. Since 1945, as in other Latin American countries, the labor unions have played a central role in the campaign against authoritarian government and in favor of democracy, although their efforts have been hampered by internal political divisions. The 1950s and 1960s were marked by a high level of labor disputes and the growth of communist support. In 1964 an anti-union military junta seized government.

It was not until 1986 that the first national labor federation, the *Central Geral dos Trabalhadores* (CGT), was formed after the reintroduction of civilian government in 1985. In 1991 three Brazilian labor federations were members of the International Confederation of Free Trade Unions (q.v.): the CGT with 4 million members, the *Central Unica dos Trabalhadores* (formed in 1983) with 3.8 million members, and the *Força Sindical* with 2.1 million members. (*See also* Argentina, Chile, Italy)

BRENNER, OTTO (1907-1972) One of Germany's main post-1945 labor leaders, Brenner was born in Hanover and began his working life as a general laborer but eventually worked his way up to electrical engineer. He joined the *Deutscher Metallarbeiter-Verband* (q.v.) (German Metal Workers' Union) in 1922. He was a co-founder of the *Sozialdemokratische Arbeiterpartei* (Social Democratic Workers' Party) in 1931. Arrested by the Gestapo in 1933, he was jailed for two years and was under police surveillance until 1945. With Hans Brümmer, he was joint leader of *IG Metall* (q.v.) from 1952 to 1956 and then led the union alone until his death. Under Brenner's leadership, *IG Metall* led the movement in West Germany for shorter working hours. In 1958 Brenner warned of the dangers of unemployment caused by technological change. In 1969 he was elected president of the European Confederation of Free Trade Unions. (*See also Deutscher Metallarbeiter-Verband, IG Metall*)

BRITISH LABOUR PARTY Formed in 1900 as the Labour Representation Committee, the British Labour Party has been one of the leading continuous political parties in the world to be based on organized labor. Labor officials first began contesting British parliamentary elections in 1847 but none were successful until 1874 when Alexander Macdonald (1821-1881) and Thomas Burt (1837-1922), two coal miners' leaders, were elected to the House of Commons. In 1867 the franchise was widened to include relatively well-off urban working-class males. Because of its ability to work with the Liberal Party for labor objectives, the Trades Union Congress (TUC) (q.v.) was slow to see the need for organized labor to support its own political party. James Keir Hardie founded the Scottish Parliamentary Party in 1888 and the Independent Labour Party in 1893, but these were not arms of the unions. In 1892 Hardie succeeded in having a resolution for separate labor representation carried at the TUC but no action followed. It was the *Taff Vale Case* (q.v.) that galvanized organized labor into supporting a separate labor party; in 1906 the Labour Representation Committee was renamed the Labour Party. Membership was at first open only to unions but in 1918 individuals were allowed to join. During World War I a number of Labour members were participants in the government.

In 1918 the Labour Party adopted a socialization objective and in 1922 became the official opposition party for the first time. In 1923-24 the Labour Party formed a minority government under Ramsay MacDonald. In the 1930s the Labour Party fared badly in elections and directed its policies towards producing detailed reformist programs. During World War II, members of the Labour Party, such as Ernest Bevin (q.v.), participated in Churchill's government. In 1945 Labour, under Attlee (who had been leader of the party since 1935), won government for the first time and proceeded to implement wide-ranging reforms. Labour was defeated in 1951 and did not win government again until 1964.

Thereafter, the Labour Party's electoral record in national British politics was mixed: Labour lost power in 1970, regained it in 1974, and lost it again in 1979. Nevertheless, the Labour Party has been more successful in winning power in elections in local government. Compared to the Australian Labor Party (q.v.), the British Labour Party is a relatively left-wing political party. (*See also* Ernest Bevin, James Keir Hardie, Labour Representation League)

BULGARIA The first labor union in what is now Bulgaria was formed in 1883 by printers. Other unions were formed after that date and a Socialist Party was set up in 1893. In 1904 two labor federations were formed: one socialist and one Marxist. Despite its small membership (there were 2,700 members in 1904 and about 29,000 union members in 1911), organized labor conducted 537 strikes up to 1910 of which 161 won gains for the strikers. During World War I Bulgarian organized labor developed a revolutionary character; in 1920, when the two labor federations merged, union membership reached 36,000 and attained its pre-1945 peak of 49,800 in 1923. Bulgaria was an affiliate of the International Federation of Trade Unions (q.v.) from 1904 to 1913 and from 1921 to 1933. A military coup in June 1923 brought a fascist-style government to power which banned many labor unions. Although there was some revival of organized labor after 1927, union membership had fallen to 18,900 by 1933. After the withdrawal of the Nazis in 1944, the Confederation of Independent Trade Unions of Bulgaria (CITUB) was formed; it became a pillar of the communist regime and was given a range of responsibilities concerning labor administration. Bulgaria was a model of communist orthodoxy until the late 1980s.

In February 1989 some members of the intelligentsia formed an independent labor union, *Prodrepka* ("Support"). In spite of the imprisonment of some of its leaders, it claimed 100,000 members by December 1989 and played a central part in the popular uprisings which broke the communist political monopoly. The challenge posed by *Prodrepka* for the leadership of organized labor prompted the CITUB to reform itself and call a general strike in December 1990, a move which helped to cause the fall of the government. As in Poland (q.v.), disputes over the ownership of union assets have been a major issue since the fall of the communist government. In December 1991 the democratically elected government seized the assets of the Communist Party, a decision which included those of the CITUB. In June 1992 the CITUB and *Prodrepka* agreed that union property should be returned to organized labor and divided between them. In 1993 *Prodrepka* was a member of the International Confederation of Free Trade Unions (q.v.) with 321,200 members.

C

CANADA Labor unions in Canada made their presence felt at Saint John, New Brunswick, as early as 1812 when they tried to exclude American immigrants to maintain the shortage of skilled labor in the building industry. Up to the early 1870s Britain, through immigration (q.v.), was the dominant influence on the shaping of Canadian organized labor as shown by the establishment of Canadian branches of the British unions such as the Amalgamated Society of Engineers (q.v.) in 1853 and the Amalgamated Society of Carpenters and Joiners (q.v.) in 1872. The first local trade assemblies were formed in 1871.

With the growth of the American economy after the Civil War and its greater inter-relationship with the Canadian economy after the early 1870s, the United States increasingly came to dominate the politics and structure of organized labor in Canada. The Knights of Labor (q.v.) formed their first assembly in Canada in 1881, the same year which saw the formation of the Federation of Organized Trades and Labor Unions of the United States and Canada (q.v.) in Pittsburgh. Its successor, the American Federation of Labor (q.v.), soon established a presence in Canada. Conflict arose with the Knights of Labor and in 1902 the Canadian Trade and Labour Congress (formed in 1886) expelled the Knights and all other unions not part of an American (or "international") union. The excluded unions formed their own federation, the National Trades and Labour Congress in Canada in 1903 which was renamed the Canadian Federation of Labour in 1908. In 1906 the International Workers of the World (q.v.) formed its first organization in Canada; as in the United States, it largely recruited the lesser skilled employees. Catholic unions in Quebec created a provincial federation in 1921. In common with other countries Canada experienced a wave of labor disputes after World War I, notably the general strike in Winnipeg in 1919. The One Big Union (q.v.) movement also found support at the same time. Despite the growth of organized labor, the proportion of employees enrolled in unions remained low. In 1920, for example, only 15 percent of Canadian employees were union members compared to 42 percent in Australia, 17 percent in the United States and 26 percent in New Zealand. Union density rose to 33 percent in 1950 but remained relatively unchanged thereafter; unlike other countries, Canada did not suffer a sharp decline in union membership during the 1980s.

For most of the twentieth century about half of Canada's union members have been members of American unions, a feature which ensured that the political divisions and events of the United States, such as the formation of the Congress of Industrial Organizations (q.v.), were also part of the history of Canadian organized labor. This particular chapter was closed in 1956 when the Trades and Labour Congress (the Canadian equivalent of the AFL) and the Canadian Congress of Labour (the Canadian equivalent of the CIO) merged to form the Canadian Labour Congress which remains the largest labor federation in the country with 2.2 million members in 1990. Since 1974 a number of Canadian unions split from the American unions to be fully independent in collective bargaining. (*See also* Rand Formula, United States of America)

CARIBBEAN CONGRESS OF LABOUR This regional international labor organization was formed in 1960 to lobby Caribbean governments on labor issues and to provide training and research. In 1990 it had seventeen member countries and represented 122,600 employees. Most of its country members are also members of the International Confederation of Free Trade Unions (q.v.).

CATHOLICISM Catholics and Catholicism have played a major role in shaping the history of organized labor. Because the growth of socialism (q.v.) in Western Europe was often associated with anti-clericalism, it led to a Catholic reaction. At Ghent, an Anti-Socialist League was set up in 1878. In France, the first Catholic labor union was formed among white-collar workers in 1887. The papal encyclical *Rerum Novarum* (Of New Things) rejected socialism but recognized and supported the need for social justice within industrial society, thereby encouraging Catholics to participate in labor unions. In Germany, the first Catholic unions were formed in 1894 and by 1919 had a combined membership of one million. In France, the first national Catholic union was formed among clerical workers in 1913. In Switzerland, Catholic unions formed their own federation in 1907. A French Catholic labor federation, *Confédération Française des Travailleurs Chrétiens*, was formed in 1919; it claimed to represent 100,000 employees. An international body, the International Federation of Christian Trade Unions (q.v.), was formed at the Hague in 1920, the culmination of efforts begun in 1908. Although Catholic labor organizations were important, they did not represent the full extent of Catholic activity in organized labor for Catholics were also active in the non-Catholic organizations which generally retained their numerical superiority over the purely Catholic ones.

The emergence of communism (q.v.) from the early 1920s presented Catholicism with its greatest ideological challenge of the century as it had many of the features often associated with a religion. Communism was officially condemned by the Vatican in the encyclical *Domini Redemptoris* (Redemption of the Lord) in 1937. From that time onwards, Catholics were important as a group in fighting communist infiltration of organized labor in the 1940s and 1950s. Catholic unions remain a feature of organized labor in Western Europe but in Germany and Austria (qq.v.) their support is limited because the pre-World War II divisions within organized unions were seen as contributing to the success of fascism. (*See also* Communism, World Confederation of Labor)

CHARTISM Chartism was a radical political movement in England in the 1830s and 1840s. The objectives of Chartism were expressed in the People's Charter which called for voting for all adult males, annual parliaments, vote by secret ballot, public payment of members of parliament, population equality of electoral districts, and the abolition of property qualifications for members of parliament. Although most of these aims were achieved in England by 1914, the most radical demand, for annual parliaments, was not; had it been agreed to, it would have drastically altered the British constitution. Chartism drew its strength from the depressed economic conditions of the time and the unemployment in many industrialized areas. The People's Charter was presented to parliament as a petition in 1839, 1842, and 1848 and was rejected each time. England's rulers saw Chartism as a revolutionary movement and treated it with hostility. The movement was marked by violence (24 were killed at Newport) and internal divisions. With the gradual economic recovery in the late 1840s, Chartism died but its ideas entered the agenda of working-class politics in other English-speaking countries through emigration. It has been suggested that the benign attitude of British governments after 1850 towards the emergence of organized labor compared to Chartism was to encourage working-class activism to take an orderly, moderate form. (*See also* United Kingdom)

CHECKOFF A formal arrangement between an employer and a union whereby the employer deducts union fees and dues from their employees' pay and remits them to the union. In Britain and Australia this arrangement referred to as check-off. Checkoff systems operated in Britain by 1894 but have have grown in importance since the 1960s. (*See also* Rand Formula)

CHILD LABOR The elimination of child labor was a general objective of organized labor in the nineteenth century, not just on the grounds of the protection of children but also to reduce their competition with adults. As children were cheaper to employ than adults, their employment tended to keep down the wages of adults. Early nineteenth century social reformers like Robert Owen (q.v.) opposed the employment of children. Union pressure for legislation to regulate factory employment and exclude child labor effectively began in 1833 in England, but progress was slow and grudging. In the United States, Samuel Gompers (qq.v.), although generally suspicious of government labor laws, supported them if they were aimed at eliminating child labor. The National Child Labor Committee (formed in 1904) induced most states to pass child labor legislation, but Supreme Court opposition delayed the passing of a national law to directly prohibit child labor until 1949. The International Labour Organisation (ILO) (q.v.) has sought to reduce the incidence of child labor but with limited success outside of Western economies. The first ILO Convention concerning child labor was adopted in 1919: the Minimum Age (Industry) Convention, 1919 (No. 5). Child labor remains widespread in Third World countries with many poor families seeing child labor as essential for their economic survival. On January 8, 1995 the Indian National Trade Union Congress and the the Centre of Indian Trade Unions signed a pact with the International Labour Organisation to work towards the elimination of child labor. (*See also* Minimum Age)

CHILE The first labor organizations in Chile were founded as mutual aid associations by artisans in 1847. The growth of unions was slowed by hostile governments which violently suppressed strikes in 1890 and 1907; the 1907 strike was led by nitrate employees of whom over 2,000 were killed by the army. The first national labor federation in Chile was set up in 1909. Anarchism (q.v.) attracted a wide following and an anarchist labor federation existed between 1931 and 1936. The number of union members was claimed to be 150,000 by 1923 and 204,000 in 1927. A new labor federation was created in 1936, but during 1946-47 it split into communist and socialist factions. A reformed national labor federation, the *Central Unica de Trabajadores* (CUT), was established in 1953; left-wing in character but independent of any political party, it became affiliated with the World Federation of Trade Unions (q.v.). During the 1960s there was a general rise in labor unrest, a reflection of the deep divisions in Chilean society. In 1970 Salvador Allende, the leader of the Popular Unity Coalition, was elected president with the CUT as his major ally. In September 1973 Allende was assassinated in a military coup which had the backing of the Nixon administration. Unions and collective bargaining were not only suppressed but 13,000 people were arrested and at least 2,200 were executed. Labor unrest during the 1980s gave rise to a new, broadly based labor federation, the *Central Unitaria de Trabajadores,* in August 1988 which actively worked for the restoration of democractic government (achieved in 1990) and labor law reform. In 1992 there were about 720,000 union members in Chile (about 24 percent of employees) of whom 425,000 were affiliated with the CUT. Between 1983 and 1993 the number of unions in Chile rose from 4,401 to 11,389. (*See also* Argentina, Brazil, Mexico)

CHINA The first Chinese labor unions were formed in the Canton region from 1895; they were followed by a union of seamen formed in the British colony of Hong Kong in 1909 who successfully defended their union by a general strike in 1922 against an attempt to suppress it . In the same year, the first national congress of Chinese labor was held which led to the formation of the All China General Labor Federation in 1925. Organized labor drew much of its support from the industrial city of Shanghai. In 1927 Chiang Kai-shek purged the communists from organized labor in Shanghai which resulted in the killing of about 5,000 people. In 1930 there were said to be 2.8 million labor union members in China, but free labor bodies were never able to get established primarily because neither the communists nor the Kuomintang supported an independent labor movement. In 1989 there was some attempt to form independent labor unions but these and the Free Trade Union Preparatory Committee (formed at the end of 1991) were suppressed by the government in 1992. Neither China nor Taiwan (q.v.) was a member of the International Confederation of Free Trade Unions (q.v.) in 1993. On January 1, 1995 a labor law came into effect which set down minimum general conditions of employment for the first time. (*See also* Japan, Taiwan)

COAL MINING With engineering, coal mining was one of the main pillars of organized labor in most Western countries. Between the mid-1900s and the late 1930s coal miners' unions were the largest single labor unions in both Britain and the United States (q.v.). Within both countries, labor unions among coal miners emerged on a regional basis after 1840, but their attempts to form effective national bodies floundered until the 1890s. The similarity in the two countries was explained not just by the geographical separation between coalfields but also by the presence of British immigrants among the union leaders in the early history of coal mining in the United States. The first labor union in the anthracite coalfields of Pennsylvania was organized by an English immigrant, John Bates, in 1849. Later, Daniel Weaver and Thomas Lloyd, both immigrant miners from Staffordshire, formed the American Miners' Association in 1861.

Between 1854 and 1902 nearly 191,000 miners of all kinds emigrated from Britain; of the 184,000 whose destinations are known, 109,200 went to the United States, 11,000 to Canada and 24,900 to Australia and New Zealand (qq.v.). The bulk of this migration occurred between 1854 and 1871 when 70,400 miners departed from Britain. In 1890 58 percent of coal miners in Pennsylvania were foreign-born; in Australia, 76 percent of coal miners in the largest coalfield, at Newcastle, New South Wales, were foreign-born.

Because coal was the main source of energy up to the 1950s, coal miners' unions were able to command considerable influence within organized labor but since that time, technological changes reduced the number of miners needed and other sources of energy lessened the reliance on coal. Between 1910 and 1940 the amount of energy supplied to the United States economy from coal fell from 85 to 50 percent. Coal mining had also been a major source of labor disputes (q.v.) in Australia, Britain, and the United States before 1950. (*See also* Immigration, Mineworkers' Federation of Great Britain, United Mine Workers of America)

CO-DETERMINATION (*See Mitbestimmung*)

COGHLAN, TIMOTHY AUGUSTINE (1855-1926) Born in Sydney of Irish parents, Coghlan became the colonial statistician of New South Wales in 1886, a post he held until 1905 when he became agent-general in London. As a statistician, he achieved acclaim both in Australia and internationally; in 1893 he was made a Fellow of the Royal Statistical Society in London. One of his special interests was organized labor and his official publications are an important source for their study in Australia. His great work was *Labour and Industry in Australia from the First Settlement in 1788 to the Establishment of the Commonwealth in 1901* published as four volumes in 1918 by Oxford University Press, which remains an important source for economic, political, and labor history in the last half of the nineteenth century. He was knighted in 1914. (*See also* Australia, Labor Statistics)

COLLECTIVE BARGAINING Collective bargaining refers to a decision-making process whereby employers and unions negotiate the wages and conditions of employment. This process may also include governments. The form of collective bargaining varies. Unions and employers may bargain directly with each other or through a third party, such as an independent negotiator or a tribunal established by the government. Bargaining structures can vary also. Bargaining can take place with just a single enterprise or across a whole industry or a whole country. The types of collective bargaining which take place reflect the particular histories and cultures of the countries concerned. For example, collective bargaining in the private sector in the United States and the United Kingdom is generally done without any government participation whereas in Australia (qq.v.) government industrial tribunals play an active part in the bargaining process. (*See also* Union-Government Agreements)

COLORED NATIONAL LABOR UNION (CNLU) The CNLU was a black American labor confederation which was formed in Washington, D.C., in December 1869 out of the refUnited Statesl of the National Labor Union (NLU) (q.v.) to accept racial integration. The two bodies also disagreed over politics. The leadership of the CNLU was inclined to favor the Republican Party whereas the leadership of the NLU supported the Greenback Party and the Democrats. Membership of the CNLU was open to any black worker. The CNLU faced too many obstacles to endure, and its last national convention was held in October 1871. (*See also* National Labor Union, Race and Ethnicity)

COMBINATION ACTS The Combination Acts were two English laws passed in 1799 and 1800 by the government of William Pitt during the war with France. The laws were part of a series of measures designed to repress political disturbances. They were enacted against a backdrop of high levels of wartime inflation and forebade combinations (that is labor unions) to press employers for higher wages and fewer hours. The intention of the legislation seems to have been to outlaw labor disputes (q.v.) rather than peaceful collective bargaining. Labor unions which did not strike seem to have continued to operate without legal harassment. The 1800 act included provision for arbitration in labor disputes. The Combination Laws were not repealed until 1824 following agitation led by Francis Place (q.v.) and Joseph Hume. Important as the repeal of the Combination Acts was, the legal advance for labor bodies it represented was severely qualified by amending legislation passed in 1825 (Combination of Workmen Act) which effectively outlawed picketing. (*See also* Francis Place)

COMINTERN Also known as the Third International, the Comintern was formed in Moscow in 1919 as a means of assuming communist leadership of international socialism. During the 1920s and 1930s, the Comintern was the means of coordinating communist parties to meet the needs and interests of the Soviet Union. Stalin formally dissolved the Comintern in 1943. (*See also* Communism)

COMMONS, JOHN ROGERS (1862-1945) Born in Ohio, Commons became a political reformer on the side of labor and one of the foremost political economists in the United States. Based in

Wisconsin, he played a significant role in drafting progressive labor laws between 1905 and 1911 and served on the state's Industrial Commission between 1911 and 1913. Outside of Wisconsin, he helped to found the American Association for Labor Legislation in 1906, served on the Commission on Industrial Relations between 1913 and 1915 and was president of the National Consumers' League from 1923 to 1935. Among his many achievements was his founding of the Wisconsin school of labor history, one of the first systematic, scholarly endeavors of its kind anywhere. His publications included *A Documentary History of American Industrial Society* (1910-11,10 vols.) and *History of Labor in the United States* (1918-35, 4 vols.).

COMMONWEALTH TRADE UNION COUNCIL   This international body, based in London, was formed in 1979 to promote the interests of employees in the fifty countries which make up the Commonwealth, that is the former British Empire. In 1990 there were 30 million employees in the Council's member countries.

COMMONWEALTH V. HUNT   *Commonwealth v. Hunt* was an early landmark legal case in American labor history. In 1842 the Massachusetts Court essentially held that labor unions were legal organizations and not a conspiracy and that the unions' goal of establishing a closed shop was not an illegal objective. The favorable decision of *Commonwealth v. Hunt* was overturned by a number of court decisions in other states concerning labor between 1885 and 1889, decisions which weakened the legal position of unions in striking for closed shops. (*See also* Right-to-Work Laws)

COMMUNICATION WORKERS' UNION OF AMERICA (CWU)   The CWU is the largest telecommunications union in the world. It claimed a total of 700,000 members in the United States and Canada in 1992. The CWU grew out of the organization of telephone workers in the 1890s by the International Brotherhood of Electrical Workers and the Commercial Telegraphers' Union. The modern union began as the National Federation of Telephone Workers which was formed at Chicago in June 1939 with 45,000 members. By 1945 the Federation had grown to 170,000 members. Following a failed strike against the American Telephone and Telegraph Company, the Federation renamed itself the Communication Workers' Association in 1947 and was reorganized along more central lines. In 1949 it joined the Congress of Industrial Organizations (q.v.) to avoid further jurisdictional or demarcation disputes with other unions in the telecommunications industry. Membership rose from 180,000 in 1950 to 260,000 in 1960 and to 420,000 by 1970. (*See also* Congress of Industrial Organizations, Postal, Telegraph and Telephone International)

COMMUNISM The successful establishment of the Bolshevik regime under Lenin following the revolution in the former Russian Empire in 1917 and the formation of communist parties in other parts of the world after 1918 began a new era in the history of organized labor. Underlying these changes were an upsurge of working-class discontent based on sharp inflation during and after World War I and the economic slump of the early 1920s. Following Lenin, communist theory and practice regarded labor unions as the primary vehicle of working-class organizations and, as such, ideal for infiltration and moblization on behalf of revolution; this was the purpose of the Comintern (q.v.) which was established in March 1919. Non-communist bodies which proved resistant to infiltration, notably the International Federation of Trade Unions (q.v.), were made the targets of propaganda wars of ridicule and scorn. As organizations, labor unions were often poorly equipped to deal with communist infiltration because of the low proportion of members who usually attended union meetings. As well, many communists gained election to union posts because of their dedication and hard work. The communist presence was notable in certain industries such as coal mining (q.v.), engineering, transportation, and the waterfront (q.v.); during the Depression of the early 1930s communists were often the leaders of moves to mobilize the unemployed into movements. With Hitler's attack on the Soviet Union in June 1941, the communist parties in the West were instructed to cooperate with their governments. In 1943 the Comintern was officially disbanded. The end of World War II and the start of the Cold War saw a renewal of the Russian-led campaign to infiltrate organized labor, a campaign which brought about a split of the World Federation of Trade Unions and the creation of the International Confederation of Free Trade Unions (qq.v.) in 1949. The improvement in the world economy after the early 1950s and determined campaigns to remove communists from key union positions (often, but not entirely, led by Catholics), largely eliminated communism as a major force within organized labor in the West. Nevertheless, individual communist leaders continued to be important in organized labor until the 1980s. (*See also* Catholicism, Comintern)

CONCILIATION AND ARBITRATION Conciliation and arbitration are two methods which can be used for settling labor disputes (q.v.). Following legislation in 1562 to fix maximum levels of wages, local courts in England acted as industrial tribunals and as wages boards. By 1769 conciliation in labor disputes had become an important part of the work of English magistrates. The Combination Act (q.v.) of 1800 included an arbitration clause. During the nineteenth century, conciliation and arbitration gradually became features of the method of resolving labor disputes. Conciliation referred to the voluntary use of a mediator who tried to reach a settlement which both employer and employees would accept. Failing that, resort could be made to arbitration where a settlement would be proposed by a board or individual. The first conciliation legislation was passed in Britain in 1867, but the system had mixed success. In the wave of labor disputes in the late-nineteenth and early-twentieth century, governments considered making conciliation and arbitration compulsory, that is the parties in dispute would be legally compelled to accept the settlement of a board or tribunal. In Britain, labor unions generally opposed compulsory conciliation and arbitration.

Nevertheless, compulsory arbitration as a means of settling disputes was used in Germany (1923-28), France (1936-39), Britain (1915-19 and 1940-51), Kansas, U.S., (1920-23), Norway, (1945-52), and Turkey (1947-63, 1980-82).

Compulsory conciliation and arbitration achieved its most lasting success in Australia and New Zealand (qq.v.). In 1894 New Zealand introduced compulsory arbitration into its legal system, and it remained there until removed by far-reaching reforms in 1991. In Australia, industrial tribunals were established under federal and state laws between 1896 and 1912. In the early 1900s there was considerable interest in these labor experiments from the United Kingdom, France, and the United States. In 1907 the British government sent Ernest Aves (1857-1917) on a fact-finding mission to Australia and New Zealand to investigate compulsory conciliation and arbitration; he reported that these systems seem to work well in their particular environments but concluded that the different legal and economic environment of the United Kingdom made their adoption inappropriate. Since the mid-1980s both federal and state governments in Australia have encouraged greater reliance on collective bargaining although the essentials of the conciliation and arbitration system remain intact. (*See also* Australia, New Zealand, Order 1305)

CONFEDERACIÓN DE TRABAJADORES DE AMERICA LATINA

(CTAL) The CTAL, or Confederation of Latin American Workers, was formed in 1938 by Vincente Lombardo Toledano, a Mexican Marxist. A left-wing international federation, it had close links with the Congress of Industrial Organizations (q.v.). During World War II, the CTAL actively promoted organized labor in Latin America and supported the work of the International Labour Organisation (q.v.). In 1945 the CTAL joined the World Federation of Trade Unions (WFTU) (q.v.) and became its regional affiliate for Latin America. The CTAL remained with the WFTU after the withdrawal of its non-communist members in 1948. In 1962 the CTAL was officially disbanded and replaced by the *Congreso Permanente de Unidad Sindical de los Trabajadores de America Latina* (Permanent Congress of Trade Union Unity of Latin American Workers). (*See also Congreso Permanente de Unidad Sindical de los Trabajadores de America Latina, Organización Regional Interamericana de Trabajadores,* World Federation of Trade Unions)

CONFEDERACIÓN INTERAMERICANA DE TRABAJADORES

(CIT) The CIT, or Interamerican Confederation of Workers, was the successor body to the Pan-American Federation of Labor. Formed on January 10, 1948 in Lima, Peru, the other founding member countries of the CIT were: the United States, Brazil, Bolivia, Chile, Cuba, Mexico, Costa Rica, Colombia, Dutch Guiana, Puerto Rico, El Salvador, and Panama. The American Federation of Labor (q.v.) represented by George Meany (q.v.) and others was the prime mover in the creation of the CIT which also had the support of the U.S. Department of State in its efforts to insulate Latin America from European fascism. The CIT soon fell victim to regional and international politics. In 1949 it was expelled from Peru by the government crackdown on organized labor and was then caught up in the politics of the Cold War. In 1951 the CIT reorganized itself into the *Organización Regional Interamericana de Trabajadores.* (*See also Organización Regional Interamericana de Trabajadores*)

CONFÉDÉRATION EUROPÉENNE DES CADRES (CEC) The CEC

or European Conferederation of Managers was formed in 1989 to represent the interests of European managers and executives. Since December 1993 it has been formally recognized by the European Commission as a "social partner" for European-level dialogue on social policy matters. In 1993 the CEC had an affiliated membership of 800,000 of whom 181,000 were French and 146,000 were Italian. (*See also* EUROCADRES, European Trade Union Confederation)

CONFÉDÉRATION EUROPÉENNE DES SYNDICATS INDÉPENDANTS (CESI)   The CESI, or Confederation of Independent European Trade Unions, was created in 1990 to represent the interests of a range of independent labor organizations. Its country membership in 1993 consisted of Belgium, Germany, Iceland, Italy, the Netherlands, Portugal, Spain, and the United Kingdom as well as Sweden, Norway (to July 1994), the Czech and Slovak Republics, and the Public Services International (q.v.). In 1993 the CESI claimed 7 million members among all its affiliates of whom about 5 million worked in the European Union. The CESI has not been granted "social partner" status for European-level dialogue on social policy matters by the European Commission. (*See also* EUROCADRES, European Trade Union Confederation)

CONFÉDÉRATION GÉNÉRALE DU TRAVAIL (CGT)   The CGT, or General Confederation of Labor, has been the oldest continuous peak labor organization in France since its formation at Limoges in 1895 when it absorbed the National Federation of *Bourses du Travail* in 1902. In 1906 the CGT adopted the radical Charter of Amiens which called for wage increases and shorter working hours by dispossessing the "capitalist class" and supported the general strike as a means of achieving that end; the charter also made the CGT independent of any political party or philosophy. Between 1914 and 1920 the number of union members represented by the CGT grew from 400,000 to 2.5 million but, as before 1914, the CGT was riven by tensions between its right and left wings. In 1921-22 the CGT split when the communists and syndicalists formed their own federation, the *Confédération Générale du Travail Unitaire* which joined the Red International of Labor Unions in 1923. In 1936 the CGT and the *Confédération Générale du Travail Unitaire* held a unity congress which resulted in its readmission to the CGT. Membership of the CGT soared to between 4 and 5 million by 1936. Nevertheless, tensions between the communists and non-communists remained.

In 1948 many of the non-communists in the CGT left to form their own body, the *Confédération Générale du Travail-Force Ouvriére* (CGT-FO), leaving the CGT effectively under the control of the French Communist Party (formed in 1920). The CGT has been the most important Western European affiliate of the communist World

Federation of Trade Unions (q.v.) since 1949. Despite a fall in the membership of the CGT from 2.3 million to 800,000 between the early 1970s and 1988, the CGT remains the largest peak labor body in France. (*See also* France)

CONFEDERATION OF HEALTH SERVICE EMPLOYEES COHSE) COHSE, a British health workers' union, was formed in 1946 from the merger of the Mental Hospital and Institutional Workers' Union (founded in 1910) and the Hospital and Welfare Services Union (founded in 1918). Between 1948 and 1982 its membership grew from 25,000 to 230,000. (*See also* UNISON)

CONFEDERATION OF SHIPBUILDING AND ENGINEERING UNIONS (CSEU) The CSEU began in 1891 as the Federation of Engineering and Shipbuilding Trades. It provided a forum for collective bargaining for British white- and blue-collar unions in shipbuilding and engineering. In its present form, it was constituted in 1936 but until World War II it was not a fully representative body. Wartime cooperation with the Foundry Union and the Amalgamated Engineering Union (AEU) (q.v.) on the national negotiating body, the National Engineering Joint Trades Movement (formed in 1941) helped to allay suspicions and in 1944 the Foundry Union joined the CSEU followed by the ASE in 1946. In 1989 the CSEU had twenty-two affiliated organizations representing 2 million members. (*See also* Amalgamated Engineering Union)

CONGRESO PERMANENTE DE UNIDAD SINDICAL DE LOS TRABAJADORES DE AMERICA LATINA (CPUSTAL) The CPUSTAL or Permanent Congress of Trade Union Unity of Latin American Workers is an international labor federation formed in 1964 with eighteen member countries from Latin America and the Caribbean. It succeeded the *Confederación de Trabajadores de America Latina* (q.v.). Closely associated with the World Federation of Trade Unions (q.v.), it had twenty-five member countries in 1990 and claimed 20 million members. The CPUSTAL has faced much opposition from right-wing governments. (*See also Organización Regional Interamericana de Trabajadores*)

CONGRESS OF INDUSTRIAL ORGANIZATIONS (CIO) The CIO was a national labor federation in the United States (q.v.) from 1935 to 1955. Unlike its competitor, the American Federation of Labor

(AFL) (q.v.), the CIO practiced industrial unionism and sought to organize the unskilled. Although there had been earlier attempts to recruit the unskilled into the ranks of organized labor, notably by the Knights of Labor and by the Industrial Workers of the World (qq.v.), the results of their efforts had been short-lived. The AFL only supported unions based on "craft" or occupation and ignored the unskilled and those employed in the mass production industries which emerged after 1900. During the 1920s the membership of American unions declined in the face of company unionism, well-organized campaigns for the open-shop, and an unsympathetic political and legal environment. In 1929 a group of Socialists and progressive labor unionists led by A. J. Muste set up the Conference for Progressive Labor Action to win the AFL over to industrial unionism and recruitment of the unskilled, but their efforts failed.

The possibility for success came in 1933 in the form of Section 7(a) of the National Industrial Recovery Act which provided for the right of employees to form unions for collective bargaining free from employer interference. Despite the known existence of a high level of support for unionism in mass production industries, the leadership of the AFL successfully resisted all efforts to charter new industrial unions at its 1934 convention. John L. Lewis, the president of the United Mine Workers of America (qq.v.), itself an industrial union, assumed the leadership of the dissidents to the AFL policy and, along with Sidney Hillman of the Amalgamated Clothing Workers, David Dubinsky of the International Ladies' Garment Workers' Union (qq.v.), and five other labor leaders formed the Committee for Industrial Organization in November 1935. In August 1936 the ten unions which had affiliated with the CIO were suspended by the AFL following successful organizing drives by the CIO in the steel, automobile, radio, and rubber industries.

The CIO unions went on to win three major industrial victories for union recognition. The first was achieved by a large-scale sit-down strike at the Goodyear Tire and Rubber Company which won union recognition for the CIO's United Rubber Workers in 1936. In March 1937 the CIO won an unexpected major victory by negotiating union recognition for the Steel Workers Organizing Committee from U.S. Steel. The committee negotiated a 10 percent pay rise, an eight-hour day, and a 40-hour week. The third victory for union recognition was won by the United Automobile Workers' Union (q.v.) (CIO) against the General Motors' Corporation also in 1937. In 1938 the CIO was expelled from the AFL. The last major victory by the CIO was the gaining of recognition by the United Automobile Workers (CIO) from the Ford Motor Company after a ten-day strike in 1941. By 1939 the CIO claimed that its affiliated unions had a combined membership of 1.8 million compared to 3.9 million for the AFL. World War II more than doubled the membership of the CIO to 3.9 million making it equal to that of the AFL.

However, the CIO never again regained the recruiting initiative it had taken in the late 1930s because the AFL began to recognize industrial unionism within its own ranks as shown by the conversion of large affiliates like the Teamsters (q.v.) into industrial unions and by the defection of John L. Lewis and his United Mine Workers of America from the CIO in 1940. The Cold War also harmed the CIO which had always been a more militant body than the AFL. On November 5, 1955 the two organizations agreed to merge as the AFL-CIO. At the time of its merger, the CIO had an affiliated membership of 4.6 million. (*See also* American Federation of Labor, John L. Lewis)

COOPERATIVE MOVEMENT The cooperative movement has been an important part of organized labor in Britain since the 1860s. The goal of the cooperative movement was greater economic democracy by means of owning and running cooperative stores for the benefit of members. The progressive factory owner, Robert Owen (q.v.), established a cooperative store as part of his model factory at New Lanark and encouraged the growth of a wider cooperative movement which resulted in five cooperative conferences between 1831 and 1833. But the present cooperative movement was begun at a store in Rochdale in 1844. Its principles were to pool the capital of members to buy and sell goods and return part of the profits back to members in the form of a dividend. The cooperative movement grew from 15,000 members in 1851 to 437,000 by 1875 and to 1.7 million by 1900, spread among 1,439 locally controlled societies. The cooperative movement was important not just for improving the living standards of members by the payment of the dividend but also as a source of unadulterated food at a time when adulteration of food by retailers was common. Cooperatives were strongest in manufacturing and mining areas. They assisted union members and their families during strikes and played an occasional part in twentieth century British labor politics. Consumer cooperatives also became a feature of retailing in Britain, Belgium, Israel, and Scandinavia but not the United States. By 1919 they claimed 4.1 million members in Britain.

Although consumer cooperatives have declined since the 1960s, the Co-operative Wholesale Society (formed in Manchester 1863) has been commercially successful and for the year ended January 1994 had a turnover of 7.1 billion pounds and represented 8.2 million members. (*See also* Robert Owen)

COUNCIL OF EUROPEAN PROFESSIONAL AND MANAGERIAL STAFF (*See* EUROCADRES)

COUNCIL OF NORDIC TRADE UNIONS   An international labor organization representing Denmark, Sweden, Finland, Norway, and Iceland (qq.v.), this Council has existed since 1972 in its present form, but its origins date back to 1886. In 1990 the Council represented 7.2 million members.

CUBA   The first Cuban labor union was formed among tobacco employees in 1868 and over the next 15 years a number of craft unions were set up. A congress of Cuban employees was held in 1892 and passed resolutions calling for independence from Spain and the eight-hour day.   Anarchism (q.v.), as in other Latin American countries, was an important force within organized labor; an anarchist labor federation was created in 1925. In 1933 there was a general strike which succeeded in gaining some progressive legislation but a second general strike in 1935 was repressed and organized labor crushed. It revived in 1938 and in January 1939 the *Confederación de Trabajadores de Cuba* (Confederation of the Workers of Cuba) was formed.   Castro's triumph over Batista was greatly assisted by a general strike in 1959. With Castro's victory, organized labor was gradually deprived of its independence.   In October 1991 an Independent Cuban General Workers' Union was created, but as of mid-1994, it had still not been officially registered by the government.

CZECHOSLOVAKIA   Before 1918 Czechoslovakia was part of the Austro-Hungarian Empire.   The first labor union was set up by journeymen drapers at Liberec in 1870 and had 3,500 members after a year. Unions became part of the political struggle for independence as well as pursuing industrial objectives. A labor federation was formed in 1897 some of whose members attended as observers at the conferences of the International Federation of Trade Unions (IFTU) (q.v.) in 1901 and 1902. Reflecting the diversity of the society, unions were divided along national, political, and religious lines. In 1905 the unions made their presence felt through protests for the eight-hour day as well as for the universal franchise. By 1913 there were 318,000 union members; some were in German unions and others were members of Catholic or Protestant unions. In 1919 the Czech and German labor federations became affiliates of the IFTU and remained affiliated until 1938. By 1920 there were 1.7 million union members in the Czechoslovak Republic. Unlike most of its neighbors, Czechoslovakia had a large industrial base; in 1921 37 percent of the labor force were employed in manufacturing. Union membership peaked at 1,738,300 in 1928 when there were 583 unions. Under the Nazi occupation (1938-45), free unions were suppressed and compliant ones created.

As result of the experiences of World War II, the communists gained much popular support. In 1945 the communists formed their own labor federation the Central Council of Trade Unions. Noncommunist unions re-established themselves but their independence was short-lived and from 1948 the communist federation was the sole national labor center. During the "Prague Spring" in 1968, the unions actively supported Dubcek's program of reforms. The twelve industrial unions were divided into fifty-eight new unions with a high degree of independence. After the Soviet invasion and the fall of Dubček in April 1969, these initiatives were suppressed. After the collapse of the communist regime in November 1989 in the so-called "Velvet Revolution," organized labor carried out its own internal reforms which produced a united federation of Czech and Slovak unions *Česka a Slovenská Konfederace odborových* (ČS-KOS) with a membership of 6 million. Following the peaceful division of the country into the Czech Republic and the Slovak Republic, the ČS-KOS was also divided along Czech and Slovak lines. In 1994 there were 2.6 million members in the Czech Republic and 1.2 million members in the Slovak Republic.

D

DEAKIN, ARTHUR (1890-1955) One of the leading British labor leaders after 1940, Deakin was born in Sutton Coldfield, Warwickshire, and moved to Wales in the early 1900s where he worked in a steel plant. During this period he became a Primitive Methodist and a teetotaller. In 1910 he moved to north Wales where he was a member of several unions including the Amalgamated

Society of Engineers (q.v.) but transferred to the Dock, Wharf, Riverside, and General Workers' Union and became a full-time organizer for the Union in 1919. When the Union became part of the Transport and General Workers' Union (TGWU) (q.v.) in 1922, Deakin became, in effect, its manager for north Wales. After holding various local government positions, he became national secretary of the General Workers' part of the TGWU and moved to London where his abilities were recognized by the general secretary, Ernest Bevin (q.v.), who made Deakin his protégé. When Bevin joined Churchill's War Cabinet in 1940, Deakin became the acting general secretary of the TGWU, and he became permanent in the position with Bevin's retirement in 1946. In the same year he also became president of the World Federation of Trade Unions (q.v.) and like his patron, Bevin, strongly opposed the communists who were against the Marshall Plan for aiding postwar Europe. Indeed, Deakin played a central role in the foundation of the International Confederation of Free Trade Unions (q.v.) in 1949. Deakin continued to play an important part in fighting communist influence within the Trades Union Congress (q.v.) of which he was president in 1951-52. (*See also* Ernest Bevin, Transport and General Workers' Union)

DEBS, EUGENE VICTOR (1855-1926)   Born in Indiana, Debs joined the railroad at fifteen, became a locomotive fireman at seventeen and served as secretary of the Terre Haute local of the Brotherhood of Locomotive Firemen for three years. He progressed quickly through the union ranks and was elected its grand secretary and treasurer and editor-in-chief of its journal, the *Firemen's Magazine*, in 1880. He served one term in the Indiana legislature as a Democrat in 1885. Despite his success in leading a craft union, Debs was a supporter of industrial unionism and wanted a single union for the railroad industry. In 1892 he resigned his union posts and organized the American Railways Union, which aimed to recruit all railroad employees. A strike by the Union against the Great Northern Railroad in 1894 succeeded but was followed by a massive defeat in a strike against the Pullman Palace Car Company later in 1894. Debs was charged with conspiring to interfere with the passage of federal mail and served a six-month jail sentence which transformed him into a socialist. In 1897 he was one of the founders of the Social Democratic Party which, following mergers with other parties, became the Socialist Party of America in 1901. Debs was a presidential candidate for the Socialist Party in 1900, 1904, 1908, 1912, and 1920. He took part in the formation of the Industrial Workers of the World (q.v.) in 1905 but disagreed with its policies and left in 1908. Opposed to America's participation in World War I, Debs was convicted under the Espionage Act; pardoned by President Harding in 1921, he served three years of a ten-year sentence. (*See also* Industrial Workers of the World)

DENMARK   Organized labor developed relatively strongly in Denmark from the mid-1850s after the abolition of the guilds. By 1890 there were 218 unions with about 31,000 union members; in 1900 there were 96,000 union members or about 14 percent of employees, a level comparable with Britain (13 percent). This strength owed much to an agreement reached between the Federation of Danish Trade Unions (the *Landorganisationen i Denmark* or LO formed in 1898) and the government in 1899 over the right to organize; the unions were also given the task of running the unemployment insurance program. This agreement enabled Danish unions to enjoy a privileged position within European countries of the time and continued to sustain them thereafter. In the post-1945 period Denmark continued to have a high level of union membership; it rose from 52 percent of employees in 1950 to 80 percent in 1980 and even by 1991 remained at 81 percent.

DEUTSCHE ARBEITSFRONT **(DAF)**   The DAF (German Labor Front) was set up by the Nazis to control the German labor movement between 1933 and 1945. After November 1933 it also covered all employers. The DAF covered the whole labor force and by 1939 had 30 million members. During World War II it was used to maintain production of war materials. The members of the DAF were organized among eighteen *Reichbetriebsgruppen* or industrial groups. Although not a free labor organization, the structure of the DAF foreshadowed the sixteen industrial groups (*Industriegewerkschaften*) in West Germany which were created between 1948 and 1950. (*See also* Hans Böckler, *Deutscher Gewerkschaftsbund*)

DEUTSCHER GEWERKSCHAFTSBUND **(DGB)**   The DGB (German Trade Union Federation) is the leading labor union federation of Germany. The first German union federation, the *Allgemeiner Deutscher Gewerkschaftsbund* (General German Trade Union Federation) was formed in 1868 and claimed to represent 142,000 employees but was able to achieve little as a result of Bismarck's repressive Anti-Socialist Laws which were in force from 1878 to 1890.

In 1890 a new labor federation, the *Generalkommission der Gewerkschaften* (General Council of Trade Unions) was formed with Carl Legien (q.v.) as its president.

In 1919 this body was reorganized as the *Allgemeiner Deutscher Gewerkschaftsbund* (General German Trade Union Federation), a title it retained until its suppression by the Nazis in 1933. After Germany's defeat in 1945, unions were at first only allowed to organize within state boundaries but, with the lifting of this restriction, the *Deutscher Gewerkschaftsbund* was set up in the British zone under the leadership of Hans Böckler (q.v.) in April 1947. With the agreement of the Americans and French, the DGB was allowed to set up in their zones in West Germany and in their sectors of Berlin in October 1949. By 1950 the DGB had a total membership of nearly 5.5 million of whom 83 percent were blue-collar employees and 15 percent were women. One union, *IG Metall* (q.v.), accounted for 24 percent of its total membership. Although not formally affiliated with the Social Democratic Party, the DGB has been closely associated with it in practice.

The DGB consists of sixteen industry unions but its power over its larger affiliates is very limited. The sixteen industrial groups covered by its affiliated unions are: building and construction; mining and energy production; chemicals, paper, and ceramic production; railroad; education and science; horticulture, agriculture and forestry; banking and insurance; wood and plastics; leather; the media; metals and engineering; food and restaurants; civil service and transport; police; post; and textiles and clothing. Following the formal reunification of Germany in October 1990, the membership of the unions affiliated with the DGB rose from 7.8 to 9.8 million members between 1989 and 1994. Its membership in 1994 consisted of 62 percent of blue-collar workers and 31 percent were women. (*See also* Germany, *IG Metall*)

DEUTSCHER METALLARBEITER-VERBAND (DMV)   The DMV (German Metal Workers' Union) was Germany's first industrial union. The first German metal workers' unions were formed in 1868-69, but membership growth was slow before 1891 when representatives of a number of separate metal unions formed a single industrial union, the *Deutscher Metallarbeiter Verband* (DMV) with 23,200 members. Because it recruited unskilled as well as skilled workers, the DMV was regarded with suspicion by the older craft metal unions. For instance, the Berlin metal workers did not join the DMV until 1897 and then only on the condition that they retain their independence. For an industrial union, the growth of the DMV was slow, 50,000 in 1896, 100,000 in 1901, and 554,900 by 1913, largely because the DMV was denied recognition by employers in the new large-scale heavy industry plants. Granted recognition during World War I in 1916, the membership of the DMV rose to 786,000 by 1918 and to 1.5 million in 1919, a level it held until 1923 making it briefly the largest single union in the world. The DMV proved incapable of retaining these gains after 1924 because of the economic crisis and because of internal organizational weaknesses. It particularly failed to recruit the young; between 1919 and 1931 the percentage of members under twenty years old fell from 23 to 12 percent. By 1928 membership had fallen to 944,000. The DMV was to the left of most of the German labor movement. It was dissolved by the Nazis on May 2, 1933 and many of its leaders were imprisoned. (*See also* Otto Brenner, *IG Metall*)

DOCUMENT, THE (*See* Yellow Dog Contracts)

DONOVAN COMMISSION The Donovan Commission was the popular term for the British Royal Commission on Trade Unions and Employers' Associations, which reported to the government in 1968. Named after its chairman, Lord Donovan, it made a comprehensive investigation of industrial relations and institutions. The commission found that Britain had two systems of labor relations, a formal and an informal system. The formal system based on law and official institutions was less important than the informal system based on the behavior of unions, shop stewards, and employers. It argued that collective bargaining should be extended with the agreement of employers and unions and that legislative reform of the formal system was not a practical option. Despite the commission's findings, which were the product of careful research including some pioneering survey investigations, British conservative governments since 1980 have placed primary reliance on the law as a means of controlling and reducing the power of organized labor. (*See also* Employment Acts)

DUBINSKY, DAVID (1892-1982) Born in Russian Poland, Dubinsky began his working life as a baker. He took part in a successful strike in 1907 after which he spent eighteen months in jail. Exiled to Siberia, he escaped on the way and went underground until he gained an amnesty in 1910. In 1911 he emigrated to the United States and joined the International Ladies' Garment Workers' Union in New

York. From 1918 he occupied various senior offices in Local 10 of the union and became secretary-treasurer in 1929 and president in 1932, a position he held until 1966. Thereafter, Dubinsky emerged as one of the main labor leaders in the United States. He was a labor adviser to the National Recovery Administration from 1933 to 1935 and an executive council member of the American Federation of Labor (q.v.) in 1935 but resigned after the suspension of the Congress of Industrial Organizations (q.v.) in 1937. Nevertheless, Dubinksy opposed the CIO as an independent body. In 1940 he reaffiliated his union with the AFL and in 1945 was again on its executive council. He also took an active part in labor politics and was a founder of the American Labor Party (q.v.) in 1936. Dubinsky was a participant in the formation of the International Confederation of Free Trade Unions (q.v.) in 1949. (*See also* American Labor Party, International Ladies' Garment Workers' Union)

E

EDUCATION   Labor unions in education have historically concerned school teachers. In Britain, the National Union of Elementary Teachers was formed in 1870; it renamed itself the National Union of Teachers in 1888 and conducted its first strike in 1914 against the Education Authority in Herefordshire. In 1919 the union agreed to admit uncertificated teachers as members, gained a national pay scale and adopted an equal pay for equal work (q.v.) policy.

In Australia (q.v.), the first teachers' union was formed at Geelong, Victoria, in 1878. Other teachers' bodies were formed in Queensland in 1889 and New South Wales in 1895. The New South Wales Teachers' Association was formed in 1918 and formally registered as a labor union in 1919. The first teachers' strike occurred in Western Australia in July 1920 when they joined the majority of the public sector in a three-week strike for increased pay to compensate for inflation; the strike was largely successful. The first teachers' strike in Victoria occurred in 1965 and in New South Wales in 1968.

In the United States (q.v.), the Chicago Federation of Teachers was formed in 1897 and affiliated with the American Federation of Labor (q.v.) in 1902. In 1916 the American Federation of Teachers was created and grew to 9,300 members by 1920. Thereafter it had a difficult history marked by a fall of membership in the 1920s (down to 3,700) and an internal struggle with communists in the 1930s. Even by 1940 only about 3 percent of teachers were members of the federation. Despite a national no-strike policy up to 1963, teachers did strike at the state level from 1946 largely because of the failure of teachers' salaries to keep pace with comparable occupations in the private sector. The federation also faced competition from the National Education Association (q.v.) from 1960. Merger negotiations between the two bodies at the national level failed because of the determination of the federation to remain affiliated with the AFL-CIO, although mergers did proceed in New York State and Florida. (*See also* National Educational Association, White-Collar Unionism)

EGYPT The first Egyptian labor union was formed among cigarette workers in 1899, and by 1911 there were eleven unions claiming a total of 7,000 members. As often happened in other colonial societies, labor unions became part of the movement for independence. They participated in the revolution of 1919 which led to the formation of a monarchical government in 1922. In the early 1920s the unions were led by the Egyptian Socialist Party (formed in 1921), but an attempted general strike in 1923 was suppressed. During the 1930s Egyptian organized labor became more intertwined with politics. Unions were legalized in 1942. After the overthrow of the monarchy in 1952 under Colonel Nasser, organized labor and the political system have been increasingly integrated. In 1962 the president of the Egyptian Federation of Labor (formed in 1956) was made minister of labor, a trend later followed by Guinea and Tanzania. The degree of independence of organized labor in Egypt from political control since 1956 is unclear. In 1995 Egypt was not a member of the International Confederation of Free Trade Unions (q.v.).

EMPLOYERS' ORGANIZATIONS Employer organizations, like labor unions, have existed at least since Adam Smith's well-known discussion of their secret activities in *The Wealth of Nations* (Book I, Chapter VIII) in 1776. As shapers of national labor policy or participants in collective bargaining, formal employers' organizations in most countries emerged after 1880 partly in response to the rise of organized labor. The general pattern was usually for employers in an industry to organize first and create a national body later. In the **United Kingdom** (q.v.), the ship owners formed a national federation in 1890, as did the engineering employers in 1896; the engineering federation organized two lock-outs in 1896 and 1922 and defeated the unions both times. In 1919 the British Employers' Confederation was formed. In 1965 the Confederation of British Industry was created from a merger of the British Employers' Confederation, the Federation of British Industries, and the National Association of British Manufactures. The Chambers of Commerce remained separate from these bodies.

In the **United States** (q.v.), the shoemakers' employers organized an association as early as 1789. In 1899 the National Metal Trades Association was formed. The National Association of Manufacturers was set up in 1895, and in 1903 it adopted an "open shop" policy to fight unions. The Chamber of Commerce of the United States was founded in 1912.

In **France** (q.v.), the *Le Chapelier* law of 1791 banned organizations by employees and employers but was largely enforced only against labor unions. The legislation which legalized unions in 1884 also legalized employers to form organizations, but those organizations that were created were confined to particular industries. A national employers' organization was only created in 1919 and even then was set up at the behest of the government; it was dissolved in 1940. The present principal employers' organization in France, the *Conseil National du Patronat Français*, was created in 1945. In **Germany** (q.v.), a national federation of employers in manufacturing (*Vereinigung der Deutschen Arbeiterverbände*) was formed in 1913; it was joined by another national body (*Reichsverband der Deutschen Industrie*) in 1919. The November Pact (Stinnes-Legien Agreement) (q.v.) of 1918 encouraged the formation of employers' organizations by making such associations responsible for representing employers in collective bargaining. In the 1930s the Nazis incorporated the employers' organizations into the *Deutsche Arbeitsfront* (q.v.). In 1950 the West German employers created the first comprehensive national employers' organization, the *Bundesvereinigung der Deutschen Arbeitgeberverbände* (Confederation of German Employers' Associations) to conduct national collective bargaining. In **Italy** (q.v.), a national employers' organization was established in 1910; it became known by its shortened title *Confindustria* after 1920. In 1923 *Confindustria* successfully opposed a proposal by the fascist government of Mussolini to integrate employers and unions in one body; it retained its autonomy and went on to remain a part of industrial relations in Italy after 1945.

In **Japan** (q.v.), a national federation of chambers of commerce was formed in 1892. In 1917 the Japan Economic Federation was formed to prevent the legal recognition of labor unions. In 1938 the government set up the Greater Japan Patriotic Industrial Association (known as *Sampō*); all employers' organizations and unions were forced to join this body as part of the war effort in June 1940. *Nikkeiren*, the Japanese Federation of Employers' Associations, was formed in 1948.

In **Australia** (q.v.), the first employers' organizations designed to deal with unions were formed by coal mine owners in 1872. The first national body was formed by building employers in 1890. In 1903 the various State Chambers of Manufactures formed a national body. Until the 1970s employer organizations were largely state-based and relatively ineffective as national organizations. In 1977 the first national umbrella employer organization, the Confederation of Australian Industry, was formed as a counterpart to the Australian Council of Trade Unions (q.v.); in 1992 this body merged with the Australian Chamber of Commerce to form the Australian Chamber of Commerce and Industry. The Business Council of Australia, a group of large employers, was created in 1983 to shape industrial policy. In **New Zealand** (q.v.), the New Zealand Federation of Employers' Associations was formed in 1902. In 1992 the New Zealand Employers' Federation had 10,000 individual employer members and 51 affiliated business organizations as members. The New Zealand Business Roundtable, an employer body made up of large firms, was created in the mid-1970s to discuss and prepare general economic policies.

The **International Organization of Employers** was formed in 1920 and remains the only international body of its kind; it provides the employers' representatives to the International Labour Organisation (q.v.). In **Western Europe**, the two main European-wide employers' organizations in 1993 were: the Union of Industrial and Employers' Confederations of Europe (formed in 1958) and the European Center of Public Enterprises (formed in 1965). (*See also* Industrial Psychology)

EMPLOYMENT ACTS Between 1980 and 1993 British Conservative governments brought in a number of laws which have had a significant impact on labor unions. The Employment Act 1980 limited picketing to employers who were party to an industrial dispute, expanded the exemptions from the closed shop, and introduced public funding for secret ballots for the election of full-time union officials and before unions engaged in labor disputes (q.v.). The idea of strike ballots was first suggested in the Conservative Party's policy paper, *Fair Deal at Work*, which was published in 1968 and was also recommended for certain kinds of strikes in a British Labour Party (q.v.) policy document, *In Place of Strife*, published in 1969. The Employment Act 1982 outlawed the pre-entry closed shop and demanded that post-entry closed shops must to be supported by 85 percent of employees in a ballot. The secret ballot provisions of the 1980 act were boycotted by the Trades Union Congress (q.v.) and had little effect.

In 1984 the government published a Green Paper (a statement of government proposals) on proposed changes to the industrial law which reintroduced the debate about public funding for secret ballots for the election of full-time union officials and before industrial disputes. This was followed by a White Paper (a statement of government intentions) and the Trade Union Act 1984, which required secret ballots for the election of full-time officials and the holding of strikes not more than four weeks before they were due to start; the strike provision came into force on September 26, 1984. The Employment Act 1988 enabled a union member to apply to the court for legal action against the union if it engaged in industrial action without the support of a ballot. The Employment Act 1990 provided for a right of complaint to an industrial tribunal for any employee refused employment because he/she did or did not belong to a union; made unions potentially liable for common law actions if any of its officials (including shop stewards) initiated industrial action without written repudiation; and employers were given greater power to dismiss employees who engaged in unofficial industrial action.

The Trade Union Reform and Employment Rights Act 1993 became law on July 1, and built on the trends evident in British labor law since 1980. Among other things, the law created a new legal right which enabled any individual, employer, or union member whose supply of goods and services was affected by a dispute which did not meet these conditions to initiate civil law proceedings against the union. The legislations also required unions about to engage in a labor dispute to conduct first an independently scrutinized postal ballot among members and to provide the employer with at least seven days written notice. (*See also* Donovan Commission)

EQUAL PAY FOR EQUAL WORK Equal pay for equal work refers to women receiving the same pay as men provided they perform work of equal value. In the United States (q.v.), the issue of equal pay for women was raised as early as 1837 in the National Trades Union (q.v.). In the United Kingdom, the Trades Union Congress (qq.v.) passed resolutions in support of equal pay for women in the 1890s. Union support for equal pay although based on human rights concerns was also influenced by the desire to prevent women from being used to undercut union wage rates. The entry of large numbers of women into jobs traditionally done by men was generally only tolerated in wartime such as in transportation, or metal working but they were expected to leave these jobs at war's end. In the United Kingdom, women were only admitted to the Amalgamated Engineering Union (q.v.) in 1942. In Australia (q.v.), industrial tribunals set women's pay rates at 55 percent that of men's in the 1920s and 1930s and raised them to 75 percent in 1950.

In 1951 the International Labour Organisation (q.v.) adopted the Equal Remuneration Convention (No. 100) which called for equal pay for men and women for work of equal value.   In 1958 the Australian state of New South Wales introduced "equal pay for equal work" legislation, which was followed by the other States by 1968. In 1969 and 1972 the Australian federal industrial tribunal handed down decisions in favor of equal pay for equal work for employees covered by federal awards (q.v.). In 1970 the United Kingdom government introduced the Equal Pay Act. Despite these changes, women's pay in the private sector still lags behind men's. (*See also* Women)

ESTONIA (*See* Baltic States)

EUROCADRES EUROCADRES is the short title for the Council of European Professional and Managerial Staff. It was formed in February 1993 to represent the interests of professional and managerial staff within the European Community. In December 1993 EUROCADRES was granted official recognition by the European Commission as a "social partner" in European-level dialogue on social policy matters. In 1994 EUROCADRES claimed a total affiliated membership of 4 million. (*See also Confédération Européenne des Cadres*, European Trade Union Confederation)

EUROPEAN TRADE UNION CONFEDERATION (ETUC) The ETUC is the major international labor organization of Western

Europe. Although the International Federation of Trade Unions (q.v.) was mainly a European body for most of its life between 1901 and 1945, the first moves to form a regional labor federation of European bodies were made in November 1950 when the International Confederation of Free Trade Unions (ICFTU) (q.v.) established the European Regional Organization. The creation of the European Coal and Steel Community prompted a number of national labor federations as well as the International Metalworkers' Federation and the Miners' International Federation (qq.v.) to form the Committee of Twenty-One to represent the interests of organized labor. Following the creation of the European Commission by the Treaty of Rome in 1958, the ICFTU formed the European Trade Union Secretariat which incorporated the Committee of Twenty-One.

Further changes in the structure of Western European organized labor were also prompted by wider changes in the supranational European political framework. In 1968 the ICFTU members of the Free Trade Area set up the Trade Union Committee for the European Free Trade Area. In 1969 the European Trade Union Secretariat reshaped itself as the European Confederation of Free Trade Unions. In February 1973 these two bodies agreed to merge as the European Trade Union Confederation (ETUC). Up to 1991 the membership of the ETUC was largely confined to noncommunist labor bodies in Western Europe; but, since that time, the ETUC has been making arrangements for the inclusion of Eastern European countries as members. The ETUC has always operated as a lobbying body for organized labor, but at its 1991 congress it resolved to take an active role in collective bargaining for the whole of Europe. Its role assumed added signficance after the signing of the European Union Treaty (February 7, 1992); appended to the Treaty was a social policy agreement which gave European-wide labor and employer federations an enhanced formal role in preparing and implementing the social policy of the European Community. In December 1993 the ETUC was one of three European-wide labor bodies which were granted formal "social partner" status by the European Commission for European-wide dialogue on social policy matters. Although both the commission and the ETUC wanted to advance this dialogue to collective bargaining, this course has been opposed by the Union of Industrial and Employers' Confederations of Europe even though the ETUC had reached an agreement with the European Center of Public Enterprises for such a move in September 1990. In 1994 the ETUC claimed 46 million members (compared to 37 million in 1973) in twenty-one countries. (*See also Confédération Européenne des Cadres*, EUROCADRES)

F

FEDERATED MISCELLANEOUS WORKERS' UNION (FMWU)
The FMWU was an Australian labor union whose members were mainly in service occupations, such as cleaning, and in certain areas of manufacturing; as a rule, it recruited employees who were not recruited by other unions. Founded in September 1915, the FMWU filled a gap in the structure of Australian organized labor. Its history was one of amalgamation (q.v.); it grew by absorbing a total of fifty smaller unions. By 1969 it had 73,000 members. In November 1990, the FMWU (with 135,000 members) merged with the 115,000 strong Federated Liquor and Allied Industries Employees' Union (formed in 1910) to create the Australian Liquor, Hospitality, and Miscellaneous Workers Union, one Australia's largest labor unions. Between 1984 and 1990 the federal secretary of the FMWU was Martin Ferguson (1953-), who was the president of the Australian Council of Trade Unions (q.v.) from 1990 to 1995. (*See also* Amalgamation, Australia)

FEDERATION OF INTERNATIONAL CIVIL SERVANTS' ASSOCIATIONS (FICSA)
Founded in 1952, the FICSA represents the staff employed by the United Nations and its specialized agencies, including the International Labour Organisation (q.v.). Based in Geneva, the FICSA had twenty-eight affiliated associations or unions in 1990 representing about 30,000 union members. (*See also* White-Collar Unionism)

FEDERATION OF ORGANIZED TRADES AND LABOR UNIONS OF THE UNITED STATES AND CANADA (FOTLU)
Like the International Labor Union (q.v.), the FOTLU had its origins in dissension over the decision of the 1877 convention of the Workingmen's Party to become the Socialist Labor Party and its adoption of a political approach to labor problems. It also represented disappointment with the Knights of Labor (q.v.). The FOTLU was formed at Terre Haute, Indiana, in August 1881 by twenty-one labor unions who called for the establishment of a new labor federation which they succeeded in doing in Pittsburgh in November 1881. The

constitution of the FOTLU was based heavily on that of the British Trades Union Congress (q.v.). Because the FOTLU did not attract significant support from the United States' national unions, it remained a weak organization despite representing 50,000 union members by 1884. Nevertheless, it was important for maintaining the idea of a national labor federation and for providing Samuel Gompers (q.v.), the president of the 1885 convention of the FOTLU, with the vehicle for launching the American Federation of Labor (q.v.). (*See also* American Federation of Labor, International Labor Union)

***FEDERAZIONE ITALIANA OPERAI METALLURGICI* (FIOM)** The FIOM (Italian Union of Metal Workers) was formed in 1901 and operated until 1924 when it was suppressed by the fascist government along with Italy's other free unions. Its membership growth was slow, a reflection of the slow industrialization of the Italian economy. From 10,000 members in 1913, it had only reached 40,000 by 1918, but by 1920 it grew to 152,000, a rise which reflected the demands of World War I. By 1923 its membership had fallen to 20,000. It was revived in 1944. (*See also* Italy)

FINLAND Organized labor in Finland emerged on a significant scale in the 1900s. In 1907, at the initiative of the Social Democratic Party, eighteen unions held a congress which claimed a total membership of 25,000 out of 175,000 nonagricultural employees. Strongly influenced by Marxism, this body was banned by the government in 1930, and the Social Democratic Party reorganized a noncommunist body, the Confederation of Finnish Trade Unions. In 1922 a separate white-collar federation was formed to restore real pay levels which had been sharply eroded by the inflation which followed World War I; the white-collar federation, unlike the other labor federation, was politically independent. In the 1920s organized labor collapsed; union density dropped to 5 percent in 1930 compared to 25 percent in 1920 but recovered strongly after 1944 with the improvement of the political climate for labor. Between 1965 and 1970 union membership in Finland rose from 642,900 to 945,300, causing the density level to rise from 42 to 57 percent, an increase brought about by diminished internal conflict within organized labor and the introduction of a centralized collective bargaining system. The *Suomen Ammattiliittojen Keskusjärjestö* (SAK), or Central Organization of Finnish Trade Unions, remained the dominant labor federation in the post-1945 period; in 1994 it had 1.1 million members. In the same year, Finland had a total of 1.8 million union members or 87 percent of all employees..

FIRST INTERNATIONAL (*See* International Workingmen's Association)

FORCED LABOR Throughout most of recorded history, the performance of the work needed by society has been linked with coercion. Labor in classical Greek and Roman society depended heavily on agricultural laborers tied to the land and slavery. With the rise of market economies in Western Europe after 1300, the first free labor forces in the modern sense of the term began to emerge slowly on a significant scale. Although most working people had effectively little economic freedom, the Industrial Revolution brought a far greater range of choices of employment and the crude notion of a forced labor force receded although pockets of feudal arrangements remained even in the United Kingdom; for example, Scottish coal miners were not fully emancipated from lifetime bondage until 1799. Slavery was abolished in the British Empire in 1807 , in the United States in 1865, and was the target of an international conference in 1890. Serfdom in Russia was abolished in 1861. Forced labor in a legal sense in Britain became confined to convicts who were exported from Britain to North America from 1655 to 1776 and Australia until 1868. Within British prisons, labor was regarded by the authorities as therapeutic and useful for offsetting administrative costs. Organized labor has generally been hostile to prison labor because it could be used to undercut the price of goods produced by union members. In 1934 the U. S. Supreme Court denied the State of Alabama an injunction to stop the sale of goods made by prisoners. Nazi Germany and Japan both made extensive use of forced labor by civilians as well as by prisoners of war. Forced labor has also been a feature of communist regimes, notably in the former Soviet Union. The International Labour Organisation (q.v.) passed a Convention against Forced Labor (No. 29) in 1930.

FRANCE Early forms of labor organization existed in France long before the effects of the Industrial Revolution became evident during the nineteenth century. For example, there is a record of a strike by vineyard workers in Burgundy as early as 1393 and by printers at Lyons in the sixteenth century. As in Britain, journeymen were the leaders in forming labor unions. Following the revolution in 1789, journeymen carpenters in Paris took advantage of its promise of political freedom by forming a union in 1790, but the employers objected and it was suppressed by the *Loi le Chaplier* (1791), which was also applied to employers' organizations and made strikes illegal. Despite the legal prohibition on strikes, there was a revolt by silk workers in Lyons after the government attempted to suppress labor unions in April 1834. Some progress towards peaceful labor relations occurred in the early 1840s as evidenced by the making of a collective agreement in the printing industry in 1843, but otherwise the government was quick to use force against the working class as shown by the "June Days" in 1848 when it shut down employment workshops for the unemployed, a move which resulted in some thousands of deaths and the arrest of thousands of others.

In 1862 a deputation of French labor leaders was allowed by Napoleon III to visit the London Exposition. They returned with a high opinion of English working conditions and unions and asked to be granted freedom of association and the right to strike. Strikes were legalized in 1864 and although legalizing unions was considered in 1868, nothing was done. In 1869 the Comte de Paris published a sympathetic study, *The Trade Unions of England,* which was reprinted six times; but the official attitude towards unions was colored by the bloodshed of the Paris Commune (1871).

By the 1880s the government realized that there were advantages to encouraging labor unions as a means of tempering revolutionary tendencies by the working class. In 1884 the government legalized labor unions and provided financial assistance to the *Bourses du Travail* (the coordinating centers for local unions) provided they remained out of the control of political extremists. The first national trade union center (the *Fédération Nationale des Syndicats Ouvriers*) was opened in 1886. A Catholic labor union was formed among white-collar workers in 1887, the first sign of an important division within French organized labor; the Catholic unions went on to form their own national labor federation in 1919. Collective bargaining began in the coal mining (q.v.) industry in northern France but remained limited in scope because of the importance of small enterprises in the economy. In 1895 a new national labor federation, the *Confédération Générale du Travail* (CGT) (q.v.), was formed; it absorbed the National Federation of *Bourses du Travail* (founded in 1892) in 1902. Syndicalism (q.v.), a doctrine which had its origins in the revolutionary tradition of France, became an important influence on organized labor, particularly with its emphasis on the use of general strikes (q.v.).

Yet French organized labor never attained the strength of its counterparts in other major European countries. In 1920, a highwater mark for organized labor in Europe, only 12 percent of French employees were members of unions compared to 53 percent in Germany, 39 percent in Italy, and 48 percent in the United Kingdom. Subsequently, French labor was weakened by divisions caused by communists. Despite the Matignon Agreement (q.v.) in 1936 which provided for the unions' right to organize, an end to anti-union practices, collective bargaining, pay increases and the election of shop stewards, French organized labor remained relatively weak even though an impression of strength might have been created by dramatic events such as the national disturbances of May 1968. Although the reasons for the weakness of French organized labor since 1945 are complicated, they stem in large part from its deep political and religious divisions. Aside from the Catholic labor federation, the *Confédération Française des Travailleurs Chrétiens* (French Confederation of Christian Workers, formed in 1919), the most important division occurred in April 1948 when the noncommunist unions of the CGT withdrew and formed their own federation, the *Confédération Générale du Travail-Force Ouvrière* (CGT-FO) (General Confederation of Labor-Workers' Strength). From a high point of 38 percent of employees in unions in 1950, there was a steady decline thereafter to 21 percent in 1960 and 17 percent in 1980. Between 1989 and 1994, union density in France fell from 11 to eight percent, the lowest level for any OECD country. (*See also Confédération Générale du Travail*, Italy, Matignon Agreement, Syndicalism)

FREEDOM OF ASSOCIATION The International Labour Organisation (ILO) (q.v.) first considered drafting a Convention on Freedom of Association to protect labor unions in 1925, a concern prompted by the incorporation of unions under government control in fascist Italy. Among the ILO member countries of the time, there were two main kinds of laws relating to unions. Under the first kind of law, unions were unlawful unless their formation and operation were authorized by the government. Under the second kind of law, unions were legally recognized and operated without government control. Examples of this second kind of law were the United Kingdom (1871), New Zealand (1878), and France (1884). However, the 1925 proposal failed mainly because the employees' representatives were unable to agree on a course of action with some fearing that such a convention could limit the freedoms the unions already had. The present ILO Convention (87) on Freedom of Association and Protection of the Right to Organize was not passed until 1948. It was augmented by Convention No. 98 (Right to Organize and Collective Bargaining) in 1949. The ILO established the Freedom of Association Committee to monitor the operation of these conventions in 1951. (*See also* Italy, International Labour Organisation)

FRIENDLY SOCIETIES Friendly societies in their modern form began to emerge from the seventeenth century to provide members with benefits to cover the cost of sickness, accidents, unemployment, and funerals. They grew out of the trade societies and clubs formed by journeymen, often in taverns and public houses, which catered for the needs of travelling artisans to find accommodation and work. They were the ancestors of labor unions in many parts of Western Europe and enjoyed steady growth after 1760 . In 1793 genuine friendly societies received legal protection in England, provided they could pass inspection by the justices of the peace that they were not really labor unions; 9,672 friendly societies were enumerated in 1803 with a total membership of 703,350. With their requirement for regular contributions, friendly societies attracted those in better paid employment with relatively high job security. After 1850 some of the better-off unions, notably the Amalgamated Society of Engineers (q.v.), also provided similar kinds of benefits to members. In Italy, the first regional meeting of friendly societies was held in 1853. (*See also* United Kingdom)

G

GENERAL AND MUNICIPAL WORKERS' UNION (GMWU) The GMWU was one of the largest labor unions in the United Kingdom from its formation on July 1,1924 following the amalgamation (q.v.) of three unions: the National Union of General Workers, which was founded by Will Thorne (1857-1946) in 1889 as the National Union of Gasworkers and General Labourers of Great Britain and Ireland (it had 202,000 members in 1924); the National Amalgamated Union of Labour (q.v.), which had about 53,000 members in 1924; and the Municipal Employees' Association, which was founded in 1894 and had about 40,000 members in 1924. Known officially as the National Union of General and Municipal Workers, the GMWU drew the bulk of its membership from lesser skilled employees, particularly those in the gas industry and local government. There was much overlap between the kinds of employees it recruited and those of similar unions such as the Transport and General Workers' Union (q.v.).

At its creation, the GMWU had 298,200 members. This number fell during the Depression to 207,700 in 1932; but by 1940 the GMWU had 493,740 members and 715,460 by 1950. Between 1945 and 1992 the GMWU was Britain's third largest union in most years. Membership rose to 786,140 by 1962 and to a peak of 964,800 in 1979. An important feature of this growth was the proportion of women members. Between 1924 and 1940 the proportion of women members in the GMWU rose from 9 to 18 percent and to 20 percent by 1950. By 1976 34 percent of the total membership were women. In 1972 the GMWU set up a new section to recruit white-collar employees.

Between 1963 and 1979 the GMWU absorbed five small unions. In 1982 it combined with the Amalgamated Society of Boilermakers, Shipwrights, Blacksmiths, and Structural Workers (itself a production of amalgamation with other unions, the oldest of which was formed in 1834) to create the General Municipal, Boilermakers' and Allied Trades Unions. In 1989 this union amalgamated with the Association of Professional Executive, Clerical, and Computer Staff (originally formed as the National Union of Clerks in 1890) to form a union known simply as the GMB. In 1994 the GMB claimed 790,000 members of whom 36 percent were women. (*See also* Amalgamation, National Amalgamated Union of Labour, Women)

GENERAL FEDERATION OF TRADE UNIONS (GFTU) The GFTU was formed in Manchester, England, in January 1899 by a number of relatively large unions, including the Amalgamated Society of Engineers (q.v.) with 85,000 members, the Gas and General Labourers' Union (with 48,000 members), the National Amalgamated Union of Labour (q.v.) with 22,000 members, and the National Union of Boot and Shoe Operatives (with 22,000 members). A moderate body, the purpose of the GFTU was to provide mutual support and resolve labor disputes (q.v.). At its formation, its constituents had about 310,400 members or about a quarter that of the Trades Union Congress (TUC) (q.v.), which regarded the GFTU as a competitor.

Although the GFTU aspired to be a large organization, it found it difficult to move beyond being a largely craft organization, a feature which won it respect and support from Samuel Gompers (q.v.). The number of members it represented rose from 884,000 in 1912 to over a million by 1920, but the withdrawal of the Amalgamated Engineers in 1915 and other unions severely weakened the GFTU. The general secretary of the GFTU from 1907-38 was William A. Appleton (1859-1940). As well as its useful role in labor dispute settlements and labor politics, the GFTU was Britain's representative in the International Federation of Trade Unions (q.v.) until it was supplanted by the TUC between 1918 and 1922. In 1988 the GFTU had 277,900 members among its constituents, which were mainly smaller, skilled unions, and its activities complemented those of the TUC. (*See also* International Federation of Trade Unions, Trades Union Congress)

GENERAL STRIKE   The British General Strike which took place between May 4 and 12, 1926 was the largest single confrontation between the government and organized labor that has ever occurred in Britain. The immediate background to the strike was the government's decision in 1925 to return Britain to the gold standard, a move which increased the price of British exports and encouraged employers to instigate pay cuts to maintain their position in world trade. At the center of the strike were grievances by the coal miners over wage cuts and their efforts to gain the support of other unions. Although employees gave a high level of support to the strike-a record 162 million working days were lost through labor disputes in 1926-the Baldwin government was well prepared and used special constables, university students, and other volunteers to take the place of strikers. The coal miners remained on strike until August when they admitted defeat and returned to work on the employers' terms. As a result of the strike, the Trades Union Congress (TUC) (q.v.) issued an invitation for talks on the reform of British industrial relations in 1927. Although the offer was ignored by the employers' association, the offer was taken up by Sir Alfred Mond, the chairman of Imperial Chemical Industries, who met with Ben Turner of the TUC in a series of talks which went into 1928; these talks led to the Mond-Turner Report which suggested that organized labor should have a role in making national economic and industrial relations policies. The idea was rejected by the employers' organizations (q.v.) and the talks were abortive. The government enacted the Trade Disputes Act in 1927 which outlawed the secondary boycott and strike, the mechanisms on which the General Strike had been based. This law, although not used, was repealed by the Attlee Labour government in 1946. (*See also* General Strikes, Labor Disputes, Trades Union Congress)

GENERAL STRIKES General strikes, in the sense of a widespread labor dispute which affects a city, region or country, feature prominently in the history of organized labor; there is no hard-and-fast definition because these labor disputes can assume a variety of forms. The followers of Anarchism and Syndicalism (qq.v.) in the late-nineteenth century and early twentieth century saw the general strike as a means of overthrowing the existing social order and replacing it with a fairer one. The strike wave of the late-nineteenth century was often an expression of working class discontent with many participants not being members of labor unions as occurred in Belgium (q.v.) in 1893. A general strike could also be international in its effects; the Maritime Strike (q.v.) which was called by unions in eastern Australia in 1890 was also supported by unions in New Zealand (q.v.). After 1900 general strikes were generally called by labor unions.

General strikes have also occurred in cities (for instance, Philadelphia in 1910, Brisbane, Australia, in 1912, Seattle in 1919, and Winnipeg, Canada, in 1919), and countries (such as in Sweden in 1909, and Argentina in 1909 and 1919). The 1920s were a highpoint of the use of the general strike: Portugal (1919, 1920, and 1921), France (1920), Norway (1921), Hong Kong (1922), Egypt (1923), South Africa (1922), and the United Kingdom (1926). Usually these general strikes were suppressed (for example, in Cuba in 1935 or in Kenya in 1950) by military force or they led to punitive legal actions by the government (for instance in South Korea in 1946-47). On occasions the general strike has achieved some improvements (for instance in Cuba after the general strike in 1933). Although general strikes have continued to occur in Western Europe since 1945-for instance in France (1947, 1968) and Denmark (1973)-their incidence has declined. Yet, they remain an option for labor in an intolerable political environment as happened in Bulgaria (q.v.) in 1990 and Bangladesh in 1994. (*See also* France, Labor Disputes)

GEORGE, HENRY (1839-1897) American journalist and single tax advocate, George was an influential figure in late-nineteenth century labor in English-speaking countries. Born in Philadelphia,

Pennsylvania, he eventually joined the staff of the *San Francisco Times* in 1866 after a variety of failed business ventures. In his *Progress and Poverty* published in 1879, he promoted a single capital tax on land as the means to eliminate poverty. A popularizer rather than an original thinker, George promoted his ideas through lecture tours to England and Australia but, although they attracted support from the urban working class, they failed to be implemented. During his career, George ran for public office a number of times unsuccessfully; for example, in 1884 he ran for mayor of New York City with union backing. Nevertheless, because of his opposition to protectionism and socialism (q.v.), George alienated many of the leaders of organized labor in the 1890s. (*See also* Edward Bellamy)

GERMANY In terms of historical importance and influence in Europe, organized labor in Germany has been second only to that of Britain. This importance derived not just from the numerical size of Germany's labor unions during the first two decades of the twentieth century but also from the pivotal role German labor leaders played in promoting international labor unionism. Organized labor came relatively late to Germany. The first national German labor union, the National Printers' Association (*Nationaler Buchdrucker-Verein*), was not formed until 1848. Despite the spread of industrialization after 1850, political repression retarded the growth of unions. In 1861 the legal ban on labor unions was lifted in Saxony, which was followed by Weimar (1863) and the North German Confederation (1869), but there was no legal right to form unions. In 1863 Ferdinand Lasalle (1825-1864) founded the German Workingmen's Association which had as one of its aims the legalizing of labor unions. Yet by 1869 there were only 77,000 union members of whom 30,000 were enrolled in Hirsch-Duncker Trade Associations (q.v.). Further progress of organized labor was retarded by Bismarck's Anti-Socialist Laws of 1878 which were not repealed until 1890.

   In 1892 German labor unions held their first national congress at which they decided to encourage the formation of national unions andagreed to work for the formation of industry-based unions. In 1894 the Catholics began organizing their own unions, a step which marked the beginning of the third division of pre-1933 German organized labor, along with the conservatives (the Hirsh-Duncker Trade Associations) and the socialists (the Free Trade Unions). By 1913 the Free Trade Unions had 2.5 million members, the Catholic unions 218,200, and the Hirsh-Duncker Trade Associations 106,600.

White-collar unions were formed after 1900, and their membership grew from 567,700 in 1906 to 941,300 by 1913. Collective bargaining also emerged during the 1900s; by 1913, 2 million employees were covered by agreements negotiated by collective bargaining. In 1913 Germany had nearly 3 million labor union members, the second highest figure in the world after the United Kingdom. World War I boosted membership to 10.5 million in 1920, but the hyperinflation of the War and the economic disruption which followed it made this level unsustainable. Nonetheless, the labor unions were largely responsible for the defeat of the right-wing Kapp *putsch* in Berlin in 1920.

In 1923 the government created an arbitration (q.v.) service to deal with labor disputes (q.v.) and even made the service compulsory if the parties could not agree. The legitimacy of organized labor was not accepted by many large employers in the late 1920s. Between October and December 1928, 220,000 engineering employees were locked out by their employers in the Ruhr; and although the dispute was settled by mediators, the employers were harshly critical of its efforts. The economic downturn turned into full depression by 1931 and its resultant very high unemployment (44 percent by 1932) destroyed the power of organized labor and made its suppression by Hitler a relatively easy matter. On May 2, 1933 Germany's unions were suppressed and many of their leaders were sent to the Dachau concentration camp.

In reviewing the relative political weakness of German organized labor before 1933, it is important to realize that for all the industrial growth after 1850, a large part of the German economy remained in agriculture; even in 1933 the proportion of the labor force employed in agriculture was 29 percent.

The revival of organized labor in western Germany began with the advancing Allied armies being petitioned for permission to form labor unions in March-April 1945. By August 1945 nearly 1 million union members had been officially recognized in unions in the British zone where official policy was favorable to their growth as a means of promoting democracy. In this they were very successful for Germany's labor unions went on to play a fundamental role in promoting and sustaining democracy in West Germany. Determined to avoid the mistakes of the past, German unions were organized along industry lines, sectarian divisions were to be avoided and unions were to have a say in the decision-making process of large enterprises, a policy which has made it possible for Germany to put pressure on the South African government to permit black labor unions. Despite the impressive gains made by organized labor since 1950, only 33 percent of employees were union members by the late 1980s, which was below that of neighboring Austria, Belgium and Denmark. Although the formal reunification of Germany in October 1990 opened up new recruiting opportunities for organized labor, it also presented many problems because of the economic backwardness of the former East Germany. (*See also* Hans Böckler, Otto Brenner, *Deutsche Arbeitsfront, Deutscher Metallarbeiter-Verband, Deutscher Gewerkschaftsbund*, Hirsh-Duncker Trade Associations, *IG Metall*, Karl Legien, *Mitbestimmung, Zentralarbeitsgemeinschaft*)

GOMPERS, SAMUEL (1850-1924) Gompers was an outstanding labor leader in the United States (q.v.) from the late 1880s until his death. He was also an important figure in international labor. Born in London, he and his family arrived in New York in 1863 where he began work as a cigarmaker and attended night classes to improve his education. He joined the Cigarmakers Local 15 in 1864 and made the union the basis of his career, serving as president of Local 144 from 1875 to 1878 and again from 1880 to 1886. Gompers was one of the principal founders of the Federation of Organized Trades and Labor Unions of the United States and Canada (q.v.) in 1881 and of its successor, the American Federation of Labor (AFL) (q.v.) in 1886; he became the first president of the AFL, a position he held, with the exception of 1894, until his death. Although originally attracted to socialist ideas in the early 1870s, Gompers turned to unionism as the means to improve the position of labor. He was an admirer of English unionism and used it as a model for reorganizing the Cigarmaker's Union, particularly its emphasis on high membership fees and unemployment, sickness, and death benefits. He based the Federation of Organized Trades on the British Trades Union Congress (q.v.). He and the socialists became enemies.

By the late 1870s Gompers had developed the set of beliefs-later known as the doctrine of voluntarism (q.v.)-that he applied throughout his labor career. He believed that unionism, organized along occupational rather than industrial lines and using strikes, was the correct path to improving the position of employees. He distrusted the state as a means of achieving this end and opposed not only unions supporting political parties but also laws designed to set maximum hours, minimum wages, and establish health and unemployment insurance. At the same time, he supported the state legislating to restrict child labor (q.v.).

Voluntarism (q.v.), as espoused by Gompers, made the United States a notable exception to the views held by organized labor in other countries and led to friction with the International Federation of Trade Unions (q.v.). With the collapse of the Knights of Labor (q.v.) from the late 1880s, Gompers and the American Federation of Labor became the undisputed center of American organized labor; but it was a narrowly based movement based on better-off employees which largely ignored the unskilled and the immigrants. Gompers's ideas prevailed until the Depression and the rise of the Congress of Industrial Organizations (q.v.) in the 1930s. Gompers also played a significant role in setting up the International Labour Organisation (q.v.). (*See also* American Federation of Labor, Federation of Organized Trades and Labor Unions of the United States and Canada)

GRAND NATIONAL CONSOLIDATED TRADES UNION (GNCTU)
The GNCTU was the first attempt in the history of organized labor to form a union that recruited unskilled as well as skilled employees. Formed by Robert Owen (q.v.) and John Doherty (c.1798-1854) in London in January 1834, the GNCTU attracted a membership of about 16,000 after three months (and not the 500,000 often claimed). Planned to be based on urban trades organized into lodges, the platform of the GNCTU included striking to gain the eight-hour day. None of the main labor unions of the time (that is, the builders, the potters, the spinners, and the clothiers) joined the GNCTU. From the beginning, there were divisions among the leaders of the GNCTU; Owen wanted peaceful collaboration with employers, but others had radical political aims. The rank-and-file of the membership tended to favor strikes to achieve objectives such as the eight-hour day and the vote for all men. Alarmed by government hostility towards unions as shown by the treatment of the "Tolpuddle Martyrs" (q.v.), Owen dissolved the GNCTU in August 1834. (*See also* Knights of Labor, Robert Owen, "Tolpuddle Martyrs", Workers' Union)

GREECE The development of organized labor in Greece was hampered by the country's lack of economic growth and dependence upon agriculture; in 1920 half the Greek labor force was employed in agriculture. The first union was formed by carpenters at the Syros shipyard in 1879, but it was not until 1918 that the General Confederation of Greek Labor was founded. Throughout the 1920s conflict between socialists and communists weakened organized labor. Beginning in 1914 legislation was passed to regulate unions, and from

1931 the state brought organized labor under its contro. This was obvious in 1946 when the government nominated the executive of the General Confederation of Greek Labor. Between 1967 and 1974 Greece was run by a military government which seized control by a coup. In 1968 sections of organized labor formed a group to work for the restoration of democracy. With the collapse of the military government, this group continued its activities but redirected its focus at improving democracy within organized labor, particularly with respect to the General Confederation of Greek Labor. Following organized labor's complaints to the International Labour Organisation (q.v.) over government interference in the confederation, a new leadership took over and conducted a strike against proposed antistrike legislation in 1990 in which more than a million participated. In 1991 there were about 300,000 union members in Greece who represented about 14 per cent of employees. (*See also* Italy)

GUILD SOCIALISM   Guild socialism was a strand of democratic socialism (q.v.) which advocated the control of production by workers through self-governing guilds based on industrial labor unions. As an idea, it was principally the creation of the British Fabian, Oxford academic, labor publicist and scholar, G. D. H. Cole (1889-1959). As a movement, guild socialism achieved some following between 1911 and 1917 but had petered out by 1920 mainly through competition from communism (q.v.). (*See also* Industrial Democracy, Socialism)

H

HARDIE, JAMES KEIR (1856-1915)   Born to unmarried parents in a poor rural environment near Holytown, Scotland, Hardie began his working life at the age of seven. He worked in coal mines in Lanarkshire from the age of 10 until he was 22. During the late 1870s he actively agitated for better pay and conditions for coal miners, activities which cost him and his two brothers their jobs. Hardie obtained some income by working as a journalist for the *Glasgow Weekly Mail* but did much unpaid work as an organizer for the coal miners. He became corresponding secretary for the Hamilton miners in 1879, led an unsuccessful strike by Lanarkshire miners in 1880, and helped to form a national union of coal miners for Scotland. By the mid-1880s, if not earlier, Hardie became a committed socialist who recognized the importance of labor representation in parliament. He advocated the nationalization of the coal mines as early as 1887. In 1888 he failed to get elected to a vacant seat and formed the Scottish Labour Party which merged into the Independent Labour Party in 1893. Hardie's activities as a labor publicist through his newspapers, *The Miner* (1887-89) and the *Labour Leader* in 1889, made him well known and assisted his election to the House of Commons in 1892 as a member for West Ham South (to 1895) for the Independent Labour Party; he scandalized the House by making his entrance in a deerstalker hat and preceded by a cornet player. In 1893 Hardie became chairman of the Independent Labour Party and held the position until 1900. He was again elected to the House of Commons as member for Merthyr Tydfil, a seat he held until his death. In 1906 he was the first leader of the British Labour Party (q.v.). Hardie also played an active role in international organized labor from 1888. He visited the United States in 1895 and was chairman of the British section of the International Socialist Bureau in 1914. He was greatly grieved by the inability of international labor to prevent World War I. (*See also* British Labour Party)

HAWKE, ROBERT JAMES LEE (1929-) Australian prime minister from March 1983 to November 1991, Bob Hawke was born in Bordertown, South Australia. He was educated at the Universities of Western Australia and Oxford, which he attended as a Rhodes scholar. In 1958 he joined the Australian Council of Trade Unions (ACTU) (q.v.) as research officer and industrial advocate. He was elected president of the ACTU in 1970 and held the position until 1980 when he was elected to the national parliament for the Victorian electorate of Wills for the Australian Labor Party (ALP) (q.v.). While at the ACTU Hawke gained national prominence through the presentation of national wage cases and as an advocate for organized labor generally. In February 1983 he became leader of the federal parliamentary ALP and, with the ALP's victory at the March 1983 election, he became prime minister. Among other things, his government encouraged greater communication between unions and employers. The deterioration of the economy after 1987, particularly the continuing adverse balance of trade and sharply rising foreign debt, were major problems for his government. The recession, which afflicted the economy from September 1990 and throughout 1991, eroded Hawke's popularity in opinion polls and made it possible for his former treasurer, Paul Keating (1944-), to successfully challenge him for the prime ministership in December 1991; he resigned from federal parliament in February 1992. (*See also* Accord, Australian Council of Trade Unions, Australian Labor Party)

HAYWOOD, WILLIAM DUDLEY (1869-1928)   Haywood was a leading American labor radical. Born into a mining family in Salt Lake City, Utah, he worked as a miner in Nevada and Utah. He became an official of the Western Federation of Miners and was prominent in the Cripple Creek strike in 1903. He was one of the founders of the Industrial Workers of the World (IWW) (q.v.) in Chicago in 1905. In 1906 he and Charles Moyer were jailed for the murder of an ex-governor of Idaho but was acquitted in the following year. The case made Haywood a national figure for radical labor. Ousted by moderates from the Western Federation of Miners in 1908, Haywood toured the United States for four years to promote the socialist cause. He was a leader of the successful strike at Lawrence, Massachusetts, in 1912 and the recruiting drive for the Agricultural Workers' Organization. Haywood was a strong supporter of industrial unionism and of the need to organize the immigrant and less well-off employees ignored by the American Federation of Labor (q.v.). Along with other IWW leaders, he was convicted under the Espionage Act in 1917. Released pending an appeal after two years, he left the United States for Russia in 1921; he died in Moscow. (*See also* Industrial Workers of the World)

HILLMAN, SIDNEY (1887-1946) Hillman was born in Lithuania. He studied to be a rabbi until 1902 when he moved to Kovno, Russia; there he studied economics. For his part in labor agitation, he spent eight months in jail. On his release, he left Russia for England and then emigrated to the United States in 1907 where he settled in Chicago. Hillman worked as a clerk for two years, then became a garment cutter and a member of the United Garment Workers' Union of America (formed in 1891). Between September 1910 and January 1911 Hillman became the leader of a strike against Hart, Schaffner, and Marx in Chicago. The success of this strike fed discontent with the conservative leadership of the union, and in 1914 Hillman led a breakaway group of members who formed the Amalgamated Clothing Workers of America (ACWA). Hillman became its first president. The second result of the 1910-11 strike was the setting up of arbitration machinery which was extended to other parts of the clothing industry. Hillman was a dedicated supporter of industrial unionism and led the ACWA through an industry-wide lock-out between December 1920 and June 1921 and the exclusion of racketeers during the 1920s. He served on the federal Labor Advisory Board (1933) and on the National Industrial Recovery Board (1935). In 1935 he became one of the leaders of the Congress of Industrial Organizations (q.v.). A political moderate, Hillman supported the American Labor Party (q.v.) and the Democratic Party. (*See also* Congress of Industrial Organizations)

HIRSCH-DUNCKER TRADE ASSOCIATIONS   Hirsch-Duncker trade associations were a group of German labor unions which operated from 1869 to 1933. They were begun by Max Hirsch (1832-1905), a mechanical engineer, and Franz Duncker, a newspaper publisher. Hirsch made a tour of England in 1868 and came back with the idea that German unions should follow those of England as he believed them to be, that is, independent from political parties and in favor of the amicable settlement of labor disputes and avoiding the use of strikes. In 1869 he and Duncker organized a national federation of unions with 30,000 members among eight trade associations. Although the Hirsch-Duncker Associations were exempt from the Anti-Socialist Law of 1878 because of their lack of political affiliation, their growth was slow; it was not until 1902 that their combined membership reached 102,600.   Despite claims of political and religious neutrality, the associations were linked with left-wing liberalism, a political area to which other groups could make better claim.   After reaching a peak membership of 226,000 in 1920, the associations' membership declined to 149,800 by 1931. They were dissolved by the Nazis in 1933. (*See also* Germany)

HOFFA, JAMES RIDDLE (1913-c.1975)   Hoffa was one of most controversial labor leaders in recent American history. Born in Brazil, Indiana, Hoffa worked in various service sector jobs before he became involved with organized labor in 1931. He became a member of the International Brotherhood of Teamsters, Chauffeurs, Warehousemen, and Helpers of America (IBT) (q.v.) in 1934. He advanced steadily in the Teamsters and was made a vice president in 1952 and was president from 1957 to 1971; in the course of his union career, Hoffa developed links with the Mafia.   In 1964 he was convicted of jury tampering, fraud, and conspiracy over the disposition of union benefit funds and began a 13-year jail sentence in 1967, which was commuted by President Nixon in 1971. As president, Hoffa's contribution to the Teamsters as a union was to enlarge its membership in the transportation and storage industry (under Hoffa, the Teamsters' membership grew from 1,417,400 to 1,789,100); to introduce the first nationwide contract in the industry (1964); and to expand the union's health and medical program. Hoffa disappeared in 1975 and has been presumed to have been murdered by the Mafia. The film *Hoffa* starring Jack Nicholson and Danny DeVito was released in 1993. (*See also* David Beck, Teamsters)

HOMESTEAD LABOR DISPUTE   The Homestead labor dispute was a milestone event in American labor history. It occurred at the Homestead Steel Works, near Pittsburgh, in 1892, a plant which had been acquired by the Carnegie Steel Company in 1882. The dispute had its origins in the struggle between the management and the steelworkers' union, the Amalgamated Association of Iron, Steel and Tin Workers, over the control of labor costs. For some time before the dispute, the association had agreed to tie wage rates to steel production, but the increasing mechanization of the industry changed this relationship. Mechanization raised output but falling steel prices made for more difficult trading conditions. In 1889 the association successfully resisted a 25 percent wage cut and the imposition of individual contracts. Before the expiration of the three-year contract signed after the 1889 dispute, Carnegie determined to rid the Homestead plant of the union.

Although 750 of the 3,800 employees of Homestead were union members before the dispute, they were mainly skilled men whose skills were being made redundant by mechanization. In April 1892 the management represented by Henry C. Frick demanded an average wage cut of 25 percent for the skilled men and a wage system which was independent of productivity. The association rejected this demand. The management closed the plant and by July 2, 1892 had locked out the employees, a move which helped mobilize all the employees behind the association. Unable to secure the cooperation of the local authorities (who were either union members or supporters), the management resorted to the use of armed strike-breakers. This action led to an armed clash which resulted in the deaths of seven strike-breakers and nine strikers and the wounding of twenty strike-breakers and forty strikers. The armed power of the strikers was broken by the use of 8,000 Pennsylvanian National Guardsmen who enabled the plant to be re-opened with strike-breakers. Former employees were evicted from company-owned housing.

By November 20, 1892 the dispute had petered out with the utter defeat of the association not just at Homestead but in the steel industry generally. Wages at Homestead were not only reduced by an average of a quarter between 1892 and 1897, but the daily working hours of skilled men were increased from eight to twelve hours. By 1897 mechanization meant that the Homestead plant could be operated with 2,900 employees compared to 3,800 before the dispute. What happened at Homestead became a model for the steel industry. In 1892 about half of the employees in the steel industry were unionized but, with the breaking of the association, only a tiny fraction were union members. In June 1909 the U.S. Steel Corporation, the successor to Carnegie's Steel Company, openly declared an "open shop" policy, and the industry remained effectively nonunion until the mid-1930s. (*See also* Labor Disputes, United Steelworkers of America)

HUGHES, WILLIAM MORRIS (1862-1952) Hughes was prime minister of Australia (q.v.) from 1915 to 1923. Born in London, of Welsh parents, he became a schoolteacher and spent some years teaching in Wales. He emigrated to Australia in 1884 as a government-assisted migrant and settled in Sydney, New South Wales, in 1890 where he opened a shop which became a meeting ground for future labor politicians. He gained his first political experience through the Single Tax League which had been formed after the visit by Henry George (q.v.). In 1894 he entered New South Wales politics as a Labor member and in 1901 entered federal politics. Hughes took advantage of his political office to reorganize the Sydney wharf laborers (1899) and remained their secretary until 1916; he also founded a union among the trolley, draymen and carters. In addition, he used his election to the federal parliament to organize a national union among Australia's longshoremen (the Waterside Workers' Federation) in 1902. Hughes was generally opposed to strikes.

In 1910 he published *The Case for Labor*, a statement of his views about the goals of organized labor in politics. He succeeded Andrew Fisher (1862-1928) as Labor prime minister in 1915 and devoted his energies to organizing Australia's war effort. This included leading two exceptionally bitter campaigns in support of conscription in 1916 and 1917, which split the Australian Labor Party (q.v.). In 1916 he switched sides and joined the conservatives to form the Nationalist Party. (*See also* Australian Labor Party, Waterfront)

HUMAN RIGHTS Organized labor has always supported human rights issues even if that support has been tinged with economic considerations. The exclusion of children from factory employment, for example, could be justified on the grounds of the protection of their welfare, but the employment of children also posed a threat to adult wages. Similarly, the attempts of the American Federation of Labor-Congress of Industrial Organizations (q.v.) to deny tariff preferences to certain countries such as Indonesia for abuses of trade union rights could also be interpreted as reducing competition from countries with low wage economies. More clearly, the support for human rights by organized labor was evident in the case of the apartheid system in South Africa (q.v.) where German and Swedish unions were able to exert pressure on the boards of their companies operating in South Africa to adopt progressive codes of conduct which excluded racist practices. In 1984 the International Confederation of Trade Unions (q.v.) began to publish annual surveys of violations of trade union rights in the world which document the murder, torture, and imprisonment of union leaders and, denial of official recognition of labor unions which are not controlled by the government. Those countries with the worst record of human rights violations also have the worst record of the violation of trade union rights. The Middle East usually attracts significant attention in this regard. (*See also* International Confederation of Trade Unions, International Labour Organisation)

HUNGARY Organized labor within the modern borders of Hungary emerged during the 1860s and grew in parallel with the Social Democratic Party which set up a council of labor unions in 1891; this was reorganized on a permanent basis in 1899. In 1898 there were 126 unions with a combined membership of 23,000. In 1907 the unions claimed a combined membership of 130,000, but the hostile political climate reduced this to 112,000 by 1912. Hungary was an affiliate of the International Federation of Trade Unions (q.v.) from 1905 to 1939. In 1919 Hungary's political framework was shattered by the attempted creation of a Communist republic which was replaced by a provisional government of labor and socialists and then by a right-wing counter-revolutionarygovern led by Admiral Miklós Horthy who suppressed the left-wing of organized labor. The imposition of communist rule meant that it was impossible for an independent labor movement to operate until 1986. By 1995 two national labor federations existed: the *Magyar Szakszervezetek Országos Szövetsége Tagszervezeteinek Címlistája* (MszOSz), or National Confederation of Hungarian Trade Unions, formed in 1990 from the former communist *Magyar Szakszervezetek Országos Tanácsá* (SZOT) or Central Council of Hungarian Trade Unions with 895,000 members and the Democratic League of Independent Trade Unions (LIGA), formed in 1989 with 98,000 members. The LIGA has been admitted to membership of the International Confederation of Free Trade Unions (q.v.). In 1994 there were 993,000 union members in Hungary who represented about 27 percent of all employees.

I

ICELAND In 1916, two years before Iceland became independent from Denmark, seven unions formed the Icelandic Federation of Labor with 650 members. The first attempt at forming a labor federation had been made in 1907 but it collapsed in 1910. By 1923 union mmebership reached 4,000. Between 1925 and 1927 three regional labor federations were created. Despite legal restrictions, many labor disputes (q.v.) have occurred in Iceland. State and local government employees organized their own labor federation in 1942. Union membership grew from 4,500 in 1927 to 30,000 in 1960 and to 72,700 in 1995. (*See also* Council of Nordic Organizations, Denmark)

ICONOGRAPHY Throughout its history organized labor has made extensive use of public symbols to express and create unity and to win support. Painted silken banners depicting the activities and aspirations of union members seem to have been derived from coats of arms in Britain and began to be used from about 1807. About three-quarters of the union banners used by organized labor in Britain from 1837 until the 1970s were made by one firm, that founded by George Tutill (1817-1887); Tutill's banners were also exported throughout the British Empire. Banners were carried on May Day or Labor Day (q.v.) and to encourage solidarity during labor disputes (q.v.). Common themes in the iconography of organized labor were the appeal to unity (for example, in slogans like "the unity of labor is the hope of the world") and secular millenarianism (the promise of a better future often symbolized by a rising sun) and how it might be achieved through socialism or communism (qq.v.). Union labels have also been used to promote products produced by union members; they were first used in the United States by the Cigar Makers' International Union in 1874. In 1884 the Knights of Labor (q.v.) and other unions used union labels as part of their boycott campaign. Organized labor has also used badges and medals to promote membership; the general strike in Brisbane, Australia, in 1912 was prompted by managements' objections to government street car employees wearing membership badges. Other outlets for the use of union iconography were the labor press from the 1880s and, from the 1930s, film. (*See also* Industrial Archaeology)

IG METALL *IG Metall* is not only the largest labor union in Germany (q.v.), it has also been the largest union in any democratic country since its formation in 1950. Since 1965 it has had over 2 million members or a third of Germany's total trade union membership. Based on engineering employees, the sheer size of *IG Metall* has made it a major force in post-1945 Germany labor history. *IG Metall* was formed at a congress in Hamburg between September 18-22, 1950 with a membership of 1.3 million. Its leader between 1954 and 1972 was Otto Brenner (q.v.). *IG Metall* played a prominent part in labor disputes (q.v.) and in gaining pay increases and shorter working hours for its members. In 1977 the first debates were held within *IG Metall* for gaining a 35-hour work week. In 1984 *IG Metall* conducted a strike which reduced the working hours of its members to 38.5 hours and in February 1988 signed an agreement which gave many of its members a work week of 36.5 hours. Following the reunification of Germany in 1989 *IG Metall* actively recruited in the former East Germany to raise its membership to 3.6 million by 1992. On April 24, 1994 *IG Metall* negotiated an agreement with the metal trades federation for a 35-hour week to begin on May 1, 1994. In 1994 *IG Metall* had 3 million members of whom 18 percent were women. (*See also* Otto Brenner, *Deutscher Metallarbeiter Verband*)

IMMIGRATION Immigration from Europe has played an important role in the spread of organized labor to other countries. In Britain, some sections of organized labor actively encouraged emigration as a way of reducing unemployment. Several English unions, notably the Amalgamated Society of Engineers and the Amalgamated Society of Carpenters and Joiners (qq.v.), were able to establish branches in North America, South Africa, and Australasia through immigration. As a major source of skilled employees, British immigrants were particularly important in the founding of labor unions in Canada, the United States, Australia, and New Zealand (qq.v.) before 1900. Similarly, organized labor in Latin America was much influenced by Spanish and Italian immigrants. In the United States immigrants were disproportionately represented in organized labor because they were the backbone of the industrialized labor force in the large cities.

Up to 1890 the industrialized labor force of the United States was dominated by British, Irish, and German immigrants but thereafter immigrants from Russia, Eastern Europe, Italy, and Scandinavia assumed greater importance. By 1910 20 percent of the labor force of the United States was foreign-born. Not only that, 72 percent of immigrants were urban dwellers compared to 36 percent for the native-born. The occupations which loomed large in the history of organized labor were immigrant dominated; in 1910, 48 percent of coal miners were foreign-born as were 45 percent of woollen textile workers and 37 percent of cotton textile workers. The harsh lot of many immigrant employees - the low pay, long hours and poor and unsafe working conditions-created justifiable discontent and created a large social divide in American society which established unions (because they tended to represent the better-off native-born) proved ill-equipped to heal. Nevertheless, union activity was one source of upward social mobility for the foreign-born. Gary M. Fink estimated in 1984 that of the 80 top labor leaders in the United States in 1900, 40 percent were foreign-born and that even by 1946 this proportion had only fallen to 20 percent. In Australia, immigration has been a feature of organized labor for over a century. In 1995 23 percent of union members were born overseas compared to 24 percent in 1976. (*See also* Amalgamated Society of Carpenters and Joiners, Amalgamated Society of Engineers, Coal Mining)

INDIA Before 1918 there was very little organized labor in India. Those unions which had been formed were confined to skilled and better-off employees. The industrialization brought by World War I created a more favorable climate for the creation of unions. In 1918 B. P. Wadia created the Madras Union, which was based on textile employees. Stimulated by low wages, wartime inflation, and the rise of the independence movement, the next two years brought an increase in unions and union members. In 1920 the All-India Trades Union Congress was formed representing sixty-four unions with about 150,000 members. In the interwar years, India's unions and labor federations became divided between moderates and communists. As in other countries, industrial and political aims (that is, for independence) became mixed. In 1947 the government sponsored a new noncommunist labor federation, the Indian National Trade Union Congress, thereby setting a precedent for the various labor federations to be associated with a particular political party. Union growth since 1950 in India has been difficult to measure, because the official figures are known to underestimate the true level but they indicate that between 1950 and 1970 the number of union members rose from 1.8 million to 4.9 million. By 1987 official union membership had reached 6.3 million or about 15 percent of the number of nonagricultural employees. Although Indian unions operate in a relatively benign legal environment compared to most other Asian countries, their power to influence governments has been limited. A national strike by millions of employees against the national government's economic reforms on September 9, 1993 had no effect on government policy. There were 10.3 million union members in 1995.

INDONESIA Indonesia was ruled by the Dutch as the Dutch East Indies from the seventeenth century to 1949. It had no organized labor until 1905 when Dutch and indigenous railway employees formed a union. A labor federation was founded in 1919, but it only lasted until 1921. Communism (q.v.) and nationalism were features of organized labor from the 1920s to the 1960s. By 1930 there were 32,000 members of unions in Indonesia and in 1931 a revived labor federation of natiive employees was admitted to the International Federation of Trade Unions (q.v.). Since independence, labor unions have been bound up with the government. Some sections of organized labor participated in communist insurgency in the 1950s and early 1960s, but these were suppressed in an extensive crackdown which followed the attempted coup of 1965. Since 1973 labor unions have been incorporated into the apparatus of government though remaining nominally independent. Although three Indonesian labor federations have been members of the International Confederation of Free Trade Unions (q.v.) since 1969, in the early 1990s their membership and those of a fourth body have been suspended because of their lack of independence from government control.

An independent union, *Sepia Kawan* (Prosperity Labor Union), was formed in November 1990; it claimed 50,000 members in 1993 but has twice been denied registration as a legal body and its leadership has been harassed by the military. In August 1993 the government banned the union's first congress. There is also another independent labor body, the Center for Indonesian Working-Class Struggle. Muchtac Pakpahan (1953 -), the leader of the Prosperity Labor Union was arrested on August 13,1994 over riots in Medan, Sumatra, which arose in April 1994 over demands for raising the minimum wage, freedom of assocation (q.v.), the investigation of the death of Rusli (a striker) and compensation for sacked rubber factory workers. On November 7,1994 Pakpahan was sentenced to three-years jail, a decision which brought protests from labor leaders in Australia and the United States (qq.v.). On January 16, 1995 Pakpahan's sentence was increased to four years by the North Sumatra High Court.

INDUSTRIAL ARCHAEOLOGY Industrial archaeology is a branch of archaeology which emerged in the 1960s devoted principally to the physical remains and technology of the Industrial Revolution. It is also associated with efforts to recreate the living conditions in industrial centers through open air museums such as those of Beamish in northeast England and at Dudley in the English Midlands. (*See also* Iconography)

INDUSTRIAL DEMOCRACY Industrial democracy is a term with a wide spectrum of meanings but indicating some degree of control by employees in the decisions and processes which affect their working lives. At its most extreme, it can mean that the employees should be the managers of their employment. This has been a particularly popular view in the left-wing of organized labor and expressed in the term "workers' control." In its milder forms, especially in the 1970s, it has been used to justify greater consultation with employees as a means for raising labor productivity. (*See also* Guild Socialism, *Mitbestimmung*, Syndicalism)

INDUSTRIAL PSYCHOLOGY Industrial psychology is primarily concerned with human relations at work. There have been a number of schools of thought within the field reflecting the kinds of employment dominant in the economy. One of the earliest was "scientific management" which was founded by an engineer, Frederick Winslow Taylor (1856-1915), one of the developers of chromium-tungsten high-speed steel, who had been employed by the Midvale Steel Company in the 1880s. Taylor developed his ideas at a time when technological changes in the steel industry enabled managements to break the power of skilled employees and replace them with lesser skilled. Employees were assumed to be relatively unintelligent and motivated largely to earn more by agreeing to close supervision in the performance of monotonous work of low skill content. Scientific management was suitable for industries engaged in high-volume production where the tasks could be broken down into a series of repetitive steps such as assembly lines.

The "human relations" school was founded by an Australian-born psychologist (George) Elton Mayo (1880-1949) who conducted a series of experiments for the management of the Western Electric Company in Chicago between 1924 and 1927. One of Mayo's findings was the important role played by informal groups in the performance of factory work and their significance for work habits and attitudes.

In 1943 A. H. Maslow published a psychological theory of motivation which proposed that employees' satisfaction depended upon a hierarchical order of needs beginning with the physiological, safety, love or social needs, self-esteem, and ending with self-fulfilment. In the 1950s and 1960s, F. Herzberg built on Maslow's work to stress the need for the work itself to have or produce a sense of achievement, advancement, and responsibility as factors which motivated employees to perform more productively. In the 1970s, "industrial democracy" (q.v.) (a term with a variety of meanings) was given more attention in the management literature as a means of promoting higher productivity and lower absenteeism. In practical terms, it has encouraged greater consultation by management of its employees. As a general rule, the results of the research carried out by industrial psychologists have been of far greater interest and use to management than they have to organized labor. This is because the research has often been commissioned by employers and because the research itself often ignored unions and why they might be supported by employees.

INDUSTRIAL SOCIOLOGY Industrial sociology is a branch of sociology concerned with work, its organization and effects. Although there were earlier investigations, industrial sociology had its origins in the work of British pioneers such as Henry Mayhew in the 1850s and 1860s and Charles Booth in the 1890s. These investigators collected data on employment, living conditions, income, and costs among the working class in London. In the United States (q.v.), important studies were carried out of particular groups such as coal miners (for example, by Peter Roberts in 1904) and clothing employees. In the 1930s studies by industrial sociologists in many countries documented the debilitating effects of long-term unemployment; for example, E. W. Bakke published *Citizens without Work* in 1940. Others published their findings as official government reports. Common themes in industrial sociology in the period from 1945 to 1980 were how the working class was responding to greater affluence, the monotony of mass production, and family relationships.

Labor unions as such were not studied much before the pioneering works of Beatrice and Sidney Webb (q.v.). In 1952 an American investigator, Joseph Goldstein, published *The Government of British Trade Unions*, which examined the workings of the Transport and General Workers' Union (q.v.) and estimated that branch attendance at union meetings never exceeded 15 percent of the membership. Subsequent studies have confirmed Goldstein's findings of low membership participation in the affairs of most large unions.

Since 1980 industrial sociologists have often been concerned with the social impact of economic change; the effects of steel plant closures on communities, for instance, have been studied in many countries. (*See also* Beatrice Webb and Sidney Webb)

INDUSTRIAL WORKERS OF THE WORLD (IWW) The IWW, popularly known as the Wobblies, was the American expression of syndicalism (q.v.) which was influential in international organized labor from the early 1900s until about 1920. Although the works of European theorists such as Marx and Sorel were known, the IWW owed its origins to the violent labor environment of the mining industry in the western United States (q.v.). The prime mover in the formation of the IWW was the radical Western Federation of Miners, a body which originated in the Butte Miners' Union established in 1878. After defeats in disputes in 1903-04, particularly at Cripple Creek, Colorado, the Western Federation of Miners called a convention in 1904 in Chicago to create a single organization for the working class which led to the creation of the IWW in 1905. The convention adopted a radical platform which declared that the employers and workers had nothing in common and agreed to build an organization which admitted all employees regardless of sex, race or nationality, an idea dormant in American organized labor since the demise of the Knights of Labor (q.v.) in the late 1880s. It also agreed that the IWW should be made up of five main industry groups: mining, manufacturing, building, transportation, and public service distribution.

By 1906 the IWW claimed 14,000 members but was able to mobilize far greater support among poorly paid and exploited workers. It campaigned for free speech in the late 1900s, which provoked vigilante violence and conducted America's first sit-down strike at the General Electric plant at Schenectady, New York, in 1906. The IWW proved adept at mobilizing working class discontent, for example among the largely immigrant textile employees at Lawrence, Massachusetts, in 1912, but not at creating lasting organizations. With the entry of the United States into World War I in 1917, the IWW, which opposed the war, came under direct attack from the federal government which raided IWW offices and arrested the bulk of the leadership. Of the 105 leaders arrested, 91 were convicted including William Haywood (q.v.). At its height, that is between 1919 and 1924, the membership of the IWW ranged between 58,000 and 100,000.

Although the IWW continued to live on after 1924, it was no longer a significant force. In its heyday, it led the mobilizing of unskilled workers in agriculture and lumber and, more importantly, drew public attention to their deplorable working conditions. The IWW also provided members for the American Communist Party. Although primarily an American organization, the IWW was an important force in Canada and was a focus for left-wing activity in Argentina, Australia, Mexico, New Zealand, and South Africa (qq.v.); it was also important for its advocacy of the One Big Union (q.v.). (*See also* Syndicalism)

INDUSTRIEGEWERKSCHAFT METALL   (*See IG Metall*)

INTERNATIONAL BROTHERHOOD OF TEAMSTERS, CHAUFFEURS, WAREHOUSEMEN, AND HELPERS OF AMERICA (*See* Teamsters)

INTERNATIONAL CONFEDERATION OF ARAB TRADE UNIONS (ICATU) The ICATU was formed in Damascus, Syria, in March 1956 by national labor bodies in Egypt, Jordan, Lebanon, Libya, and Syria. The aims of the ICATU included the improvement of living standards of Arab employees but also support for national struggles for independence against colonial rule. The ICATU promoted training and study courses for union officials from 1969. Two forces weakened the potential effectiveness of the ICATU: the repression of organized labor by Arab governments and the left-wing character of the ICATU. The ICATU split in 1978 and its headquarters were transferred from Egypt to Syria. In 1992 the ICATU had sixteen member nations and had close links to the World Federation of Trade Unions (q.v.).

INTERNATIONAL CONFEDERATION OF FREE TRADE UNIONS (ICFTU) The ICFTU has been the largest international body representing organized labor in noncommunist countries since its formation in 1949. After the replacement of the International Federation of Trade Unions by the World Federations of Trade Unions (qq.v.) in 1945, there was growing concern over infiltration of the new body by communist organizations controlled by the Soviet Union. This concern was strongest in the United States, Britain, and the Netherlands which set up the ICFTU in 1949. At its foundation, the ICFTU had members in fifty-one countries, which represented 48 million union members of whom 43 percent were in Western Europe and 31 percent in North America. Despite its strong support for independent labor unions from its formation, many of the ICFTU's members in Latin America, Africa, and Asia were guilty of violations of this principle. By the 1960s the ICFTU had broadened its perspective to include progressive social goals. In 1969 the politically conservative AFL-CIO (q.v.) withdrew from the ICFTU and did not rejoin until 1981. In 1984 the ICFTU began to conduct annual surveys of violations of trade union rights in the world. After 1989 some labor federations from former East European communist countries were admitted to membership of the ICFTU. By 1995 organized labor in Eastern Europe accounted for nine percent of the 125 million members in the ICFTU. As well as country members, International Trade Secretariats (q.v.) have been associated with the ICFTU although retaining their autonomy. (*See also* International Federation of Trade Unions, International Trade Secretariats, World Federation of Trade Unions)

INTERNATIONAL FEDERATION OF BUILDING AND WOODWORKERS (IFBWW) The IFBWW trade secretariat was formed in 1934 through the union of the Woodworkers' International (formed in 1904) and the Building Workers' International (formed in 1903). In 1934 two other trade secretariats, the Painters' International (formed in 1911) and the Stoneworkers' International (formed in 1904), joined the IFBWW which has been based in Geneva since 1970. The affiliated membership of the IFBWW was 2.2 million in 1975 and 3.5 million in 1992. (*See also* International Trade Secretariats)

INTERNATIONAL FEDERATION OF CHEMICAL, ENERGY, AND GENERAL WORKERS (IFCEGW) The IFCEGW trade secretariat was created in 1964 from the merger of the International Federation of General Factory Workers (formed in 1907) and the International Federation of Industrial Organizations and General Workers' Unions (formed in 1947). The IFCEGW faced competition from the International Federation of Petroleum and Chemical Workers (formed in 1954) until its denouncement by Victor George Reuther (1912-) as a "front" for the U.S. Central Intelligence Agency, an action which led to the folding of the federation in 1976. Between 1976 and 1992 the affiliated membership of the IFCEGW rose from 4 to 6.3 million members. (*See also* International Trade Secretariats)

INTERNATIONAL FEDERATION OF CHRISTIAN TRADE UNION (*See* World Confederation of Labour)

INTERNATIONAL FEDERATION OF COMMERCIAL, CLERICAL, PROFESSIONAL, AND TECHNICAL EMPLOYEES (IFCCPTE) The IFCCPTE trade secretariat was formed in 1921 from a failed earlier international clerical body which operated from Hamburg, Germany, between 1909 and 1914. The IFCCPTE was primarily a European body until 1949 after which time it expanded into other continents. The main industries represented by the IFCCPTE were banking, insurance, commerce, retailing, and social services. Between 1976 and 1994 the affiliated membership of the IFCCPTE had risen from 6.2 to 11 million. It is based in Geneva. (*See also* International Trade Secretariats, White-Collar Unionism)

INTERNATIONAL FEDERATION OF FREE TEACHERS' UNIONS (IFFTU) The IFFTU trade secretariat was originally formed as an entirely European body in 1928 but was reorganized as a global labor body in 1951 in Paris. Its membership increased from 2.3 million in 1976 to 19 million in 1994. It is based in Brussels. In 1993 it was reorganized as the Educational International. (*See also* International Trade Secretariats, World Confederation of Organizations of the Teaching Profession)

INTERNATIONAL FEDERATION OF JOURNALISTS (IFJ) The IFJ was formed in 1952 by noncommunists who split from the communist-dominated International Organization of Journalists. The primary goals of the IFJ have always been the defense of freedom of the press and its journalists. Up to the late 1980s the IFJ was neither a trade secretariat nor a formal associate of the International Confederation of Free Trade Unions (q.v.), but it was both by 1993. Membership of the IFJ was 81,900 in 1976 and 350,000 in 1994. It is based in Brussels. (*See also* International Trade Secretariats, White-Collar Unionism)

INTERNATIONAL FEDERATION OF PLANTATION, AGRICULTURAL, AND ALLIED WORKERS (IFPAW) The IFPAW trade secretariat was created in 1960 by the merger of the International Landworkers' Federation, which was formed by some European agricultural labor unions in 1921, and the Plantation Workers' International, which was organized by the International Confederation of Free Trade Unions (q.v.) in 1957 to represent Third World plantation employees. Between 1976 and 1992 the affiliated membership of the IFPAW was stationary at 3 million. (*See also* International Confederation of Free Trade Unions, International Trade Secretariats)

INTERNATIONAL FEDERATION OF TRADE UNIONS (IFTU) The IFTU was the first continuous general international organization of labor unions. Officially called the International Secretariat of the National Trade Unions Federations until 1919, the IFTU was formed in Copenhagen on August 21, 1901 by labor representatives from Britain, Belgium, France, Germany, Denmark, Sweden, Norway, and Finland. The original impetus for the formation of the IFTU came from J. Jensen, the leader of the Danish labor unions, who had attended a conference held by the General Federation of Trade Unions (q.v.) in London in 1900. Its largest affiliates between 1901 and 1913 were Britain and Germany. The American Federation of Labor (AFL) (q.v.) joined the IFTU in 1911 but left officially in 1919; it did not reaffiliate until 1937. Before 1913 the IFTU devoted itself to collecting money to help unions and strikers and to exchanging information. World War I split the IFTU along national lines, and it was not reestablished until 1919. Up to 1919 the IFTU was ably led by Carl Legien (q.v.).

After 1919 the IFTU participated in European politics, a policy which led to the withdrawal of the AFL. The IFTU invited the Russian trade unions to its conferences, but these moves were met with hostility from the Communist government which regarded the IFTU as a competitor for the leadership of organized labor. The Russians established Profitern, the labor arm of the Comintern (q.v.), as a rival to the IFTU. The IFTU continued to aid labor unions in affiliated countries and carried out fact-finding missions of workers' conditions in Austria and Belgium (1920) and the Saar and Upper Silesia (1921). Throughout its life, the IFTU was essentially a moderate, European-based organization and the voice of organized labor in the International Labour Organisation (q.v.). In 1927 the IFTU established an International Committee of Trade Union Women which lasted until 1937 ; it considered issues such as equal pay for equal work (q.v.), domestic service, working from home, and the women's peace campaign.

In the 1930s the IFTU tried to widen its membership; India joined in 1934, Mexico in 1936, New Zealand in 1938, and China (qq.v.) in 1939. The Australian Council of Trade Unions (q.v.) was invited to join in 1936 but did not accept. At conferences in 1931 and 1932 the IFTU adopted the 40-hour work week and a comprehensive social program as objectives.

Despite its best efforts, the IFTU was weakened by the suppression of organized labor by fascism and undermined by communism (q.v.) and lack of support from the AFL for most of its life. The IFTU gave way to the World Federation of Trade Unions (q.v.) and ceased to exist on December 31, 1945. (*See also* American Federation of Labor, Comintern, General Federation of Trade Unions, International Confederation of Free Trade Unions, Carl Legien, Social Democratic/Socialist/Labor Parties, World Federation of Trade Unions)

INTERNATIONAL GRAPHICAL FEDERATION (IGF) The IGF was founded in Stockholm in 1949 through the amalgamation (q.v.) of three international printing and graphical trades bodies-the International Typographical Secretariat (formed in 1889), the International Federation of Lithographers (formed in 1896) and the International Federation of Bookbinders and Kindred Trades (formed in 1907)-and eight British graphical trades labor unions. Based in Brussels, the IGF is mainly a European body. Its affiliated membership increased from 806,300 in 1976 to 1.2 million in 1994. (*See also* International Trade Secretariats, Printing)

INTERNATIONAL LABOR UNION (ILU) The ILU grew out of dissidents at the 1877 convention of the Workingmen's Party which wasrenamed the Socialist Labor Party. The leading dissidents, George McNeill, Ira Stewart and J. P. MacDonnell, organized the ILU in Boston in February 1878, and by the end of the year it claimed 8,000 members. The aims of the ILU included the eight-hour work day, higher wages, unemployment relief, government factory and mine inspection, and restrictions on child labor. The ILU also sought to amalgamate all labor unions in one body. Despite some early successes in strikes in the textile industry of the Northeast, the ILU was defeated thereafter and by 1887 had ceased to exist. Nevertheless, it made the first wholesale attempt to organize the unskilled, thus anticipating the Knights of Labor and the Congress of Industrial Organizations (qq.v.). (*See also* Federation of Organized Trades and Labor Unions, Knights of Labor, One Big Union)

INTERNATIONAL LABOUR ORGANISATION (ILO) Created in 1919 as part of the peace process to end World War I, the ILO is a permanent world organization comprised of representatives of governments, employers, and unions whose function is the protection and improvement of working people through the setting of legal minimum standards and technical assistance. The first steps towards the creation of such a body were taken in Switzerland in the late 1880s. The Belgian government supported the Swiss initiatives, and the International Congress of Civil Reforms in Brussels in 1897 called for the setting up of an international body to protect labor. The Swiss-based International Association for Labor Legislation was formed in 1900 and held a number of international conferences which stimulated government interest in forming a permanent body to protect employment conditions. An important precedent for the creation of the ILO occurred in 1904 when France and Italy (qq.v.) signed a treaty regulating the employment conditions of their nationals working in each other's country.

World War I disrupted these efforts but the need for the active support of labor to fight the war gave organized labor an enhanced standing with the British, French, and German governments. In 1916 a congress held by organized labor in Britain was attended by representatives from France, Italy, and Belgium (q.v.); it prepared specific proposals to be incorporated into the treaty expected to end the war and suggested an international commission to implement them. In Germany, Carl Legien (q.v.), concerned that the International Federation of Trade Unions (q.v.) might be broken up, convened a counter-conference at Berne in 1917. Organized labor in France and Germany strongly supported the idea of an international body to safeguard the interests of labor. During the preparations for the Versailles Treaty, a Labor Commission was formed of fifteen members drawn from the United States, France, United Kingdom, Italy, Japan, Belgium, Cuba, Czechoslovakia, and Poland and chaired by Samuel Gompers (qq.v.).

Overcoming many political and ideological differences, the commission succeeded in having these principles incorporated in the treaty: respect for labor; the right of association; adequate wages; an eight-hour work day or 48-hour week; abolition of child labor (q.v.); equal pay for equal work (q.v.); migrant workers to be given the same treatment as nationals; and an inspectorate system for protecting labor. Although the final outcome of the peace process was a disappointment for organized labor in Europe, the compromises reflected the political reality of the time. Under the ILO constitution, the governing body was to have twelve representatives from governments, six from employers and six from employees; although, in practice, employee representation was dominated by the International Federation of Trade Unions. The ILO became an affiliated agency of the League of Nations.

The ILO was able to achieve relatively little in its first twenty years. The fascist suppression of free unions in Italy raised the issue of freedom of association (q.v.) in a very stark way, but the ILO was unable, as an organization, to agree on a course of action. Its representation was also inadequate; the United States did not join until 1935. Its recommendations for reducing the mass unemployment of the early 1930s through increased government spending were ignored by member governments. Despite its difficulties, the ILO succeeded in starting the first continuous collections of international labor statistics (q.v.).

In 1946 the ILO became the first specialized agency to be associated with the United Nations. In the late 1940s the ILO adopted two fundamental propositions regarding organized labor: Convention 87 (Freedom of Association and Protection of the Right to Organise, 1948) and Convention 98 (Right to Organise and to Bargain Collectively). In 1951 the governing body of the ILO set up a standing Freedom of Association Committee to oversee the operation of these and other conventions relating to organized labor. Although there is no specific ILO convention setting down the right to strike, Article 3 of Convention 87 stating that unions had the right to "draw up their constitutions and rules, to elect their representatives in full freedom, to organise their administration and activities and to formulate their programmes" has been interpreted as including a right to strike. The extent of ratification by member governments of the ILO of these and similar conventions varies as does the degree of respect for them among those governments which have. The United States withdrew from the ILO between 1977 and 1980 because of disagreements with its policies. (*See also* Employer Organizations, International Federation of Trade Unions, Labor Disputes, Occupational Health and Safety, Albert Thomas)

INTERNATIONAL LADIES' GARMENT WORKERS' UNION (ILGWU) The ILGWU has played a significant role in the history of organized labor in the United States (q.v.). Formed in New York City in March 1900, the ILGWU received a charter from the American Federation of Labor (AFL) (q.v.) three months later. Its membership grew from 2,200 in 1904 to 58,400 in 1912, many of whom were Jewish and East European immigrants. Successful strikes in New York City in 1909 and 1910 secured the union's future. The 1910 cloakmakers' strike gained a 54-hour work week over six days, the closed shop, arbitration for the settlement of disputes, and the abolition of home-based work and subcontracting which were important means of keeping wages in the trade low. Other important initiatives of the ILGWU in this period were union health centers (1913) and the preparation of an employer-funded unemployment plan (1919). By 1920 the ILGWU had grown to 195,400, but this success was undermined by communists who dominated the leadership until 1928. The new leadership of Benjamin Schlesinger and David Dubinsky (q.v.) took over a union with debts of $800,000 and a financial membership of only 40,000. Assisted by the National Industrial Recovery Act (q.v.), the ILGWU was rebuilt; by 1935 its membership had grown to 168,000 and most of the debts had been repaid. Under Dubinsky's leadership, the ILGWU was at the center of the struggle within organized labor to promote industrial unionism and in the formation of the Congress of Industrial Organizations (q.v.). It left the AFL in 1938 but rejoined in 1940. In 1973 the union had a membership of 427,600 of whom about 80 percent were women. Racial and ethnic diversity remained characteristic of its membership. In 1992 the ILGWU had 143,000 members. (*See also* David Dubinsky)

INTERNATIONAL METALWORKERS' FEDERATION (IMF) The IMF is the largest of the International Trade Secretariats (q.v.). It began as the International Metallurgists' Bureau of Information in 1893 and took its present name in 1904. In 1921 the IMF accepted a new constitution which included a call for international cooperation to improve wages and conditions and for workers to take over the means of production. In 1931 the IMF had a membership of 1,742,000. The IMF played a major role in defeating the attempt of the communist-led World Council of Trade Unions (q.v.) to absorb the various International Trade Secretariats in 1948-49 and in the formation of the International Confederation of Free Trade Unions (q.v.) in 1949. In 1994 the IMF claimed 16 million members among its 165 affiliated unions. (*See also* International Confederation of Free Trade Unions, International Trade Secretariats)

INTERNATIONAL ORGANIZATION OF EMPLOYERS (*See* Employers' Organizations)

INTERNATIONAL SECRETARIAT FOR ARTS, MASS MEDIA, AND ENTERTAINMENT TRADE UNIONS (ISAMMETU) The ISAMMETU trade secretariat was set up in 1965 in Brussels at a conference of the International Confederation of Free Trade Unions (q.v.) as the International Secretariat of Entertainment Trade Unions. It has not been a success: between 1973 and 1992 its membership fell from 470,000 to 100,000. Since 1984 it has been an autonomous part of the International Federation of Commercial, Clerical, Professional, and Technical Employees (q.v.). (*See also* International Trade Secretariats)

INTERNATIONAL STANDARD-SETTING International standard-setting refers to the work of the International Labour Organisation (ILO) (q.v.) in devising suitable standards for the protection and improvement of working conditions especially in relation to working hours (q.v.), the protection of women and children, adequate wages, social security (q.v.), freedom of association (q.v.), and vocational and technical education. The framing of such standards is difficult because the standard of living in the member countries of the ILO differs so greatly. At the same time, there is an obvious need for such standards. (*See also* International Labour Organisation)

INTERNATIONAL TEXTILE, GARMENT, AND LEATHER WORKERS' FEDERATION (ITGLWF) The ITGLWF trade secretariat was formed in 1970, although international bodies among European textile labor unions dated from 1894 and among shoemakers and leather employees from 1907. In 1960 the Textile Workers' Asian Regional Organization was created with 1.5 million members. Other similar regional bodies were formed and these were the basis of the ITGLWF. Based in Brussels, the membership of the ITGLWF was 5.2 million in 1976 and 7 million in 1994. (*See also* International Trade Secretariats)

INTERNATIONAL TRADE SECRETARIATS International Trade Secretariats have been an important feature of the European labor movement throughout the twentieth century and of the international labor movement since 1945. The secretariats represented individual occupations or particular industries. They emerged as formal organizations among hatters (Paris, 1889); cigar makers (Antwerp, 1889); shoemakers (Paris, 1889); miners (Manchester, 1890); glass workers (Fourmies, France, 1892); typographers (Berne, 1892); tailors (Zurich, 1893); metalworkers (Winterthur, Switzerland, 1893); textile workers (Manchester, 1894); furriers (Berlin, 1894); lithographers (London, 1896); brewery workers (Berlin, 1896); transportation workers (London, 1897; this secretariat absorbed the railroad workers who had formed a secretariat in Zurich in 1893); foundry workers (1898); stone workers and stone cutters (1902, 1904); building workers (Berlin, 1903); carpenters (Hamburg, 1903); wood workers (Amsterdam, 1904); pottery and china workers (1905, 1906); diamond workers (Antwerp, 1905); bookbinders (Nuremberg, 1907); hairdressers (Stuttgart, 1907); municipal and public services (Mainz, 1906); factory and unskilled workers (this secretariat lasted from 1908 to 1914); postal workers (Marseilles, 1910); hotel and restaurant workers (Amsterdam, 1911); and painters (Hamburg, 1911).

By 1913 the trade secretariats claimed a total membership of 5.6 million of which the largest were those of the miners (1.2 million), metalworkers (1 million), transportation workers (860,000), and textile workers (533,000). By 1939 important new secretariats had emerged among government employees (1935) and teachers.

After 1945 international labor organizations along occupational lines were important among civil servants, journalists, transportation workers, metal workers, miners, teachers, postal workers, textile workers, and plantation and agricultural employees. Despite attempted communist infiltration in 1948-49, the international trade secretariats have preserved their independence. Since 1949 they have been associated with the International Confederation of Free Trade Unions (q.v.). In 1995 there were sixteen of these bodies: International Federation of Building and Woodworkers; International Federation of Chemical, Energy, and General Workers' Unions; International Federation of Commercial, Clerical, Professional, and Technical Employees; International Federation of Free Teachers' Unions; International Federation of Journalists; International Federation of Plantation, Agricultural, and Allied Workers; International Graphical Federation; International Metalworkers' Federation; International Secretariat for Arts, Mass Media, and Entertainment Trade Unions; International Textile, Garment, and Leather Workers' Federation; International Transport Workers' Federation; International Union of Food and Allied Workers' Associations; Miners' International Federation; Postal, Telegraph and Telephone International; Public Services International; and the Universal Alliance of Diamond Workers (qq.v.). (*See also* International Metalworkers' Federation, International Transport Workers' Federation, Public Services International)

INTERNATIONAL TRANSPORT WORKERS' FEDERATION (ITWF) The ITWF grew out of the International Federation of Ship Dock and River Workers which was formed by Tom Mann (q.v.) and some European labor leaders who were attending a conference of the Second International Workingmen's Association (q.v.) in London in 1896. It became the ITWF in 1898. World War I disrupted the ITWF and it was reestablished in 1919 though the efforts of Dutch, Swedish, and British labor unions. In 1920 the ITWF had three million members, all of them in Europe; by 1931 membership had fallen to 2.3 million. The ITWF provided valuable services to the Allied war effort during World War II. From 1948 the ITWF began to seek affiliates from outside Europe. By 1976 half of the claimed membership of 4.1 million members of the ITWF was in developing countries. In 1994 the ITWF had 400 union affiliates which represented 5 million members. (*See also* International Trade Secretariats)

INTERNATIONAL UNION OF FOOD AND ALLIED WORKERS' ASSOCIATIONS (IUFAWA) The IUFAWA trade secretariat was established in 1920 from the amalgamation (q.v.) of the international federation of brewery employees (formed in 1896) and baking and meat employees. Until 1945 the IUFAWA was a European body, but afterwards it expanded into North America (1950), Latin America (1953), Africa (1959), and East Asia (1961). Membership of the Geneva-based IUFAWA was 2.1 million in 1978 and 2.3 million in 1992. (*See also* International Trade Secretariats)

INTERNATIONAL UNIONS International labor unions are those which have branches in more than one country. The term is commonly applied to American unions with branches in Canada but could also be applied to Ireland (q.v.). Other international unions have been the Amalgamated Society of Carpenters and Joiners and the Amalgamated Society of Engineers (qq.v.). (*See also* Canada, Immigration)

INTERNATIONAL WORKINGMEN'S ASSOCIATION (IWMA) Also known as the First International, the IWMA was the first attempt at the formation of an international body to protect and advance the interests of the working class although a precedent for such a body existed in the Society of Fraternal Democrats (q.v.). The IWMA was formed in London in September 1864 against a background of a depressed economy (the late 1850s saw a slump in the building trades in London and Paris and the American Civil War hurt employment in the British textile industry) and the presence in Britain of some French labor leaders, there to support the Polish revolt against Russian rule in 1863. Once established, Marx and Engels took the leading role in its affairs. The IWMA was mainly composed of the leaders of English organized labor and political emigres from continental Europe. A split developed between these two groups, particularly after 1867 when the better-off English urban working class was given the vote; they tended to support reformist solutions for labor's problems whereas the members from continental Europe could not envisage their governments granting the necessary concessions with the result that they tended to support revolution.

These tensions eventually proved fatal to the IWMA. It broke up at its Hague conference in 1872 when Marx moved it to New York to avoid it coming under anarchist control. It was formally wound up in Philadelphia in 1876. Although primarily a radical political organization, the IWMA assisted the campaign in northeast England in 1871-72 for the nine-hour work day and frustrated the employers' attempt to recruit strike-breakers from continental Europe. In return, the IWMA was allowed to raise money in Britain to assist strikers in other parts of Europe. A short-lived off-shoot body of the IWMA, the Democratic Association of Victoria, operated in Australia in 1872. (*See also* Second International Workingmen's Association, Society of Fraternal Democrats)

INTERNATIONAL WORKING UNION OF SOCIALIST PARTIES
Also known as the Vienna Union, this body, which was dubbed the Two-and-a-Half International by Lenin, was formed in 1921 by the socialist parties of Austria, France, Switzerland, the German Independent Social Democratic Party, and the British Independent Labour Party rather than join either the Second International or the Comintern (qq.v.). A unity conference between these three bodies in Berlin in 1922 broke down and in May 1923, at a second congress in Hamburg, the International Working Union of Socialist Parties joined the remnants of the former Second International (q.v.) to form the Labor and Socialist International (q.v.). (*See also* Labor and Socialist International)

IRELAND The existence of unions by the eighteenth century in Ireland is known from a law of 1729 which outlawed combinations among journeymen with a penalty of three months hard labor. Similar laws were passed in 1743 and 1757. Despite the intimidating legal climate, unions were formed. In May 1788 journeymen cabinetmakers in Belfast formed a union; their minute book survives, making it one of the oldest documents of its kind. As a part of the United Kingdom until 1922, Irish organized labor was much influenced by the English model, but it also took some important initiatives of its own. In 1844 the Regular Trades' Association was formed in Dublin; it perished in the 1847 depression, but it was one of the first city labor councils in Britain.

British unions were active in Ireland from 1851, beginning with the Amalgamated Society of Engineers (q.v.). By 1900 about three-quarters of the 67,000 union members in Ireland belonged to British unions; in 1940 this proportion had fallen to 30 percent and was stable at about 14 percent between 1955 and 1985.

In 1894 the Irish Trades Union Congress was formed with 50,000 members among its affiliates. Originally intended to act as an auxiliary to the Trades Union Congress (q.v.), it went its own path from 1901; in 1945 it was challenged by the formation of a new peak labor body, the Congress of Irish Unions, but in 1959 these two bodies merged to become the Irish Congress of Trade Unions. Union membership in Ireland rose from 189,000 in 1922 to 285,000 in 1950 and to a peak of 490,000 in 1980. Despite some losses in the 1980s, union membership had recovered to 677,600 by 1995 which was 47 percent of employees. Irish immigrants have played a significant role in the history of organized labor in the United States and Australasia. (*See also* United Kingdom)

ISRAEL Organized labor in what is now Israel began in 1920 with the formation of leagues by both Arab and Jewish workers. The creation of the *Histadrut* (General Federation of Labor in Israel) in December 1920, representing 4,400 workers, was a pivotal event in the history of organized labor in Israel. Unlike the labor federations in most other countries, the socialistic *Histadrut* was a state in miniature with wide political and economic goals within its promotion of Zionism and consumer cooperation (q.v.). In 1933 there were 35,400 union members within the present borders of Israel. In the next year, some members of the *Histadrut* formed the National Labor Federation which rejected the idea of class struggle and supported separate bodies for employees and employers. Nevertheless, the *Histadrut* continued to be the dominant labor organization after the declaration of Israel in 1948; in 1945 it claimed 150,000 members. By 1995 the *Histadrut* had about 300,000 union members and about the same number who were self-employed or housewives. Individuals join the *Histadrut* directly and are then placed in the union which covers their occupation; there were 43 unions within the *Histadrut* in 1991. The *Histadrut* has close ties with the Labor Party which was formed in 1968. Labor unions also operate among the Palestinians who live in Israel. There is a Palestinian Trade Union Federation which is affiliated with the World Confederation of Trade Unions (q.v.) and a General Federation of West Bank Trade Unions.

ITALY Although organized labor in its modern form developed during the last half of the nineteenth century, there is evidence of earlier organizations in cities such as Florence from the fourteenth century. In 1675 an estimated 10,000 silk workers in Genoa rioted over the introduction of French ribbon looms which enabled a single worker to weave 10 to 12 ribbons at a time; the workers burnt the new looms. The system of medieval guilds lasted longer in Italy than in other parts of Western Europe and was only abolished piecemeal on a regional basis between 1770 and 1821. At the same time, as in other parts of Western Europe, artisan journeymen were the vanguard of organized labor. In 1853 they held a regional conference of friendly societies (q.v.), bodies which were forerunners of labor unions. Although the first labor union was formed by printers in Turin and a national printers' body was created in 1872, there was little in the way of unions elsewhere until after 1880. Nevertheless, the absence of formal unions did not indicate the absence of labor disputes; 634 occurred between 1860 and 1878, mainly in the north and mostly over wages.

The example of the French *bourse*, particularly that founded at Marseilles in 1888, was influential in Italy and led to the formation of chambers of labor (*Camera del Lavoro*) beginning in Milan in 1891. By 1893 the chambers had about 41,000 members. Government policy towards organized labor turned hostile in the 1890s, and they tried to suppress the unions between 1894 and 1899.

After a last attempt at official suppression in Genoa in 1900, labor unions began to emerge and create new national organizations, exemplified by the formation of the *Confederazione Generale di Lavoro* (CGL) or General Confederation of Labor in 1906. Although there was impressive national growth in Italian union membership after 1900, the labor movement was divided on political and religious lines. Revolutionary syndicalism (q.v.) attracted much support from rural workers employed on large estates and claimed 200,000 members in 1908. The syndicalists formed their own labor federation, the *Unione Syndicale Italiano,* in 1912 and were opposed by the socialist unions. As well, the Catholic unions which were first formed in 1894 and claimed 107,600 members by 1910 made up a separate strand of organized labor. In 1920 they formed their own federation, the *Confederazione Italiana dei Lavoratori* with 1.2 million members of whom 79 percent were employed in agricultural activities or textiles. The socialist federation, the CGL, had 2.2 million members of whom about 34 percent worked as farm laborers and most of the others in manufacturing.

Politically, Italy was immature in 1920; universal manhood suffrage was only granted in 1912 and there was little opportunity for labor leaders to gain the experience of government they needed. There was much labor unrest in 1919 and 1920, but the Socialist Party failed to translate this into practical political gains and continued to preach revolution; it was further weakened by a split caused by the communists in 1921. Divided, organized labor lost support and declined. Between 1920 and 1924, the membership of the CGL collapsed from 2.2 million to 201,000. On January 24, 1924 Mussolini's fascist government abolished the nonfascist labor unions of Italy. The CGL voted itself out of existence in 1927. The fascist government introduced a number of important principles into Italy's system of industrial relations which were to have lasting consequences. It brought in a centralized system of collective bargaining under which unions that were part of the Confederation of Fascist Corporations were legally recognized as partners as well as a compulsory system of pay deductions for union dues. Italy's example in these areas was imitated by Germany, Greece, Spain, Portugal, and Brazil.

On June 3, 1944 all three sections of organized labor-socialist, communist, Christian Democrat (Catholic)-agreed to the "Pact of Rome" which provided for the setting up of a new united labor confederation, the *Confederazione Generale Italiana del Lavoro* (CGIL), which was made up of equal representation from these three groups. This unity did not last; following a wave of strikes and unrest led by the communists of the CGIL, the Christian Democratic unions formed their own federation in 1948 as did the republican and democratic socialists in 1949. The Christian Democratic federation, the *Libera Confederazione Generale Italiana dei Lavarotori*, received support for its establishment not only from the Catholic church but also the AFL-CIO (q.v.) and the U.S. Central Intelligence Agency as a counter to the communist-dominated CGIL. In 1972 the three labor federations formed an alliance which collapsed in 1984 and was only partly restored. Rank-and-file dissatisfaction with the three federations in 1987-88 led to the formation of grassroots committees known as *comitati di base* or "cobas" which sought the repeal of a law of 1970 which gave the federations legal rights in collective bargaining. In June 1990 the government prohibited strikes in a wide range of essential services. In 1994 Italy's ten "autonomous" labor unions (which operate mostly in the public sector) formed a federation, the *Intesa Sindicati Autonomi* (Pact of Autonomous Unions) which claimed to represent 6 million employees. In all, there were 10.6 million union members in Italy in 1994. *(See also Federazione Italiana Operai Metallurgici*, Syndicalism)

J

JAPAN The first recorded labor disputes in Japan date from 1870 and the first union was formed among steelworkers in 1897. Other unions were formed among employees in printing, railroads, teaching, and firefighting; their total membership reached 8,000 in 1900, but they were suppressed by law. Japanese government opposition to unions continued until 1945, and unions were denied legal recognition. Nevertheless, a Japanese labor movement did emerge from 1912 when Bunji Suzuki formed a labor union called the *Yuai-kai* (Workers' Fraternal Society); government hostility forced it to pretend it was a cultural and moral body in its early years. In 1917 some employers formed the Japan Economic Federation to prevent the legal recognition of labor unions. By 1920 there had been significant growth in organized labor in Japan with total membership reaching 103,000. In 1921 the *Yuai-kai* established Japan's first labor federation, the *Nihon Rodo Sodomei*. In the 1920s and 1930s Japanese organized labor was split between social democrats and reformers, socialists and communists. In 1940, when all independent unions and employers' organizations (q.v.) were compulsorily merged into a body run by the government, there were only 9,500 union members compared to 408,700 in 1935.

As in Germany (q.v.), the end of World War II brought an explosive growth in organized labor; in December 1945 Japanese employees were legally allowed to form unions, to bargain collectively, and to strike. The release of communists and other radicals from jail enabled them to rejoin the unions and exploit the hardship and poverty of the immediate postwar period through strikes. In 1948 the right to strike was withdrawn from public sector employees. Between 1945 and 1950 the number of labor union members increased from 380,700 to 5.8 million and the number of unions rose from 509 to 29,144.

Three labor federations were formed in 1946 and multi-federations based on political as well as industrial differences remained a feature of Japanese organized labor thereafter. The largest federations were the *Domei* (or Japanese Confederation of Labor which evolved out of *Sodomei*, the Japanese Federation of Trade Unions, originally formed in 1946 to cover private sector employees) and the socialist, mainly public sector *Sohyo*, General Council of Trade Unions of Japan. *Sohyo* was formed in 1950 when the noncommunists split from the communist dominated *Sanbetsu-Kaigi* (or Congress of Industrial Unions of Japan, originally formed in 1946). In 1987 *Domei* and some other federations as well as unaffiliated unions formed a new private sector federation, now referred to as "old" *Rengo* (Japanese Trade Union Federation). In 1989 this body merged with *Sohyo* to create "new" *Rengo*, which claimed 7.7 million members by 1992 or about two-thirds of total labor union membership. New *Rengo* has also supported opposition candidates in Japanese elections.

From 1946 to 1960 the level of labor disputes (q.v.) in Japan was relatively high; an annual average of 458 working days per thousand employees were lost through labor disputes between 1946 and 1950, 468 between 1951 and 1955, and 437 between 1956 and 1960. In 1956 the *Shunto* (q.v.), or Spring Offensive, was begun by *Sohyo* and became an annual coordinated drive to gain wage increases. Since the mid-1970s the level of industrial disputes in Japan has decreased.

As a proportion of employees, union membership has declined steadily since its peak of 56 percent in 1950 to 24 percent in 1994. This decline has largely occurred in the private sector with union density remaining high among government employees. In 1992 29 percent of employees in manufacturing were union members compared to 72 percent in the public sector. Nevertheless, since 1945 organized labor in Japan has become very important in world terms; with 12.7 million members in 1995 Japan accounted for about a tenth of all world members. There were 32,581 unions in 1994. *See also* Employers' Organizations, China, *Rengo*, South Korea)

JOB SHARING Job sharing generally refers to the splitting of a full-time job into two part-time positions in Western countries. Although first proposed in the 1970s, job sharing is largely a development of the 1980s and has been especially beneficial to female employees with young children. Although it came to be accepted by most unions when it was done on a voluntary basis, it was often treated with suspicion at first as a possible threat to the conditions of full-time employees. (*See also* Women)

K

KIRKLAND, JOSEPH LANE (1922-) Lane Kirkland was president of the AFL-CIO (q.v.) from 1979 to 1995. Born in Camden, South Carolina, he was employed as a merchant marine pilot between 1941 and 1946 and as a nautical scientist in the Hydrographic Office of the U.S. Navy Department between 1947 and 1948. In 1945-46 he was a member of the International Organization of Masters, Mates, and Pilots (formed in 1887). He graduated with a science degree from Georgetown University in 1948. In the same year he joined the AFL (q.v.) as a researcher and was assistant director of its social security department between 1953 and 1958. His writing ability was recognized in the AFL-CIO, and in 1961 he was made executive assistant to its president, George Meany (q.v.). In 1969 he was elected secretary-treasurer of the AFL-CIO. In the 1960s he coordinated the AFL-CIO's civil rights campaign and fought racial discrimination in unions. He lobbied for a fair employment clause in the Civil Rights Act (1964), played an active role in the war on poverty, and helped to raise over $2 million for the A. Philip Randolph Institute's antighetto programs. In 1979 he negotiated a national accord with the Carter administration in which the AFL-CIO promised to restrain wage claims to help control inflation in return for greater measures to protect the poor, limits on corporate profits, and an undertaking not to use unemployment as a means of lowering inflation. As AFL-CIO president, Kirkland followed a more moderate path than Meany. Under him, the AFL-CIO rejoined the International Confederation of Free Trade Unions (q.v.) in 1981. In 1986 Kirkland was elected president of the Trade Union Advisory Committee to the Organization of Economic and Community Development (founded in 1948). (*See also* American Federation of Labor-Congress of Industrial Organizations, George Meany)

KNIGHTS OF LABOR Officially known as the Noble and Holy Order of the Knights of Labor, the Knights were the first labor organization in the United States (q.v.) to recruit unskilled workers as well as African-Americans and women. Originally formed in 1869 as a secret society by some garment cutters in Philadelphia, the Knights rejected the wage system and supported cooperation and education as means of improving the position of workers. The organization began in secrecy to avoid its members being blacklisted for work by employers.

Between 1878, when it became a national body, and 1881, membership of the Knights rose from 9,000 to 19,000. It ceased to be a secret organization by January 1882. Its membership was open to all who earned their living through manual labor either as employees or as small farmers. Between 1881 and 1893 the Knights were led by Terrence V. Powderly (q.v.). The Knights supported the abolition of child labor (q.v.), government inspection of mines and factories, and the nationalization of banks and railroads. A centralized organization, the membership of the Knights grew from 49,500 in 1883 to a peak of 703,000 in 1886 of which about 10 percent were Afro-Americans and 10 percent were women. Most of this growth occurred as a result of successful strikes against railroad companies in 1884.

After 1886 the membership of the Knights declined rapidly following their defeat in a strike against Jay Gould's South-Western Railroad (1886), factional fighting within the Knights, and a prolonged struggle with the craft unions represented by the American Federation of Labor (q.v.). One of the major problems faced by the Knights was the gulf between the expectations of the rank-and-file and the moderation of the senior leadership, a gulf exposed by the leadership's refusal to endorse the nationwide eight-hour campaign in 1886. The Knights were also active outside the United States, forming off-shoots in Canada (1881), Britain (where they claimed 10,000 members by 1889), Belgium, Ireland, Australia (1890), and New Zealand. Within the United States, the membership of the Knights ebbed rapidly from 511,400 in 1887 to 220,600 by 1889. Although a spent force after 1890, the Knights claimed 20,200 members in 1900 and continued to publish a journal until 1917. Some of their ideas were carried on by the Industrial Workers of the World (q.v.) after 1905. (*See also* Labor Day, Terrence Vincent Powderly)

L

LABOR AND SOCIALIST INTERNATIONAL (LSI) The Labor and Socialist International was formed in 1923 in Hamburg, Germany, by 620 delegates from 30 countries representing socialist and labor parties drawn from the remnants of the Second International and the International Working Union of Socialist Parties (qq.v.). It considered the class struggle to be a means of achieving socialism (q.v.). Competition from the Comintern (q.v.) and the rise of fascism greatly reduced the effectiveness of the LSI even though it claimed 6.2

millionmembers in Europe and North America in 1931. The LSI had close links with the International Federation of Trade Unions (q.v.). Its main achievement was to provide assistance for refugees from fascism. The LSI was made defunct by World War II and was replaced by the Socialist International, a noncommunist body, in 1951. (*See also* Second International Workingmen's Association)

"LABOR ARISTOCRACY" The term "labor aristocracy" was used by Marx and Engels to describe the emergence of labor unions by skilled, relatively well-paid employees in Britain after 1850. Such employees included stonemasons, engineers, railroad engine drivers, carpenters, and printers. Because of their better-off condition, such unions were less likely to support radical social change and more likely to identify with middle-class ideas and values. A leading British historian, E. J. Hobsbawm, estimated that about 15 percent of working-class employees in late-nineteenth century Britain would have qualified as the labor aristocracy. (*See also* Marxism-Leninism)

LABOR DAY Labor Day, a public holiday celebrated in the United States and Canada on the first Monday of September, was begun by the Knights of Labor (q.v.) as a march in New York City in 1882; other marches were held in 1883 and 1884 to celebrate labor. Oregon was the first U.S. State to legislate Labor Day as a public holiday in 1887. The U.S. Congress declared it a public holiday in 1894. (*See also* Second International Workingmen's Association)

LABOR DISPUTES Labor disputes, whether arising from strikes or lock-outs, are the most consistently visible sign of the presence of organized labor. There have been labor disputes since the earliest times-the first recorded labor dispute occurred in Egypt in 1152 B.C. among the pharoah's tomb-makers-and they predate unions as formal, continuous organizations. In eighteenth century England, 383 labor disputes were recorded between 1717 and 1800 and these led to the first sustained efforts to create legal mechanisms for their resolution. As the Industrial Revolution developed, labor disputes and other kinds of collective action such as rallies and demonstrations began to replace older forms of social protest such as food riots and tax revolts.

From about 1830 the first systematic efforts were made to collect information on disputes both by officials and by individuals. In France, official monitoring began in 1830 even though strikes were treated as a crime before 1864. Elsewhere in Europe, monitoring of disputes in some form had begun in Britain (1870) and Italy (1871), activities which often grew into official national statistical collections by the 1890s. In 1888 the Massachusetts Bureau of Statistics published a time series for its industrial disputes from 1825 to 1886 and continued to publish statistics into the twentieth century as did New York State even though a national series of American dispute statistics was begun in 1881. Other countries followed: Denmark (1897), Germany (1901), Sweden and Norway (1903), Canada (1901), New Zealand and South Africa (1906), Finland (1907), Australia (1913), and Japan (1914). In 1927 the International Labour Organisation (q.v.) began publishing dispute statistics for all the countries which collected them.

This monitoring was in response to a general rise in the level of disputes in Western Europe and North America from the late 1860s to the outbreak of World War I in 1914 and from 1917 to about 1930. General national disputes occurred in some countries such as in Belgium (1893), Sweden (1909), Britain (1926), and France (1968). The year 1920 was one of the high points of disputes based on high inflation and falling real wages. The causes of these waves of disputes included political as well as economic objectives and, before 1890, many employees who were not union members.

Governments before 1914 were more concerned with disputes as a threat to political stability than as a cost to the economy. Labor disputes are unlike most other social phenomena in that they can change greatly from one year to the next and often occur in waves. There have been three major international waves of labor disputes: 1869 to 1875, 1910 to 1920, and 1968 to 1974. The relationship between labor disputes and the trade cycle is complicated, but there is a clear association between the frequency of disputes and the state of the trade cycle: in good economic times, there are usually more disputes than when the cycle is depressed.

On occasions, particularly intense labor disputes have politicized some of their participants. For instance, two of the thousands of strikers who were victimized after the great railroad strike of 1917 in New South Wales, Australia, were drawn into politics: one was Joseph Benedict Chifley (1885-1951) who was Australia's prime minister from 1945 to 1949 and the other was John Joseph Cahill (1891-1959) who was premier of New South Wales from 1952 to 1959.

In 1984 two Danish economists, Martin Paldam and Peder J. Pedersen, examined data for eighteen OECD countries between 1919 and 1979 and found a positive link between nominal wage rises and the number of disputes. They found that changes in real wages were only negatively related to changes in disputes in the United States and that in the other countries the relationship was either positive or insignificant They also suggested that there was a cultural-linguistic divide in the dispute record of the eighteen OECD countries between 1919 and 1979. They distinguished high-conflict countries as belonging to the Anglo-Saxon group (United Kingdom, Ireland, United States, Canada, Australia, and New Zealand) or the Latin group (France and Italy), low conflict countries as belonging to the German-Nordic group (Austria, Netherlands, Norway, Germany, Denmark, Sweden , and Switzerland) and a fourth group which did not fit easily into any category (Belgium, Japan, and Finland). They could not discern any long-term pattern in the dispute levels of the Anglo-Saxon or Latin groups, but in the German-Nordic group, there was a strong falling trend of disputes since the peak level of the early 1920s.

Labor disputes are unevenly distributed in the economy. Certain industries, particularly coal mining (q.v.), engineering, and transportation have frequently accounted for a major part of the disputes in many countries. Since 1980 the number of disputes has fallen to very low levels in most countries, a trend which has been attributed to the decline in the strength of organized labor and profound economic shifts.

The study of labor disputes has been approached from two main directions: the socio-historical approach which examined their statistical characteristics within and between countries over time and that of the "rational expectations" approach which treats labor disputes as one possible result of rational decision making by bargainers with incomplete information. This latter approach has been popular among labor economists since about 1970, although it was first suggested by the economist John R. Hicks in 1932. Although the two approaches proceed from widely different attitudes and assumptions, it is clear that there is no agreed single model which can be applied to labor disputes for all periods.

For all the drama which can accompany large labor disputes, they account for only a tiny proportion of the work days lost in most Western economies compared with other sources of loss such as illness and industrial accidents. The lost production caused by disputes is usually quickly made up. Nevertheless, governments remain sensitive to the level of disputes as an indicator of political stability and the countries' reliability as international traders. Consequently, the legal right to strike is circumscribed in various ways even in many Western countries. Legal notice of a strike is required in Belgium, Netherlands, Greece, Spain, Portugal, the United Kingdom (since 1984), and New Zealand (since 1991). In Japan most of the public sector is denied the right to strike as are federal government employees (since 1912) and most state employees in the United States with the exception of those in Hawaii and Pennsylvania. Finally, the international statistics on disputes for any period must be treated with caution as many countries understate their true level of disputes and use incomparable definitions. (*See also* Conciliation and Arbitration, General Strike, General Strikes, Luddism, Machine Breaking, Order 1305, Police Strikes)

LABOR-MANAGEMENT REPORTING AND DISCLOSURE ACT
(*See* Landrum-Griffin Act)

LABOR PARTIES (*See* Social Democratic/Socialist/Labor Parties)

LABOR STATISTICS Most of the earliest labor statistics were collected through the census of population and housing: the United Kingdom census included a question on occupation from 1811 and the United States census included a question on industry from 1820. From the 1860s there was growing demand for better statistical information about labor. Several American states, notably Massachusetts (1869), Pennsylvania (1870), and Ohio (1877), established statistical bureaus which collected data on wages, prices, and labor disputes (q.v.).

The demand for better statistics did not just come from governments and employers; sections of organized labor were well aware of the importance of accurate statistics. Aim III of the Knights of Labor (q.v.) was the establishment of a Bureau of Labor Statistics "so that we may arrive at correct knowledge of the educational, moral and financial condition of the laboring masses." The U.S. Bureau of Labor was created in 1884 and made an independent organization in 1888. From about 1890 many countries began to publish official statistics on labor topics, such as disputes, union membership, wages, prices, employment, and unemployment. In 1893 the British government began to issue a national statistical publication with commentary, the *Labour Gazette*, which continues to the present as the *Employment Gazette*. In Australia, the federal government began publishing a compendium of national labor statistics, the *Labour Report*, in 1912 and continued it until 1972. The U.S. Bureau of

Labor Statistics began to publish the *Monthly Labor Review* in 1915, a publication which continues to the present.

In 1940 the United States began to collect labor force statistics from a regular household survey, an example followed by Canada (1954), and Australia (1960) and many other countries since. One important by-product of these surveys has been their ability to match labor union membership with a range of socioeconomic and demographic characteristics. Such information began to be available for the United States in 1973 (although the present survey began in 1983), in 1976 for Australia (with subsequent surveys in 1982, 1986, 1988, 1990,and 1992 to 1995), in 1984 for Canada, in 1987 for Sweden, and in 1989 for the United Kingdom.

The main agency for the collection of international labor statistics is the International Labour Organisation (ILO) (q.v.) which has been publishing its *Year Book of Labour Statistics* since 1927. ILO Convention 160 (Labor Statistics, 1985) called on member countries to regularly compile and publish statistics on employment, unemployment, earnings, working hours, consumer prices, household expenditure, occupational injury and diseases and labor disputes. This convention was a revision of Convention 63 (Statistics of Wages and Hours of Work, 1938). (*See also* Timothy Augustine Coghlan)

LABOUR REPRESENTATION LEAGUE This league was formed by organized labor in Britain in 1869 to promote the election of working-class candidates to parliament. Despite some electoral successes in 1874, political concessions to labor and lack of resources doomed the league. It was defunct by 1889 but its activities were continued by the Parliamentary Committee of the Trades Union Congress (q.v.). (*See also* British Labour Party)

LANDRUM-GRIFFIN ACT This act, known officially as the Labor-Management Reporting and Disclosure Act, was a major piece of American federal labor law which was passed in September 1959. It was aimed at reducing corruption within unions as exemplified by the Teamsters (q.v.). It set down minimum standards to ensure democratic elections, but it also extended the ban of the Taft-Hartley Act (q.v.) on secondary boycotts and allowed the states to assume jurisdiction in relatively minor labor disputes (q.v.). (*See also* Teamsters)

LATVIA (*See* Baltic States)

LAW (*See* Combination Laws, *Commonwealth v. Hunt*, Employment Acts, Landrum-Griffin Act, National Industrial Recovery Act, Osbourne Judgement, Right-to-Work Laws, *Rookes v. Barnard*, Taff Vale Case, Taft-Hartley Act, Wagner Act, Yellow Dog Contracts)

LEGIEN, CARL (1861-1920) Carl Legien was one of the leading labor leaders in Germany before 1914. Born in Marienburg, he was raised in an orphanage after the death of his parents. Apprenticed as a turner in 1875 he settled in Hamburg after military service. He joined the turner's union in 1886 and became its chairman. In 1890 he was elected chairman of the *Generalkommission der Gewerkschaften*, the National Federation of Trade Unions, a position he held until his death. He used his position to build a strong national union organization and to maintain the independence of the union movement from the control of the Social Democratic Party. He was a strong opponent of the general strike as advocated by Syndicalism (q.v.). He was president and secretary of the International Federation of Trade Unions (q.v.) from 1901 to 1919. Ironically for someone who opposed general strikes, it was Legien who issued the call for the general strike in Berlin which defeated the proto-fascist Kapp Putsch in 1920. (*See also* International Federation of Trade Unions)

LEWIS, JOHN LLEWELLYN (1880-1969) John L. Lewis was the most important miners' leader in the United States (q.v.) in the twentieth century. He was born in Lucas, Iowa, and began working as a coal miner at sixteen. In 1909 he gained his first office with the United Mine Workers of America (UMWA) (q.v.) progressing to vice president in 1917 and president in 1920, a position he held until 1960. Lewis was a controversial figure who devoted much of his energies in the 1920s to fighting and expelling rivals from within the union, the membership of which fell from 500,000 to 75,000 between 1920 and 1933. Lewis realized the need for legal support in rebuilding the union and was a prime mover behind Section 7(a) of the National Industrial Recovery Act (q.v.) of 1933 which gave employees the right to collectively organize and bargain without employer interference. A supporter of industrial unionism, Lewis saw the potential for organizing the semiskilled and led the campaign to form the Congress of Industrial Organizations (q.v.). He served as its president from 1938 to 1940, resigning in opposition to the policies of President Franklin D. Roosevelt. In 1946 and 1948 Lewis led a series of strikes which resulted in the coal mine owners paying a bounty on each ton of coal mined which was used to finance health, welfare, and retirement benefits for miners. Lewis's last major achievement was the first federal Mine Safety Act (1952). (*See also* Coal Mining, Congress of Industrial Organizations, United Mine Workers of America)

LITHUANIA (*See* Baltic States)

LUDDISM   Luddism was the name given to a systematic if sporadic campaign organized by employees in the English textile industry between 1812 and 1818 which aimed to destroy new machinery. It was characterized by secret organizations, oaths of loyalty, masked men, midnight raids, violence and sometimes deaths. It had three centers each with its own particular grievances. In the Midlands, Luddism was based on Nottingham with the main grievances being the alleged poor quality of the products of the new equipment and their threat to the reputation of the industry and hence loss of trade and employment; the campaign was also intended to defend customary ways of working. Luddism in Yorkshire was largely concerned with job losses from the new machinery. In Lancashire and Cheshire, rising prices were also a factor in the local Luddite movement. Luddism drew its name from an imaginary leader, Ned Ludd, who was also referred to as Captain Ludd and General Ludd. Luddism was defeated by the deployment of strong military forces and a law which made frame breaking an offense punishable by death. (*See also* Machine Breaking)

LUXEMBOURG   Luxembourg has been a sovereign nation since 1867 when organized labor also began to develop. Like its neighbor, Belgium, its organized labor has been divided by religion. The *Confédération Générale du Travail*, the main labor federation, was formed in 1919. A Catholic labor federation was formed in 1920. Union membership was 18,000 in 1930. Unions were suppressed by the Nazis and, although an attempt was made to build a unified labor movement after 1944, it had failed by 1948 through the defection of communists and Catholics. Between 1970 and 1990 the number of union members in Luxembourg rose from 52,000 to 75,000 divided among labor federations which cater for white- and blue-collar unions, Catholic unions, private sector white-collar unions, and craft unions. (*See also* Belgium)

M

MACHINE BREAKING Machine breaking, that is, the wrecking of new machinery by employees, was a form of industrial protest dating from at least the seventeenth century and a feature of industrial relations before the recognition of labor unions. It was most common in the textile industry. In 1675, 10,000 silk workers in Genoa, Italy, rose up over the introduction of ribbon looms from France which enabled a single worker to weave 10 to 12 ribbons at a time; the workers burnt the new looms. In England there was occasional machine breaking by Spitalfields weavers from the seventeenth century. Although Luddism (q.v.) was the best known example of these activities in the early nineteenth century, it was by no means unique. Both France and Germany experienced episodes of machine breaking, especially in the 1830s and 1840s. In 1841 Paris textile employees wrecked sewing machines in large workshops. (*See also* Labor Disputes, Luddism)

MALAYSIA The first labor unions in the Malayan Peninsula were created by the Chinese in the Singapore (q.v.) area, starting with a union of engineering mechanics in 1875. Other unions were formed later by Indian employees. In 1939 there were 43 unions. By 1947 there were about 200,000 members of labor unions of which about half belonged to unions controlled by communists. The Malaysian Trades Union Congress (originally called the Malayan Trade Union Council) was formed in 1950. The development of Malaysian labor unions was retarded by the economic dominance of agriculture until the late 1980s and by the period of the Emergency (1948-1960), which forced governments to devote their efforts to fighting the communist insurgency. Since becoming independent from Britain in 1957, Malaysian governments have tolerated rather than encouraged labor unions. In 1967 the Industrial Relations Act gave the government the power to use compulsory arbitration to settle disputes if conciliation (q.v.) failed. From 1981, to encourage foreign investment, labor unions were excluded from special free-trade zones which mainly produced electronic goods. Under pressure from the American Federation of Labor-Congress of Industrial Organizations (q.v.), this policy was relaxed in September 1988 to permit in-house unions in these zones. In 1992 there were 350,000 union members in Malaysia which represented about seven percent of employees. (*See also* Singapore)

MANN, TOM (1856-1941)   Tom Mann was one of the leaders of
organized labor in England and a radical political activist who
operated internationally. Born near Coventry, his mother died when
he was two years old and he received only three years of formal
schooling. His working life began at the age of nine; he was employed
as a pit worker at the age of ten and was apprenticed as a toolmaker in
1872. Mann benefitted directly from the successful campaign by the
Tyneside Nine Hours League and used the shorter work day for further
study. He also concluded that labor unions alone could not achieve
such victories. In 1881 he joined the Amalgamated Society of
Engineers (q.v.) and read *Progress and Poverty* by Henry George
(q.v.) but rejected its central idea of the single tax. Mann was a friend
of Engels and Marx's daughter Eleanor, friendships which
strengthened Mann's political radicalism as was shown by his role in
the eight-hours campaign in the 1880s. In 1889 he became the first
president of the London Dockers' Union, a post he held until 1893. He
was one of the main founders of the International Federation of Ship,
Dock, and River Workers in 1896 which became the International
Transport Workers' Federation and the Workers' Union (qq.v.) in
1898. Mann visted the United States twice, in 1886 and 1913.
Between 1901 and 1910 he lived in New Zealand and then Australia
(qq.v.) where he was active in organized labor and in the Socialist
Party of Victoria. In 1919 he became general secretary of the
Amalgamated Society of Engineers and held the position until 1921
when it became the Amalgamated Engineering Union (q.v.). Mann
was a founding member of the British Communist Party in 1920. (*See
also* Waterfront, Workers' Union)

MANNHEIM AGREEMENT   The Mannheim Agreement was the name
given to a declaration passed at the conference of the Social
Democratic Party of Germany (*Sozialdemokratische Partei
Deutschlands*) in Mannheim in September 1906 which recognized the
party and the labor unions as equal partners in the leadership of the
working-class movement. Carl Legien (q.v.) was prominent in the
debate. The agreement was rescinded by Resolution A.7 passed by the
German Free Trade Union Congress at its conference in Nuremberg
between June 30, and July 5, 1919 which declared that the congress
was to be politically neutral following the split in the Social
Democratic Party of Germany. (*See also* Germany)

MARITIME STRIKE The Martime Strike was a milestone in the history of organized labor in Australia and New Zealand (qq.v.). Despite its name, it was actually a series of large, interconnected labor disputes (q.v.) which occurrred between August and November 1890. The Maritime Strike was essentially a power struggle between a union movement grown confident by five years of unprecedented membership growth and well-organized employers determined to resist the unions' challenge to their authority. The unions' claim for the "closed shop" (that is, for workplaces where the employees were union members) was countered by the employers' principle of "freedom of contract" (that is, their freedom to employ whom they wanted). The Maritime Strike had two immediate sources: a dispute in the wool shearing industry which began in late 1889 and a dispute between the Mercantile Marine Officers' Association of Australia and New Zealand (formed in 1889 with 187 members) and the shipowners who refused to negotiate with the association after it decided to affiliate with the Melbourne Trades Hall Council. After the dismissal of a member of the association, it declared a strike which attracted general support from organized labor on the waterfront, in mining and sheep shearing.

The strike soon enveloped New South Wales, Victoria, South Australia, Queensland, and New Zealand. British organized labor subscribed 4,000 pounds (about US$ 9,600) to support the strike, but the employers were too strong and had the backing of the governments which used the police and military forces to defeat the strikers. By September 1890 about 50,000 men were estimated to have gone on strike in Australia and about 10,000 in New Zealand. The defeat of the Maritime Strike and other large strikes in wool shearing in 1891 and 1894, combined with the onset of a severe economic depression which was aggravated by drought, greatly reduced union membership and power; between 1890 and 1901 the number of union members in Australia fell from 150,000 to 97,000. Within organized labor these defeats encouraged the unions to give greater prominence to politics as a means of achieving their goals. (*See also* Australian Labor Party, New Zealand)

MARXIST-LENINISM Marx and Engels recognized that the emergence of organized labor was a natural outcome of the capitalism which forced employees to unite against wage cuts and labor-saving technology. They saw unions primarily as defensive bodies which although they might defend wage levels were unable on their own to raise them beyond their value as determined by the capitalist trade cycle. To advance their position against the concentration of capital and downturns in the trade cycle, Marx and Engels believed that the workers would have to unite in class action; they saw the National Association of United Trades for the Protection of Labour (q.v.) as an example of this trend. After the 1850s they became disillusioned with organized labor in Britain, particularly with the rise of unions of skilled workers which they called a "labor aristocracy" (q.v.) and their tendency to identify with middle-class ideas and values. Lenin saw labor unions as representing a retarded form of class consciousness and incapable of carrying out revolution on their own. In his view, they could act as training schools for communists but, for the revolution to succeeed, well-trained and motivated individuals organized as a party operating outside the ranks of organized labor were required. (*See also* Communism)

MATERNAL PROTECTION The provision of legal safeguards for employed mothers was recognized by the International Labour Organisation by Convention No. 3 (Maternal Protection) in 1919 which was revised in 1952 as Convention No. 103. Paid leave for maternity (that is, during and after pregnancy), however, generally only became a feature of women's employment in the 1980s. (*See also* Women)

MATIGNON AGREEMENT The Matignon Agreement was a landmark agreement in French labor history reached between the Socialist government of Léon Blum, the *Confédération Générale du Travail* (CGT) and employers on June 7, 1936. The agreement provided for the unions' right to organize, an end to anti-union practices, collective bargaining, pay increases of seven to twelve percent ,and the election of shop stewards. One problem with the agreement was that by extending bargaining rights to all representative unions rather than to a single bargaining body, it tended to inhibit the development of strong collective bargaining units representing employees. (*See also* France)

MAY DAY (*See* Second International Workingmen's Association)

MEANY, GEORGE (1894-1980) Meany was president of the American Federation of Labor (AFL) from 1952 to 1955 and of the American

Federation of Labor-Congress of Industrial Organizations (qq.v.) from 1955 until 1979. Born in New York City, Meany completed an apprenticeship as a plumber in 1915 and based his union career on the United Association of Plumbers and Steam Fitters of the United States and Canada. In 1939 he was elected secretary-treasurer of the AFL, but it was not until the late 1940s that he could exercise any real power. He was the first director of the AFL's League for Political Education (1948) and served on the executive board of the International Confederation of Free Trade Unions (q.v.) in 1951. A skilled negotiator, he played a major role in negotiating the merger of the AFL with the Congress of Industrial Organizations (CIO) to form the AFL-CIO in 1955. A Catholic, Meany waged a determined campaign against communism (q.v.) and labor rivals such as Walter Reuther (q.v.); he was also opposed to racial or religious discrimination in organized labor. A right-wing Democrat, Meany refused to give the AFL-CIO's endorsement to the left-wing George S. McGovern, the Democratic nominee for president in 1972. (*See also* American Federation of Labor, American Federation of Labor-Congress of Industrial Organizations, Joseph Lane Kirkland, Walter Philip Reuther)

MEXICO As in Western Europe, the first organizations among workers in Mexico were friendly societies (q.v.) which were formed in the main urban areas between 1835 and 1864. Although unions emerged after 1876, it was not until after 1900 that organized labor made its presence felt though strikes by miners (1905) and textile workers (1906) which were violently suppressed. The Constitution of 1917 recognized labor unions and was a tangible victory from the revolution of 1910. The *Confederación Regional Obrera Mexicana* (Confederation of Mexican Wage Earners or CROM) was established in May 1918 with seventy-five organizations which claimed a million members. Militant at first, the CROM became more allied with the government, a trend which promoted the creation by anarchists of a radical alternative labor federation, the *Confederación General de Trabajo* (General Confederation of Labor or CGT) in 1921. By 1923 union membership in Mexico had fallen to about 800,000 but had risen to 2.1 million by 1927.

The Depression reduced membership to 500,000 by 1932, but by 1934 organized labor in Mexico claimed 2.6 million members. In 1936 a third labor federation, the *Confederación de Trabajadores de Mexico* (Confederation of Mexican Workers or CTM) was formed.

Because the CTM had the affiliation of metal workers, railroad employees and peasants, it became the dominant federation and developed close links with the ruling political party. The other labor federations formed since 1936 have been to the left of the CTM. Mexico has been an active participant in pan-American labor bodies such as the Pan-American Federation of Labor (q.v.) and the *Organización Regional Interamericana de Trabajadores* (q.v.). In 1966 the *Congreso del Trabajo* (Congress of Labor) was set up to provide a single voice for organized labor. In 1994 the level of union membership in Mexico was unclear because of inflated claims made for the CTM (which vary from 2 to 5 million) but it is estimated that union membership covers between 25 and 30 percent of Mexican employees.

MINERS' ASSOCIATION OF GREAT BRITAIN AND IRELAND (MAGB)   The MAGB was the first national organization of British miners. Established in November 1842, it was largely based on the coal mining unions of Durham, Northumberland, and Lancashire counties which had been set up in the 1830s. During 1843 its membership grew from 5,000 to 50,000. Membership was open to any kind of miner. Two of its leaders, William Dixon and William P. Roberts, made history in 1847 by being the first Britsh union members to stand for election to parliament. Despite its rapid rise, the MAGB was short-lived because of strong hostility from coal mine owners as shown in the defeat of Durham and Northumberland miners in the disastrous strike of 1844, the economic crisis of 1847, and the imprisonment of its general secretary, William Grocott, a Chartist activist. (*See also* Miners' National Union)

MINERS' INTERNATIONAL FEDERATION (MIF)   The MIF was set up in Belgium in 1890 by representatives of miners' unions from Austria, Belgium, France, Germany, and Britain. Between 1913 and 1931 its claimed membership rose from 1.2 to nearly 1.5 million. In the late 1950s the MIF began to prepare standards for miners; it released a miner's charter in 1957 and a charter for young miners in 1958. In 1976 the MIF had 887,500 members of whom 628,700 were in Europe, 203,800 in Asia, and 8,800 in the United States. In 1994 the MIF had fifty-eight affiliated unions which represented 4.2 million members. (*See also* International Trade Secretariats)

MINERS' NATIONAL UNION (MNU) The MNU was formed in 1863 with the official title of the National Association of Coal, Lime, and Ironstone Miners' of Great Britain. It saw its main role as lobbying parliament for better laws to regulate and improve working conditions in mines, and to promote conciliation and arbitration (q.v.) in the settlement of labor disputes (q.v.). It drew its main support from the relatively better-paid coal mining districts of Durham, Northumberland, and Yorkshire. Because the MNU disapproved of strikes, it proved to be a disappointment to many miners, and they expressed their opposition by forming the Amalgamated Association of Miners (q.v.) in 1869. Although the MNU achieved the passing of the Coal Mines Regulation Act in 1872 and claimed 123,400 members by 1873, its national membership and influence disintegrated thereafter. It was formally disbanded in 1898. (*See also* Amalgamated Association of Miners)

MINEWORKERS' FEDERATION OF GREAT BRITAIN (MWF) From the early 1890s to the late 1930s, the Mineworkers' Federation (its official title from 1932) was the largest labor union in Britain. The federation grew out of discussions among delegates representing regional groups of miners who met in 1888 and 1889 to coordinate wage claims on the mine owners. The Yorkshire Miners' Association (formed in 1858) took the initiative to form the federation in 1889. In 1890 the MWF showed its strength by leading a campaign which resulted in a five percent wage rise. In 1892 the federation claimed 150,000 members among its affiliates compared to only 36,000 in 1889. Thereafter, the federation's membership grew rapidly as large affiliates joined: the Scottish Miners' Federation joined in 1894, the South Wales Miners' federation in 1898, and, finally, the Durham Miners' Federation in 1908. Originally formed in 1869, the Durham Miners' Federation had 121,800 members when it affiliated with the MWF. Between 1900 and 1910 the membership of the federation rose from 363,000 to 597,000, but it continued to be an umbrella organization covering a multitude of labor unions often with a regional rather than a national outlook. In 1944, when the federation had 603,000 members, it was made up of no less than twenty-two largely autonomous districts. Wartime centralization of coal mining organization and bargaining hastened the conversion of the federation into the National Union of Mineworkers in January 1945. (*See also* Coal Mining, United Mine Workers of America)

MINIMUM AGE   The legal specifying of a minimum age of employment in an industry has been one way of controlling the exploitation of children and teenagers in the labor force. The first effective factory legislation in England in 1833 outlawed the employment of children under nine years of age. In 1919 the International Labour Organisation (q.v.) approved Convention No. 5 which set fourteen as the minimum age for entry into industrial employment. This convention was revised in 1937 to raise the minimum age to fifteen for most forms of employment. (*See also* Child Labor)

MINIMUM WAGE The term minimum wage refers to the principle that an employee in a country or an industry should be paid a minimum amount. The idea of a minimum (or living) wage was an important aspiration in the history of organized labor, naturally so in the nineteenth century when wages were often barely adequate to live on, particularly in certain industries such as clothing manufacturing. In 1773 the Spitalfields Act gave English silk weavers a minimum wage which lasted as a principle until about 1820, but other textile employees were not successful. In 1779 English stocking hand-loom workers rioted after a proposed minimum wage law for the industry was rejected by parliament. In 1811 petitions from weavers in England and Scotland with a total of 77,000 signatures for a minimum wage were also rejected by parliament.

In 1796 the English parliament debated a minimum wage law which had been proposed by Samuel Whitebread, but the measure failed to attract support. Pressure for minimum wages caused governments to act in various ways to provide a minimum wage. Some countries (the United States in 1938 and France in 1950) have provided a minimum wage through national legislation. Others such as Australia and New Zealand have used conciliation and arbitration (qq.v.) to set minimum wages in particular industries. There is no legal minimum wage in the United Kingdom although the British Labour Party (qq.v.) adopted it in principle in the early 1990s. The effects of minimum wage laws have been criticized by some economists since the 1970s as hurting rather than helping low-skilled employees. They have argued that such laws raise the cost of their labor above the market rate and thereby increase their unemployment. The economic effect of a minimum wage depends upon the level at which it is set and whether employers have a monopoly on the labor they wish to hire. Too high a minimum wage rate could add to unemployment but, where employers enjoy monopoly conditions, a minimum wage can help low-skilled workers because the additional labor cost could be paid out of profits. (*See also* Wages)

MITBESTIMMUNG *Mitbestimmung* is a German term meaning the right to have a voice in the economic decision making process of firms; it is usually translated as co-determination. *Mitbestimmung* was expressed though direct labor representation at the various levels of decision-making within a firm. The idea of co-determination came from the desire of organized labor to replace the authoritarian order of pre-1918 Germany with one which embodied both political and economic democracy. This goal was given practical expression in the Works' Councils Law of February 1920, which provided for elected employee-employer councils in enterprises employing more than twenty employees and for the election of a works' steward in enterprises with less than twenty employees; the idea for these councils grew out of the government's attempts during World War I to enlist the support of organized labor for the war effort in return for recognition. The principles of co-determination remained popular in German organized labor throughout the 1920s. In 1928 the *Allgemeiner Deutscher Gewerkschaftsbund* (German General Trade Union Federation) formally adopted *Wirtschaftsdemokratie* (or economic democracy), a philosophy designed to counter Leninism. In contrast, what little support there was for co-determination among large employers in the early 1920s rapidly declined as the decade progressed.

With the revival of free German labor unions in 1945, co-determination was widely adopted and was first applied at the Klöckner steel works in early 1946. The principle of co-determination was encouraged in the British occupational zone (but not in the American) as a means of promoting and sustaining democracy in the economy.

An extended form of co-determination, *Montanmitbestimmung*, was applied to companies which derived more than half their income from steel, iron, or coal in 1951. Under legislation passed in 1952 and 1972 all enterprises with five or more employees were able to have works' councils. In 1976 the principle of co-determination was extended to the supervisory boards of enterprises with 2,000 or more employees. Although in theory works' councils are distinct from labor unions, in practice, those elected to the councils from the unions are usually shop stewards. Although only 39 percent of German firms had works' councils in 1992, the proportion varied according to the size of the firm with 13 percent among those with five to twenty employees, 34 percent among those with twenty-one to fifty employees, 53 percent among those with fifty-one to 159 employees, 97 percent among those with 151 to 300 employees and 88 percent among those with more than 300 employees. (*See also* Austria, Hans Böckler, November Pact, *Zentralarbeitsgemeinschaft*)

MITCHELL, JOHN (1870-1919)   Mitchell was president of the United Mine Workers of America (q.v.) from 1898 to 1908, the period when it became the largest labor union in the United States.   Born in Braidwood, Illinois, Mitchell received only about five years of public education which he supplemented by evening classes. He began his working life as a coal miner in 1882 and joined the Knights of Labor (q.v.) in 1885. Present at the formation of the United Mine Workers of America in 1890, he was first elected secretary-treasurer of District 12 in Illinois in 1895, then appointed international organizer in 1897 and finally elected president in 1898. Mitchell proved to be a shrewd and able labor leader. Under his presidency, the union's membership grew from 34,000 to 300,000 and its reserves from $12,000 to $900,000. Mitchell's reputation was greatly enhanced by the skillful settlement of the anthracite coal strike in 1902 which gained the miners a 14 percent pay increase and shorter work hours. Mitchell served as fourth vice-president of the American Federation of Labor (q.v.) in 1899-1900 and as second vice president from 1900 to 1914. He was chairman of the New York State Industrial Commission from 1915 until his death. (*See also* Coal Mining, United Mine Workers of America)

MOLLY MAGUIRES   The Molly Maguires was the name given to a secret Irish society which operated in the coal mining districts of Schuylkill County, Pennnsylvania, between about 1862 and 1876. Poor working and living conditions and oppressive management encouraged some of the Irish immigrants in the region to resort to violence to achieve their ends. Opposition to conscription during the Civil War was another source of grievance. Between 1863 and 1865 fifty-two murders were committed in Schuylkill County, some of which were associated with the management of the coal mines. The mine owners used the Pinkerton agency to collect information on the miners; one of them found there was a secret society within the Ancient Order of Hiberians, a discovery used to justify the conviction and hanging of twenty miners in 1876. The Molly Maguires were the subject of a film (*The Molly Maguires*) with Sean Connery in 1984. (*See also* Coal Mining)

MOHAWK VALLEY FORMULA (*See* Rand Formula)

MURRAY, PHILIP (1886-1952)   Murray was the first president of the United Steelworkers of America (q.v.). He was born in Blantyre, Scotland, and began work as a coal miner at the age of ten. His father was a local coal mining union official. In 1902 he emigrated with his family to the United States (q.v.) where he began working as a coal miner in western Pennsylvania. In 1904 he was elected to his first position within the United Mine Workers of America (UMWA) (q.v.) and in 1912 was elected to its executive board. Thereafter Murray sat on a number of important labor bodies including the National Bituminous Coal Production Committee (1917-18) and the Labor Industrial Advisory Board of the National Recovery Administration (1933). In 1936, as a vice president of the UMWA, he was put in charge of the campaign to unionize the steel industry by the UMWA's president, John L. Lewis (q.v.). His efforts eventually led to the formation of the United Steelworkers of America which Murray led from 1942 to his death. In 1940 he took over the presidency of the Congress of Industrial Organizations after Lewis's resignation. Lewis had Murray expelled from the UMWA for a combination of personal and political differences; Lewis was a Republican and Murray was a Democrat. After World War II Murray led major strikes in the steel industry (1946, 1949, and 1952) for better pay and conditions. Murray was also active in community affairs; for example, he was a member of the National Association for the Advancement of Colored People. (*See also* John L. Lewis, United Mine Workers of America, United Steelworkers of America)

N

NATIONAL AMALGAMATED UNION OF LABOUR (NAUL)
Called the Tyneside and National Labour Union until 1892, this British general labor union was formed in 1889 originally to recruit plater's helpers and boilermaker's assistants but soon broadened its recruiting base to include waterfront workers in northeast England. The NAUL competed with the National Labour Federation (q.v.) for members and, although it had fewer members (35,000 in 1890), it was

far stronger financially and was able to recruit the membership of the federation as it declined after 1891. By 1900 the NAUL had only 21,000 members, but it survived to be one of the three amalgamating unions which formed the General and Municipal Workers' Union (q.v.) in 1924. (*See also* General and Municipal Workers' Union, National Labour Federation)

NATIONAL AND LOCAL GOVERNMENT OFFICERS' ASSOCIATION (NALGO) NALGO was one of the largest unions in Britain from 1946 to 1993. It was founded in 1905 as a provincial federation catering for local government officers and was called the National Association of Local Government Officers (NALGO). Between 1905 and 1946 its membership grew from 5,000 to 140,000. In 1946 NALGO broadened its recruitment of members to include those in other parts of the public sector such as the National Health Service, gas, and electricity. Its title was officially changed to National and Local Government Officers' Association in 1952 to reflect these changes in membership, but the acronym NAGLO was retained. In 1964, when it became affiliated with the Trades Union Congress (q.v.), its membership had reached 338,300. Like other white-collar unions, NALGO was opposed to strikes and connections with the political and industrial aspects of organized labor for most of its life. It was not until 1970 that NALGO authorized its first strike. By 1981 NALGO's membership had reached 706,150; its membership rose to 750,000 by 1986, but by 1991 had only increased to 760,000. (See also National Union of Public Employees, UNISON, White-Collar Unionism)

NATIONAL ASSOCIATION OF UNITED TRADES FOR THE PROTECTION OF LABOUR (NAUTPL) The NAUTPL was the first attempt in Britain to form a federation of unions to protect the interests of organized labor through resistence to wage cuts and by securing laws favoring labor. It was formed in Sheffield, England, in March 1845, and although never gaining general support from organized labor, it advocated a number of significant policy proposals which later became important issues for organized labor both in Britain and in other countries. Its chairman was Thomas Slingsly Duncombe, an aristocrat and supporter of Chartism (q.v.). The NAUTPL supported the setting of wages by wage boards which were to be made up of representatives of employers and unions and the use of conciliation and arbitration (q.v.) to resolve disputes. Its lobbying was largely responsible for the Molestation of Workmen Act of 1859 which legalized peaceful picketing and the Conciliation Act of 1867 after which time the NAUTPL had ceased to exist. After 1868 the Trades Union Congress (q.v.) assumed the role of national lobbyist for labor. (*See also* Conciliation and Arbitration, Trades Union Congress)

NATIONAL CONVENTION OF COLORED LABOR (*See* Colored National Labor Union)

NATIONAL EDUCATIONAL ASSOCIATION (NEA) In 1987 the NEA became the largest labor union in the United States (q.v.). Formed in 1857 in Philadelphia, it operated as a professional association of school administrators until 1905 when it admitted teachers as members. Before 1963 it opposed unionism and collective bargaining for teachers. Since 1963 the NEA has been a participant in collective bargaining as evidenced by its victories in ballots for exclusive bargaining rights against its industrial rival, the AFL-CIO American Federation of Teachers. In 1995 the NEA claimed 2.2 million members, making it the largest white-collar union in the world. (*See also* Education, White-Collar Unionism)

NATIONAL INDUSTRIAL RECOVERY ACT The National Industrial Recovery Act of 1933 was the cornerstone of modern collective bargaining in the United States (q.v.). Under Section 7(a), employees were given the right to organize labor unions to collectively bargain with employers without harassment, provisions which had been included previously in the federal Railway Labor Act (1926). The National Industrial Recovery Act was declared unconstitutional by the Supreme Court in *Schecter Poultry Corporation v. U.S.* in 1935 and was replaced by the Wagner Act (q.v.). Nevertheless, the shift in the legal environment towards a more favorable view of labor unions indicated by these laws was the basis of a massive recruitment drive by organized labor in the mid-1930s. (*See also* American Federation of Labor, Congress of Industrial Organizations, United Steelworkers of America)

NATIONAL LABOR RELATIONS ACT (*See* Wagner Act)

NATIONAL LABOR UNION (NLU) The NLU was a body created by American organized labor in Baltimore, Maryland, in August 1866, to bring about progressive political reforms. Its agenda included the eight-hour work day, the reduction of monopolies, producer and consumer cooperatives, and racial integration of labor unions. The delegates at the inaugural congress represented about 60,000 employees. The main achievement of the NLU was the gaining of the eight-hour work day law for laborers, workmen, and mechanics working for the federal government. In 1869 it sent a delegate to the first conference of the International Workingmen's Association (q.v.) in Basle, Switzerland. In 1870 the NLU formed a political wing which created the Labor Reform Party in 1872. The emphasis on the political wing cost the NLU the support of organized labor and by 1876 it was defunct. (*See also* Working Hours)

NATIONAL LABOUR FEDERATION   The National Labour Federation was formed in Newcastle-upon-Tyne, England, in 1886 with the goal of organizing men and women of all trades. Any labor union could also join. Its founders were some members of the Amalgamated Society of Engineers (q.v.) and Edward R. Pease (1857-1955), a socialist and founder member of the Fabian Society. The federation claimed 60,000 members in 1890, mostly in semi-skilled jobs in engineering, chemicals, shipbuilding, and construction. By 1892 the federation's membership had fallen to 6,000 and it was dissolved in 1894, largely as a result of the depression of the early 1890s and defeats in strikes. (*See also* Knights of Labor, National Amalgamated Union of Labour)

NATIONAL TRADES UNION (NTU)   The NTU was the first attempt by American organized labor to form a national federation. It was created after failed political participation by organized labor between 1828 and 1832 and the creation of city councils of labor unions in New York and Philadelphia in 1833. The New York council invited representatives from the unions in other cities to a conference in 1834; thirty delegates attended representing about 21,000 union members and formed the NTU. Although the NTU was swept away by the financial panic and depression of 1837, it provided a forum for expressing support for the ten-hour work day, the legal recognition of unions, higher pay, and equal pay for women. Ely Moore (1798-1860), a journeymen printer, was the first president of the NTU (1834-35) and was elected to the U.S. Congress in 1834. (*See also* National Labor Union)

NATIONAL UNION OF PUBLIC EMPLOYEES (NUPE) The NUPE grew out of the London County Council Employees' Protection Society which was formed in 1888 and which became the basis of the Municipal Employees Association in 1894. As a result of a split in 1907, a new body was created, the National Union of Corporation Workers with a membership of 8,000. In 1928 this body changed its name to the NUPE and set about recruiting all employees employed by local governments in Britain, a policy which led to conflict with the General and Municipal Workers' Union (q.v.) and the Transport and General Workers' Union (q.v.) which managed to exclude the NUPE from affiliation with the Trades Union Congress (q.v.) until the 1970s. The membership of the NUPE grew from 10,000 in 1948 to 215,000 in 1962 as a result of recruiting the lower grades of the local government and the National Health Service. Between 1934 and 1962 the NUPE was led by its general secretary, Bryn Roberts, a strong supporter of industrial unionism. In 1982 the NUPE had 710,450 members of whom 65 percent were women; membership declined to 658,000 in 1986 and to 551,000 in 1992 of whom 70 percent were women. (*See also* UNISON)

NETHERLANDS Organized labor in the Netherlands began in 1866 when printers and diamond cutters formed unions. A non-religious labor federation was established in 1871 and a Protestant labor federation in 1877. Organized labor was divided by politics as well as religion. In 1893 a social democratic labor union center, the National Labor Secretariat, was created which claimed to represent 16,000 members. The secretariat came to be infiltrated by supporters of anarchism (q.v.) which caused its alienation from mainstream labor supporters. Union growth was slow; by the early 1900s there were only about 19,000 union members. Nevertheless, there were major labor disputes (q.v.) organized by longshoremen and railroad employees in 1903. These failures led to the formation of a new national labor federation in 1905. In 1909 a combined Catholic and Protestant labor federation was created, but the Catholics withdrew on orders from their bishop.

As in other countries, there was considerable growth in union membership between 1913 and 1920, rising from 234,000 to 684,000. This growth took place along deep religious and political divisions not just because these divisions were present in Dutch society but also because many unions were created by socialists or clergy in the absence of large-scale concentrations of manufacturing employment. In 1920, 23 percent of Dutch union members belonged to Catholic unions, 12 percent to Protestant unions, 37 percent to Socialist unions, 7 percent to syndicalist/communist unions, and 21 percent to some other category. Although these proportions changed over time, the fundamental divisions remained part of the Dutch labor movement despite the formation of a non-denominational association of labor federations in 1929. During the Nazi occupation, organized labor was banned.

In 1943 secret meetings between the leaders of the employers and the unions led to a new understanding about the conduct of industrial relations after the war. This agreement produced a permanent employer-union body, the Foundation of Labor in May 1945 which received recognition by government as the leading policymaker in socio-economic matters. By 1950 there were nearly 1.2 million union members covering 42 percent of all employees, but since that time the proportion of employees enrolled by unions has steadily declined. In 1976 a new national labor federation, the *Federatie Nederlandse Vakbeweging*, sought to merge the social democratic and Catholic divisions of organized labor; the merger was completed in 1981. The Dutch labor movement was significantly reduced by the recession of the early 1980s which cut the proportion of employees in unions from 32 percent in 1980 to 23 percent in 1989.

NEW ZEALAND New Zealand has an importance in the history of organized labor which belies its small size and location in the southwest Pacific Ocean . It was first settled by Maoris in the mid-fourteenth century and by Europeans from 1840. Exploiting shortages of skilled labor, the first unions emerged in the building trades from 1842. Sustained British immigration brought union members as well as the example of labor unions. Printers (1862) and tailors (1865) formed unions and the British international unions, the Amalgamated Society of Engineers (1864) and the Amalgamated Society of Carpenters and Joiners (1875) (qq.v.), set up New Zealand branches. The first urban trades council was formed in Auckland in 1876, an example followed by other cities and towns in the early 1880s. In 1879, following the successful election of S. P. Andrews, a plasterer, to parliament, a Working Men's Political Association was formed which was concerned with land tax, tariff protection for local industries, and the prohibition of Chinese immigration.

The most powerful influences on organized labor in New Zealand were Australia and the United Kingdom. In 1878 New Zealand followed the British example and legalized labor unions. In January 1885 the first New Zealand Trades Union Congress was held in Dunedin following the example set by Australian labor unions from 1879. As in other countries, there was a surge of union growth between 1886 and 1890. In 1886, for example, the Amalgamated Shearers' Union of Australia set up a New Zealand branch and made a special effort to recruit Maoris; in the same year, Christopher Leek founded a mass railroad union and called it after the union he had belonged to in England, the Amalgamated Society of Railway Servants. Between 1885 and mid-1890 the number of union members rose from 3,000 to 63,000.

The participation of New Zealand labor in the great Australian Maritime Strike of 1890 (q.v.) (August-November) and the economic depression which set in after it largely destroyed the unions' growth of the late 1880s. It was at this time that New Zealand embarked on a series of social experiments which attracted international attention in the early 1900s. In 1894 New Zealand became the first country in the world to introduce a compulsory conciliation and arbitration system for labor disputes (qq.v.). Amending legislation was passed in 1898 which, although it encouraged union formation and growth through official registration, denied unions the right to strike once an award of the arbitration court was in force. The New Zealand experiment attracted interest and visits from France (F. Challye in 1903), Britain (Beatrice and Sidney Webb [q.v.] in 1898, Ramsay Macdonald in 1906, and Ernest Aves in 1907), and the United States (Henry Demarest Lloyd in 1900, V. S. Clark in 1906 and Colonel H. Weinstock in 1909). The use of compulsion in conciliation and arbitration in labor disputes was adopted by Australia but remained unusual in the rest of the world. The constraints of the arbitration system led to labor disputes particularly as radical unions found they could legally strike if they were not registered organizations under the conciliation and arbitation legislation. There was a disastrous waterfront strike in 1913 which, despite Australian support, depleted the finances of the unions for four years. Radical ideas, particularly for the One Big Union (q.v.), came though the Industrial Workers of the World (q.v.) which formed a branch in New Zealand in 1912. A gold miners' strike at Waihi and Reefton in 1912 was marked by police and employer violence which led to the death of a picketer.

In July 1916 the New Zealand Labour Party was formed and claimed 10,000 members. Yet, compared to Australia, organized labor was weak; in 1920 only 26 percent of employees were union members compared to 42 percent in Australia. In 1928 a coalition government abolished compulsory arbitration to enable wage reductions. In 1935 the Labour Party won a landslide victory and enacted legislation which established a strong regulatory role for government in economic and social management. In 1936 the Industrial Conciliation and Arbitration Act was amended to make union membership compulsory for any employee subject to a registered award of industrial agreement, a change which naturally led to a substantial growth in union membership. In 1937 the New Zealand Federation of Labour was formed and joined the International Federation of Trade Unions (q.v.) in 1938. Another feature of the period was the growth of industrial unionism in engineering and printing. With the exception of the 1951 waterfront strike, developments among organized labor were not especially noteworthy again until the late 1960s when the white-collar unions formed a federation; it amalagamated with the New Zealand Federation of Labour in October 1987 to form the New Zealand Council of Trade Unions.

In the mid-1980s, in response to New Zealand's severe economic difficulties, a series of radical reforms were introduced which again made New Zealand a social laboratory, this time for economic deregulation and the free exercise of market forces. In 1984 the first move was made to abolish compulsory arbitration in interest disputes (a distinction between rights and interest disputes was first introduced into New Zealand legislation in 1973) except in "essential" industries. Yet much of the system first created in 1894 remained in place up to 1991 when the Employment Contracts Act was enacted. The act abolished the arbitration system and its awards and changed the basis of the industrial relations system to one based on the law of contract. It also ended the system of compulsory union membership which had been introduced into bargaining arrangements in 1936. Largely because of the economic problems faced by the New Zealand economy, but also because of the removal of the protection of compulsory membership, organized labor has fared poorly since 1991. In 1985 there were 683,000 union members in New Zealand covering 44 percent of employees but by December 1994 there were only 375,900 covering 23 percent of full-time employees. (*See also* Australia, Conciliation and Arbitration)

NIGHT WORK   Night work is an integral feature of industrial economies particularly in certain industries, such as transportation, storage and communication, and in some parts of manufacturing, such as baking. The problem of night work was recognized in an English law of 1802 designed to protect the health and morals of pauper children taken on as apprentices; it forebade any apprentice to work between 9 p.m. and 6 a.m. from June 1, 1803. Night work has long been held to be harmful to young employees and women, hence the efforts made by the International Labour Organisation (q.v.) to limit night work to adult males by Conventions No. 4 and No. 6 in 1919. These conventions were revised in 1948 to remove exceptions in the earlier conventions. (*See also* Working Hours)

NIHON RODOKUMIAI SORENGOKAI (*See Rengo*)

NORRIS-LAGUARDIA ACT   The Anti-Injunction (Norris-LaGuardia) Act was a fundamental piece of American federal labor law which was passed in 1932 and designed to give organized labor full freedom of association. It outlawed yellow dog contracts (q.v.) and prohibited federal courts from issuing injunctions (court orders restraining union activity on the grounds of the prevention of injury to property or other rights) during labor disputes (q.v.) except under particular circumstances. The effect of the Norris-LaGuardia Act was weakened by a series of Supreme Court decisions in the 1970s concerning the issuing of injunctions during disputes where there were contracts or arbitration machinery. (*See also* National Industrial Recovery Act, Yellow Dog Contracts)

NORWAY   Organized labor in Norway began to emerge from the 1860s. As in other countries, mutual aid or friendly societies (q.v.) preceded the formation of unions. The first union was founded by printers in Oslo in 1872. Labor federations were formed in the cities from 1882. In 1887 a political Labor Party was formed. Two pivotal events in Norwegian labor were the establishment of the *Landsorganisasjonen i Norge* (LO), the Labor Union Federation of Norway in 1899 and a parallel national organization by employers in 1900. In 1902 the LO and the employers' organization signed their first agreement. A lock-out in 1911 gave rise to a law on labor disputes (q.v.) passed in 1915 and revised in 1927 which introduced the concepts of rights and interests in disputes in an attempt to control strikes. In 1919 another law brought in the eight-hour work day. There was a failed general strike in 1921 and other major labor disputes in 1924 and 1931. In 1935 the Labor Party, which had become Norway's largest political party in 1927, won government. In the more cooperative political climate which followed, the first Basic Agreement (1935) was concluded between the LO and the employers' organization thereby founding a tradition of collective bargaining characterized by a mixture of national and industry bargaining. The proportion of employees who were union members in Norway declined from a peak of 63 percent in 1960 to 55 percent in 1994. (*See also* Denmark, Sweden)

NOVEMBER PACT (STINNES-LEGIEN AGREEMENT) The November Pact (also known as the Stinnes-Legien Agreement) was signed between the largest employer associations and the Free (or Social Democratic labor unions), the Hirsch-Duncker Trade Associations (q.v.) and the Christian (Catholic) unions in November 1918. Designed to stabilize the revolutionary political climate that prevailed in Germany following its defeat in World War I, the agreement recognized the legitimacy of unions to bargain for employees, granted the eight-hour work day and provided for workers' committees in enterprises employing more than fifty employees to ensure that the conditions of employment of collective agreements were carried out. The November Pact led to the formation of the *Zentralarbeitsgemeinschaft* or Central Labor Association. (*See also* Carl Legien, *Mitbestimmung, Zentralarbeitsgemeinschaft*)

O

OCCUPATIONAL HEALTH AND SAFETY The term occupational health and safety covers all aspects of health at work from the hazards which can cause injury or death to ways of improving the working environment. Knowledge about the risks of particular occupations and from handling certain materials dates from antiquity; the Roman architectural writer Vitruvius (c. 25 B.C.) was aware that lead smelting and lead pipes were harmful to producers and consumers. Over the past two centuries, occupational health and safety has grown as an area of concern for organized labor, particularly in occupations with a high risk of injury or death, such as coal mining (q.v.). The International Labour Organisation (q.v.) published its first encyclopedia on occupational health and safety in 1930. Since the 1930s there has been a growth in joint management-union committees with responsibilities for occupational health and safety. (*See also* International Labour Organisation)

ONE BIG UNION (OBU) The idea of uniting all employees into one union dated from 1834 when Robert Owen (q.v.) organized the Grand United Consolidated Trades Union. In the United States, the International Labor Union (q.v.) made the first determined effort to recruit unskilled as well as skilled in the late 1870s, an idea followed by the Knights of Labor (q.v.) in the 1880s. In Britain, the idea of an OBU was expressed by unions, such as the Workers' Union, in 1898 and through federations of existing unions, such as the General Federation of Trade Unions (qq.v.) in 1899, organizations both created following the defeat of the Amalgamated Engineers (q.v.) in the lock-out of 1897. The idea of the OBU was revived by the Industrial Workers of the World (q.v.) and was an important topic of debate internationally up to the early 1920s. It has found practical expression in union amalgamations (q.v.). (*See also* Amalgamation, Grand United Consolidated Trades Union, Industrial Workers of the World)

ORDER 1305 British Order in Council 1305 was a wartime regulatory measure issued in June 1940. It set up a National Arbitration Tribunal to enforce compulsory abitration as a final resort in labor disputes (qq.v.). Strikes and lock-outs were illegal. To be effective, Order 1305 depended upon the cooperation of labor unions. Despite it, labor disputes continued. Order 1305 was withdrawn in August 1951, but the tribunal survived until 1958. (*See also* Conciliation and Arbitration)

***ORGANIZACIÓN REGIONAL INTERAMERICANA DE TRABAJADORES* (ORIT)** The ORIT, or Inter-American Regional Organization of Workers, was formed out of the *Confederación Interamericana de Trabajadores* (q.v.) or Inter-American Confederation of Workers in Mexico City in January 1951 by the representatives of twenty-one countries. The United States delegation was led by George Meany of the American Federation of Labor, and the International Confederation of Free Trade Unions (ICFTU) (qq.v.) was represented by Sir Vincent Tewson, the general secretary of the British Trades Union Congress (q.v.). Since 1953 the ORIT has been based in Mexico. It was created within the framework of Cold War politics with the aim of resisting communist influence in Latin

America. Despite its promotion of strong, democratic labor unions, the ORIT came under suspicion of being too close to the American Department of State. The ORIT has faced competition from rival inter-American labor federations, the Marxist *Confederación de Trabajadores de America Latina* (CTAL) (q.v.), a Catholic labor federation formed in 1954, and the radical *Congreso Permanente de Unidad Sindical de los Trabajadores de America Latina* formed in 1964. Nevertheless, the ORIT is the primary body for representing the Americas in the ICFTU. (*See also Confederación de Trabajadores de America Latina, Confederación Interamericana de Trabajadores*, International Confederation of Free Trade Unions)

ORGANIZATION OF AFRICAN TRADE UNION UNITY (OATUU)
The OATUU was formed in 1973 from the merger of the All-African Trade Union Federation (AATUF), the African Trade Union Confederation (ATUC), and the Pan-African Workers' Congress. TheAATUF was formed in Casablanca in May 1961. It was the first international trade union federation designed to reprepresent African countries only and was formed to exclude influence of both the International Confederation of Free Trade Unions and the World Confederation of Labor (qq.v.) which were regarded as too conservative. Those national organizations that did not accept this view formed the ATUC in January 1962 as a rival organization. The merger of the AATUF and the ATUC to form the OATUU was made at the behest of the Organization of African Unity. The affiliation of African labor organizations with international labor bodies created discord within the OATUU with both the ICFTU and the WCL claiming affiliates among bodies affiliated with the OATUU. In 1988 the OATUU and the WCL signed a formal statement of cooperation. In 1992 the OATUU claimed to represent seventy countries with a combined membership of 30 million.

OSBOURNE JUDGEMENT The Osbourne Judgement was a landmark decision by the British House of Lords in December 1909 which declared that it was illegal for labor unions to contribute funds to the British Labour Party (q.v.). The action had been brought by W. V. Osbourne, a branch secretary of the Amalgamated Society of Railway Servants, who, as a member of the Liberal Party, objected to the society's funds being used to support the Labour Party. The Lord's decision was based on the omission of any mention of political parties in the functions of labor unions as set out in the original legislation of 1871 and the amending legislation of 1876. Organized labor was only able to get redress from the Osbourne Judgement after the Liberal Party, led by Lloyd George, was elected to government in 1911. The government brought in payment of members of parliament from public money in 1911, a measure which relieved the immediate financial pressures on the members of the parliamentary Labour Party. In 1913 the government passed the Trade Union Act which permitted unions to contribute to a political party provided they maintained a separate political fund from which members could opt out. In addition, a ballot of members in favor was needed first before the political fund could be set up. (*See also* British Labour Party)

OWEN, ROBERT (1771-1858)   Owen was a British visionary and social reformist whose influence extended to the United States (q.v.). Born in Newtown, Montgomeryshire, Wales, he left school at nine and completed an apprenticeship as a draper. He then worked in London and Manchester (1787-88). He entered the cotton spinning industry in 1791 with a business partner. Bought out, he started a cotton spinning factory on his own, prospered and, in 1799, he and another, bought the New Lanark mills near Glasgow, Scotland, from David Dale.   Owen continued and greatly extended the tradition of philanthropy and educational reform which had been begun by Dale. New Lanark became an industrial showcase which attracted many visitors from Britain and other parts of Europe.   In 1813 Owen published his best-known work, *A New View of Society*, which argued that a person's character was formed by his or her environment; explained the reforms of New Lanark and advocated a national educational system, public works for the unemployed, and reform of the Poor Laws. In 1818 Owen presented a memorial to the Congress of Aix-la-Chapelle in which he urged that the governments of Europe should appoint a committee to visit his factory at New Lanark and use its lessons to place legal limits on the normal working hours (q.v.) in manufacturing in their countries; his initiative was ignored.

By the mid-1820s Owen had developed a theory of utopian socialism based on communities, social equality, and cooperation. To this end, he bought the community of New Harmony from a German religious sect, the Rappites, in Indiana in 1825, a move which cost him most of his fortune. Owen was too autocratic and paternal a figure to become a direct leader of organized labor, but his many initiatives provided a focus for its activities, particularly the formation of the

Grand National Consolidated Trades Union (q.v.) in 1834 and the cooperative congresses held between 1831 and 1835. As well, Owenism as an ideology became influential among working-class leaders. Owen was also important among the social critics of his time in his acceptance of industrialization and the possibilities it offered for general material improvement. Four of Owen's sons settled in the United States. The eldest, Robert Dale Owen, was elected to the state legislature of Indiana in 1835 and to the house of representatives in 1843. In 1958 a Robert Owen Association was formed in Japan to study and promote his ideas. (*See also* Cooperative Movement, Grand National Consolidated Trades Union)

P

PACIFIC TRADE UNION COMMUNITY (PTUC)   Originally called the Pacific Trade Union Forum, the PTUC was set up in 1980 to improve cooperation between organized labor in Australasia and the South West Pacific countries, as well as to campaign against the testing of nuclear weapons in the region. In 1992 the PTUC had fourteen country members representing about 3.2 million union members with the bulk of these members living in Australia, New Zealand, and Papua New Guinea. The Australian Council of Trade Unions provides the secretariat for the PTUC. (*See also* Australian Council of Trade Unions)

PAN-AMERICAN FEDERATION OF LABOR (PAFL)   The PAFL was the first international labor federation formed in the Americas; it operated between 1918 and 1940. It was formed at Laredo, Texas, on November 13, 1918 primarily through the efforts of Santiago Iglesias, the president of the labor federation of Puerto Rico, and John Murray of the International Typographical Union in California working in conjunction with Samuel Gompers (q.v.). The original members of the PAFL were: the United States, Mexico, Guatemala, Costa Rica, El Salvador, Colombia, and Puerto Rico. Iglesias began lobbying the American Federation of Labor (q.v.) for the creation of a pan-American labor federation since 1900, but his efforts did not begin to bear fruit until 1915. The value of good relations betweeen organized labor in the United States and Mexico was shown in 1916 when Gompers secured the release of Americans taken prisoner during an illegal military raid in Mexico to capture Pancho Villa. The PAFL worked for peace between the United States and Mexico, concerned itself with the international migration of labor in the Americas and opposed American invervention in the internal affairs of Central American and Caribbean countries. Although the Dominican Republic, Nicaragua, and Peru joined the PAFL, its effectiveness was reduced by the deaths of its key personnel: Murray in 1919, Gompers in 1924, and Iglesias in 1939. The last conference of the PAFL was held in New Orleans in 1940. (*See also Confederación Interamericana de Trabajadores*, Samuel Gompers)

PERMANENT CONGRESS OF TRADE UNION UNITY OF LATIN AMERICAN WORKERS (*See CONGRESO PERMANENTE DE UNIDAD SINDICAL DE LOS TRABAJADORES DE AMERICA LATINA*)

PHILIPPINES Although labor unions were not legalized in the Philippines until 1908, craft unions were formed after 1899; these unions set up a national federation of labor (*Union Obrera Democratica Filipina*) in 1902. Tolerated by the American administration rather than encouraged, union growth was slow; by 1930 there were estimated to be only 67,000 union members. The labor movement was also divided between communists and noncommunists; the communists were more successful in enlisting union support for independence. After 1945 Cipriano Cid, an official of the Congress of Industrial Organizations (q.v.), set up the Philippines Association of Free Labor Unions. A Catholic labor federation, the Federation of Free Workers, was formed in 1950. In 1954 the Republic Act 875 gave the unions legal protection and the right to engage in collective bargaining. Because of deep internal divisions, hostile management, legal complexities, and lack of public support, organized labor was unable to utilize fully the advantages of this law. In 1950 there were only 150,000 union members out of 2 million nonagricultural employees. In 1963 organized labor created the Workers' Party but it fared poorly in the Manila elections of that year. In 1965 a new national labor federation, the Philippines Labor Center, was formed but it did not result in a unified labor movement. From the early 1970s industrial and political protests in the Philippines became intertwined.

President Marcos declared a state of emergency in September 1972 which was used to suspend the right to strike and to arrest labor leaders. In 1974 a new labor code aimed at reorganizing the unions along industrial lines. In 1975 the Trade Union Congress of the Philippines was established; it claimed a million members and remains the largest labor federation in the country. After the overthrow of Marcos in 1986, a new constitution was adopted in February 1987 which promised full legal protection for labor, organized and unorganized. Despite an improvement in the political and legal climate for organized labor, the International Confederation of Free Trade Unions (q.v.) complained to the Philippine government about restrictions on the right to collective bargaining and discrimination against unions in 1991-92. It has also noted the continuation of violence against labor officials and striking employees. In 1988 there were only 475,000 union members in the Philippines who represented only about five percent of non-agricultural employees.

PLACE, FRANCIS (1771-1854) A radical English political figure, Place began his working life as an apprentice leather breaches maker in 1785. In 1793 he led an unsuccessful strike by members of his trade which was in decline. Self-educated, Place played an active role in the London Corresponding Society. He ran a successful tailor's shop before gradually returning to political life from 1810. In 1824 he and Joseph Hume (1777-1855), a member of parliament, were able to prevent the reenactment of the Combination Acts and thus secured their repeal thereby enabling labor unions to openly emerge. This was not what Place had expected; in his view the repeal of the acts should have removed the need for unions altogether. (*See also* Combination Acts)

POLAND Organized labor in what is now Poland emerged during the late nineteenth century in Galicia, then under Austrian control. Other unions were formed in German-controlled Poland but not in the Russian Partition where unions were illegal before 1906. Organized labor and the Polish Socialist Party (formed in 1892) were closely linked. A national labor federation was created in 1918. Despite the difficult conditions for organizing and the heavily rural nature of the Polish economy, union growth was impressive. In 1920 there were 947,000 union members who were mostly organized by industry groups. Political pressure by the Socialist Party gained exclusive rights for unions in collective bargaining in the 1920s, but the economic difficulties of the period reduced union membership from its peak of 1 million in 1921 to 539,100 by 1924. In 1926 the government forced employees of government-owned enterprises to belong to a government-sponsored union. Nevertheless, union membership reached 979,000 by 1930 and, despite the Depression, there were still claimed to be 738,900 members in 1933. This growth was to some extent a reflection of the increase in manufacturing employment which nearly doubled from 1.3 to 2.5 million between 1921 and 1931. With the imposition of communist rule in 1948, an independent labor movement ceased to exist in Poland although the trend towards an industrialized economy continued. Between 1950 and 1969 the number employed in manufacturing rose from 2.8 to 4 million.

In the 1970s the first sustained popular challenge to the communist-dominated labor movement and society in Eastern Europe occurred in Poland. From December 1970 to January 1971 there was a wave of labor disputes in the Baltic cities which resulted in forty-four deaths. Poland's continued economic problems-particularly its high inflation and large overseas debts-depressed living standards and maintained discontent. In September 1976 the workers' defense committee (KOR) was set up to help those who had lost their jobs in labor disputes. In May 1976 a committee of free labor unions was formed in the Baltic cities. The visit to Poland of the newly elected first Polish Pope, John Paul II, in June 1979 provided a focus for economic grievances as well as nationalist, political, and religious feelings. A round of government-decreed price rises in the 1980s led to rolling strikes at the Lenin shipyard in Gdansk (the former German city of Danzig) which was the catalyst for the government conceding on August 31,1980 the right not only to form independent labor unions but also the right to strike, broadcast religious programs, and more civil liberties. It was from these origins that Solidarity (*Solidarnosc*) was formed on September 22, 1980 with a former unemployed electrician, Lech Walesa, as its chairman. By December 1980 forty independent labor unions had been formed and there was a growing movement to create a rural version of Solidarity. On January 1, 1981 the communist labor federation was disbanded.

These gains proved short-lived. The pace of change raised the threat of Russian intervention, a threat that had hung over Poland since the first Partition in 1772. In October 1982 Solidarity was driven underground by new labor laws which dissolved all labor unions. The government declared martial law in December 1981. Solidarity continued to survive but its membership fell from 10 to 1.3 million by 1995. There was much debate about Solidarity's goals and a splinter organization, Solidarity 80, was formed. In November 1984 the former communist labor federation reformed itself as the *Ogolnópolskie Porozumienie Zwiazków Zawodowych* (OPZZ) or All-Poland Alliance of Labor Unions, a non-authoritarian body which recognized the independence of labor unions. The OPZZ derived its strength from its control of the assets of Solidarity which enabled it to offer members benefits such as the use of holiday homes. In 1992 the OPZZ had 3 million members and another 1.5 million pensioner members. Despite these national divisions, organized labor in Poland cooperates closely through joint councils at the enterprise level which has enabled it to conduct many labor disputes since the end of communist rule in early 1990 and to obtain the election of Walesa as the new republic's first president.

POLICE STRIKES Although often overlooked in the history of organized labor, the police have on occasions engaged in labor disputes (q.v.). The inflation of World War I and the failure of police pay to be increased accordingly was the background to strikes by the police in Britain in 1918 and 1919, incidents which led to the suppression of police unionism. Other police strikes took place in Boston (1919) and in Melbourne, Australia (1923). The Boston strike was the result of the suspension of some of the police who had joined a new union sponsored by the American Federation of Labor (q.v.). The governor of Massachusetts, Calvin Coolidge, strongly opposed the strike, thereby gaining a greatly enhanced standing with the public which assisted his election as president. Since the 1920s other police labor disputes have occurred such as the dispute in New York City in January 1971. During the 1970s, 245 illegal police strikes occurred in the United States. (*See also* Labor Disputes)

PORTUGAL Unions and left-wing political groups developed in parallel in Portugal after 1870, a response to Portugal's poverty and its political conservatism. A Socialist Party was set up in 1875 and syndicalism (q.v.) attracted much support. There was considerable labor unrest from the 1880s to the revolution of 1910 which caused the fall of the monarchy and the creation of a republic. By 1913 there were claimed to be 90,000 union members and a national labor federation, named the *Confederaçao Geral de Trabalho* (General Confederation of Labor) from 1913, was created. The next fifteen years were chaotic with general strikes being declared in 1919, 1920, and 1921. Collective bargaining was legalized in 1924. In 1926 a fascist military-backed dictator, Salazar, took power and dissolved the *Confederaçao Geral de Trabalho.* Using the examples of fascist Italy and the Nazi *Deutsche Arbeitsfront* (q.v.), Salazar established a corporate network of government-controlled unions which required compulsory membership in 1933. A general strike called by the left-wing of organized labor in 1934 only led to more repression. An independent labor movement did not begin to emerge once more until 1970 when the present *Confederaço Geral dos Trabalhadores Portugueses-Intersindical Nacional* (General Confederation of Portuguese Workers-National Labor Unions) was formed illegally. After the revolution in 1974, conditions for organized labor began to improve. The right to strike was conditionally granted in 1974 and the right was extended in 1977. A rival socialist labor federation, the *União Geral de Trabalhadores* (General Workers' Union), was formed in 1978. In 1989 about 55 percent of Portugese employees were members of unions. (*See also* Spain)

POSTAL, TELEGRAPH, AND TELEPHONE INTERNATIONAL (PTTI) The PTTI was founded in Milan, Italy, in 1920, although the first international conference of postal, telegraph, and telephone employees was held in Paris in 1911. As with other International Trade Secretariats (q.v.), the PTTI was a European body up to 1950 after which time it began to expand globally. Membership of the Geneva-based PTTI was 3.2 million in 1975 and 4.0 million in 1994. (*See also* Communication Workers' Union of America)

POWDERLY, TERRENCE VINCENT (1849-1924) Powderly was the head of the Knights of Labor (q.v.) from 1881 to 1893. He was born in Carbondale, Pennsylvania and left school at thirteen to work on the railroads. He completed an apprenticeship as a machinist, joined the Machinists and Blacksmiths' Union in 1871, and became an organizer for the union in 1873. In 1876 he was initiated into the Knights of Labor and was elected corresponding secretary of the Scranton, Pennsylvania, district assembly in 1877. He was mayor of Scanton three times through the support of the Greenback Labor Party. As grand master workman of the Knights, Powderly presided over an explosion in its membership from 19,000 to 703,000 between 1881 and 1886 which converted the organization from a secret society to the first mass labor organization in the history of the United States (q.v.). There were elements of utopianism in Powderly's thinking; for example, he opposed the wage system and considered it could be replaced by a system of producer cooperatives. Ironically, although he supported the recruitment of lesser skilled employees, he proved an inept leader for the times. He opposed strikes when most of the new rank-and-file supported them and advocated conciliation (q.v.) and mediation to settle disputes rather than confrontation. When he was removed from his leadership of the Knights of Labor in 1893, it had ceased to be an effective force and continued to decay. Powderly served in several federal government positions after 1893 but never again played a significant role in organized labor. (*See also* Knights of Labor)

PRINTING Printing has an important place in the history of organized labor. Printing was an unusual trade in that it demanded not just superior technical skills but also a high level of literacy. It was this combination which often placed printers at the forefront of employees both in terms of power at the workplace and as leaders within organized labor. Printing was also a leading industry in technological change, a fact which created problems as well as opportunities for its employees. Labor disputes in printing occurred as early as the sixteenth century: 1504 (Venice), 1539, 1572 (Paris and Lyons), and 1560 (Geneva). The disputes in Lyons concerned long hours. The printers formed a union and attacked strikebreakers, but they were beaten in both disputes. Printers were among the first to form formal unions in many countries although they had been informally organized long before; for instance, in 1829 printers conducted one of Australia's first strikes. In 1848 printers formed the first national German labor union, the *Nationaler Buchdrucker-Verein* (National Printers' Association). The printing industry was often a pacesetter for other industries. The first collective agreement made in France in 1843 set wage rates for printers.

Philadelphia printers carried out the first strike of employees in a single trade in the United States in 1786 and a short-lived union existed among New York printers in the late 1770s. In 1804 the New York printers formed a union which lasted until 1815. Ely Moore, the first president of the National Trades' Union (q.v.) in 1834, was a printer. In 1852 the National Typographical Association was formed which, after the affiliation of printing unions in Canada, renamed itself the International Typographical Union (ITU) in 1869. As a strong craft union, the ITU played an influential role in the creation of the Federation of Organized Trades and Labor Unions of the United States and Canada in 1881 and the American Federation of Labor (qq.v.) 1886.

Hierarchical occupational divisions were an important feature of the organization of printing work with compositors being the highest group; their dominance of the ITU led to the creation of separate unions by other printing employees such as stereotypers and electroplaters, photoengravers, bookbinders, and journalists in the last decades of the nineteenth century. Ethnicity also played a role in the history of the ITU. In 1873 printers employed by the German language press formed their own union, the German-American *Typographia*, but in 1894 this body merged with the ITU. In 1906 the ITU conducted a successful campaign in book and job-printing firms for the eight-hour work day, laying the foundation for its adoption elsewhere in the printing industry. In 1911 the ITU and other unions formed a printing industry body, the International Allied Printing Trades Association.

Until the 1960s the printing industry unions throughout the world enjoyed considerable power but, with the coming of new technology, that power waned as many of the older mechanical skills were replaced by electronic machines and, more recently, by computers. Symptomatic of the decline of their power was the defeat of London printing unions over the introduction of new technology at Rupert Murdoch's Wapping plant in London, in 1986. (*See also* International Graphical Association)

PRIVATIZATION   Privatization refers to the sale or partial sale of a government-owned enterprise or agency either to a private sector company or through the sale of shares offered to the general public. Privatization was adopted by the Conservative governments in Britain since 1979 as a means of improving the efficiency and productivity of the economy. The economic effects of privatization have been much debated, but privatized concerns can achieve higher productivity at least in the short term if they are able to significantly reduce the number of employees. Generally, organized labor has opposed privatization because of the job losses it usually brings. From the early 1980s a number of Western countries have used privatization to varying degrees as a means of improving their economic performance (for example, Australia and New Zealand). Since the late 1980s the former communist countries of Eastern Europe have used privatization as part of the transition from planned to market economies. In Asia, privatization has been used both in noncommunist countries (for example, Indonesia and Thailand) and communist countries such as Vietnam (qq.v.). (*See also* Public/Private Sector)

PROFITERN (*See* Comintern)

PUBLIC/PRIVATE SECTOR In most Western countries one of the most significant trends in the structure of union membership over recent decades has been the large increase in the proportion of union members employed by the public sector (government or government agencies) compared to the private sector. Precise measurement of this trend is difficult because the statistics have not always been collected in a convenient form or because frequent changes of national policy (such as over the nationalization of industries in the United Kingdom since 1945) drain the meaning from longer term comparisons even if the data are available.   Nevertheless, the industry data on the distribution of labor union membership for the United Kingdom (taking the public sector to be a combination of union membership employed by national government, local government and education, gas, electricity, water, post and telecommunciations) suggest that 10 percent of union members were employed by the public sector by 1920, 20 percent by 1940 and 22 percent by 1960. In 1960 only 6 percent of union members in the United States (q.v.) were public sector employees. The growth of government employment after 1960 and structural changes in the private sector in the 1970s and 1980s (specifically the decline in mass manufacturing employment and the growth of the service sector) combined to raise the proportion of union members employed by the public sector to a historic high. In the United States the proportion of union members employed by the public sector rose from 11 percent in 1970 to 32 percent in 1983 and to 42 percent in 1995. In 1994 50 percent of union members were public sector employees in the United Kingdom and 42 percent in Australia in 1995.   (*See also* White Collar Unionism, Women)

PUBLIC SERVICES INTERNATIONAL (PSI) The PSI is one of the largest International Trade Secretariats (q.v.) in the world. It was formed in 1935 with the merger of the International Federation of Workers in Public Administration and Utilities (IFWPAU) and the Civil Servants' International.   The IFWPAU was founded by representatives of local government unions from Denmark, Germany, Hungary, the Netherlands, Sweden, and Switzerland in 1907 at the suggestion of the Dutch. The Civil Servants' Association was created in 1925 in the Netherlands and represented employees of central governments. The activities of the PSI were severely restricted first by the disaffiliation of the British civil servants in 1927 (which was forced by legislation passed after the General Strike [q.v.] in 1926) and then by the suppression of organized labor by the Nazis in Germany in 1933. After World War II the PSI was re-established in London and its membership broadened to take in countries outside Europe. In 1957 persistent lobbying of the International Labour Organisation (q.v.) by the PSI resulted in the formation of a committee for the public services, although it was not until the early 1970s that the public sector was given greater attention by the ILO. Between 1976 and 1994 the membership of the PSI rose from 4.8 to 16 million and the number of member countries from fifty-six to 110. (*See also* International Trade Secretariats, White-Collar Unionism)

R

RACE AND ETHNICITY Racial divisions have been both a unifier and divider in the history of organized labor. There were many instances of the use of different ethnic groups to break strikes in the nineteenth century. In the United Kingdom (q.v.), Welsh, Irish, and Cornish miners were brought in by employers to break strikes. In the United States (q.v.), immigrants were used as strikebreakers in the steel industry. In the 1870s and 1880s, violent anti-Chinese feelings, particularly in the mining industry, helped to promote labor unions in the western United States and southeastern Australia. In the United States, one of the objectives of the National Labor Union (q.v.) was the restriction of Chinese immigration (q.v.). It was the refusal of the NLU to accept racial integration that led to the formation of the Colored National Labor Union (q.v.) in 1869. In the United States, and later in South Africa, organized labor tended to be the preserve of European males although cooperation could occur as was shown by the successful biracial strike of 1893 in New Orleans. The Knights of Labor (q.v.) were unusual in the mid-1880s in their practice of racial integration.

Attempts at racial integration in the United States for much of the twentieth century floundered on the racism of many labor unions. In 1924 the Central Trades and Labor Council of Greater New York supported the creation of the Trade Union Committee for Organizing Negro Workers, but this body was defunct by 1927. In 1935 the Negro Labor Committee was formed in New York State and organized a march on Washington in 1941 which led to the setting up of the Fair Employment Practices Commission in 1943 which was designed to eliminate discrimination in employment in war industries or government on the grounds of "race, creed, color, or national origin." In 1960 A. Philip Randolph and other black leaders set up the Negro American Labor Council to fight racial discrimination in unions affiliated with the American Federation of Labor-Congress of Industrial Organizations (AFL-CIO) (q.v.); the council operated throughout the 1960s and its relations with the AFL-CIO were often difficult. In the late 1960s more radical black union groups came into being which challenged the leadership of the NALC within organized labor.

In the United States, 15 percent of American labor union members were Afro-Americans in 1995 compared to 14 in 1983. The percentage of Hispanics among union members rose from 6 percent in 1983 to 8 percent in 1995. African-Americans were more likely to be union members than white or Hispanic Americans; in 1995 20 percent of African-American employees were union members compared to 14 percent of white and 13 of Hispanic employees.

In the United Kingdom, an official household survey of labor union members also found that there were significant variations in the proportions of employees by race who were union members; in 1995 32 percent of white employees were union members compared to 41 percent for Blacks, 28 percent for Indians, 18 percent for Pakistanis and Bangladeshis and 29 percent for other minority groups. In Australia, the proportion of all union members born in non-English speaking countries fell from 18 percent in 1982 to 13 percent in 1995. (*See also* Immigration, National Labor Union, South Africa)

RAILROADS The railroads have been one of the main battle grounds of organized labor between 1870 and 1920. Railway employment was characterized by long hours, dangerous working conditions, and management devices to control employees such as company towns (for instance, Pullman in Illinois and Crewe in England). Management attitudes and organization were based on the army. Occupations were divided horizontally as well as vertically. Despite these drawbacks, the railroads were attractive because they usually offered relatively secure employment and the prospect of promotion with experience and length of service. Under these conditions, unions were slow to emerge although a friendly society (q.v.) was set up by English locomotive engine drivers and firemen as early as 1839 and may have had some features of a labor union; locomotive enginemen are known to have formed unions in 1848 and in 1860.

In 1865 an attempt to form a provident society by the guards of the Great Western Railway Company was crushed by the sacking of its leaders. In 1866 locomotive engine drivers and firemen formed a union which demanded the ten-hour work day. The other unions present within the railroad industry before 1870 were those of tradesmen working in the repair workshops. In 1871 the Amalgamated Society of Railway Servants of England, Ireland, Scotland, and Wales was formed and it became the largest railroad union in Britain; this union was the subject of the Taff Vale Case (q.v.) in 1901. It amalgamated with two other unions in 1913 to become a genuine industrial union and changed its name to the National Union of Railwaymen.

In the United States (q.v.), the Brotherhood of Locomotive Firemen and Enginemen was formed in New York in 1873 with the original aim of providing sickness and funeral benefits for members but soon became a labor union. In 1883 the formation of the Brotherhood of Railroad Trainmen represented the first attempt to form an industrial union in the railroad industry.

In Australia (q.v.), a locomotive engine drivers' union was formed in Victoria in 1870 and general railway unions, based on the Amalgamated Society of Railway Servants of England, Ireland, Scotland, and Wales, were formed in the various colonies between 1884 and 1899 and in New Zealand in 1886.

The railroad industry was the focus of some major conflicts between management and its employees. In the United States, there were three national clashes before 1900: the strikes and riots from July 16, to August 5, 1877 sparked off by wage cuts, the Burlington railroad strike of 1888-89, and the Pullman strike and boycott of 1894. There was a national railroad strike in France in 1898. The first national railroad strike in Britain was in 1911 and lasted two days; it was followed by another one in 1919. One of Australia's largest strikes, that from August to September 1917, was centered on the railroads. (*See also* Eugene Victor Debs, Taff Vale Case)

RAND FORMULA This term has two meanings. In Canada, it refers to a form of checkoff (q.v.) in which the employer deducts part of the wages of all employees within a bargaining unit (regardless or not of whether those employees are union members). The system was named after Mr Justice Ivan Rand, a judge of the Supreme Court of Canda, who used it to arbitrate in a strike in 1946, and it has since spread in a modified form thoughout Canada. In the United State, the term refers to a method of anti-unionism used by the Remington Rand Corporation in which unions were discredited among their members and other members of the community. This second meaning is also known as the Mohawk Valley Formula. (*See also* Checkoff)

REAGAN, RONALD (1911-) Reagan was the first U.S. president to have also been an executive officer in a national labor union; between 1959 and 1960 he was president of the Screen Actors' Guild (formed in 1933). Despite this background, his presidency (1981-89) was hostile to organized labor as shown by his crushing of the strike by the Professional Air Traffic Controllers' Organization (PATCO) in August 1981 by firing over 11,000 strikers and replacing them with military controllers and civilian controllers who returned to work.

RENGO *Rengo*, an abbreviation for *Nihon Rodokumiai Sorengokai* (Japanese Trade Union Confederation), is the largest labor union federation in Japan. It is the product of a series of amalgamations (q.v.) with other labor federations. The largest part of *Rengo* began as *Sodomei* (Japanese Federation of Trade Unions) in 1946 which became *Domei* (Japanese Confederation of Labor) in 1964, by which time it had 2.1 million members. In 1987 *Domei* joined with *Sorengo* (National Federation of Trade Unions of Japan; formed in 1979), and *Shinsanbetsu* (National Federation of Industrial Organizations; formed in 1952) to form *Zenmin Roren* (Japanese Private Sector Trade Union Federation, now referred to as old *Rengo*). The second part of *Rengo* was the public sector labor federation *Sohyo* (General Council of Trade Unions of Japan) which was formed in 1950 when the noncommunist unions split from the communist dominated *Sanbetsu-Kaigi* (Congress of Industrial Unions of Japan) which had been formed in 1946. Left-leaning and militant, *Sohyo* was largely responsible for beginning the *Shunto* (q.v.) or Spring Offensive for wage increases in 1956. In November 1989 *Zenmin Roven* and *Sohyo* merged to form *Rengo*. In 1993 *Rengo* represented 7.8 million union members or 62 percent of all Japan's labor union members. (*See also* Japan, *Shunto*)

REUTHER, WALTER PHILIP (1907-1970) Reuther was one of the chief labor leaders in the United States (q.v.) in the post-1945 period through his presidency of the United Automobile, Aircraft, and Agricultural Implement Workers of America (UAW) (q.v.) which he held from 1946 until his death. Born in Wheeling, West Virginia, he completed three years of secondary education before entering a tool and die maker apprenticeship with the Wheeling Steel Corporation. Fired for union activities by the corporation, he moved to Detroit in 1926. In 1931 he was fired by Ford, again for union activities. Unemployed, he took a world tour during 1933 to 1935 which included Europe, the Soviet Union, China, and Japan. On his return, he became an organizer and then an official of the UAW in Detroit. He was elected to the executive board of the UAW in 1936 and was one of the leaders of the UAW's campaign of sit-down strikes during 1937 against General Motors and Chrysler Motors. The UAW's campaign for recognition against Ford was met with violence in which Reuther and Richard Frankensteen were beaten up by Ford's private police. During World War II, Reuther served on a number of federal government boards.

In 1946 his moderate faction won control of the UAW and Reuther became its president. The UAW's strike campaign for better pay and conditions in the motor industry culminated in a contract with General Motors in 1948, which included pay increases based on the official cost of living index. In the same year, Reuther was wounded by a shotgun in an attempted assassination. He became president of the Congress of Industrial Organizations (q.v.) in 1952 and supported its merger with the American Federation of Labor in 1955. He served as a vice president but led the UAW out of the AFL-CIO in 1968 following disagreements with its conservative president, George Meany (q.v.). Before his death in a plane crash, Reuther's last major activity was his leadership of the Alliance for Labor Action (q.v.). (*See also* Alliance for Labor Action, "Battle of the Overpass," George Meany, United Auto Workers' Union)

RIGHT-TO-WORK LAWS Under the federal Taft-Hartley Act (q.v.) of 1947, American states were given the right to ban the union (or closed) shop within their borders. Under most union shop agreements, new employees typically had thirty days in which to join the union. Right-to-work laws make it possible for employees in unionized workplaces to remain nonunionists and have the general effect of inhibiting union membership growth. By 1988, twenty-one American states had such laws; they included all of the South and most of the Midwest. (*See also* United States of America)

ROMANIA Organized labor first emerged in what is now Romania among printers who formed mutual benefit societies, beginning at Brasov in 1846. During the 1860s other employees formed associations which were much influenced by socialist ideas. In 1872 a general union was formed which was open to all employees without regard to occupation, sex, or religion. In 1893 the Romanian Social Democratic Party was formed and a national labor federation was set up in 1906. The unions supported the peasant uprisings in 1907. The labor federation was an affiliate of the International Federation of Trade Unions (q.v.) from 1909 to 1918 and from 1923 to 1938. Between 1914 and 1920 union membership rose from 40,000 to 300,000 divided among 350 unions. In 1921 the Communist Party was constituted from the former Socialist Party and competed for the leadership of organized labor. Both parties sponsored their own labor federations. After a short period of cooperation, the Communist Party broke away from the united labor federation and was banned by the government in 1923; in 1929 its labor federation was banned too. There were many labor disputes (q.v.) in Romania in the late 1920s and early 1930s, a reflection not just of the deterioration in economic conditions but also the rise in manufacturing employment from 318,000 in 1913 to 953,000 in 1930. In 1936 a new labor federation was formed with 310 individual unions representing 80,000 members but when the fascist government came to power two years later, unions and strikes were outlawed.

During World War II, the Romanian government was an ally of the Nazis until its overthrow in 1944. With the establishment of a communist republic in 1947, organized labor became part of the machinery of government. An attempted formation of an independent union was made in 1979 but it was harshly suppressed. A second clandestine effort was made in 1988 but it was suppressed too. Communist rule in Romania was ended by a violent popular uprising between December 1989 and January 1990. In December 1989 *Fratia* ("Fraternity"), a broadly based independent labor union, was formed. The former communist labor federation (UGSR) was dissolved early in 1990 and replaced by what became the *Confederatia Nationala a Sindicatelator Libere din România* (CNSLR) or National Free Trade Union Confederation of Romania. A third independent labor body, *Alfa-Cartel*, was formed by 1991. As in Bulgaria and Poland (qq.v.), there have been conflicts between the independent labor organizations over the control of the assets of the former communist labor federations, but in Romania these have been minimized by a high degree of cooperation. In 1995 the CNSLR and *Fratia* joined forces to become the Romanian member of the International Confederation of Free Trade Unions (q.v.) with a claimed membership of 3.2 million which represented 39 per cent of employees.

ROOKES V. BARNARD *Rookes v. Barnard* was an important legal case concerning the operation of labor unions in Britain. In 1955 Douglas Rookes, an employee of the British Overseas Airways Corporation, resigned from his union, the Association of Engineering and Shipbuilding Draftsmen. The union, wanting to maintain a closed shop, instigated his dismissal. Rookes sued the union and was awarded substantial damages; the association appealed to the house of lords but it upheld the original decision in 1964. The case, which reflected poorly on the attitude of a union towards an individual, opened up a loophole in the Trades Disputes Act (1906) by making union officials liable for damages for threatening to strike in breach of contracts of employment. This loophole was closed by the Trades Disputes Act (1965). (*See also* Taff Vale Case)

RUSSIA Before March 1906 unions were illegal throughout the Russian Empire. Their brief legalization produced a surge of membership growth to 123,000 by 1907 in the wake of the 1905 Revolution, but this development was wrecked by a government crackdown. There was some revival by organized labor between 1911 and 1914, but it was able to achieve little beyond conducting protest strikes. The revolutionary period between mid-1917 and 1920 saw an explosion of union membership from 1.5 to 5.2 million. The main division in the Russian labor movement was between those who supported the autonomy of organized labor from the political arm of labor (led by the Mensheviks) and the Bolsheviks who held that the function of the unions was to help overthrow the government and transfer power to industrial wage earners, the proletariat. During 1919 and 1920 the Bolsheviks achieved control of the Russian labor movement. At first, the unions played an important role in the program of economic reconstruction known as the New Economic Plan, but from 1922 under Lenin, and then Stalin, the unions operated as agents of centralized communist rule whose main role was to increase economic output.

In 1978 some dissidents tried to form an independent union for professional employees, but it was suppressed by the Soviet government and its leaders imprisoned. The first sign of a mass independent labor movement came in mid-1989 with a wave of strikes in northern Russia, the Ukraine, and the Urals which gave rise to Workers' Committees and the formation of an independent miners' union which joined an independent Confederation of Labor when it was set up in May 1990. In October 1990 the All-Union Central Council of Trade Unions, the central communist body formed in November 1924, transformed itself into the General Confederation of Unions of the USSR which recognized the rights of the newly independent nations within the former Soviet Union and pledged itself to protect union rights.

After the creation of the Commonwealth of Independent States on December 8, 1991, the General Confederation of Unions again reshaped itself to become the Federation of Independent Trade Unions of Russia made up of seven of the new states (excluding the Ukraine) in April 1992. The organizational continuity of these moves was important for maintaining control of the assets of the former communist labor organization, a vexed issue in most other East European countries. Aside from the emergence of the independent labor organizations in the former Soviet republics, the main independent Russian labor organization is *Sotsprof*, a federation of social democratic and socialist unions formed in about 1990. In 1995 none of the Russian labor bodies were members of the International Confederation of Free Trade Unions (q.v.).

S

"SAINT MONDAY" "Saint Monday" was a custom observed from about the mid-seventeenth century by shoemakers, tailors and other journeymen of taking Monday as a holiday and sometimes even Tuesday. The custom also seems to have been observed by French textile employees. By 1764 it was observed by bricklayers, painters, and hand loom employees. Work not performed on Monday was made up later in the week at night. The purpose of the custom was to create a period of leisure and to exert more control over when work was done. Its opponents claimed that "Saint Monday" was observed mainly in ale-houses and taverns. The custom was gradually eliminated by the factory system and replaced by a regulated system of hours. The idea of the weekend as a defined period of leisure did not emerge until late in nineteenth century England; the first recorded use of the term "weekend" dates from Staffordshire in 1879. (*See also* Working Hours)

SECOND INTERNATIONAL WORKINGMEN'S ASSOCIATION
The Second International Workingmen's Association or, as it is more usually known, the Second International, was a loose association of socialist parties which was founded in Paris in 1889 and was dissolved in 1914 when World War I began. Its founding was a logical extension of moves towards creating International Trade Secretariats (q.v.) by unions in particular occupations. From the start, the Second International was subject to many disagreements but it did manage to initiate May 1, as a day for international demonstrations by labor unions in favor of the eight-hour work day. May Day, which owed its origins to Labor Day (q.v.) in the United States, was first celebrated in this way in Europe in 1890. The Second International, which did not have a secretariat until 1900, proved unable to agree on many important issues, specifically whether socialism (q.v.) could be achieved through parliamentary means and whether socialist parties should join in parliamentary coalitions with other parties, a practice condemned by the 1905 conference in Amsterdam. The Second International opposed anarchism (q.v.), and after 1896 anarchists were excluded from membership. The outbreak of a European war in 1914 in which nationalism would override the interests of the working class was foreseen by the Second International but, despite efforts to prevent it, nationalism proved stronger and destroyed the organization. A number of bodies since 1914 have claimed to be the rightful successor to the Second International. (*See also* Comintern, James Keir Hardie, Labor and Socialist International)

SHORTER WORKING HOURS   From as early as the sixteenth century, unions have attempt to reduce working hours or at least resist them being lengthened. There were two disputes in the printing industry in Lyons, France (q.v.), in 1539 and 1572 over long working hours. In both the United Kingdom and the United States (qq.v.), there were moves by organized labor to gain a maximum working day of ten hours in the 1830s. In the 1880s there was an international movement by organized labor to reduce the work day to eight hours, but for most employees this was not achieved until the twentieth century. Since 1945 metal workers' unions have generally been the vanguard for the reduction of working hours in the UK, Germany, and Australia (qq.v.). (*See also* Working Hours)

SHUNTO   *Shunto* is a Japanese term meaning "Spring Offensive" and refers to the national process of bargaining over wages, conditions of employment, and other issues between unions, employers, and the government.   The *Shunto* was begun in February 1956 by *Sohyo* (General Council of Trade Unions of Japan) as a way of strengthening the power of the unions and of reducing earning differentials between enterprises and the thousands of unions based on them.   As it has developed, the *Shunto* begins with an agreement by the unions about the amount of the pay increase they want and a corresponding decision by the employers' organization (*Nikkeiren*) about the size of the unions' demand which they are prepared to accept; the unions then formally present their demands.   The *Shunto* then proceeds by industry groups in the private sector beginning with the iron and steel, shipbuilding, electrical equipment, and automobile industries.   Later the *Shunto* moves on to industries such as textiles, petroleum, and food.   Gains made in the larger enterprise are then applied to medium and smaller enterprises.   The *Shunto* reaches its climax in April.   The outcome of increases gained by the *Shunto* in the private sector form the basis for the increase for government employees and employees in national enterprises.   The *Shunto* has been responsible for gaining wage increases higher than the consumer price index.   In 1975 the *Shunto* delivered a pay increase of 32.9 percent but since 1976 these increases have been less than 10 percent; in 1995 the *Shunto* pay increase was 2.8 percent, its lowest level.   (*See also* Japan, *Rengo*)

SINGAPORE   Labor unions emerged in Singapore from 1946 and soon became part of the struggle against British rule.   In the early 1950s Singapore's high strike record was a reflection of the political militancy of organized labor.   In 1955 strikes were forbidden in essential services.   The National Trade Union Congress was officially registered in 1964 but had its origins in a body formed in the 1950s, the Singapore Trade Union Congress.   Between 1946 and 1962 the number of labor union members in Singapore grew from 18,700 to 189,000.   In 1965 Singapore left the Malayasian federation and has been sovereign since that time.   With the defeat of political leftists in the early 1960s, organized labor in Singapore was increasingly brought under government control.   Despite its lack of freedom, the National Trade Union Congress with its 150,000 members, which represented about 11 per cent of employees, was a member of the International Confederation of Free Trade Unions (q.v.) in 1995.   (*See also* Malaysia)

SOCIAL DEMOCRATIC/SOCIALIST/LABOR PARTIES   Social democratic/socialist/labor political parties grew out of the recognition that labor unions alone were not sufficient to improve the economic and social condition of working-class people. Usually composed of a diversity of groups and opinions, these parties developed their own characteristics depending upon their country of origin but they were united by their vision of themselves as the political arm of the working class. Despite the formation of socialist groups in the 1880s, such as the Social Democratic Federation, the Socialist League, and the Fabians, it was the relative success of the political alliance of labor unions with the Liberal Party in Britain which delayed the formation of an independent political party based on unions. It was not until 1893 that the Independent Labour Party was formed; it cooperated with the Trades Union Congress (q.v.) to form the Labour Representation Committee in 1900 and was renamed the Labour Party (q.v.) in 1906. In Norway, a Labor Party was formed in 1887.   In Australia, the Labor Party (q.v.) was established separately in New South Wales and South Australia in 1891. Labor parties were formed in South Africa in 1909 and in New Zealand in 1916.

In continental Europe, the generally authoritarian political climate encouraged political parties with labor connections to be far more radical, even revolutionary. They drew the bulk of their political ideas from Marxism.   This tendency was reinforced by their relative weakness of labor unions for most of the nineteenth century. The first European social democratic party was formed in Germany in 1863 by Ferdinand Lassalle (1825-1864), as the German Workingmen's Association, and the second, also in Germany, by Wilhelm Liebknecht (1826-1900) and August Bebel (1840-1913) as the Social Democratic Party of Germany in 1866. In 1875 these two parties fused to form the Social Democratic Party. Socialist parties soon emerged in other Western European countries: Denmark (1871), Czechoslavakia (1872), Portugal (1875), Spain (1879), and France (1880), Belgium (1885), Austria and Switzerland (1888), Sweden (1889), Italy (1892), Romania (1893), the Netherlands (1894), and Finland (1899). Socialist parties were formed in Eastern Europe too: Armenia (1890), Poland (1892), Bulgaria (1893), Hungary (1894), Lithuania (1896), Russia (1898), and Georgia (1899); a social democratic party was formed in Latvia in 1904 and in the Ukraine in 1905. In the United States, a socialist labor party was formed in 1876, a Greenback-Labor Party in 1878, and a Socialist Party in 1901. A Socialist Party was formed in Argentina in 1892.

The Second International Workingmen's Association (q.v.), set up in 1889, was the international forum for many of these parties. Although there was agreement about the need for change, there was much disagreement about the methods for achieving it. By the late-nineteenth century, there were two main tendencies at work in these parties both within their national borders and internationally: those who wanted change by gradual reform within the political order and those who wanted change by full-scale social revolution. The second strand was incorporated into communism (q.v.) from 1917.

Electorally successful labor parties, that is political parties built solely on organized labor have been relatively rare since 1900 outside of Australia, Britain, and Scandinavia. Conflict can, and does, arise between the political and industrial wings of organized labor. One early instance of this occurred in Germany in 1906; it was resolved by the Mannheim Agreement (q.v.) which declared the equality between the Social Democratic Party and the unions in providing the leadership for the working class. In France (q.v.), the trade unions declared their independence from all political parties in the Charter of Amiens, also in 1906. (*See also* Australian Labor Party, British Labour Party)

SOCIAL SECURITY Social security has been defined by the International Labor Organisation (q.v.) as embracing social insurance schemes (for occupational injury, health, pensions, and unemployment), public health, family allowances, war benefits, and special transfers to government employees. The growth of social security systems in Western economies during the twentieth century was sought by organized labor not just to improve the conditions of employees generally but also as a means of reducing the competition for positions in the paid labor force from dependent groups such as children, mothers, and the aged. Of special importance was the introduction of unemployment benefits because the unemployed were the pool from which strikebreakers were traditionally drawn by employers. In the 1980s there has been increased concern by governments about the adverse economic effects of spending on social security. Nevertheless, social security systems are the main means for the redistribution of income from the better-off to the less well-off in Western societies. (*See also* Minimum Wage)

SOCIALISM The term socialism derives from the Latin "socius" or ally, but as a political ideology it took shape during the nineteenth century. Although the term was applied to a wide range of beliefs, a common concern was the need to assume some kind of collective control over the means of production, distribution, and exchange and to use this control for the greatest good of the members of society. Despite great interest in socialist ideas in organized labor, there was often little understanding of how to translate socialist theories into practice. In many countries from about 1910 socialists within labor unions began to divide between reformists and revolutionaries. The inflationary effects of World War I caused a heightened sense of economic injustice among working people and led to the incorporation of explicit socialist objectives into the platforms of the British Labour Party (1918) and the Australian Labor Party (1919) (qq.v.). (*See also* Guild Socialism, Second International Workingmen's Association)

SOCIETY OF FRATERNAL DEMOCRATS The Society of Fraternal Democrats was a British political group made up of English Chartists and political refugees from continental Europe. It was founded in 1845 and was the first real attempt at democratic internationalism. Its motto was "all men are brethren,," and its founding manifesto denounced all forms of political inequality. One of its leaders, George Julian Harney (1817-1887), knew Karl Marx and Friedrich Engels. Although short-lived, the society was a precedent for the International Workingmen's Association (q.v.). (*See also* Chartism)

SOUTH AFRICA The first labor union in South Africa was the Amalgamated Society of Carpenters and Joiners (q.v.) which was formed by Europeans in Cape Town in 1881. Miners in the Kimberley set up a union in 1884 and the Amalgamated Society of Engineers (q.v.) formed a branch in Cape Town in 1891. A Federation of Unions was formed in 1911. One remarkable feature of this development was the very low membership of organized labor in South Africa compared to similar societies such as Australia and New Zealand. There were only 3,800 union members in 1900 and only 11,900 by 1914 of whom 2,800 were members of the Amalgamated Society of Engineers. As in other countries, the following six years saw a large increase in union membership to 135,100 by 1920, but this represented only about 12 percent of nonagricultural employees.

A second feature of European organization, though not one confined to South Africa, was its hostility to other racial groups. The South African Industrial Federation which was formed in 1914 was aimed at protecting skilled Europeans and maintaining racial divisions. The South African branch of the Industrial Workers of the World (q.v.) was unique in setting up a multiracial body, but it could not survive in the racially divided society. The first black union was formed in 1917 but the largest body, the Industrial and Commercial Workers' Union, was set up in 1919; it claimed 100,000 members by 1925 but was made defunct by 1930. Gandhi also helped to form unions among Indian workers, but the growth of non-European unionism alarmed the Europeans who went on strike in 1922; in the ensuing conflict, 230 strikers were killed by the army. The incident led to moves by European organized labor to reduce economic opportunities for non-Europeans, a policy which greatly harmed non-European unionism. Membership of all South African unions grew from 118,300 in 1930 to 272,500 in 1940 and to 408,600 in 1950. In 1941 some black unions formed the Council of Non-European Trade Unions; it claimed 158,000 members by 1945.

With the victory of the National Party in the 1948 elections, full apartheid became government policy and this also entailed a hostile attitude towards non-European unions which led to their politicalization. In 1954 the Trade Union Council of South Africa was formed with unions from all the country's racial groups. In 1955 the South African Congress of Trade Unions was formed from the merger of some independent black unions and the Council of Non-European Trade Unions, but it was crushed by the government between 1962 and 1965 because of its radicalism. After strikes by black workers in Durban in 1972-73, the government arrested the leaders and tried to suppress black unionism. The government reaction led to concerted support for black unions by international unionism through bodies such as the International Metalworkers' Federation (q.v.) and through pressure from the union representatives on the boards of Swedish and German multinational companies operating in South Africa.

In 1979 the government appointed the Wiehahn Commission to investigate trade unionism; the commission successfully recommended that black labor unions be legally recognized and the system of racial reservation of occupations be abandoned. The recommendations did not mean complete freedom for black organized labor. Rural and domestic workers and state employees were denied access to collective bargaining and unions could not affiliate to a political party or support illegal strikes. Nevertheless, black unionism grew despite continued violence; in April 1987, for instance, seven strikers were killed during a railroad strike. In December 1985 the Congress of South African Unions, a mainly black labor federation, was formed; nonracial by policy, it claimed 1.3 million members by 1991. A radical black labor federation, the National Council of Trade Unions was formed in 1986 and claimed 327,000 members in 1994. (*See also* Race and Ethnicity)

SOUTH KOREA The first labor disputes (q.v.) on the Korean peninsula date from the 1890s, and the first labor union was formed by longshoremen in 1898. The country was a colony of Japan from 1910 to 1945. Following the suppression of a revolt for independence in 1919, Japanese policy was one of toleration until 1925. In this period three labor federations were formed (1920, 1922, and 1924). In 1925 the Japanese repressed organized labor by their Public Peace law; at this time there were about 123,000 union members in Korea. With Japan's defeat in 1945, organized labor revived and set up a large, broadly based, communist labor federation. It was challenged by an anticommunist, nationalist labor federation, the General Federation of Korean Trade Unions, in March 1946. After it led two general strikes, the communist federation was outlawed in 1947.

Although in theory organized labor was able to organize, collectively bargain and strike under the constitution of 1948, in practice it was controlled by the government. In 1958 an independent labor federation was formed, but after a military coup in 1961 all labor unions were broken up and reorganized by the military into fourteen industrial unions based on organized labor in Germany (q.v.). Under the labor laws of 1953 (and subsequent years), most public sector employees were denied the right to strike. In 1963 unions were legally forbidden from participation in politics.

Following the promise of constitutional reforms in June 1987, there was an outburst of independent activity among white- and blue-collar employees; it is estimated that 400,000 employees joined these unions by August 1987. An independent labor federation, the National Council of Labor Unions, was set up in January 1990 from a body originally formed in March 1984; it claimed about 200,000 members in 1992. Despite the lack of freedom of organized labor in South Korea since 1953, its labor federation has been a continuous member of the International Confederation of Free Trade Unions (q.v.) since 1949. (*See also* Japan)

SPAIN Organized labor developed slowly in nineteenth century Spain, a reflection of the country's economic and political backwardness. In 1871 printers formed a union in Madrid but unions were not legalized until 1881, an event which led to the formation of the first labor federation, the *Federación de Trabajadores de la Región Española* which claimed to represent 58,000 members. This body was replaced in 1888 by the *Unión General de Trabajadores* (General Union of Workers) (UGT) and continued to be Spain's largest labor federation; it was dominated by the socialists. Anarchism (q.v.) was one of the distinguishing characteristics of Spanish labor. It found particular appeal in rural areas and envisaged the overthrow of the state by a general strike and its replacement by democratically run cooperative groups covering the whole economy. In 1910 the anarchists formed their own federation, the *Confederación Nacional del Trabajo* (National Labor Federation), which continues to the present. Unions and union growth were relatively weak. Between the early 1900s and 1913 the number of union members rose from 26,000 to 128,000.

Violence was also a feature of Spanish labor. During "Tragic Week" (July 1909) over 175 were shot in riots led by revolutionary syndicalists in Catalonia over calling up of reservists for the war in Morocco. The rioters' attacks on churches and convents led to the execution of anarchist leader Francisco Ferrer despite international protests. After World War I unions grew strongly; between 1920 and 1930 the number of union members increased from 220,000 to 946,000 and by 1936 the UGT claimed 2 million members.

The Civil War (1936-39) and the repression which followed under General Francisco Franco eliminated organized labor from political life. The UGT continued as an organization in exile in France. During the 1960s the communists organized employees at the workplace and even led illegal strikes. With the restoration of democracy following Franco's death in 1975, labor unions were legalized in 1977 although full legalization was not granted until 1985. As well as the UGT, the communists organized their own federation from the workplace groups they formed under Franco, the *Confederación Sindical de Comisiones Obreras* (Union Confederation of Workers' Commissions) (CCOO) and the anarchists reemerged but with only a shadow of their pre-1936 strength. In 1984 the government and the *Unión General de Trabajadores* agreed to a social and economic pact to control wage claims as an anti-inflationary measure. The pact, which was opposed by the CCOO, broke down after 1986. In 1980 Spain had about 1.7 million union members, but this figure had declined to about 1.2 million by 1990. (*See also* Anarchism)

SPENCE, WILLIAM GUTHRIE (1846-1926) One of Australia's leading labor leaders in the late nineteenth century, Spence was born on one of the Orkney Islands of Scotland and emigrated with his family to Geelong, Victoria, in 1852. He had no formal education and worked as a butcher's boy, miner, and shepherd. He assisted with the recruiting drive which led to the formation of the Amalgamated Miners' Association (AMA) at the goldmining town of Bendigo in 1874. In 1878 he became secretary of the Creswick Miners' Union. Spence was an early supporter of industrial unionism and wanted the AMA to cover all miners in Australia and New Zealand (qq.v.). A number of mining unions did affiliate with the AMA but the idea of a single union for the whole mining industry did not survive beyond the nineteenth century. At the 1884 Intercolonial Trade Union Congress, Spence tried unsuccessfully to persuade the unions to amalgamate along trade or industry lines and to set up a Federal Council to "deal with matters affecting the well-being of the working classes generally," a move which foreshadowed the formation of the Australian Council of Trade Unions (q.v.) in 1927. Although he supported conciliation (q.v.) as a means of settling disputes with employers, he was quite willing to use strikes as well. An excellent organizer and negotiator, he was appointed the first president of the Amalgamated Shearers' Union of Australasia in 1886 and in 1894 combined this union with several others to form the Australian Workers' Union (q.v.) in 1894; Spence served as its secretary from 1894 to 1898 and as its president from 1898 to 1917. He also wrote a history of the union in 1911. From the mid-1880s Spence was a supporter of the need for organized labor to have political representation. He served as a Labor member in the New South Wales parliament from 1898 to 1901 and in the federal parliament from 1901 to 1917. In 1917 he was permitted to resign from the Australian Labor Party (q.v.) rather than be expelled for his support of conscription. (*See also* Australian Workers' Union)

SPRING OFFENSIVE (*See Shunto*)

STEELWORKERS (*See* United Steelworkers of America)

SWEDEN The first true labor unions in Sweden were formed in the 1880s by skilled men some of whom had contact with trade unionism in the United Kingdom and Germany (q.v.). In 1886 the first of what became regular conferences was held between labor leaders of Sweden, Denmark, and Norway. In 1889 the unions formed the Social Democratic Party. But union membership growth was very slow;

there were only 9,000 members or about 1 percent of nonagricultural employees by 1890. Thereafter, union membership grew steadily to 67,000 or 5 percent of employees by 1900. In 1898 a labor federation for blue-collar employees, the *Landsorganisationen i Sverge* (LO) or Labor Union Federation of Sweden was formed, but the union movement faced a difficult political environment. In 1899 the government enacted a law which prevented strikebreaking; it remained law until 1938.

Yet the unions demonstrated their power by conducting a general strike in 1902 for universal suffrage which led to the formation of the *Svenska Arbetsgivaresöforreningen* (SAF) or Swedish Employers' Confederation. In 1906 the SAF and the LO signed their first agreement which, although it recognized the unions' right to organize and engage in collective bargaining, forced the unions to accept the employers' right to hire and fire employees and to make working arrangements. A massive but unsuccessful general strike in 1909 (the number of working days lost per thousand employees was 12,677, making it one of the biggest disputes in Sweden's history) hurt organized labor although union membership after 1910 continued to grow. Between 1913 and 1920 the number of union members rose from 134,000 to 403,000 and the proportion of employees in unions rose from 8 to 28 per cent. Despite large-scale protests, the government enacted laws in 1928 which regulated collective bargaining contracts and set up a labor court to settle disputes. In 1931 white-collar employees in the private sector formed their own labor federation.

In 1932 the political climate for labor changed for the better with the election of the first Social Democratic government. In 1936 the government passed a second major labor law which provided for the recognition of unions and the opening of negotiations by either employers or unions and outlawed the victimization of union members for taking part in legal union activities. National government employees formed a labor federation in 1937 and were granted the right to bargain in that year; the benefit was extended to employees of local government in 1940. Of particular significance was the Saltsjobaden Agreement in 1938 between the LO and the SAF; it specified dispute settlement procedures, the avoidance of disputes and, by implication, the avoidance of government intervention. This agreement is generally credited with securing a high degree of industrial peace until the economic problems of the 1970s. By 1940 there were 971,000 union members covering 54 percent of employees.

Since 1950 Sweden has had one of the highest levels of union membership in the world. In 1994 Swedish unions covered 96 percent of employees. (*See also* Council of Nordic Trade Unions)

SWITZERLAND Organized labor in Switzerland began effectively in the late 1860s through contact with German socialist labor bodies. In 1873 an unsuccessful attempt was made to form a national federation ,but in 1880 the socialist labor unions created the *Schweizerischer Gewerkschaftsbund* (Swiss Trade Union Confederation or SGB). In 1890 the Canton of Geneva passed a law which recognized agreements between unions and employers; it seems to have been the first legislation of its kind in Europe. In 1900, when the SGB declared its political neutrality, Switzerland had about 90,000 union members covering about 10 percent of its nonagricultural employees. A white-collar labor federation was established in 1903 and a Catholic labor federation in 1907. A general strike in 1918 was crushed by the army. By 1920 there were 313,000 union members representing about 26 percent of non-agricultural employees. Swiss organized labor developed and grew in a tolerant political climate and in a relatively wealthy economy. In 1937 a peace accord was made in the engineering industry which became the basis for a national social partnership between unions and employers from the 1950s. It provided for bargaining in good faith and avoiding strikes or lock-outs during the life of agreements. The consensus approach adopted so successfully in industrial relations reflected a wider respect for Switzerland's diversity of people, language, and religion. Spared the ravages of World War II, the Swiss labor movement continues to be formally divided by religion unlike those of Germany and Austria. In 1994 there were 541,400 union members representing about a quarter of nonagricultural employees.

SYNDICALISM Syndicalism was a set of practices and ideologies developed by French organized labor in the 1890s and 1900s. It derived from the French "syndical" meaning simply trade union but, as an ideology, syndicalism (or revolutionary syndicalism) meant the aggressive use of unions to gain political and social change. The class war was central to syndicalist thought which saw governments and political parties, including socialist parties, as instruments of working-class oppression. Syndicalist thought stressed direct action, particularly the general strike (q.v.), as the means to gain its objectives. It owed as much, if not more, to work experience than ideas.

Syndicalism grew out of conditions peculiar to France (q.v.), namely, its revolutionary tradition (1789, 1830, 1848, 1871), the self-reliant attitude of its working class, the relatively slow growth of industrialization, and the importance of small enterprises in the economy. The French Charter of Amiens (1906) which was adopted by the national organization of French labor, the *Confédération Générale du Travail* (q.v.), called for wage increases and shorter hours to be won by the taking over of the capitalist class and the general strike. In Italy (q.v.), syndicalism began to emerge after 1902 as a reaction to reformism in the Italian Socialist Party and developed into an unstable combination of Marxism and populism. Some of the Italian syndicalists became fascists. For example, Edmondo Rossini (1884-1965), the head of the fascist labor union federation from 1922 to 1928, had been a revolutionary syndicalist labor organizer in Italy and New York before 1914. In Spain (q.v.), syndicalism remained important until the late 1930s. (*See also* Industrial Workers of the World, One Big Union)

T

TAFF VALE CASE   The Taff Vale Case was a pivotal legal case in the history of British organized labor. It arose from picketing by the Amalgamated Society of Railway Servants to prevent the use of non-union labor during a strike in August 1900 on the Taff Vale railroad in South Wales. The general manager of the railroad, Ammon Beasley, sued the officials of the society for damages to the property of the railroad. The strike was settled through mediation after eleven days, but the company continued to press its claim through the courts. The company won the first round but lost in the court of appeal after which it went to the house of lords which decided against the society in July 1901 and, in a consequent case, declared that the society would have to pay the company 23,000 pounds plus its legal costs of 19,000 pounds (about $100,000 in total) which were huge sums for the time. The Taff Vale Case was immediately followed by two other anti-union decisions by the house of lords over picketing and boycotting (*Lyons v. Wilkins* and *Quinn v. Leathem*). The Taff Vale Case had three major results. First, it cast doubt on the legal status of labor union activity not just in Britain but in all countries which used British law, particularly Canada, Australia, and New Zealand (qq.v.). Second, it swung opinion within British organized labor round to the idea that it needed its own political party. The Labour Representation Committee, which had been formed in 1900, was upgraded; in 1903 a compulsory levy was made of unions to pay for Labour members of parliament and the committee itself was renamed the Labour Party (q.v.) in 1906. Third, pressure from organized labor on the Liberal government led to the Trade Disputes Act (1906) which granted the unions immunity from actions such as happened in the Taff Vale Case. (*See also* British Labour Party, *Rookes v. Barnard*)

TAFT-HARTLEY ACT   The Taft-Hartley Act, known formally as the Labor-Management Relations Act, was a piece of American federal law passed in 1947 to redress the imbalance in the law alleged to have been caused by the Wagner Act (q.v.) of 1935. Conservative politicians and employer groups claimed that the Wagner Act only dealt with coercive actions by employers and ignored such acts by unions. The legislation was passed at a time of increasing labor disputes (q.v.) generally and in coal mining and steel production in particular. Although the Taft-Hartley Act maintained the fundamental freedoms of unions, it imposed a number of important restrictions on them; it outlawed the union or closed shop and allowed the states to pass their own anticlosed shop or right-to-work laws (q.v.). Unions were also made liable to be sued in the federal courts for breaches of contract and had to give at least sixty days notice of the ending or amending of an agreement. Finally, unions were forbidden to spend any of their funds on political campaigns. (*See also* Right-to-Work Laws, United Mine Workers of America, United Steelworkers of America, Wagner Act)

TAIWAN   Following the imposition of martial law in 1949, strikes on Taiwan were outlawed and unions controlled by the Kuomintang Party encouraged. Between 1955 and 1989 the number of members in government-controlled unions rose from 198,000 to 2.4 million. The continuance of martial law was justified by the government on the grounds that Taiwan was still at war with mainland China (q.v.); it was only lifted in 1987, a step which led to a pent-up wave of labor disputes (q.v.). Strikes were permitted by the Arbitration Dispute Law which allowed employees to strike after mediation but required them to return to work. Nevertheless, striking union members were jailed for striking in 1988 and 1989. In November 1987 a Labor Party was formed and there was significant growth in the membership of independent labor unions. (*See also* China)

TEAMSTERS   Officially known as the International Brotherhood of Teamsters, Chauffeurs, Warehousemen, and Helpers of America, the Teamsters was the largest labor union in the United States (q.v.) from the mid-1950s to 1987 when it was overtaken by the National Educational Association (q.v.). The Teamsters began as the Team Drivers' International Union in January 1899 with a membership of 1,700 based on drivers of horse teams. In 1902 part of the Chicago membership formed a rival body, the Teamsters' National Union, but in 1903 the two organizations agreed to merge as the International Brotherhood of Teamsters. In its early years, the Teamsters was a sprawling confederation of local unions controlled by powerful bosses rather than a unified national organization. It owed much of its organizational success to Daniel J. Tobin who was its president from 1907 to 1952. In 1910 Tobin gained jurisdiction over truck drivers from the American Federation of Labor (q.v.), a decision which enabled it to grow with the fastest parts of the American economy and placed it in a strong bargaining position in many related industries. Even so, membership growth was slow between 1912 and 1930 (from only 84,000 to 98,800) but after 1935, it grew strongly reaching 441,600 in 1939 and 644,500 by 1945.

In 1955 the Teamsters had 1,291,100 members, the largest membership of any American labor union. Under presidents Dave Beck (1952-57) and James R. Hoffa (1957-71) (qq.v.), the Teamsters continued to expand into employment sectors which were related to transportation, such as cold storage, warehousing, baking, laundry work, and canning, despite the conviction of Beck and then Hoffa for corruption and other offenses. In 1957 the Teamsters were expelled from the AFL-CIO but were readmitted in November 1987. During the 1980s the leadership of the Teamsters backed Ronald Reagan (q.v.) for president but the reformed leadership which gained power in the late 1980s supported Bill Clinton's presidential campaign. The Teamsters claimed 1.4 million members in 1992. (*See also* David Beck, James Riddle Hoffa)

THAILAND   Unofficial organizations among Thai employees existed from the early 1880s. They conducted a number strikes to gain formal recognition, but this was not granted until 1932 and then only lasted until 1934. Legal recognition of unions was not restored until after the Japanese were expelled in 1944; it was withdrawn in 1948, restored in 1955, and revoked in 1958. Unions were again legally recognized between 1972 and 1976 but the military government which took power in October 1976 once again withdrew recognition. The bulk of union members in Thailand work in state-owned enterprises which have been vulnerable to changes in government policy, particularly privatization (q.v.). Following a campaign by the unions, the right to strike was restored in January 1981 but was withdrawn for those employees working in state-owned enterprises in April 1991 following the military coup on February 23, 1991. In June 1991 the president of the Labor Congress of Thailand (formed in 1978), Thanong Po-arn, disappeared and was presumed murdered. Between 1989 and 1991 the number of union members in Thailand dropped from 309,000 to 160,000. In 1993 there were 800 unions and twenty-six labor federations in Thailand.

THOMAS, ALBERT (1878-1932) French labor scholar, newspaper editor and politician, Thomas was the first director of the International Labour Organisation (ILO) (q.v.) between 1920 and 1932. During the early 1900s he carried out research in Germany, Russia, and the eastern Mediterranean into socialism, syndicalism, and consumer cooperatives (qq.v.) which he published in 1903. In 1904 he was made assistant editor of the socialist newspaper *L'Humanité*. In 1910 he was elected to the Chamber of Deputies for the Socialist Party, a position he held until 1921. In 1915 he became Under-Secretary of State for Artillery and Munitions and Minister for Munitions in 1916. In 1917 he was ambassador to Kerensky's government in Russia. As ILO director, he worked tirelessly for the adoption of its conventions by member countries in a very difficult political climate. (*See also* International Labour Organisation)

THOMPSON, EDWARD PALMER (1924-1993) One of Britain's leading Marxist historians, Thompson exerted considerable influence on the writing of the history of organized labor. As the author of *The Making of the Working Class*, first published in 1963 and made more widely available in paperback by Penguin Books in 1968, he was one of the founders of modern social history in English-speaking countries. Thompson examined English working class history "from below," that is, through the life-experiences of particular groups among the working-class between 1780 and 1830. This approach, although extraordinarily influential, has been criticized for not taking sufficient account of the role played by other groups in society.

"TOLPUDDLE MARTYRS"   The "Tolpuddle Martyrs" were a group of six English agricultural laborers who were convicted of unlawful oaths and conspiracy at the village of Tolpuddle in Dorset. Led by George Loveless (1797-1874), who was also a lay Methodist preacher, the six men seemed to have used an initiation ceremony in the process of setting up a union to seek higher wages. Their union may have been part of the expansion of the Grand National Consolidated Trades Union (q.v.). After a summary trial in March 1834, the six were convicted under conspiracy and mutiny laws of 1797 and 1819 and transported to New South Wales, Australia. It was only in 1838 that sustained protests gained the six a pardon. The incident was important for showing government hostility to unions and led to the dissolution of the Grand National Consolidated Trades Union. (*See also* Grand National Consolidated Trades Union)

TRADES UNION CONGRESS (TUC)   The TUC has been the largest national labor union organization in Britain since its formation in 1868. Its constitution provided the model for the Federation of Organized Trades and Labor Unions of the United States and Canada (q.v.) in 1881, the organization which was the forerunner to the American Federation of Labor (q.v.). In 1894 Samuel Gompers (q.v.) initiated an annual exchange of fraternal delegates between the American Federation of Labor and the TUC. The TUC played only a minor role in international labor unionism before 1913; this role was taken by the General Federation of Trade Unions (q.v.). Between 1868 and 1898 the number of members in unions affiliated with the TUC rose from 118,400 to 1,093,200. By 1914 most British unions were affiliated with the TUC. The TUC is essentially a policy-making body for its affiliates; it has no power to direct them although it acts as the national voice of organized labor in Britain. From 1871 it acted through its parliamentary committee as a lobby to government in the interests of labor. It also provided a national forum for delegates to debate policy matters at its annual congresses. In 1892 Keir Hardie (q.v.) was able to persuade the TUC to pass a motion calling on its parliamentary committee to draw up a scheme for a fund to pay for the direct representation of labor members of parliament. Nothing came of the proposal and it was not until a conference of the parliamentary committee (representing less than half of the TUC) in 1900 that Hardie succeeded in setting up the Labour Representation Committee, the body which became the British Labour Party (q.v.).

As organized labor grew, the TUC was drawn into adjudicating in disputes between its affiliates over which union had the right to recruit particular employees. In 1924 it drew up formal rules for the transfer of members between unions to avoid jurisdictional or demarcation conflicts. In 1939 these rules were codified into six principles known as the Bridlington Agreement. The operation of these procedures has been criticized as favoring larger over smaller unions. Under section 14 of the Trade Union Reform and Employment Rights Act 1993, the unions' power to exclude or expel employees was curtailed thus giving individuals greater choice about which union to join and so substantially reducing the power of the TUC in deciding on jurisdictional disputes between affiliates. In 1981 the membership of affiliates with the TUC reached its highest point of 12.2 million, but by 1992 this membership had fallen to 7.8 million or the level it had in 1950. Over the same period, the number of affiliated unions fell from 109 to 72. (*See also* James Keir Hardie, Ireland, United Kingdom)

TRANSPORT AND GENERAL WORKERS' UNION (TGWU) From 1937 to 1993 the TGWU was been Britain's largest labor union. Formed in January 1922 by the amalgamation of fourteen unions from various industries, it began with 350,000 members. In 1929 it absorbed the declining Workers' Union (q.v.) which gave it a recruiting foothold in industries which were to grow strongly in later years. In 1933 the TGWU had 371,000 members, which made it the second largest union in Britain after the Mineworkers' Federation of Great Britain (q.v.). By 1937 the TGWU had 654,500 members. Membership continued to rise from the 1930s: 984,000 by 1945, 1.3 million by 1956, and 2.1 million by 1979. Between 1922 and 1978, the TGWU absorbed eight-four smaller unions in a wide range of industries. In 1994 the TGWU had 914,000 members or 11 percent of all British labor union members. (*See also* Ernest Bevin, Workers' Union, UNISON)

TURKEY The first attempts to form labor unions in what is now Turkey began in 1871. Unions in a number of crafts were formed after the 1908 revolution but, faced with a well-organized right-wing government under Ataturk from 1920 and limited industrial development, a mass movement was unable to emerge. The first Turkish labor law was adopted in 1936 and set down minimum standards for employees at workplaces where ten or more worked but banned unions, strikes, and collective bargaining. Unions were legally permitted from 1947 and compulsory arbitration (q.v.) was introduced for labor disputes. The Confederation of Turkish Trade unions (*Türk-Is*) was formed in 1952. In 1963 new laws were brought in to regulate labor unions and to introduce a system of collective bargaining.

A left-wing labor federation, the Confederation of Progressive Trade Unions (DISK), was formed as a breakaway organization from *Türk-Is* in 1967 which had about 400,000 members by 1980. The deterioration in the economy during the 1970s led to a military coup in September 1980. The military government suppressed the DISK because of its militancy and leadership in labor disputes: 1,477 of its members were charged and 264 sentenced to varying jail terms in 1986. Several thousand others fled Turkey. The sentences were revoked in 1991. The military government also restored compulsory arbitration in labor disputes. In 1982 a new constitution was introduced which was the basis for revised labor laws that recognized labor unions (provided they restricted their activities to one sector of the economy and avoided any links with political parties) and reintroduced collective bargaining. Despite the repressive political and legal environment of Turkey and many international complaints about its human rights record, Turkey has continued to be an affiliate of the International Confederation of Free Trade Unions (q.v.). In 1991 there were 2,076,700 union members in Turkey, covering about 37 percent of eligible employees.

TWO-AND-A-HALF INTERNATIONAL (*See* International Working Union of Socialist Parties)

U

UNION-GOVERNMENT AGREEMENTS One of the features of relations between governments and unions since the 1960s has been efforts to enlist the support of unions in assisting economic growth. In Britain, Sweden, and the United States (qq.v.), governments experimented with freezes on wages in the 1960s and 1970s as means of controlling inflation; these schemes had mixed results. In 1974, for example, the British Labour Party and the Trades Union Congress (qq.v.) agreed to a Social Contract which provided for a range of economic and social reforms in return for voluntary wage restaint by the trade unions.

It became evident that such schemes had little chance of success without a high level of cooperation by organized labor which was difficult to achieve in inflationary periods. The acute economic difficulties of the late 1970s and early 1980s prompted governments in a number of countries to sign formal agreements with peak union organizations to achieve improved productivity, higher growth, and a range of other objectives. In September 1979 the AFL-CIO (q.v.) and the Carter administration reached a national accord under which the unions agreed to restrain wage claims in return for a package of economic and social measures, but the accord lapsed with Carter's defeat by Ronald Reagan (q.v.).

One of the most successful union-government agreements was made in Australia (q.v.). Named the Accord, it was formally agreed to between the Australian Labor Party (ALP) and the Australian Council of Trade Unions (ACTU) (qq.v.) regarding economic and social policy in February 1983. The Accord set out details of policies to be implemented when the ALP was elected to the federal government. It covered prices, wages and working conditions, nonwage incomes (for instance, earnings from dividends and interest), taxation, government expenditure, social security and health. The Accord grew out of conferences between the ALP and the ACTU in 1979 over new approaches to economic management. The Accord was renegotiated seven times, but ceased with the defeat of the ALP in the national elections of March 1996. The Accord has been credited with modest general increases in wages and lower levels of labor disputes (q.v.) since 1983.

In Spain (q.v.) a social and economic pact between the government and the noncommunist federation of unions (*Unión General de Trabajadores*) was agreed on in October 1984 but broke down after 1986. A accord between unions, the government and the employers was signed in Portugal in 1990 and was judged to have been a success in helping to modernize the economy and introduce social reforms; a new accord was signed in January 1996. Ireland (q.v.) has also experimented with union-government agreements. In 1987 the Irish Congress of Trade Unions suggested to the government that there should be a conference to produce a national plan for economic growth including pay and a range of social issues. Such a plan was produced; it was called the Programme for National Recovery. It operated for three years (1988-90) and was generally judged to have been a considerable success. It was replaced by a second and broader Programme, the Programme for Economic and Social Progress, in

April 1991. The third Programme, the Programme for Competitiveness and Work, was negotiated in April 1994 and was intended to run until 1997. Unlike the Australian Accord, these Programmes have included employers and have been negotiated with conservative governments. (*See also* Australia, Ireland)

UNION WAGE DIFFERENTIAL The union wage differential refers to the generally higher earnings of union members compared to employees who are not union members. This differential is one way of directly measuring the economic effects of unions. In the United States (q.v.), H. G. Lewis estimated that union members earned on average between 10 to 15 percent more than nonunion members between 1923 and 1929; this figure rose to about 25 percent for the period 1931-33 and fell to between 10 and 20 percent during 1939-41. Between 1945 and 1949 union members were estimated to earn only about 5 percent more than nonunion members. This gap widened to between 10 to 15 percent in 1957-58 and has continued to widen since. By 1995 the median earnings of full-time male employees who were union members was 14 percent above those employees who were not union members; for female full-time employees, the gap was even higher: 27 per cent.

In contrast, in Australia (q.v.), a country with a higher level of unionization than the United States, the union wage differential was much less though it has widened in recent years. In August 1995 Australian full-time male employees who were union members earned 8 percent more than nonunion members compared to 10 percent for females. The reasons why union members earn more than employees who are not union members include their tendency to work in larger enterprises (which usually pay higher wages than smaller ones) and in manufacturing or public sector industries. It has been suggested that the high union differential in the United States in the 1980s has contributed to the decline in the proportion of employees who were union members. (*See also* Table 15, Statistical Appendix)

UNISON UNISON, the shortened title of UNISON-The Public Service Union, was formed in the United Kingdom (q.v.) on July 1, 1993 from the merger of three white-collar unions, the Confederation of Health Service Employees, the National Union of Public Employees, and the National and Local Government Officers' Association (qq.v.). Negotiations for the merger began in 1978 but took on greater urgency with declining membership in the late 1980s. In 1994 UNISON claimed 1,369,000 members of whom 71 percent were women. It is the largest labor union in Britain and the largest public sector union in Western Europe. (*See also* Confederation of Health Service Employees, National and Local Government Officers' Association, National Union of Public Employees)

UNITED AUTO WORKERS' UNION (UAW) The UAW-the United Automobile, Aerospace, and Agricultural Implement Workers of America, International Union-has been one of the leading unions in the United States (q.v.) since the 1930s. The UAW grew out of the Carriage and Wagon Workers' International Union which was formed in the early 1900s. Because of the metalworking nature of the industry, the union became party to many jurisdictional disputes with other unions which led to the suspension of its charter by the American Federation of Labor (AFL) (q.v.) in 1918. The union was renamed the Automobile, Aircraft, and Vehicle Workers' Union of America; although its membership reached 40,000 in 1920, it collapsed during the 1920s.

Its revival in the 1930s occurred through the passage of the National Industrial Recovery Act (q.v.) in 1933 and the campaign by the AFL to recruit members in the auto industry. These efforts led to the formation of the National Council of Automobile Workers' Unions in 1934, but this did not satisfy the employees' demands for the AFL to charter an industrial union for the industry. The AFL issued a limited charter for the United Automobile Workers of America in 1935. As before 1918, the new union became embroiled in jurisdictional disputes with other unions. In 1936 it joined the Committee for Industrial Organization, the forerunner of the CIO (q.v.), a move which led to the revocation of its charter by the AFL in 1938. The UAW was boosted by the militancy of the employees in the auto industry and during 1937 led successful campaigns for recognition by General Motors and Chrysler, campaigns which raised membership to 478,500 by 1939. Recognition by Ford came after violence against union organizers in the "Battle of the Overpass" (1937) and pressure from the federal government in 1941. In 1946 the moderate leader Walter Reuther emerged as the winner from a long factional battle within the UAW and dominated the union until his death in 1970. In 1945 the UAW had 891,800 members making it briefly the largest union in the United States. Thereafter its membership reflected the fortunes of the automobile industry;

membership reached a peak of 1.3 million in 1955 but declined slowly after that time. In 1992 the UAW had 840,000 members. (*See also* "Battle of the Overpass," Congress of Industrial Organizations, Walter Philip Reuther)

UNITED KINGDOM Although covert organizations among employees are known to have existed throughout history, it was in eighteenth century England that organized labor in the form that it is most familiar today began to emerge. Between 1717 and 1800, 383 labor disputes (q.v.) are known to have occurred despite legal prohibitions on unions (called "combinations") and strikes. Most of the strikes and unions were organized by journeymen tailors and weavers. These actions led to the first efforts at large-scale industrial relations legislation (as opposed simply to the repression of unions and strikes). For instance, the Spitalfields Act (1773) provided for the statutory setting of wages and piece-rates; the level of wages could be proposed by a joint board of masters and journeymen.

From the late-eighteenth century onwards, organized labor was shaped by two great forces: the Industrial Revolution and the gradual growth of democracy in Britain. These two forces, particularly the indigenous development of the Industrial Revolution in Britain, meant that its organized labor assumed a different character from that of organized labor in other parts of Western Europe. Because of the Combination Acts (q.v.) of 1799 and 1800, unions often disguised their activities as those of friendly societies (q.v.). Although these acts were repealed in 1824, they were followed by amending legislation in 1825 which reintroduced the common law of conspiracy for certain union actions such as picketing.

Nevertheless, unions survived; indeed, the modern use of the word "union" was current in the ship and shipbuilding trades by the mid-1820s. In 1826 a union was formed by Manchester engineers which was the ancestor of the Amalgamated Society of Engineers (q.v.). In 1827 carpenters and joiners formed a union. Better communications, especially the introduction of a national postal service and the expansion of the railroads, assisted with the creation of national labor bodies. In 1842 the Miners' Association of Great Britain and Ireland (q.v.) was formed; it claimed 70,000 members but had collapsed by 1848. In his investigations into the social condition of London in the 1850s, Henry Mayhew estimated that only about 10 percent of skilled trades were members of unions (which he called "societies").

Significantly, he noted that the union men were paid for their work on the basis of custom and that the nonunion men were paid by market rates. According to the first directory of British labor unions, there were 290 unions in London in 1861.

Organized labor had also begun to play some role in the political system even though the restrictive franchise and the absence of payment of members of parliament limited its activities to lobbying and supporting occasional union officials as parliamentary candidates. In 1859 the National Association of United Trades for the Protection of Labour (q.v.) secured the Molestation of Workmen Act which freed "peaceful" picketing from common law actions. In 1851 the Amalgamated Society of Engineers was formed and it was followed by the formation of the Amalgamated Society of Carpenters and Joiners (q.v.) in 1860. Both unions were distinctive in founding branches in other countries. Another important development was the creation of federations of unions (trades councils) in the cities and large towns; the London Trades Council was formed in 1860.

The 1860s were a formative period in shaping British unionism. Its relative success and moderate behavior attracted favorable interest and comment from French and German visitors. In 1867 the Second Reform Act gave the vote to the better-off urban working class who made up the bulk of union members at the time. In 1868 the Trades Union Congress (TUC) (q.v.) was formed; it became the largest labor federation in Britain and was used as the model for the Federation of Organized Trades and Labor Unions of the United States and Canada (q.v.) in 1881.

Before 1870 union membership was largely confined to skilled urban workers and to industries which relied for their labor on large, long-established working-class communities such as mining and textiles. In the comparatively prosperous early 1870s other groups of employees formed unions: railroad employees (1871), gas workers, agricultural laborers, longshoremen, and builders' laborers (1872). The depression of the late 1870s reduced union numbers but, they rose again with the return of better conditions in the 1880s. The number of union members affiliated with the TUC rose from 289,000 in 1870 to 464,000 in 1880 and to 581,000 by 1886. As not all unions were affiliated with the TUC, these figures underestimate the real level of union membership. During the 1890s the number of union members doubled from 1 to 2 million. The 1890s also saw the rise of a regional consciousness within Britain as shown by the formation of the Irish Trades Union Congress in 1894 and the Scottish Trades Union

Congress in 1897.

The ability of British organized labor to work within the political system through the Liberal Party reduced the imperative for it to form a separate political party despite pressure from its left-wing led by James Keir Hardie (q.v.). It took the Taff Vale Case (q.v.) in 1901 to transform the Labour Representation Committee into the Labour Party (q.v.) in 1906. Despite the legal uncertainties created by the Taff Vale Case and the Osbourne Judgement (q.v.) in 1906, the number of union members grew from 2 to 4.1 million between 1900 and 1913. As well, the Labour Party increased in support and political experience. During World War I the demands of total war led to governments coopting the support of organized labor as also occurred in France, the United States, and Germany. In Britain, members of the Labour Party were included in the cabinet for the first time in 1915. In 1917 Whitley councils, made up of representatives from unions and management ,were set up in a number of industries. One unintended consequence of the Whitley councils was the promotion of unionism among employees of the national government. Between 1913 and 1920 the number of union members who were national government employees rose from 20,800 to 136,200.

In 1920, largely as a result of official encouragement of organized labor during World War I, union membership reached 8.3 million or 48 percent of employees. Other aspects of this growth were an increase in white-collar unionists (who made up 15 percent of total union members by 1920) and the growth in the proportion of women labor union members (from 11 to 16 percent between 1913 and 1920). These changes reflected the rise in the number of public sector union members (whose numbers rose from 394,100 in 1913 to 854,900 in 1920).

The generally depressed economic conditions of the 1920s gave rise to high levels of unemployment which sapped union strength. There was a lock-out by engineering employers in 1922, the first since 1897-98, which forced a wage cut on the industry. The return to the gold standard increased the price of British exports and encouraged employers to reduce wages in order to compete, steps which added to labor unrest and erupted in the disastrous General Strike (q.v.) of 1926. Persistent high unemployment for the rest of the 1920s cut union membership to 4.8 million by 1930 and lowered its coverage rate to 26 percent of employees. The main positive developments of the 1920s among the unions were the formation of the Transport and

General Workers' Union (q.v.) in 1922 and the decision of the Amalgamated Engineering Union (q.v.) to admit lesser skilled employees as members in 1926. After the severe depression of the early 1930s union membership began to grow again to reach 6.6 million by 1940.

During World War II, as in World War I, there was a resurgence of organized labor with the coopting of both the Labour Party and the unions into the government and in the management of the economy. At the end of the war in 1945, union membership had grown to 7.8 million. As in other Western countries, organized labor in Britain had to expend some of its energy on resisting communist influence in a number of key unions. The World Federation of Trade Unions (q.v.) was set up in London in 1945, but its promise of a united global labor movement was dashed by its infiltration by the Soviet Union, a development which led organized labor in Britain, the United States, and other countries to form the International Confederation of Free Trade Unions (q.v.) in 1949. Within Britain, union membership in the 1950s was stable: in 1960 44 percent of employees were union members (the same level as in 1950) and 74 percent worked in blue-collar jobs. The importance of organized labor in the management of the postwar economy was recognized by governments, but their experiments with wage restraint schemes from 1948 to 1950 and from 1951 to 1964 did not attract general union cooperation. The Wilson (Labour) government, which was elected in 1964, was able to secure the participation of the unions in the Prices and Incomes Board, but its efforts to raise productivity were disappointing.

In the mid-1960s the unions were the subject of close scrutiny by the Donovan Commission (q.v.) which presented its report in 1968. But the voluntary approach advocated by the Donovan Commission was swept aside by official concern over Britain's poor economic performance and by frustration over unofficial labor disputes. Both the Conservatives (1968) and the Labour Party (1969) published policy papers which suggested ballots before unions could conduct strikes.

In 1979 organized labor in Britain claimed its highest ever membership-13.4 million-but this high-water mark was not maintained for long. Since 1980 the British labor movement has been a case study of the "decline of labor" caused by a mixture of economic and political forces. The recession of the early 1980s drastically cut employment in the older parts of manufacturing such as steelmaking and shipbuilding, industries which were strongholds of organized labor. Union membership figures from the Certification Office of Trade Unions and Employers' Associations show a fall of 3.7 million between 1980 and 1991 of which nearly 2.5 million occurred between 1980 and 1985. When considered annually, these falls corresponded closely to falls in manufacturing employment.

The decline was not offset by the growth in services employment because of the diversity of this employment and its often part-time or casual nature which made union recruitment difficult. Neither did the unions show an understanding of the need for recruiting drives in these new areas of employment. The 1980s were also notable for the continued decline in the number of small unions which were usually absorbed by larger ones. From a peak of 1,384 unions in 1920, the number of unions fell to 453 by 1979 and to 254 by 1993. The most important union amalgamations in the early 1990s were those between the Amalgamated Engineering Union and the Electrical Electronic Telecommunication and Plumbing Union in 1992 and the creation of UNISON (q.v.) from the merger of three public sector unions in 1993.

The defeat of the Labour government in 1979 and the victory of the Conservatives under Margaret Thatcher also signalled a radical change for the worse in the political and legal climate for organized labor. The process of consultation between the national government and the TUC which had begun during World War I and had accelerated during and after World War II was abruptly brought to a halt. The Thatcher government also introduced a number of Employment Acts (q.v.) from 1980 which aimed at restricting closed shops, picketing, and strikes without a ballot of members. The government also showed a determination to win confrontations with unions, a policy which was made plain by its defeat of the twelve-months coal miners' strike in 1984-85. In 1995 a government household survey found that union membership had fallen to 7.3 million compared to 9 million in 1989 when the survey was first conducted and that the proportion of employees who were union members had fallen from 39 to 32 percent. (*See also* Trade Union Congress)

UNITED MINE WORKERS OF AMERICA (UMWA) From the mid-1900s to 1939, the UMWA was the largest labor union in the United States (q.v.). As in Britain, the home of many of the first generation of U.S. coal miners, organization among miners began at a regional level. A Miners' Association was formed in St. Clair County, Illinois, in 1861; it became the American Miners's Association in 1863 by which time it had spread to the coalfields of Missouri, Ohio, and Pennsylvania. Its success proved short-lived; although it claimed 20,000 members, it had largely collapsed by 1866. Unionism was revived in the late 1870s by the miners of the Hocking Valley, Ohio, who formed a new union in 1882. In 1883 the Amalgamated Association of Miners of the United States was formed based largely on the coalfields of Ohio and Pennsylvania. A new body, the National Federation of Miners and Mine Laborers, was formed in Indianapolis in 1885. In 1886 the Knights of Labor (q.v.) formed a second national miners' union, the Miner and Mine Laborers' National District Assembly No. 135. To avoid competition between the two bodies, a joint conference agreed to the organization of the National Progressive Union of Miners and Mine Laborers, but the Knights of Labor body continued to operate more or less independently.

Finally, in January 1890 the National Progressive Union of Miners and Mine Laborers was reformed as the United Mine Workers of America and was recognized by the American Federation of Labor (AFL) (q.v.). Major defeats in strikes and the economic depression of the 1890s reduced the UMWA to only 10,000 members in the mid-1890s but an unexpectedly successful general strike (q.v.) in the bituminous coal mining industry in 1898 (which gained its participants a standard wage and the eight-hour work day) boosted membership from 97,000 in 1898 to 250,100 by 1904. The UMWA's leader, John Mitchell (q.v.), used the victory to organize the miners on the anthracite coalfields of western Pennsylvania. In 1902 the UMWA won a famous victory in its strike on the anthracite coalfields after the personal intervention of President Theodore Roosevelt.

Despite the failure to organize the miners of West Virginia and elsewhere, the membership of the UMWA grew to nearly 4 million by 1920 when the controversial John L. Lewis (q.v.) became its president, an office he held until 1960. Under Lewis, the UMWA became a far more centralized body and played a notable role in labor politics, notably through the formation of the Congress of Industrial Organizations (q.v.). When it withdrew from the AFL in 1947, it followed an independent path.

Lewis's leadership and the diminished importance of coal as an energy source reduced the membership of the UMWA to 213,100 by 1973 compared to its peak of 500,000 in 1945. In 1989 the UMWA claimed a membership of 150,000. (*See also* Coal Mining, Congress of Industrial Organizations, John L. Lewis, John Mitchell, Mineworkers' Federation of Great Britain)

UNITED STATES OF AMERICA Organized labor in the United States emerged in the late-eighteenth century but was largely confined to Philadelphia and New York. British immigration (q.v.) injected journeymen and their working habits and attitudes into the colonial economy. A register of emigrants to North America compiled between 1773 and 1776 showed that, of the 6,190 emigrants whose occupations were known, 49 percent were artisans, mechanics, or craftsmen. During the 1780s journeymen and their employers in Philadelphia began to meet annually to negotiate their wages. The first strike in a single trade (printing, 1786) and in the building trade (1791) also occurred in Philadelphia. The first formal labor union likewise was formed in Philadelphia in 1794 by cordwainers or shoemakers. The union lasted until 1806 when it was made defunct by an adverse court decision. What little union growth there was after 1806 was destroyed by the depression of 1819. Unions began to reappear in 1822. In 1827 the first citywide federation of unions was formed at Philadelphia. This, and other federations, were the basis of the twelve Workingmen's political parties which operated in the late 1820s and early 1830s. The General Trades Union (q.v.) was formed in New York in 1833. Despite these activities, union membership was small; there were only about 44,000 in 1835 and in the financial crash of 1837 organized labor collapsed.

In 1864 there were 270 unions with a total membership of about 200,000. The growth of industrialization after the Civil War accentuated the worst features of the capitalist economy that had been previously evident, namely long hours and low wages. Old skills became obsolete and the general trend of economic development reduced opportunities for self-employment and independence. Agriculture no longer offered the escape valve it had before the Civil War. In addition, mass immigration kept the wages of the unskilled low in the major cities. In 1869 the National Labor Union (q.v.) was formed but was unable to provide leadership for labor either politically or industrially. In any case, organized labor suffered greatly following the financial crisis of 1873 which reduced the number of national unions from thirty to nine by 1877 and the number of union members from 300,000 to about 50,000. Although organized labor was weak in the late 1870s, there was no shortage of discontent as proved by the massive violent national railroad strikes in 1877 or of labor activity as shown by the conversion of the Knights of Labor (q.v.) into a national body and the formation of the International Labor Union (q.v.) in 1878.

The 1880s saw the emergence of mass unionism in the United States for the first time; there were over a million union members by 1886, mainly members of the Knights of Labor, but this success disguised serious weaknesses. What successes labor achieved were through the cooperation of union members in skilled occupations but, without this support, the unskilled union members could achieve little. Moreover, much of the membership was new to unionism and its discontent over wages and hours of work applied to immigrants in the large cities. This, and the association of labor with violent protests, made it possible for organized labor to be portrayed as something foreign and outside of mainstream American society which still had strong agricultural roots.

The demise of the Knights of Labor in the 1890s and the relative success of the better-paid employees represented by the craft unions of the American Federation of Labor (AFL) (q.v.) also reinforced, as well as reflected, the far wider dispersal in earnings between the skilled and unskilled compared to the United Kingdom. The barriers to organized labor achieving the fairly high coverage of nonagricultural employees that prevailed in Western Europe and Australasia by 1913 were formidable. They included enormous racial and ethnic divisions, a generally hostile legal environment, and strong, well-organized employers. The AFL added to these barriers by its unwillingness to build a mass union movement among the unskilled, leaving the task to alternative bodies such as the Industrial Workers of the World (q.v.) and the Congress of Industrial Organizations (q.v.) in the 1930s.

But it was in its attitude to politics that American organized labor showed its greatest distinctiveness from the labor movements of other Western nations. In Western Europe and Australasia, labor unions by 1900 were closely associated with social democrat or socialist political parties. In the United States this kind of permanent relationship did not exist (though this is not to say that the AFL did not participate in the political process). The AFL's leadership regarded these relationships with intense suspicion and developed its own peculiar conservative ideology of voluntarism (q.v.) which put it at odds with bodies such as the International Federation of Trade Unions (q.v.). By 1930 only 9 percent of American employees were union members or the same level that had been reached in 1913.

The election of the Roosevelt administration in 1933 and its pro-labor stance, as shown by its National Labor Relations Act (q.v.), enabled the emergence of the Congress of Industrial Organizations

(CIO) (q.v.) and its recruitment of millions of semi-skilled employees into the ranks of organized labor. It was the main reason for raising the proportion of employees in unions to 28 percent by 1950, a good result for American labor but a low figure by Western European and Australasian standards. The proportion of American employees who were union members peaked at 32 percent in 1953 but declined steadily thereafter. The public reputation of organized labor suffered in the 1950s and 1960s with well-publicized inquiries into corruption within certain unions, notably the Teamsters (q.v.). As in other Western economies, the impact of technological change whittled away at the parts of the labor force where labor was traditionally strong such as coal mining (q.v.), steel, printing, (q.v.) and the railroads (q.v.). At the same time, the labor force saw a general shift towards white-collar employment and a rising number of women employees. Union recruitment of new members was also hampered by right-to-work laws (q.v.) in many states.

Politically, organized labor was just one interest group among many; since 1936 it had been allied with the Democratic Party but this alliance has not protected it from anti-labor forces within the party. Among reformers organized labor also suffered from its conservative posture, particularly its slowness in dealing with racial discrimination. From 1980 organized labor in the United States, as in other countries, entered a prolonged crisis which was epitomized by severe slumps in steelmaking and automobile manufacturing, industries characterized by outmoded production methods. It also faced a hostile political climate under the presidency of Ronald Reagan (q.v.). Between 1983 and 1995, the proportion of employees who were union members fell from 20 to 15 percent. (*See also* American Federation of Labor, Knights of Labor, Congress of Industrial Organizations, Samuel Gompers)

UNITED STEELWORKERS OF AMERICA (USWA)   The steel industry of the United States (q.v.) was a mainly nonunion industry during its formative period in the first thirty-five years of the twentieth century. The first union was formed by skilled British puddlers in Pittsburgh in 1857. They were joined by the formation of a union among skilled workers in the furnaces and rolling mills in 1861. A united industry union of skilled workers, the Amalgamated Association of Iron and Steel Workers of the United States, was formed in Pittsburgh in 1876. By 1891 this union claimed 24,068 members, but in 1892 it suffered a crushing defeat in a strike to resist wage cuts by the Carnegie Steel Company at Homestead, Pennsylvania. In the following years, the association proved incapable of meeting the enormous managerial and technological changes which came into steelmaking in the 1890s and 1900s. In particular, the unions faced a general de-skilling of jobs which greatly reduced their bargaining power. Lesser skilled jobs meant that wages could be kept low and that immigrants could be easily recruited. In 1909 the largest steel company, the United States Steel Company, refused to recognize the association and defeated it in a strike. The company was able to maintain a union-free labor force until 1937. By 1912 the United States steelmaking industry was a byword for high productivity but with low wages and long working hours. Discontent among its employees led to the great strike of 1919 which was organized by the American Federation of Labor (AFL) (q.v.) through its Iron and Steel Organizing Committee. Despite 300,000 taking part, the strike ended after three and a half months on January 8, 1920 in the utter defeat of the strikers.

The National Industrial Recovery Act (q.v.) of 1933 laid the foundation for a revival of unionism in the steel industry. In 1934 the AFL began a campaign to recruit union members in the steel industry but these efforts were frustrated by the amalgamated's leadership, which wanted its almost defunct union to lead the campaign, and was then swept aside in 1936 by the Congress of Industrial Organizations (CIO) (q.v.) which launched its own campaign to unionize the industry. Led by Philip Murray on behalf of John L. Lewis (qq.v.), the aim of the campaign was to build an industrial union for the steel industry and to increase the bargaining power of the United Mine Workers of America (q.v.) in negotiating with steel companies which owned coal mines. The CIO recruited 200,000 steelworkers for the Steel Workers' Organizing Committee and in secret discussions Lewis secured not only recognition for the Committee from U.S. Steel in March 1937 but also a 10 percent wage increase, an eight-hour work day, and a 40-hour work week. However, the CIO's campaign against the independent steel producers was defeated by violence and a downturn in the demand for steel. Ten strikers were killed and eighty wounded by police at the steelworks of the Republic Steel Company in South Chicago in May 1937.

In 1942 the Steel Workers' Organizing Committee was reorganized as the United Steelworkers of America and was forced to use the National War Labor Board to compel the independent steel producers to engage in collective bargaining. Murray led the USWA from its formation to his death in 1952. In 1946 the USWA conducted a month-long strike throughout the industry which yielded it a large pay increase. Through strikes in 1949 and 1952 and bargaining, the USWA gained the closed or union shop and a pension scheme for members. Defeat in the strike of 1959 against management's attempt to change work rules and a downturn in the national economy caused the USWA's membership to fall from 1.2 million in 1956 to 876,000 in 1965. By 1975 membership had recovered to the 1 million mark, but the worldwide crisis in the steel industry in 1982-83 caused membership to fall to 572,000 by 1985. In 1992 the USWA had only 459,000 members. (*See also* Homestead Labor Dispute, John Llewellyn Lewis, Philip Murray)

UNIVERSAL ALLIANCE OF DIAMOND WORKERS (UADW)
The UADW International Trade Secretariat (q.v.) was formed in Antwerp in 1905, although international conferences among diamond employees began in 1889. By 1913 the UADW had 22,700 members. Between 1975 and 1992 membership of the UADW was stationary at about 10,000. The UADW was one of sixteen International Trade Secretariats associated with the International Confederation of Free Trade Unions (q.v.) in 1995. (*See also* International Trade Secretariats)

V

VIETNAM Organized labor in Vietnam originated in the participation by some Vietnamese intellectuals in labor affairs in France (q.v.) during World War I. Using this experience, they set up some unions in Vietnam (then French Indochina) beginning in Hanoi in 1920. Most labor organizing thereafter was carried out by communists. In 1929 the communists formed a labor federation as part of the struggle for independence from French rule. By 1930 the federation claimed 6,000 members, but it was crushed in 1930-31 during a major peasant uprising against the French. Despite a new labor code and more toleration of labor organizations in the Popular Front period (1936-39), these initiatives proved short-lived in the face of widespread discontent in Vietnam, the fall of the Blum government in France and the start of World War II. During the war, Vietnam was occupied by the Japanese.

In 1946 the North Vietnamese government set up the Vietnamese Confederation of Labor Unions on the Soviet model. In what was South Vietnam, the French Catholic labor federation, the *Confédération Française des Travailleurs Chrétiens*, was instrumental in forming the *Confédération Vietnamienne du Travail* (Vietnamese Confederation of Labor) which was based on unions among rice growers and employees in river transportation and later claimed 500,000 members. Two other labor federations were formed in 1952 and 1953, but they never had more than 70,000 members between them. After the military reunification of Vietnam, the Vietnam General Federation of Labor Unions was created in June 1975 which subsumed the labor organizations of the South.

With the opening up of the Vietnamese economy to foreign investment and enterprises in the late 1980s, there was widespread exploitation manifested in long hours, low pay, and physical abuse. The federation, with assistance provided by the Australian chapter of the International Labour Organisation (q.v.), persuaded the National Assembly at the end of June 1994 to approve a new labor code. The code obliged every foreign joint venture to establish a trade union within six months of beginning operations, allowed the employees of such enterprises the right to strike, set up independent courts of conciliation and arbitration (q.v.), protected these employees from wrongful dismissal, and required retrenched employees to be paid severance pay. The first legal strike under the code occurred in August 1994. (*See also* France)

VOLUNTARISM Voluntarism is a term with two meanings. In the United States (q.v.), it referred to a doctrine subscribed to by the American Federation of Labor (AFL) (q.v.) from the late 1890s to the early 1930s which stressed the need for organized labor to rely on its own resources for gaining improvement of pay and conditions and not on political parties. Voluntarism saw a separation between the political process and organized labor though the doctrine did not exclude lobbying political parties for favors. Voluntarism was strengthened within the AFL after its crushing failure to organize the steel industry in 1919. The doctrine suited workers in skilled unions which could provide welfare benefits to members but ignored the lesser skilled employees.

In the United Kingdom (q.v.), the term voluntarism usually refers to the abstaining by the state from intervention in labor relations, particularly labor disputes (q.v.), except to support or extend collective bargaining. For example, the Advisory Conciliation and Arbitration Service, the British government agency which was established in 1974 to resolve labor disputes, can only operate if the parties to the dispute agree to its participation. Since 1980 British governments have shown a greater willingness to intervene in labor relations and have passed laws to regulate their internal management and behavior. (*See also* American Federation of Labor, Employment Acts)

W

WAGES Wages, together with working hours, have traditionally been central topics for organized labor in collective bargaining (q.v.) with employers. Although the amount of wages was usually of most concern, the method and timing of payment also figured as issues in the nineteenth century. Payment in goods instead of money (or "truck") was widespread in the United Kingdom (q.v.) in the early-nineteenth century even though it was outlawed as early as 1701. Similarly, the common practice of monthly payment of wages imposed undue hardship on employees and forced them into debt to meet day-to-day living costs. The ability of organized labor to raise wages largely depends on the condition of the trade cycle. One area of wages where organized labor has been traditionally most active is in maintaining the differentials between wages in occupations by means of margins such as for skill or seniority. With the generally higher level of union strength between 1940 and 1980 in most Western countries, organized labor has sought to use economic growth to extend wages claims to cover holidays, severance, and redundancy. It has also tried to use increased productivity as a means of raising wages. The importance of unions in economic management, particularly to control inflation, was recognized by government through various experiments in prices and incomes policies in the United Kingdom and the United States (qq.v.) in the 1970s which attempted to limit general increases in wages. (*See also* Shorter Working Hours, Union-Government Agreements)

WAGNER ACT Officially known as the National Labor Relations Act, this American federal law, named for its promoter, Senator Robert F. Wagner, was passed by the Senate eleven days before the National Industrial Recovery Act (1933) was declared unconstitutional by the Supreme Court. The Wagner Act reaffirmed the legal right of organized labor to recruit and represent employees in collective bargaining without interference from employers. A National Labor Relations Board was created to administer the act. The scope of the act was amended by the Taft-Hartley Act in 1947. (*See also* National Labor Relations Act, Taft-Hartley Act)

WEBB, BEATRICE (1858-1943) AND WEBB, SIDNEY JAMES (1859-1947)   Married in 1892, the Webbs created one of the most productive working partnerships in modern British intellectual history. Committed Fabians, their contribution to the scholarship of organized labor was enormous and included *The History of Trade Unionism* (1894), *Industrial Democracy* (1897), and *The Consumers' Cooperative Movement* (1921). *The History of Trade Unionism* was revised in 1920 and exerted a major influence, particularly in encouraging an institutional approach to labor unions. They defined a labor union as a "continuous association of wage earners for the purpose of maintaining or improving their conditions of employment," a definition that has been criticized for neglecting the role of noncontinuous labor bodies in the history of organized labor.

Sidney Webb, a lawyer by training and gifted with a remarkable memory, was an adviser to organized labor during World War I, and he greatly assisted the Miners' Federation of Great Britain (q.v.) before the Royal Commission on the Coal Mines in 1918. He served three terms as a Labour member of parliament in the 1920s.

WHITE-COLLAR UNIONISM   Up to the 1950s white-collar employees were a minor part of organized labor in most Western countries with unions of manual employees being the dominant force. Not only that, manual unions tended to regard white-collar unions poorly because their members did not perform "real" work. Typically, white-collar occupations included teachers, salaried government workers, and clerks in all industries. For most of history, distinctions of social class underlay manual and white-collar work. Manual workers were, by general definition, the working class whereas white-collar employees came from the middle class and often saw themselves as socially superior. In Germany (q.v.), federal laws from 1911 even recognized a "collar line" which treated white-collar workers better than blue-collar or manual workers. As members of the middle class, white-collar employees were less likely to join unions, particularly if they enjoyed advantageous conditions by their employers.

Although lacking the stature of manual unions within organized labor, unions of white-collar employees have a long history. In the United States (q.v.), the first white-collar unions emerged among retail clerks in the 1830s who wanted employers to adopt a standard early closing time; in 1864 dry goods employees in New York went on strike to prevent the imposition of longer hours. In the United Kingdom (q.v.), the first white-collar unions were formed among teachers in the 1860s as a result of school managers being given the right to appoint and dismiss teachers. Yet it was not until the 1880s that sustained growth in the number of white-collar unions occurred. In the United States, the first national white-collar union, the Retail Clerks' National Protective Association, joined the American Federation of Labor (q.v.) in 1888. In the United Kindom, white-collar unions were formed among national government clerks (1890) and postal workers (1891).

As the economies of Western nations matured, the tertiary sector (that is, those parts of the economy which were not in agriculture, mining, or manufacturing) grew and with it the number of white-collar employees. Between about 1910 and 1930, the proportion of white-collar employees in the labor forces of the United States, Germany, and Britain rose from about 13 to about 20 percent. Within organized labor in Britain, Denmark, and Germany, a fifth of labor union members were white-collar employees by 1930. After 1950 white-collar unions grew with the growth in public sector employment, particularly as government was more likely to concede recognition to unions than the private sector. At the same time, manual occupations grew relatively slowly. During the 1960s white-collar employees became more willing to join unions. By 1991 over 40 percent of union members in Britain and the United States were white-collar employees and, in both countries, white-collar unions were the largest single unions. (*See also* Education, Federation of International Civil Servants' Associations, National Educational Association, UNISON, Women)

WOMEN One of the biggest changes in the post-1950 structure of union membership has been the rising proportion of women. In 1913 women made up only 11 percent of labor union members in Britain, 8 percent in Germany, and 4 percent in Australia and the United States. By 1950 women made up 18 percent of labor union members in Britain and Germany, 19 percent in Australia, and 23 percent in Japan. The entry of women into the labor force gathered pace after

1960 both in numbers and in the proportion of women working, making them more liable to be recruited by the largely male-dominated labor unions. Increasingly, women moved into the expanding white-collar occupations and were no longer just to be found in low-paid manufacturing occupations such as in the clothing industry. Between 1970 and 1990 the International Confederation of Free Trade Unions (q.v.) estimated that the proportion of women members among its affiliates rose from 22 to 34 percent. In 1994 the proportion of women in labor unions was: 44 percent in Britain, 40 percent in Australia and 40 percent in the United States or about double what it had been in 1960. In contrast, the proportion of women in labor unions in Germany and Japan changed very little over this period. (*See also* Table 11, Statistical Appendix, White-Collar Unionism)

WORKERS' UNION (WU) The WU was one of the largest general unions in Britain in the early-twentieth century. Formed in May 1898, it set out to recruit all employees whether skilled or unskilled and, through militancy, work towards the creation of a socialist society. The WU was formed in the wake of the major defeat suffered by the Amalgamated Society of Engineers (q.v.) in London in 1897 by the leading labor left-wing leader Tom Mann (q.v.). The new union barely survived its first few years: membership reached 2,000 by the end of 1898, 4,170 by 1899, but fell to 1,000 by 1902. With the recovery in the economy after 1906, membership rose to 91,000 in 1913 and to 140,000 by 1914. Much of this growth was achieved through the recruitment of poorly paid employees, particularly in engineering and agriculture. By 1918 membership reached a peak of 379,000, a quarter of them women. Although the WU affiliated with the Trades Union Congress (q.v.) in 1917 (after two failed attempts), it was disliked by a number of other unions such as the Agricultural Labourers' Union and especially the Amalgamated Engineers as a competitor for members. In 1916 the WU began negotiations for amalgamation (q.v.) with the National Amalgamated Union of Labour (q.v.) and the Municipal Employees' Association which resulted in the formation of a new but only partly amalgamated organization, the National Amalgamated Workers' Union in January 1919; this body claimed 500,000 members in 1920. Thereafter, membership of the WU plummeted to 140,000 in 1923 through economic depression, high turnover of members, and hostility from other unions. The WU never recovered and in 1929 was absorbed into the Transport and

General Workers' Union (TGWU) (q.v.), but the WU gave the TGWU an organizational foothold in a number of industries whose employment growth helped it to become Britain's largest union by the late 1930s. (*See also* Transport and General Workers' Union)

WORKING HOURS   Although there are few statistics on working hours before the Industrial Revolution, there is an impression that working hours, although long, were more varied before it than after it. Where work was monotonous, customs like "Saint Monday" (q.v.) were observed by the eighteenth century. Figures for the Amalgamated Society of Engineers (q.v.) in England show that the number of hours its members worked in a week varied from 57 to 63 in 1851 and from 56 to 60 by 1869. In Germany, the typical work week in manufacturing was 78 hours in the 1860s, 66 hours in the 1870s, and between 58 and 60 hours between 1911 and 1914. The long, monotonous week brought by the Industrial Revolution made the reduction of work hours an important issue for organized labor in Europe and North America.

The Ten Hours movement began with textile employees in England in the 1830s, and the short-lived radical body, the National Regeneration Society (1833-34), advocated an eight-hour work day. In Australia, James Stephens (1821-1889), an English Chartist, played an important role in winning the eight-hour work day in a number of skilled trades in Victoria in the mid-1850s. In 1869 the National Labor Union (q.v.) succeeded in gaining the eight-hour work day for American federal employees. In 1871-72 engineering and building employees in northeast England won the nine-hour work day through strikes. Yet most governments before 1900 avoided legislating for maximum work hours. The English Factory Act of 1875 laid down a maximum work week of 56.5 hours for women and teenagers but ignored men. In the 1880s and early 1890s there was international agitation for the eight-hour work day by organized labor. British railroad employees did not get the eight-hour work day until 1920 and then only after a national strike in 1919. Since 1945 metal unions have been at the forefront of reducing work hours in Australia, Germany and the United Kingdom. (*See also* Knights of Labor, *IG Metall*)

WORLD CONFEDERATION OF LABOR (WCL)   The WCL began as the International Federation of Christian Trade Unions (IFCTU) which was formed in the Hague in 1920. In turn, the origins of the

IFCTU lay in the Ghent Anti-Socialist League set up in 1878. The IFCTU represented labor unions which objected to the anti-clericalism of the socialist and anarchist labor unions which dominated European organized labor. The entry of the IFCTU into the International Confederation of Free Trade Unions (q.v.) was opposed by socialist labor unions in Western Europe, and the IFCTU turned its attention to the Third World and recruiting affiliates from Muslim and Buddhist countries. The main criterion of membership was belief in a religion rather than adherence to Christianity. In 1968 the IFCTU changed its name to the World Confederation of Labor. In 1992 it claimed 19 million members compared to 14.5 million in 1973. (See also International Confederation of Free Trade Unions)

WORLD CONFEDERATION OF ORGANIZATIONS OF THE TEACHING PROFESSION (WCOPT) The WCOPT was made up of two federations, the International Federation of Teachers' Associations and the International Federation of Secondary Teachers from its foundation in 1952 until February 1993 when it agreed to merge with the International Federation of Free Teaching Unions (q.v.). Claiming to be an independent, non-political body, the WCOPT had 13 million members in 191 countries at the announcement of its merger. (*See also* International Trade Secretariats)

WORLD FEDERATION OF TRADE UNIONS (WFTU) The WFTU was formed in Paris on 25 September 1945 at an international conference of labor organizations as a replacement for the International Federation of Trade Unions (q.v.). The WFTU was ruptured by the Cold War and communist opposition to the Marshall Plan. In December 1949 the non-communist countries withdrew from the WFTU and set up their own international labor organization, the International Confederation of Free Trade Unions (ICFTU) (q.v.). The WFTU held its 12th congress in Moscow in November 1991 where it claimed 214 million members in 81 countries. (*See also* International Congress of Free Trade Unions)

Y

YELLOW DOG CONTRACTS One of the means by which English employers defeated the Grand United Council of Trade Unions (q.v.) in 1834 was by requiring employees to sign "The Document" by which they would give an undertaking to leave a union and not join another one. In the United States (q.v.), this measure was known as a yellow dog contract, from "yellow dog" meaning a contemptible person. In the 1890s yellow dog contracts which forbade union membership became more common. In 1898 section 10 of the Erdman Act outlawed such contracts but this section was declared unconstitutional by the Supreme Court in 1908 in *Adair v. United States*, thereby increasing their use by employers as an anti-union measure in their general campaign against organized labor. The Kansas legislature outlawed yellow dog contracts, but its legislation was declared invalid by the Supreme Court in 1915. In 1917 the Supreme Court again defended the use of yellow dog contracts in *Hitchman Coal and Coke v. Mitchell*. A change in the legal climate was signalled in 1927 when the Court of Appeals of New York State found that a yellow dog contract was binding neither on the signer nor on the union. The use of yellow dog contracts was outlawed by the Anti-Injunction (Norris-LaGuardia) Act in 1932 and subsequent cases were dealt with by the National Relations Labor Board. (*See also* Norris-LaGuardia Act)

YUGOSLAVIA The former federal republic of Yugoslavia was created in 1918 from part of the Austro-Hungarian Empire and lasted until 1991 when it was torn apart by a murderous civil war. Within the borders of the former republic, organized labor first emerged in the form of mutual aid societies in the 1870s. The first labor unions were formed in 1894 in Slovenia, in 1904 in Croatia and Serbia, and in 1905 in Bosnia-Herzegovina, Macedonia, and Montenegro. In 1904 when it became affiliated with the International Federation of Trade Unions (q.v.), Serbia had about 5,100 union members; Croatia became an affiliate in 1907 and Bosnia in 1910. By 1913 the number of union members in these countries was 10,000 in Serbia, 7,000 in Croatia, and 5,000 in Bosnia. After the creation of Yugoslavia, a Communist Party and a national labor federation were formed in 1919. By 1920 there were 25,000 union members; but, following a number of strikes, the Communist Party and the labor federation were banned by the government. A new labor federation was formed by the communists and those unions not affiliated with any political party. In 1922 the Social Democrats set up a labor federation called the United Federation of Workers' Unions of Yugoslavia which was an affiliate of the International Federation of Trade Unions (q.v.) until 1939. From 1934 the United Federation of Workers' Unions of Yugoslavia became more militant through communist influence; in 1935 the government challenged its power by setting up a labor federation modelled on the fascist example of Italy (q.v.) and Germany. Before its suppression in 1940 the federation claimed 100,000 members.

After the Nazi withdrawal in December 1944, a new labor federation was established in 1945 which adopted its present title, *Savez Sindikata Jugoslaviji*, in 1948. Reflecting Yugoslavia's independence from Soviet control, it withdrew from the World Federation of Trade Unions (q.v.) in 1950 although relations improved after 1969. Organized labor in Yugoslavia was given greater freedom than elsewhere in Eastern Europe between 1948 and 1988 (for example, in being able to conduct local strikes). In late 1988 the first independent demonstrations occurred among Yugoslav employees. Independent labor unions were formed during 1989 by railroad engineers and airline pilots. In 1995 none of the present states created from the breakup of Yugoslavia were members of the International Confederation of Free Trade Unions (q.v.).

Z

***ZENTRALARBEITSGEMEINSCHAFT* (ZAG)** The ZAG or Central Labor Assocation was an organization established by German employers and organized labor to develop a common management-union approach to economic, social, and legal issues affecting labor. The ZAG, which was formally agreed to in December 1918, grew directly out of the November Pact (q.v.) of the previous month. Like the November Pact, it was an attempt to counter the revolutionary climate of the period by organizing the regulation of major parts of the economy through industry groups consisting of equal representatives of employees and employers. Fear of anarchy and communism encouraged support by employers for the ZAG but, as this threat waned after 1924, so did their support. Despite its idealistic intentions, the ZAG achieved little beyond hobbling the movement for the socialization of the economy led by the soldiers' and workers' councils which organized labor regarded as revolutionary. The ZAG was defunct by 1929 as a result of employer resistance to organized labor. (*See also* November Pact)

APPENDICES

Appendix 1   GLOSSARY OF TERMS

Like any other movement, organized labor has its own specialized terms which can appear in the primary sources or in the secondary literature. What follows is a sample of terms which are intended to provide a starting point for a reader; further information about some of them can be found in the specialized works listed in the bibliography. Cross-references to other terms in the glossary are in **bold**.

Angestellte
German noun for private sector white-collar employee in contrast to *Beamte*.

Apprenticeship
A system of trade training in which an individual is legally bound or indentured to an employer. The word was first recorded in 1362. Labor unions favor apprenticeship as one means of controlling the supply of labor.

Arbeiter
German noun for manual or blue-collar workers in contrast to *Angestellte* and *Beamte*.

Beamte
German noun for public sector employees including civil servants and employees in state-run enterprises, such as postal services, railroads and schools, in contrast to *Angestellte*.

Brownfield site
A workplace where there are established unions and a long-standing system of industrial relations characterized by customs and practices recognized by employers and unions in contrast to a **greenfield** site.

Ca'canny
Originally a Scottish term meaning to go carefully, it was first recorded in 1896 to refer to employees deliberately reducing the pace of their work or the quantity of their output. By 1918 "ca'canny" had entered standard English usage in Britain.

Candy men

Term used in nineteenth century England to describe the men employed by coal owners to evict miners from company-owned housing during labor disputes. The term originated in the English coal miners' strike of 1844 when some sellers of "dandy candy" in Newcastle upon Tyne were employed as bailiffs to evict miners from company-owned houses.

Closed (or union) shop

A workplace where union membership is a condition of employment; closed shop is British usage, union shop is American usage. There are two main forms of the closed shop: workplaces where an individual must be a member of a particular union before being employed and those where the individual must join a particular union after being employed at the workplace. The opposite term is **open shop**.

Company union

A company union is one formed by the management of a company among its employees and run for the benefit of the employer. Such unions are also variously called house unions, yellow unions, and even employee representation plans. Although a company union was formed in France in 1899, company unions were largely a feature of American labor relations. They flourished in the 1920s and early 1930s but were effectively killed off by the National Labor Relations Act in 1935. Some observers regard the relatively docile unions of large Japanese companies as a form of company union.

Corporatism

The organization of large interest groups in society into corporate bodies. The term specifically refers to industry groups, unions, and government. The creation of such umbrella organizations was a feature of the fascist governments of Italy and Germany. Hence, the term "neocorporatism" has been coined to describe the close cooperation between government, business and unions in Western European countries since the 1960s to develop and implement economic policies such as over wages or managing technological change.

Craft union

A union whose members have a recognized, specialized manual skill gained from serving an **apprenticeship**. Craft unions have been very important in the engineering, building, and printing industries. The bases of such unions are vulnerable to technological change which can reduce the value of such skills.

Demarcation (see **Jurisdiction**)

Gheraos

A term used in India to describe labor disputes in which employees harass employers and prevent them from leaving the workplace until the employees' claims are granted.

Greenfield site

A new workplace where there are no established unions or system of industrial relations. Often such sites are objects of competition between unions to recruit members and to gain exclusive recognition from management in contrast to a **brownfield site**.

Industrial relations

A general term for the interaction between management and its employees; it implies that both sides are organized. Industrial relations can also include governments and their representatives. As a term, industrial relations dates from the 1920s. Since 1945 the term labor-management relations, or just labor relations, has also come into use.

Industry

A general description of the type of goods or services produced or provided by the various sectors of the economy. Industries can be classified in a number of ways. One approach is to divide the economy into three parts: Primary (Agriculture and Mining), Secondary (Manufacturing), and Tertiary (other industries, also called service industries). For statistical purposes, most countries use a variant of the United Nations' International Standard Industrial Classification. Generally, unions recruit their members by occupations rather than industries.

Inflation/deflation

These terms refer to movements in the level of prices of goods and services in an economy. Inflation refers to rising prices and deflation refers to falling prices. If **real wages** do not match the changes of prices in an inflationary period, organized labor is more likely to engage in disputes for higher wages.

Internal labor market

The labor market which operates in a large enterprise such as the railroads. In the past, it has often been characterized by clearly defined points of entry, vertical organization, bureaucratic rules, and promotion of employees within the organization.

Journeymen

Term first recorded in England by the fourteenth century to describe an artisan or mechanic who had completed an **apprenticeship** and then worked as an employee. Journeymen were the main groups in the formation of early labor unions in eighteenth century-England and the United States.

Jurisdiction

Jurisdiction refers to the work boundaries recognized by unions for recruiting members for a particular union. Unions can, and do, disagree over which union has the right to recruit members carrying out certain kinds of work and this can lead to disputes. Work boundaries can also be altered by technological change. In British usage, jurisdiction is demarcation.

Kragenlinie

German noun literally meaning "collar line" but really referring to the social distinction between blue- and white-collar employees.

Labor economics

The branch of economics which studies the supply and demand for human beings. Theoretical advances and the availability of computerized data sets have enabled labor economics to advance greatly since the 1960s through the use of quantitative analysis or econometrics. One topic which has received attention from labor economists has been the economic effects of organized labor.

Labor force

The economically active part of the population. It includes those who are employed (the employed labor force) and the unemployed.

Lock-out

A labor dispute initiated by an employer or group of employers in contrast to a **strike**. The word was first recorded in 1860 to describe a labor dispute in which the employees were literally locked out of their workplace. In practice, lock-outs are difficult to measure because provocation by an employer can mean that the dispute takes the form of a **strike**. An example of a national lock-out occurred in Sweden in May 1980.

Nominal wages

The amount of money received by an employee without taking account of inflation in contrast to **real wages**.

Normative

In economic and sociological literature, normative refers to what ought to be, that is, the outcome predicted by a theory in contrast to positive or what actually happens.

Occupation

The specific job an individual is paid to carry out. There are two main kinds of occupation: manual or blue-collar occupations and non-manual or white-collar occupations. Unions generally base their recruitment of members on groups of occupations. Historically, unions drawn from manual occupations tend to be more militant than those drawn from white-collar occupations.

Occupational status

Refers to the division of the employed **labor force** into employers, self-employed, employees, and unpaid helpers.

Open shop

In contrast to a **closed shop**, an open shop is a place of employment where employees are not union members either by choice or by coercion by the employer.

Picketing

Picketing refers to the use of persuasion or deterrence by a group of union members outside a place of employment where there is a dispute between the union and the employer. The term was first recorded in Britain in 1867.

Primary labor market

A labor market characterized by high or difficult entry qualifications, high pay, good working conditions, and good promotion prospects in contrast to the **secondary labor market**.

Real wages

Real wages are **nominal wages** taking account of **inflation/deflation**. Changes in levels of real wages, particularly falls, have been a potent cause of labor unrest. An older term for real wages was effective wages.

Rights and interest

A distinction sometimes made between types of labor disputes: **rights** refers to the interpretation of the rights of unions and management in the interpretation of a contract or employment agreement whereas **interest** refers to the making of those terms. For example, an interest dispute could be over the recognition of a union by management; rights disputes are usually about alleged violations of agreed conditions of employment by one of the parties to the agreement.

Scab

Scab is a pejorative term used by organized labor in the United States and elsewhere to describe persons brought in by employers to replace employees on strike. In the United States, its use was first recorded in 1806 to describe employees who would not join a union of their occupation. Used as a term for strikebreaker, its usage was recorded in the United Kingdom by 1890.

Secondary labor market

A labor market usually characterized by low entry qualifications, low pay, poor working conditions, and limited opportunities for promotion in contrast to a **primary labor market**.

Segmented labor market

A labor market that is dominated by one sex, race, or other group. Sex is a common characteristic of a segmented labor market. For example, most librarians are female and most engineers are male.

Shop stewards

Also known as delegates, shop stewards are the representatives of a union at the workplace but are not officials of the union. Shop stewards have been very important in British labor unions since 1918.

Sliding scale

A system of payment which linked wages directly to the price obtained for the good being produced by an industry. In 1795 agricultural laborers in Norfolk, England, suggested a sliding scale which would have tied their wage rate to the price of wheat. Sliding scales which linked wages to the price of coal were prevalent in the coal mining industry in the 1870s and 1880s in Britain and the United States. Although the system could yield higher wages when coal prices were high, it could have disastrous effects on miners' earnings if the coal price fell sharply.

Social dumping

A term coined in Western Europe in the late 1980s to refer to the adverse effects on affluent countries of economic competition from poorer countries. These effects can take the form of unemployment caused by the displacement of relatively highly paid employees because of the import of goods produced by poorly paid employees, the relocation of centers of employment from countries of high pay to ones with low pay, and attemptation to lower the pay and conditions of employment in affluent societies to compete with Third World countries. The term has also been applied to the migration of workers from low-wage countries to high-wage countries.

Strike

A labor dispute initiated by a labor union or a group of unions in contrast to a **lock-out**. The origin of the word is unclear. It does not seem to have a nautical origin as has been suggested. It was used in its modern sense in a hiring bond in 1763 between coal owners and miners at Newcastle in northern England and in connection with London tailors in 1764.

Tripartite

Bodies made up of representatives of employers, unions, and government. Tripartite bodies of this kind are usually designed to address a problem of labor relations such as a dispute, training, or occupational health and safety.

Truck

A term first recorded in England in 1665 to describe the payment of employees' wages in kind rather than money. The abuse arose from the goods often having a lesser value than the wages owed. Truck was first outlawed in 1701 but remained an abuse throughout the nineteenth century despite laws passed in 1831, 1887, and 1896. Truck was also an abuse in Germany and the United States. By the late-nineteenth century the term was extended to refer to an employer's fines or unauthorized deductions from an employee's wages.

Unemployment rate

The number of unemployed as a percentage of the total **labor force**. The level of unemployment is important for labor unions as a factor in determining their strength in negotiations with employers.

Union density

Union members as a percentage of potential union members.

Appendix 2   **CHRONOLOGY**

1152 BC Egypt: strike by the pharaoh's tomb makers over the failure
of their employers to supply grain.

———

AD

301   Roman Empire: the emperor Diocletian issued an Edict of
Maximum Prices which also set maximum wage rates.

544   Byzantine Empire: the emperor Justinian forbade laborers,
sailors, and others to demand or accept wage increases on
penalty of having to pay the treasury three times the amount
demanded.

1345   Florence: Cinto Brandini hanged for attempting to form an
organization among woolcombers.

1351   England: the Statute of Labourers prohibited laborers from
demanding wage increases and employers from granting
them. .

1383   England: early use of the term "journeyman" in connection
with a union of London saddlers who had combined to raise
their pay.

1387   England: a group of London journeymen cordwainers
(shoemakers) were accused of forming a union.

1393   France: strike by vineyard workers in Burgundy.

1411   England: Colchester municipal authorities outlawed payment
in kind for weavers.

1448   England: maximum wage law.

1490   Genoa: shipbuilding employees organized to resist wage reductions; they did so again in 1526.

1504   Venice: labor dispute in printing.

1524   England: municipal authorities in Coventy fixed maximum wage rates in the textile industry, specified payment in money, and forbade payment in kind.

1539   France: strike by printing employees in Lyons over long hours. They formed a union and attacked strikebreakers.

1548   England: parliament passed the Bill of Conspiracies of Victuallers and Craftsmen which introduced the concept of combinations as conspiracies into English law.

1560   England: some London saddlers combined to raise their pay.

1562   England: the Statute of Artificers gave justices of the peace the power to set the wages of artisans and laborers and provided penalties for breach of contract by employers and employees. It also required a seven year apprenticeship as a qualification to be a journeyman.

1675   Italy: 10,000 silk workers in Genoa rose up over the introduction of ribbon-looms from France which enabled a single workers to weave ten to twelve ribbons at a time; the use of the same ribbon-looms also led to attacks on French immigrant silk workers in London.

1696   England: organized journeymen feltmakers in London tried to resist a wage cut.

1701   England: payment in kind outlawed in the textile and iron industries.

1706   England: journeymen weavers in the west were accused by their employers of trying to force them to only employ members of their union.

1718   England: the free emigration of skilled artisans and skilled operatives was prohibited by law. Similar legislation was again passed in 1750 and 1765.

1721   England: London journeymen tailors were accused by their employers of forming a "combination" of 7,000 to raise their wages and reduce their work day by one hour.

1726   England: parliament passed the Act to Prevent Unlawful Combinations of Workmen Employed in the Woollen Manufactures.

1731   England: first recorded use of the "round robin" in the British navy as a method of voicing grievances.

1765   England: first sign of organization among coal miners at Newcastle in northeast England.

1768   England: the Tailors' Act imposed jail terms of two months on any London journeyman who demanded pay above the legal maximum and on any master who paid a higher amount.

1769-73 England: unrest among London's silk workers in the Spitalfields district over mechanized looms and French competition. Workers' clubs evolved into unions which threatened industrial sabotage to gain standardized wages. The protests led to the Spitalfields Act in 1773 which provided for the setting of wages and piece-rates; wage rates could be proposed by a joint board of masters and journeymen.

1772   England: London journeymen tailors petitioned parliament for higher pay because of rising living costs.

1773   Scotland: trial of twelve leaders of weavers from Paisley, near Glasgow. Thousands had taken part in the strike and used force to prevent the use of strikebreakers. The leaders threatened to take all their followers to North America if their demands were not met. Seven were found guilty.

1773   England: strike by London cabinetmakers and tradesmen in the royal dockyards for higher pay.

1773-76   England: register of emigrants to North America showed that of the 6,190 emigrants whose occupations were known, 49 per cent were artisans, mechanics, or craftsmen.

1780s   United States: formation of trade societies by journeymen in Philadelphia to meet annually with masters to settle the price of their labor.

1786   United States: first strike of employees in a single trade (Philadelphia printers).

1790   France: journeymen carpenters in Paris formed a union. Following complaints by employers, it was suppressed by the law *Le Chaplier* (1791) which was also applied to employers' organizations and made strikes illegal.

1791   United States: first recorded strike in the building trades by Philadelphia carpenters.

1792   England: seamen's strike in the northeast.

1794   United States: formation of the Federal Society of Journeymen Cordwainers (shoemakers) in Philadelphia; the society lasted until 1806.

1794   England: rises in the cost of living because of the war with Napoleon led to some successful strikes for higher pay by London journeymen tradesmen between 1794 and 1813.

1796   England: debate in the House of Commons concerning a proposal to empower justices of the peace to fix a minimum wage.

1797   England: Henry Maudslay invented a metal cutting lathe with a slide rest; perfected in 1800, the lathe played a major role in shaping the working conditions of metal workers.

1799   England: first Combination Act passed. This act, and the second act of 1800, outlawed labor disputes but did not prohibit employees from improving wages and conditions.

1799   Scotland: abolition of serfdom for coal miners.

1800   England: second Combination Act passed. The act included provision for arbitration in labor disputes.

1810   France: the Penal Cole prohibited strikes.

1812   Canada: in Saint John, New Brunswick, building unions attempted to exclude American immigrants to maintain the shortage of skilled labor.

1812   England: frame breaking made an offense punishable by death in a move aimed at the Luddites.

1812-14 England: Luddites organized attacks on machinery in the woollen industries.

1813   England: repeal of the wage clause of the Statute of Artificers of 1562.

1814   England: repeal of the apprenticeship clause of the Statute of Artificers of 1562. One of the petitions to parliament opposing their repeal was signed by 30,517 journeymen.

1817   England: suppression of the "Blanketeers" march planned from Manchester to London.

1818   Robert Owen's memorial to the Congress of Aix-la-Chapelle which urged the governments to legally limit ordinary working hours of employees in manufacturing.

1819   England: "Peterloo" Massacre at Manchester.

1824   England: repeal of the Combination Acts of 1799 and 1800.

1825   England: picketing effectively outlawed by the Combination of Workmen Act.

1825   United States: Boston construction workers struck unsuccessfully to reduce their work day to ten hours; they tried again, unsuccessfully, in 1830.

1825   United Kingdom: repeal of a law which had prohibited the emigration of artisans to continental Europe.

1826   England: Journeymen Steam Engine Makers' Society formed in Manchester; known as "Old Mechanics," it was the forerunner of the Amalgamated Society of Engineers.

1827   United States: journeymen in Philadelphia formed the Mechanics' Union of Trade Associations, the first citywide federation of local unions in the United States.

1827   England: general union of carpenters and joiners formed.

1829   Australia: a labor union was founded among shipwrights in Sydney, New South Wales.

1833   United States: General Trades Union formed in New York; it was a confederation of tradesmen which was copied by more than twelve other American cities; it lasted until 1837.

1833   England: the Factory Act outlawed the employment of children under nine years and set a maximum of nine hourswork day for employees aged between nine and thirteen years. The act appointed inspectors to enforce its provisions and was the ancestor of modern factory laws.

1833   England: the National Regeneration Society in Lancashire, advocated general strikes for the eight-hour work day.

1834   England: "Tolpuddle Martyrs" sentenced to transportation to Australia for forming a union (March 18).

1834   France: revolt by silk workers in Lyons, after the government attempted to suppress labor unions (April 9-13).

1839   England: the Chartist Convention voted in favor of a national strike to achieve its objectives (July 28).

1841   France: first factory legislation; it concerned child labor.

1842   United Kingdom: Miners' Association of Great Britain and Ireland formed. It claimed 70,000 members or a third of the coal mining industry.

1842   United States: a Massachusetts judge ruled that it was not illegal for a union to strike for higher pay in *Commonwealth v. Hunt.*

1843   France: first collective agreement in France; it set wage rates for printers.

1844   Ireland: Dublin Regular Trades' Association formed; it perished in the 1847 depression.

1844   United Kingdom: four-month coal miners' strike in Durham and Northumberland; the strike was unsuccessful.

1845   United Kingdom: the National Association of United Trades for the Protection and Employment of Labour advocated Boards of Trade, that is, bodies to conciliate and arbitrate in labor disputes.

1845   Prussia: labor unions prohibited.

1846   Chile: artisans formed a mutual aid society.

1847   United Kingdom: William Dixon and W. P. Roberts, two of the leaders of the Miners' Association, became the first union officials to stand for election to parliament.

1847-48   United Kingdom: collapse of the Miners' Association of Great Britain and Ireland.

1848   Germany: formation of the first national German labor union, the National Printers' Association (*Nationaler Buchdrucker-Verein*).

1848   France: government forcibly closed down the national workshops that had been set up to provide employment;

several thousands were killed and thousands of others were arrested during the "June Days."

1848   Marx and Engels published the *Manifesto of the Communist Party*.

1849   United States: first labor union organized in the anthracite coalfields of Pennsylvania by an English immigrant, John Bates.

1850   United States: two picketers killed by police in New York, the first labor fatalities in a United States strike.

1851   United Kingdom: formation of the Amalgamated Society of Engineers in England.

1852   United States: formation of the National Typographical Union, the first national labor union in the United States.

1852   United Kingdom: William Newton (1822-1876), a leader of the Amalgamated Society of Engineers, stood for a seat in the British House of Commons.

1857   Argentina: mutual aid society among the printers; the society was made into a union in 1877.

1858   Scotland: Glasgow Trades' Council formed.

1859   United Kingdom: Molestation of Workmen Act made "peaceful" picketing lawful.

1859-60   United Kingdom: strike by London building employees; one outcome of the strike was the formation of the London Trades Council in 1860.

1860   United Kingdom: formation of the Amalgamated Society of Carpenters and Joiners.

1861   Germany: the legal ban on labor unions was lifted in Saxony which was followed by Weimar (1863) and the North

German Confederation (1869), but there was no legal right to form unions.

1862   United Kingdom: a delegation of French workers was allowed to visit the London Exhibition; on their return, they demanded freedom of association and the right to strike.

1863   England: foundation of the Co-operative Wholesale Society at Manchester.

1864   United Kingdom: formation of the International Workingmen's Association, or the First International, in London (September 28).

1864   France: the legal ban on strikes was lifted.

1866   United States: the National Labor Union formed in Baltimore (August); seventy-seven labor union delegates claimed to represent 60,000 members. The union lasted until 1872.

1866   Netherlands: unions formed by printers and diamond cutters.

1867   England: Second Reform Act gave the vote to the better-off urban working class.

1867   United Kingdom: a Conciliation Act became law.

1868   United Kingdom: foundation of the Trades Union Congress.

1869   United States: formation of the National Colored Labor Union (December) by black intellectuals and labor leaders; it tried to affiliate with the National Labor Union but was refused.

1870   Austria: labor unions legalized.

1871   United Kingdom: labor unions legalized (June 29), but objections by organized labor led to an improved law in 1876.

1871   Spain: formation of a printers' union in Madrid.

1871   Canada: first local trade assemblies formed.

1872   United Kingdom: Joseph Arch founded the Agricultural Labourers' Union.

1874   United Kingdom: two coal mining labor leaders were elected to the House of Commons: Alexander Macdonald and Thomas Burt.

1874   France: a factory law introduced a system of inspectors and outlawed child labor and women working underground.

1877   United States: nationwide railroad strikes (July 16 to August 5) marked by rioting and use of the U.S. Army and State guards.

1878   United States: International Labor Union formed.

1878   New Zealand: labor unions legalized.

1879   France: first national labor union formed by hatters.

1879   Australia: first Intercolonial Trade Union Congress held in Sydney; subsequent congresses were held in 1884, 1886, 1888,1889, 1891, and 1898.

1880   Switzerland: formation of the *Schweizerischer Gewerkschaftsbund* by socialist labor unions.

1881   South Africa: the Amalgamated Society of Carpenters and Joiners formed a branch at Cape Town.

1881   Canada: the Knights of Labour formed its first assembly.

1881   Spain: after the legalization of labor unions, the *Federación de Trabajadores de la Región Española* was formed.

1881   United States: formation of the Federation of Organized Trades and Labor Unions of the United States and Canada, the forerunner of the American Federation of Labor, in Pittsburgh.

1883   United States: first attempt to form an industrial union in the railroad industry, the Brotherhood of Railroad Trainmen.

1883   Bulgaria: printers' union formed.

1884   France: labor unions legalized (March 21).

1886   Canada: formation of Canadian Trades and Labour Congress.

1886   France: formation of the first national trade union center (*Fédération Nationale des Syndicats Ouvriers*).

1886   United States: founding of the American Federation of Labor (December 8).

1886   United States: labor riots in Chicago (May 4).

1886   Beginning of regular conferences between labor leaders of Sweden, Denmark, and Norway.

1887   France: first Catholic labor union formed among white-collar workers.

1888   United States: Burlington railroad strike (February 27, 1888 to January 5, 1889).

1888   United Kingdom: strike by women match workers in London for higher pay and improved health and safety.

1888   Denmark: Blacksmiths and Ironworkers' Union formed.

1888   Spain: formation of the *Unión General de Trabajadores*.

1888   United Kingdom: international labor union conference held in London; it claimed to represent 850,000 British union members and 250,000 European union members.   The conference was a failure.

1889   France: Second International formed in Paris.

1889   Germany: strikes for higher wages and regulation of women and children's work.

1889   United Kingdom: London longshoremen's strike (August-September).

1890   Australia: 50,000 workers took part in the Maritime Strike (August-December) over freedom of contract; the strike, which extended to New Zealand, failed.

1890   Switzerland: the Canton of Geneva legally recognized agreements between employers and unions; it was one of the first laws of its kind.

1890   Austro-Hungarian Empire: Austrian Union of Metalworkers and Miners formed.

1891   Germany: defeat of a strike by 20,000 German coal miners in the Ruhr; formation of the *Deutscher Metallarbeiter-Verband* (German Metalworkers' Union), Germany's first industrial union.

1891   Norway: Iron and Metal Workers' Union formed.

1891   Australia: Labor Party founded in New South Wales and South Australia.

1891   France: first collective agreement in the mining industry.

1892   France: voluntary conciliation and arbitration law in France.

1892   United States: major labor dispute at the Homestead Steel plant near Pittsburgh (June-November).

1892   France: foundation of the National Federation of *Bourses du Travail.*

1892   Germany: first Congress by German labor unions. It decided to encourage the formation of national unions and agreed to work for the formation of industry-based unions.

1893   Belgium: general strike (April).

1893   United States: first successful biracial strike in the Uunited States, in New Orleans.

1894   Ireland: Irish Trades Union Congress formed.

1894   Australia: Australian Workers' Union formed.

1894   New Zealand became the first country in the world to introduce a compulsory conciliation and arbitration system for labor disputes.

1894   United States: Pullman railroad strike.

1895   China: first unions formed in Canton region.

1895   France: *Confédération Générale du Travail* founded in France; it absorbed the National Federation of *Bourses du Travail* in 1902.

1896   Uruguay: formation of the first union federation *Federación Obrera Regional Uruguay*.

1897   Japan: steelworkers formed a union.

1897   United Kingdom: Workmen's Compensation Act; the law applied only to blue-collar employees.

1897   United Kingdom: Scottish Trades Union Congress formed.

1897   Austro-Hungarian Empire: Czechoslovak Trade Union Federation formed.

1898   United Kingdom: Workers' Union formed.

1898   France: failure of first general railroad strike.

1898   Korea: longshoremen form a union.

1899   Austro-Hungarian Empire: Hungarian Trade Union Council (formed 1891) was set up on a permanent basis.

1899   Australia: first Labor Party government in the world in Queensland; it lasted one week.

1899   France: first company union formed.

1899   Egypt: first labor union formed among cigarette workers.

1900   Japan: unions formed among employees in metalworking, printing, railroads, teaching, and firefighting; they were suppressed by legislation later in 1900.

1901   United Kingdom: the House of Lords upheld an appeal by the Taff Vale Railway Company against the Amalgamated Society of Railway Servants which cost the society 23,000 pounds in damages (July).

1901   Denmark: international labor union conference in Copenhagen (August 21); the conference set up the International Secretariat of the National Trade Union Federations which was officially renamed the International Federation of Trade Unions in 1919.

1901   Argentina: formation of the first union federation, the *Federación Obrera Regional Argentina (FORA)* ; it soon split into anarchist, syndicalist and socialist factions. The same happened in Chile, Brazil, Uruguay and Paraguay.

1901   Italy: Italian Metal Workers' Union (*Federazione Italiana Operai Metallurgici*) formed.

1902   United States: major strike by anthracite coal miners brought about the formation of a presidential arbitration commission by President Theodore Roosevelt.

1902   Philippines: creation of a national federation of craft labor unions, the *Unión Obrera Democratica Filipina*.

1903   Brazil: strike by textile workers in Rio de Janeiro.

1903   Netherlands: major strikes by railroad and longshoremen.

1903   Switzerland: white-collar unions formed their own federation.

1903   Canada: formation of the National Trades and Labour Congress by organizations excluded by the Trades and Labour Congress (that is, the Knights of Labour and unions not part of American unions).

1904   Australia: first national Labor government formed with Protectionist support (April 27 to August 12).

1904   Bulgaria: creation of socialist and Marxist labor union federations; the two bodies merged in 1920.

1905   United States: creation of the Industrial Workers of the World in Chicago.

1905   Dutch East Indies (modern Indonesia): first labor union formed by Dutch and indigenous railway employees.

1905   Nigeria: formation of first substantive labor union of indigenous employees in Africa (civil servants in Lagos).

1905   Russia: All-Russian Conference of Trade Unions held.

1906   Russian Empire: unions legalized (March) but a government crackdown was begun after 1907.

1906   Bolivia: formation of the first labor union, the *Centro Social Obrero*.

1906   Italy: foundation of the *Confederazione Generale di Lavoro* (General Confederation of Labor).

1906   France: the *Confédération Générale du Travail* adopted the radical Charter of Amiens which advocated the general strike to eliminate capitalism and affirmed the independence of trade unions from political parties.

1906   Germany: the Mannheim Agreement declared the equality of unions and the Social Democratic Party in providing leadership for the working-class movement.

1906   United Kingdom: the Trades Disputes Act in Britain protected unions from prosecution by employers over breach of contract under common law.

1907   Canada: the Industrial Disputes Investigation Act enacted; the act enabled the federal government to appoint a tripartite board to try to resolve labor disputes on application by the employers or the unions.

1907   Argentina: general strike in Buenos Aires by 93,000 employees.

1907   Switzerland: Catholic unions formed their own federation, the *Christlicher Gewerkschaftsbund der Schweiz*.

1909   Hong Kong: first labor union formed.

1909   Sweden: general strike by 300,000 employees in Sweden.

1909   Spain: "Tragic Week" (July) when over 175 were shot in riots led by revolutionary syndicalists in Catalonia over calling up of reservists for the war in Morocco. Attacks on churches and convents. Execution of anarchist leader Francisco Ferrer.

1909   United Kingdom: the House of Lords upheld the Osbourne Judgement declaring political levies by labor unions illegal (December 2).

1910   Spain: formation of the *Confederación Nacional del Trabajo* by anarchists.

1910   France: first old age pension law.

1911   United Kingdom: first national railway strike; it lasted for two days.

1912   United States: the Lloyd-LaFollette Act and other legislation forbade American federal employees from going on strike.

1912   Italy: formation of the *Unione Syndicale Italiano*.

1912   Japan: a labor union formed by Bunji Suzuki.

1913   France: first national Catholic union formed among clerical workers.

1913   United Kingdom: twelve countries represented at an attempt to form a Syndicalist International in London.

1917   Russia: Bolshevik Revolution (November).

1918   India: the Madras Union formed by B. P. Wadia.

1918   Greece: formation of the General Confederation of Greek Labor.

1918   Germany: November Pact (Stinnes-Legien Agreement) made between major employers and organized labor.

1918   Pan-American Federation of Labor formed (November 13).

1919   Argentina: the army suppressed a general strike with much bloodshed.

1919   France: formation of the *Confédération Française des Travailleurs Chrétiens* (November) representing 100,000 Catholic workers in 321 unions.

1919   United Kingdom: seven-day national railroad strike; it resulted in the employees gaining the eight-hour work day in 1920.

1919   Caribbean: formation of the British Guiana Labour Union.

1919   United States: defeat of general steelworkers' strike.

1919   International Labour Organisation formed.

1919   Soviet Union: formation of the Third International (Communist) (March); known as the Comintern, it was disbanded in 1943.

1919   Canada: six-week general strike in Winnipeg; sympathetic strikes also occurred in other Canadian cities, notably in Vancouver.

1920   United Kingdom: Amalgamated Engineering Union formed.

1920   France: split in the Socialist Party resulted in the formation of the Communist Party.

1920   International Organization of Employers formed.

1920   India: All-India Trades Union Congress (AITUC) formed representing sixty-four unions with about 150,000 members.

1920   France: Failure of railway and general strike.

1921   Canada: Catholic Confederation of Labour formed in Quebec.

1921-22   France: split in the *Confédération Générale du Travail*. The Communists and syndicalists formed the *Confédération Générale du Travail Unitaire* which joined the Red International of Labor Unions in 1923.

1922   South Africa: 230 strikers killed by the army during a general strike.

1922   Hong Kong: successful general strike by seamen against an attempt to suppress their union.

1922   United Kingdom: Transport and General Workers' Union formed.

1924   Italy: the non-fascist labor unions of Italy were abolished (January 24).

1924   United Kingdom: General and Municipal Workers' Union formed.

1925   China: formation of the All China General Labor Federation.

1926   France: the syndicalists formed their own labor federation, the *Confédération Générale du Travail Syndicaliste Révolutionnaire*.

1926   Portugal: the government dissolved the *Confederaçao Geral de Trabalho* (the peak labor organization formed in 1913).

1926   United Kingdom: general (May 4-12) and coal mining (May-November) strikes.

1927   Australia: formation of the Australian Council of Trade Unions in Melbourne, Victoria.

1927   China: Chiang Kai-shek purged the communists from organized labor in Shanghai; about 5,000 were killed (April).

1927   Canada: formation of the All-Canadian Congress of Labour.

1928   Colombia: the army killed several hundred strikers during a dispute with the American-owned United Fruit Company.

1930   United Kingdom: the British government began to encourage the development of labor unions in its colonies in Africa, Asia, and the Caribbean; the policy was formalized by the Colonial Development Act 1940 which linked the payment of assistance funds to fostering labor unions.

1930   Argentina: formation of the *Confederación General del Trabajo* (General Confederation of Labor).

1930   Colombia: labor unions legalized.

1932   United States: Anti-Injunction (Norris-LaGuardia) Act designed to provide full freedom of association to organized labor.

1933   Germany: suppression of labor unions in Germany (May 2); imprisonment of labor leaders in Dachau concentration camp.

1933   United States: unions were given the undisputed legal right to recruit employees and collectively bargain for employees by Section 7(a) of the National Industrial Recovery Act.

1933   Dutch East Indies (Indonesia): joined the International Federation of Trade Unions.

1934   France: first successful general strike over the need to resist fascism.

1935   Norway: basic agreement concluded between the peak union and employer bodies.

1935   United States: National Labor Relations Act (Wagner Act) protected the right of labor unions to organize and engage in collective bargaining.

1936   France: the *Confédération Générale du Travail* and the *Confédération Générale du Travail Unitaire* held a unity congress (March). The election of the Popular Front led to new laws on a 40-hour work week, paid holidays, collective bargaining, and compulsory conciliation and arbitration (this last law was suspended in 1939).

1936   France: the Matignon Agreement between the Socialist government of Lèon Blum, the *Confédération Générale du Travail*, and employers (June 7). The agreement provided for the unions' right to organize, an end to anti-union practices, collective bargaining, pay increases of 7 to 12 percent and the election of shop stewards.

1936   New Zealand: the Industrial Conciliation and Arbitration Act was amended to make union membership compulsory for any employee subject to a registered award of industrial agreement. This provision remained part of New Zealand law until 1991.

1937   New Zealand: Federation of Labour formed.

1937   British East Africa: the Labour Trade Union of East Africa
          was banned; its successor, the East African Trade Union
          Congress was founded in 1949 and also banned.

1937   French-speaking Africa: the first labor unions formed in
          Tunisia among white-collar workers, in Bamako (Mali) and
          in Dakar (Senegal).

1937   Switzerland: an accord between employers and unions in the
          engineering industry eventually became the model for a
          national social partnership in Swiss industrial relations.

1938   Sweden: Saltsjobaden Agreement between unions and
          employers.

1938   United States: the Congress of Industrial Organizations (CIO)
          was founded; John L. Lewis became president.

1938   Caribbean: the West Indies Royal Commission (Lord Moyne)
          recommended the encouragement of organized labor.

1939   Canada: expulsion of the Canadian branches of the CIO
          international unions from the Trades and Labour Congress.

1939   Cuba: formation of the *Confederación de Trabajadores de
          Cuba* (Confederation of the Workers of Cuba).

1939   France: the *Confédération Générale du Travail* expelled
          communist affiliates over their support of the Soviet pact
          with Nazi Germany.

1939   United States: the Hatch Act prohibited federal employees
          from active participation in federal election campaigns and
          from providing organizational support for candidates. (An
          attempt to reform the Hatch Act failed in Congress in 1990.)

1940   Canada: the expelled CIO unions and the All-Canadian
          Congress of Labour merged to form the Canadian Congress
          of Labour.

1940   Japan: suppression of all independent labor unions and employers' organizations (June).

1940   France: dissolution of all three national labor organizations (November 9).

1942   Egypt: labor unions legalized.

1943   Canada: the Order-in-Council P.C. 1003 created a legal framework for collective bargaining and mechanisms for resolving disputes.

1944   France: the provisional government restored free labor unions (July).

1945   United Kingdom: the World Trades Union Conference was held in London, attended by representatives from fifty-three countries (February 6-17). The conference led to the creation of the World Federation of Trade Unions (WFTU) in Paris on September 25. The IFTU ceased to exist after December 31.

1945   Austria: formation of the *Österreichischer Gewerkschaftsbund* (Austrian Federation of Trade Unions) (April 13).

1945   Germany: resurgence of labor unions at the factory level in West Germany (March-August). By August 1945, nearly one million union members had been officially recognized in unions in the British zone.

1945   Netherlands: a permanent union-employer policy body, the Foundation of Labor, formed (May).

1946   United Kingdom: major dispute in the transportation industry over the closed shop.

1946   Belgian Congo (modern Zaire): Africans were allowed to form labor unions; European labor unions had been permitted in the Congo since 1921. A multiracial labor federation was formed in 1951 but split along racial lines.

1946   Canada: Rand Formula introduced into industrial relations.

1947   France: general strike.

1947   United States: Congress passed the Taft-Hartley Act which outlawed political levies by labor unions and the closed shop (June 23). The act provided for the immediate dismissal of striking American federal government employees and prohibited their re-employment by the government for three years.

1948   Peru: the *Confederación Interamericana de Trabajadores* formed (January 10) in Lima.

1948   International Labour Organisation Convention No. 87 (Freedom of Association and Protection of the Right to Organize).

1948   The Universal Declaration of Human Rights proclaimed the right of individuals to form and join trade unions to protect their interests (Article 23, Part 4).

1948   France: strike by coal miners accompanied by much violence; 30,000 troops sent in by the government.

1948   West Germany: the number of union members reached five million.

1948   Japan: public sector employees were forbidden to strike.

1949   International Labour Organisation Convention No. 98 (Right to Organize and Collective Bargaining)

1949   Formation of the International Confederation of Free Trade Unions (December) which claimed 54 million members.

1949   Australia: communist-led coal miners strike. The federal government sent in troops to mine the coal.

1949   United States: the General Schedule in its present form was introduced for white-collar employees of the American federal government; its origins go back to pay reforms of 1923 which were in turn based on pay legislation of the 1850s.

1949   United States: the communists were expelled from the CIO.

1950   Kenya: crushing of general strike in Nairobi by the army.

1950   Germany: *IG Metall* (Metal Workers' Industrial Union) formed.

1950   The International Confederation of Free Trade Unions established the European Regional Organization (November).

1951   Mexico: the *Organización Regional Interamericana de Trabajadores* formed (January) in Mexico City from the *Confederación Interamericana de Trabajadores*.

1951   Guatemala: Castillo Armas, supported by the United States, overthrew President Jacobo Arbenz and executed labor organizers and suppressed the country's 533 unions.

1955   United States: the American Federation of Labor and the Congress of Industrial Organizations (CIO) agreed to merge with George Meany as president.

1956   Canada: the Trades and Labour Congress and the Canadian Congress of Labour merged to form the Canadian Labour Congress.

1956   Japan: first *Shunto* or Spring Offensive.

1959   United States: Wisconsin legislature passed the first public-sector bargaining law which gave state employees the right to join unions.

1960   Canada: merger of the Canadian and Catholic Confederation of Labour to form the Confederation of National Trade Unions.

1964   United Kingdom: the House of Lords upheld the original
          decision in the *Rookes v. Barnard* case which gave Douglas
          Rookes damages for his dismissal from his job at the
          instigation of his union after he had resigned from the
          Association of Engineering and Shipbuilding Draftsmen in
          1955. This loophole in the Trades Disputes Act (1906) made
          union officials liable for damages for threatening to strike in
          breach of contracts of employment; it was closed by the
          Trades Disputes Act (1965).

1967   United States: the Taylor Act in New York State imposed
          penalties on public-sector employees who went on strike; the
          penalties were increased in 1969, 1974, and 1978 and have
          been enforced.

1968   United Kingdom: Report of the Royal Commission on Trade
          Unions (Donovan Commission).

1969   United States: the AFL-CIO disaffiliated from the
          International Confederation of Free Trade Unions (February)
          and set up the Asian-American Free Labor Institute (AAFLI)
          with the U.S. State Department. The AFL-CIO had
          accounted for a quarter of the budget of the ICFTU.

1970   United States: the Pay Comparability Act applied the
          principle of pay comparability with the private sector to
          American federal government employees in its present form,
          but the principle was first inserted in federal law in 1962.

1970   United States: a successful national strike by postal workers
          led to the Postal Reorganization Act 1970 which separated
          pay determination in the postal service from the rest of
          federal employment, outlawed strikes, gave the unions the
          right to engage in collective bargaining, and provided for
          compulsory arbitration in case of disputes.

1970   United States: President Nixon attempted to delay the
          statutory federal pay adjustment deadline during his freeze
          on pay and prices; the National Treasury Employees Union
          (founded in 1938) took its case to the Supreme Court and

won what has been claimed to be the largest back pay award in history: $600 million.

1970 European Economic Community: creation of the Standing Committee of Employment, the first formal European-level committee of its kind to include representatives from organized labor (December).

1972-73 South Africa: strikes by black workers in Durban. The government arrested the leaders and tried to suppress black unionism.

1973 Formation of the European Trade Union Confederation; it claimed 37 million members.

1974 United Kingdom: Social Contract agreed to between the Labour Party and the Trades Union Congress.

1974 India: strike by railway workers.

1976 West Germany: the Co-determination Law was applied to companies with 2,000 or more employees.

1976 Poland: formation of an Organizing Committee for Free Trades Unions in Silesia and a free trades union committee (KOR) following a strike wave.

1977 Spain: legislation passed which granted minimum legal freedom to labor unions; full legal freedom was not granted until 1985.

1977 Soviet Union: Vladimir Klebanov and five others announced the formation of an Association of Free Trade Unions of Workers in Moscow (November).

1979 South Africa: the government appointed the Wiehahn Commission to investigate trade unionism; the commission successfully recommended that black labor unions be legally recognized.

1979   Romania: a dissident, Paul Goma, announced the formation of the Romanian Workers' Free Union (SLOMR).

1979   United States: the AFL-CIO and Carter administration reached a national accord under which the unions agreed to restrain wage claims in return for a package of economic and social measures (September).

1980   Brazil: five-week strike by metalworkers.

1980   Turkey: a military coup resulted in restrictions on labor unions.

1980   Sweden: national lock-out by employers (May).

1980   Poland: formation of Solidarity (September 22).

1981   Chile: formation of a centrist labor union in Chile (UDT).

1981   United States: a strike by the Professional Air Traffic Controllers' Organization (PATCO) (August 3) led to the firing of strikers and their replacement by military controllers and civilian controllers who returned to work.

1981   Reaffiliation of the AFL-CIO with the International Confederation of Free Trade Unions (November).

1982   Germany: 500,000 joined in union protests about cuts to social services.

1982   Turkey: trial of fifty-two labor leaders (February-March).

1982   United States: PATCO stripped of its rights to bargain collectively (February) after its defeat in the 1981 strike.

1983   Australia: the Australian Council of Trade Unions and the Australian Labor Party (ALP) negotiated an accord covering economic policy to be followed if the ALP won the federal election (February). The accord operated between 1983 and 1996.

1984   United Kingdom: the Employment Act required secret ballots for labor union officials and for strikes.

1984   New Zealand: abolition of access to compulsory arbitration in interest disputes except in "essential" industries.

1984   The International Confederation of Free Trade Unions began publishing annual surveys of violations of trade union rights in the world.

1984   Germany: thirty-eight-hour work week introduced into the steel industry.

1984   Spain: the government and the *Unión General de Trabajadores* agreed to a social and economic pact to control wage claims as an anti-inflationary measure. The pact broke down after 1986.

1985   United States: Hormel strike, Austin, Minnesota.

1986   United Kingdom: defeat of London printing unions over the introduction of new technology at Rupert Murdoch's Wapping plant.

1986   Germany: *Neue Heimat* affair; the mismanagement of the cooperative housing project damaged the prestige of labor unions.

1987   Germany: *IG Metall* gained the 37-hour work week for members as of April 1, 1988. Other unions also gained reductions in their working time.

1987   Ireland: the Programme for National Recovery agreed to between government, union,s and employers (April). Two other three-year programmes have been agreed to since 1990.

1987   Taiwan: formation of a Labor Party (November) after the lifting of martial law.

1989   Japan: merger of two major labor federations, *Rengo* and *Sohyo*, to form *JTUC-Rengo* (November 21) with 7.6 million members.

1990   Italy: strikes in a wide range of essential services legally prohibited (June).

1990   United States: the Federal Employees Pay Comparability Act was signed into law by President Bush (November 5, 1990).

1991   New Zealand: the Employment Contracts Act was enacted. The act abolished the arbitration system and the system of compulsory union membership which operated since1936.

1991   Cuba: formation of the Independent Cuban General Workers' Union (October 4); it has been denied official recognition by the government.

1992   China: suppression of the China Free Trade Union Preparatory Committee (formed at the end of 1991).

1992   European Union Treaty signed at Maastricht (7 February); appended a social policy agreement which gave European-wide labor and employer federations an enhanced formal role in the social policy of the European Community.

1993   The European Commission formally recognized the European Trade Union Confederation, EUROCADRES, and the *Confédération Européene des Cadres* as "social partners" for European-wide dialogue on social policy matters.

1993   Poland: strikes by Solidarity over low pay and staff cuts (May).

1993   United Kingdom: the Trade Union Reform and Employment Rights Act became law (July 1).

1993   Indonesia: the government banned the first congress of the independent Indonesia Prosperity Labor Union (August). The union, formed in November 1990, claimed 50,000 members but had twice been refused official registration by the Department of Manpower.

1993   India: national strike by millions of employees against the national government's economic reforms (September 9).

1994   The International Labour Organisation adopted a Convention and Recommendation designed to protect the conditions of part-time workers (June 7-24).

1994   Vietnam: a new labor law which forced every foreign joint enterprise to establish a labor union within six months (June).

1994   The International Confederation of Free Trade Unions launched a campaign against child labor (June).

1994   Indonesia: Muchtac Pakpahan, the leader of the independent Indonesia Prosperity Labor Union, sentenced to three years jail for allegedly inciting riots in Medan in April (November 7). His sentence was extended to four years in January 1995.

1994   European Commission's White Paper on Social Policy (August); it recognized employers' organizations, unions, and voluntary associations as partners in the development of social policy.

1995   The International Confederation of Free Trade Unions announced that 528 union activists were murdered during 1994 (June).

1995   United States: the United Steelworkers, the United Auto Workers, and the International Association of Machinists agreed to a merger (July). Lane Kirkland stepped down as president of the AFL-CIO (August) and was replaced by John J. Sweeney (October).

1995   Merger of the the Miners' International Federation and the International Federation of Chemical, Energy, and General Workers' Unions to form the International Federation of Chemical, Energy, Mine, and General Workers' Unions (November).

1996   Campaign by the International Federation of Commercial, Technical, and Clerical Employees for union recognition by the U.S. firm Toys "R" Us in 60 countries.

Appendix 3 UNION MEMBERSHIP STATISTICS

The neglect of labor union statistics

The following tables trace the growth and main features of labor union membership in the world since about 1870, data which do not seem to have been collected in this way before. I found them useful in placing the growth of labor unionism in the wider historical perspective and I hope others do too. Collecting them was an arduous exercise, especially as I was concerned to collect as much published data as I could find by country before 1940. By and large, the figures refer to labor unions able to engage in collective bargaining in a reasonably free political and legal environment. Therefore, they exclude countries whose unions were (or are) under the effective control of an authoritarian government such as under fascism or communism.

I realize that these statistics present many problems of their own, but I felt there was more to be gained by collecting them than leaving them in their widely scattered sources. I have been strengthened in this view by the absence of data on labor unions in the main readily available reference books on historical statistics. B. R. Mitchell, *International Historical Statistics: Europe, 1750-1988* (New York: Stockton Press, 1992), follows his earlier international statistical works and gives data on the negative side of organized labor, that is labor disputes, but ignores labor union membership despite the time series information available in George S. Bain and Robert Price, *Profiles of Union Growth: A Comparative Statistical Portrait of Eight Countries* (Oxford: Basil Blackwell, 1980). The second volume of Peter Flora and others' monumental data book, *State, Economy, and Society in Western Europe, 1815-1975* (Chicago: St. James Press, 1987), had been planned to include labor union membership data but this chapter was never completed.

Despite their social and economic importance, neither the United Nations nor the International Labour Organisation (ILO) accepts the responsibility to regularly collect and publish labor union statistics for the whole world. This is a staggering omission from the global statistical record given that there were 128 million labor union members in the world in 1995. Some aggregate data *are* gathered by the International Confederation of Free Trade Unions but their results could hardly be described as readily available compared to those of the United Nations or the ILO; nor are they complete for a number of Western European countries (for example, Germany and Switzerland) but despite these defects this is the only single international source available from 1949.

The record of the ILO is particularly strange in this field. Since 1927 it has been publishing world labor dispute statistics-information of often dubious accuracy-but ignores the union membership data which are available for many member countries. After all, if a lone researcher with a young family can build a world time series for union membership figures in his spare time why can't the International Labour Organisation make greater efforts in this area?

The statistics as a source

There are two major problems with preparing historical statistics on the membership of labor unions. One is the nature of the membership data themselves. Labor union membership is often very difficult to measure accurately because of high labor turnover in some occupations, retirees who continue to be union members (this is an important feature of labor union membership in the United Kingdom and Germany), and the difficulty of keeping track of members who remain members but have ceased to pay their dues. Also, unions may exaggerate their membership to increase their bargaining power with employers or to gain greater representation at general conferences of unions.

The second major problem posed by union membership figures is linking them to the labor force of their particular countries. The concept of the labor force is a fairly recent one in statistical history, only being adopted widely since the 1930s. Before that, a variety of concepts and definitions were used which severely hampers international comparisons over time.

The labor force

Understanding the structure of the labor force is essential to studying organized labor and how it fits into the broader society. The main components of the labor force are set out in the following diagrams. The first diagram shows how the principal groups which make up the labor force can be identified within the total population. For the purposes of studying organized labor, the main groups are employers and employees. It must be stressed that this is a comparatively modern way of looking at the labor force and that the relative importance of the relationships shown has changed over time. For example, the proportion of the self-employed and those who worked in family enterprises was far higher before 1900 than after it.

Schema of the labor force

Total population				
Labor force (includes unemployed)				
Employed labor force				
Employer	Self-employed	Employee		
		Union member	Non-union member	

Within the employed labor force, it is important to grasp the distinction between an individual's industry and occupation to appreciate how the various divisions within the labor force have been a source of conflict within organized labor, particularly the century-old debate over whether unions should be organized by occupation or by industry.

The following diagram sets out some of the main features of the relationship between industry and occupation. It is based on how the United States classifies its labor force, but the broad principles are used by many other countries. Again, this is a modern way of examining the labor force and the diagram makes no attempt to capture the large shifts in the industrial and occupational composition of the labor force which have occurred since 1900. Chief among these shifts have been the decline of the primary industrial sector and, since about 1950, the rise of the tertiary or service sector. As well, the occupational composition of the labor force has been greatly altered by technological change and the general maturing of Western economies. This has been most evident in the growth of white-collar jobs and the stagnation in the number of blue-collar jobs. Further consideration of these trends is outside the purpose of this appendix, but it is sufficient to draw the reader's attention to an analytical framework which is also useful as a tool for historical research.

Schema of the relationship between industry and occupation

INDUSTRIES		
Primary	**Secondary**	**Tertiary**
Agriculture and Mining	Manufacturing	Service (all other industries)
OCCUPATIONS		
White-collar:	**White-collar:**	**White-collar:**
Managerial and professionals	Managerial and professionals	Managerial and professionals
Technical, sales, and administrative support	Technical, sales, and administrative support	Technical, sales, and administrative support
Blue-collar:	**Blue-collar:**	**Blue-collar:**
Service occupations	Service occupations	Service occupations
Precision production	Precision production	Precision production
Operators, fabricators and laborers	Operators, fabricators and laborers	Operators, fabricators and laborers
Farming, forestry and fishing		

Only a few countries in the world are fortunate enough to possess labor force statistics covering the last hundred years. The main source for this information is the population census which can be used to generate estimates of the number of employees at work not just for the whole economy but for particular industries and occupations. Union membership is related to the labor force by the concept of *union density*, that is the number of union members as a percent of the total number of employees at work or of a particular sub-group of those employees, for example the percentage of employees in the manufacturing industry who are union members.

In 1940 the United States became the first country in the world to collect labor force statistics from a regular household survey, an example followed by other countries since 1945. The timing of these surveys varies but in 1996 there were only four countries in the world which conducted monthly surveys: United States, Canada, Japan, and Australia. As well as collecting standard labor force data, these surveys can be used to monitor labor union membership, data which began in 1973 for the United States (although the present survey began in 1983), in 1976 for Australia (with follow-up surveys held in 1982, 1986, and thereafter every two years to 1992, and then annually), in 1984 in Canada, in 1987 in Sweden, and annually in the United Kingdom since 1989.

Comparisons of reported membership by unions and by those estimated from household surveys of trade union membership in Australia, the United Kingdom, and Canada in the 1980s suggest that unions tend to overestimate their memberships. Although subject to sampling error, the household surveys are a far more reliable source and provide a wide range of socio-demographic information not available elsewhere, such as age, sex, birthplace, and income. Of course these surveys cannot provide reliable information on the composition of individual unions.

Finally, a reminder to the reader that statistics need to be subjected to the same critical scrutiny as any other historical source. As mentioned earlier, what is presented here is done in the spirit of capturing a general picture of changes in union membership over the past 120 years. For many countries, the information is approximate only. Blanks indicate not just lack of data but also times when free trade unionism has been suppressed. Because data for a number of countries are not always available for the year shown, the data for the closest year has been used.

For further information on the problems in building time series for labor unions, I refer the reader to the extremely valuable discussions in George S. Bain and Robert Price, *Profiles of Union Growth: A Comparative Statistical Portrait of Eight Countries* (Oxford: Basil Blackwell, 1980).

Structure of the appendix

The following statistical tables are designed to illustrate the principal statistical features of the history of organized labor in the world. Tables 1 to 5 set out the growth of organized labor in the world since 1870. Tables 6 to 8 provide details of the membership of the main democratic international organizations of labor unions from 1901 to 1993. Tables 9 and 10 examine the relationship of union members to the number of employees in various countries since 1890. The composition of labor union membership by sex, white-collar membership, and industry for selected countries is presented in Tables 11, 12, and 13. Finally, Tables 14 to 18 address some features of labor unions for selected countries since 1980.

A. World Membership of Labor Unions

1. Growth of Organized Labor in the World, c.1870-1995

2. Labor Union Membership in Selected Countries, c.1870-1885/86

3. Labor Union Membership in Selected Countries, c.1890-1930

4. Labor Union Membership in Selected Countries, 1939/40-1970

5. Labor Union Membership in Selected Countries, 1980-1990

B. Membership of International Labor Union Bodies

6. Membership of the International Federation of Trade Unions, 1901-1945

7. Membership of the International Confederation of Free Trade Unions, 1949-1995

8. International Confederation of Free Trade Unions: Membership by Region, 1949-1995

C. Proportion of Employees in Labor Unions

9. Labor Union Density in Selected Countries, c.1890-1930

10. Labor Union Density in Selected Countries, 1950-1990

D. Structure of Labor Union Membership

11. Women in Labor Unions in Selected Countries, 1892-1994

12. White-Collar Membership of Labor Unions in Selected Countries, 1892-1994

13. Distribution of Labor Union Members by Selected Industry Groups: Australia, New Zealand, UK, and USA, 1900-1990

E. Features of Organized Labor since 1980

14. Percentage Distribution of Union Members by Age: Australia and USA, 1982/83, 1990, and 1995

15. Median Weekly Earnings of Union Members, Australia and USA, 1982/83-1995

16. Labor Union Members as a Percentage of All Employees by Age and Sex: Australia, UK, and USA, 1993

17. Labor Union Members by Sex, Industry and Other Features: Australia, UK and USA, 1995

18. Labor Union Members by Public/Private Sector and Occupational Groups: Australia, UK and USA, 1994-95

1. GROWTH OF ORGANIZED LABOR IN THE WORLD, c.1870-1995

Year	Europe	North America	Other	Total
Membership in thousands				
1870	490	300	-	790
1880	545	50	11	606
1886	828	1,010	53	1,891
1890	1,867	325	263	2,455
1900	4,361	869	133	5,363
1913	10,675	2,764	612	14,051
1920	36,038	5,149	2,431	43,618
1930	19,839	3,484	7,543	30,866
1940	11,461	8,239	4,022	23,722
1950	33,241	14,436	10,288	57,965
1960	33,267	18,508	14,604	66,379
1970	40,321	23,421	20,863	84,605
1980	53,934	23,492	20,377	97,804
1990	43,178	14,120	31,149	88,447
1995	56,608	14,559	57,133	128,300

2. LABOR UNION MEMBERSHIP IN SELECTED COUNTRIES, c.1870-1885/86

Country	c.1870	c.1880	c.1886
Membership in thousands			
UK	289	464	581
USA	300	50	1,010
France	120	60 (a)	110
Germany	77	21	137
Austro-Hungarian Empire (Czech lands)	4	-	-
Australia	-	11	50
New Zealand	-	-	3
TOTAL	790	606	1,891

(a) Paris only.

3. LABOR UNION MEMBERSHIP IN SELECTED COUNTRIES, c.1890-1930

Country	Early 1890s	Early 1900s	1913	1920	1930
Membership in thousands					
Western Europe					
Finland	-	-	28	59	15
Sweden	9	67	134	403	554
Iceland	-	-	-	1	4
Norway	20	20	64	143	140
Denmark	31	96	153	362	339
Luxembourg	-	-	-	-	18
Germany	357	850	2,974	10,517	6,925
Austria	47	119	263	1,004	817
Switzerland	-	90	122	313	320
Belgium	-	42	203	920	671
Netherlands	16	19	234	684	625
France	232	492	1,027	1,053	900
Spain	5	26	128	220	946
Portugal	-	-	90	100	-
Italy	41	280	435	3,410	-
Ireland (a)	50	67	70	189	102
UK	1,109	2,025	4,135	8,348	4,842

(a) Irish data are also included in the UK figure up to 1920; the 1920 figure shown refers to 1922. They are included here separately for their intrinsic interest.

3. CONTINUED

Country	Early 1890s	Early 1900s	1913	1920	1930
Membership in thousands					
Eastern Europe					
Greece	-	-	-	-	83
Russia	-	123	-	5,200	-
Bulgaria	-	3	30	36	19
Poland	-	15	160	947	979
Romania	-	4	40	300	80
Hungary	-	23	115	343	141
Estonia	-	-	-	-	13
Latvia	-	-	-	-	26
Lithuania	-	-	-	-	18
Bosnia	-	-	5	-	-
Croatia	-	-	7	-	-
Serbia	-	5	10	-	-
Yugoslavia	-	-	-	25	49
Czecho-slovakia	-	62	318	1,650	1,213

3. CONTINUED

Country	Early 1890s	Early 1900s	1913	1920	1930
Membership in thousands					
Americas					
USA	325	869	2,588	4,775	3,162
Canada	-	-	176	374	322
Argentina	-	-	23	68	280
Brazil	-	-	-	-	270
Cuba	-	-	-	-	71
Chile	-	-	-	150 (a)	204 (b)
Mexico	-	-	-	1,000	1,837
Peru	-	-	-	-	25
Uruguay	-	-	-	-	28

(a) 1923. (b) 1927.

3. CONTINUED

Country	Early 1890s	Early 1900s	1913	1920	1930
Membership in thousands					
Africa, Asia, Middle East and Oceania					
Australia (a)	200	97	498	685	856
New Zealand	63	24	72	96	102
Japan	-	8	-	103	354
Korea	-	-	-	-	123
India	-	-	-	150	242
Ceylon	-	-	-	-	114
South Africa	-	4	12	135	118
Egypt	-	-	7	40	-
Palestine	-	-	-	4	20
Dutch East Indies	-	-	-	-	32
Philippines	-	-	-	-	67
China	-	-	-	-	2,800

(a) The Australian figure for 1890 was supplied by Michael Quinlan and Margaret Gardner of Griffith University from their data base on Australian labor unions and labor disputes.

4. LABOR UNION MEMBERSHIP IN SELECTED COUNTRIES, 1939/40-1970

Country	1939/40	1950	1960	1970
Membership in thousands				
Finland	66	269	468	950
Sweden	971	1,278	1,879	2,546
Norway	307	488	542	759
Denmark	543	714	987	1,143
Germany	-	5,513	7,687	8,251
Austria	-	1,291	1,501	1,520
Switzerland	385	627	728	843
Belgium	350	1,173	1,468	1,606
Netherlands	798	1,160	1,354	1,585
France	1,300	4,000	2,592	3,549
Italy	-	7,200	3,908	5,225
Ireland	163	285	319	381
UK	6,558	9,243	9,835	11,178
USA	7,877	13,430	17,049	21,248
Canada	362	1,006	1,459	2,173
Australia	956	1,605	1,912	2,331
New Zealand	248	267	332	379
India	511	1,821	3,077	4,887
Japan	9	5,774	7,662	11,605

5. LABOR UNION MEMBERSHIP IN SELECTED COUNTRIES, 1980, 1990 ,AND 1994

Country	1980	1990	1994
- Membership in thousands -			
Finland	1,646	1,895	1,802
Sweden	3,486	3,855	3,372
Norway	1,049	1,291	1,351
Denmark	1,796	2,107	1,971
Germany	9,261	9,620	11,685
Austria	1,661	1,644	-
Switzerland	954	892	-
Belgium	2,310	2,291	-
Netherlands	1,741	1,426	-
France	3,374	1,970	1,632
Italy	8,772	9,568	-
UK	12,947	8,611	-
Ireland	381	490	-
USA	20,095	16,740	16,748
Canada	3,397	4,031	-
Australia (a)	2,568	2,660	2,283
New Zealand	516	437	376
Japan	12,369	12,265	12,898
India (b)	3,727	6,329	-

(a) The 1980 figure shown refers to 1982.

6. MEMBERSHIP OF THE INTERNATIONAL FEDERATION OF TRADE UNIONS, 1901-1945

Year	Number of country affiliates	Membership of affiliates (thousands)	Percentage of world union members
1901	8	1,168.0	21.8
1905	14	2,949.5	-
1910	18	6,118.7	-
1913	21	7,702.4	54.8
1920	21	22,701.1	52.0
1925	21	13,366.4	-
1930	26	13,578.8	44.0
1935	23	9,078.3	-
1939	26	14,638.0	61.7
1945	21	24,751.8	-

7. INTERNATIONAL CONFEDERATION OF FREE TRADE UNION: MEMBERSHIP , 1949-1995

Year	Number of country affiliates	Membership of affiliates (millions)
1949	51	48.0
1955	75	54.3
1959	97	56.0
1965	96	60.3
1969	95	63.0
1975	88	51.8
1979	87	67.0
1989	97	80.3
1995	135	124.9

8. INTERNATIONAL CONFEDERATION OF FREE TRADE UNIONS: MEMBERSHIP BY REGION, 1949-1995

Region	1949	1959	1969	1979	1989	1995
Percentage						
Africa	(a)	2.3	0.9	0.5	0.8	5.3
Asia	13.7	17.6	10.8	18.4	21.7	19.3
Middle East	(a)	(a)	1.9	4.3	2.2	1.2
Western Europe	43.0	46.7	39.8	55.2	43.6	33.6
Eastern Europe	0	0	7.3	0	0	9.0
North America	30.5	26.3	22.4	2.5 (b)	17.6	11.7
Latin America and Caribbean	12.3	6.5	14.6	15.8	11.5	17.7
Oceania	(a)	0.5	2.3	3.3	2.7	2.3
Total	100	100	100	100	100	100
Total members (millions)	48	56	63	67	80	125

(a) Less than 0.5 percent.
(b) Fall caused by the withdrawal of the AFL-CIO between 1969 and 1981.

9. LABOR UNION DENSITY IN SELECTED COUNTRIES, c.1890-1930

Country	Early 1890s	Early 1900s	1913	1920	1930
Percentage of employees					
Finland	-	-	14	25	5
Sweden	1	5	8	28	36
Norway	-	3	8	20	19
Denmark	-	14	15	35	32
Germany	3	6	18	53	34
Austria	1	3	5	51	38
Switzerland	-	10	13	26	24
Belgium	-	3	10	45	28
Netherlands	2	2	17	36	30
France	3	7	13	12	9
Italy	-	6	6	39	-
Ireland	-	-	-	36	19
UK	10	13	16	48	26
USA	3	6	9	17	9
Canada	-	-	7	15	14
Australia	23	8	34	46	51
New Zealand	-	8	19	26	24
Japan	-	-	-	-	3

10. LABOR UNION DENSITY IN SELECTED COUNTRIES, 1950- 1990

Country	1950	1960	1970	1980	1990
Percentage of employees					
Finland	29	39	62	82	71
Sweden	68	73	73	88	84
Norway	50	63	51	57	57
Denmark	52	63	64	86	88
Germany	35	38	38	41	33
Austria	62	66	64	59	58
Switzerland	39	36	30	33	31
Belgium	49	58	57	46	53
Netherlands	42	39	37	32	23
France	38	21	22	17	11
Italy	50	35	38	54	47
Ireland	46	54	53	57	42
UK	44	44	47	51	38
USA	28	26	27	22	16
Canada	33	35	35	31	36
Australia	59	58	50	49	41
New Zealand	44	44	39	48	40
Japan	56	32	35	31	25

11. WOMEN IN LABOR UNIONS IN SELECTED COUNTRIES, 1892-1994

Year	UK	Germany	Australia	USA	Japan
Women as a percentage of total members					
1892	-	2	-	-	-
1896	9	-	-	-	-
1900	8	3 (a)	-	-	-
1913	11	8	4	4 (b)	-
1920	16	-	11	8	-
1930	16	8 (c)	14	-	-
1940	17	-	16	9	-
1950	18	18	19	17 (d)	23
1960	20	18	20	18	26
1970	25	16	24	24	-
1980	29	21	32	24 (e)	-
1990	38	26	37	37	28 (f)
1994	44	32	40	40	(g)

(a) 1902-03. (b) 1910. (c) 1931. (d) 1954. (e) 1978. (f) 1991. (g) Not published.

12. WHITE-COLLAR MEMBERSHIP OF LABOR UNIONS IN SELECTED COUNTRIES, 1892-1994

Year	UK	Denmark	Germany	USA
Percentage of total union members				
1892	3	-	-	-
1901	5	8	-	-
1911	13	13	-	-
1921	15	20	13	-
1930	22	21	20	-
1940	23	21	-	11 (a)
1950	23	25	15 (b)	14 (c)
1960	26	30	16	12
1970	33	38	20	22
1980	40 (d)	46	24	38 (e)
1990	35	47	25	43
1994	33	-	28	45

(a) 1939. (b) 1951. (c) 1956. (d) 1979. (e) 1983.

13. DISTRIBUTION OF LABOR UNION MEMBERS BY SELECTED INDUSTRY GROUPS BY PERCENTAGE, 1900-1990

Year	Australia	New Zealand	UK	USA
MINING				
1900	-	20.7	28.1	15.1
1913	8.1	3.6	23.4	15.9
1920	6.1	4.3	15.1	8.7
1930	5.0	2.6	13.5	6.8
1940	5.2	1.6	11.7	8.7
1950	3.0	0.8	8.2	3.2
1960	2.0	0.5	7.5	0.6
1970	1.5	0.2	3.3	1.0
1980	2.7 (c)	0.1	3.3	1.0 (d)
1990	2.2	0.9 (a)	1.9	0.7
MANUFACTURING				
1900	-	37.7	43.7	34.2
1913	29.2	27.5	39.2	29.3
1920	32.5	36.6	42.2	37.9
1930	34.7	27.3	39.2	23.2
1940	39.5	31.5	38.0	38.3
1950	38.4	38.5	41.0	42.8 (b)
1960	36.1	37.6	41.7	51.3
1970	35.4	38.6	45.0	41.9
1980	24.7 (c)	34.6	29.4	29.9 (d)
1990	19.6	22.3 (a)	25.2	25.1

(a) 1991. (b) 1953. (c) 1982. (d) 1983.

13. CONTINUED

Year	Australia	New Zealand	UK	USA
TRANSPORTATION AND COMMUNICATIONS				
1900	-	30.6	10.6	21.8
1913	25.2	30.4	18.8	20.5
1920	21.7	28.5	16.0	24.9
1930	19.1	28.7	19.4	26.0
1940	15.6	17.0	17.6	21.8
1950	15.2	14.8	16.0	26.6
1960	12.1	15.2	14.5	13.2
1970	10.3	7.1	12.3	12.0
1980	12.0 (c)	10.0	6.1	12.3 (d)
1990	11.1	10.2 (a)	7.8	11.6
ALL OTHER INDUSTRIES				
1900	-	11.0	17.6	28.9
1913	37.5	38.5	18.6	34.3
1920	39.7	30.6	26.6	28.5
1930	41.2	41.4	27.9	44.0
1940	39.7	49.9	32.7	31.2
1950	43.4	45.9	34.8	27.4 (b)
1960	49.8	46.7	36.3	34.9
1970	52.8	54.1	39.4	30.3
1980	60.6 (c)	55.3	61.2	56.8 (d)
1990	67.1	66.6 (a)	65.1	62.1

(a) 1991. (b) 1953. (c) 1982. (d) 1983.

14. PERCENTAGE DISTRIBUTION OF UNION MEMBERS BY AGE: AUSTRALIA AND USA, 1982/83, 1990, AND 1995

Country	1982/83 (a)	1990	1995
Percentage of total labor union members			
UNDER 25 YEARS			
Australia	22.3	17.9	15.3
USA	9.9	7.0	6.2
25-34 YEARS			
Australia	27.7	28.4	25.8
USA	28.8	25.9	22.0
35-44 YEARS			
Australia	21.9	27.3	28.3
USA	26.2	31.8	32.1
45-54 YEARS			
Australia	17.1	17.8	22.8
USA	20.1	22.0	27.4
55 YEARS AND OVER			
Australia	10.9	8.7	7.9
USA	15.1	13.2	12.2
Number of union members (thousands)			
Australia	2,568	2,660	2,252
USA	17,717	16,740	16,360

(a) Australia (March to May 1982) and USA (1983).

15. MEDIAN WEEKLY EARNINGS OF UNION MEMBERS, AUSTRALIA AND USA, 1982/83-1995

Year	AUSTRALIA		USA	
	Union members ($)	Percentage over non-union members	Union members ($)	Percentage over non-union members
FULL-TIME EMPLOYEES - MALES				
1982/83	295	3.05	411	14.11
1986	391	4.86	482	18.26
1988	445	6.07	506	17.79
1990	506	4.15	542	15.68
1992	538	4.46	589	18.51
1995	637	8.48	640	20.78
FULL-TIME EMPLOYEES - FEMALES				
1982/83	234	1.71	307	22.48
1986	319	5.02	368	25.54
1988	368	7.61	403	25.56
1990	426	7.51	448	27.23
1992	480	9.17	484	25.41
1995	555	9.73	527	26.76
FULL-TIME EMPLOYEES - PERSONS				
1982/83	276	6.88	398	27.64
1986	372	7.80	444	26.80
1988	423	8.98	480	25.83
1990	484	8.06	509	23.38
1992	521	7.29	547	24.50
1995	601	8.49	602	25.75

16. LABOR UNION MEMBERS AS A PERCENTAGE OF ALL EMPLOYEES BY AGE AND SEX: AUSTRALIA, UK AND USA, 1993

Ages (years)	Birth period	Australia	UK	USA
Union members as a % of employees in same category				
MALES				
Under 25	1969-78	28.3	18.6	18.4
25-34	1959-68	40.1	35.0	15.1
35-44	1949-58	46.3	44.8	21.6
45-54	1939-48	47.5	47.2	27.1
55-64	1929-38	44.7	41.7	25.7
65 and over	Before 1928	23.8	13.0	9.4
FEMALES				
Under 25	1969-78	25.7	17.5	4.7
25-34	1959-68	33.4	32.6	10.6
35-44	1949-58	38.1	36.1	15.8
45-54	1939-48	36.6	35.9	19.0
55-64	1929-38	38.1	35.0	15.6
65 and over	Before 1928	17.0 (a)	4.9	7.8
PERSONS				
Under 25	1969-78	27.0	18.1	5.9
25-34	1959-68	37.2	33.9	13.0
35-44	1949-58	42.6	40.5	18.8
45-54	1939-48	42.7	41.5	23.1
55-64	1929-38	42.5	38.7	20.8
65 and over	Before 1928	21.2	9.2	8.6

(a) Subject to a relative standard error of over 25 percent.

17. LABOR UNION MEMBERS BY SEX, INDUSTRY, AND OTHER FEATURES: AUSTRALIA, UK, AND USA, 1995

Selected feature	Australia	UK	USA
Number ('000)	2,252	7,275	16,360
% Males	60	55	61
% Females	40	45	39
Proportion of employees in same category (%)			
Males	36	35	17
Females	29	30	12
Persons	33	32	15
Full-time (a)	39	36	17
Part-time (a)	23	21	8
Mining	46	36	14
Manufacturing	39	32	18
Construction	31	26	18
Transportation	50	49	27
Wholesale and retail	20	11	6
Finance and property	23	19	2
Public administration and defense	50	59	38

(a) The data for full-time and part-time proportions for Australia refer to 1994.

18. LABOR UNION MEMBERS BY PUBLIC/PRIVATE SECTOR, OCCUPATIONAL GROUPS: AUSTRALIA, UK AND, USA, 1994-95

Selected feature	Australia (a)	UK	USA
Number ('000)	2,2252	7,275	16,360
Proportion of employees in same category (%)			
Public sector	56	61	38
Private sector	25	21	10
White collar	31	32	12
Blue collar	42	33	19
Managers and administrators	19	21	6
Professional	39	52	21
Associated professional and technical	53	47	12
Clerical	28	27	13
Craft and related	41	37	23
Sales	24	12	5
Plant and machine operators	55	43	24
Laborers and related	37	28	20
All occupations	33	32	15

(a) The data shown for Australia from Public sector to Laborers and related relate to 1994.

NOTES AND SOURCES FOR TABLES

1. GROWTH OF ORGANIZED LABOR IN THE WORLD, c.1870-1995

SOURCES: Tables 2, 3, 4, 8. The membership of the International Confederation of Free Trade Unions has been used as the basis of the world total of union membership from 1950. It should be noted that figures compiled by the the International Confederation of Free Trade Unions are incomplete for a number of countries in Western Europe and therefore require some adjustment.

2. LABOR UNION MEMBERSHIP IN SELECTED COUNTRIES, c.1870-1885/86

SOURCES: **UK:** B. C. Roberts, *The Trade Union Congress, 1868-1921* (London: George Allen & Unwin, 1958), p. 379. Data are for 1871, 1881, and 1885. [Note: these data refer only to TUC affiliates and so underestimate total union membership, but this seems to be the only time series available for this period.] **USA:** Estimates in Lance E. Davis and others, *American Economic Growth: An Economist's History of the United States* (New York: Harper & Row, 1972), p. 220. Data are for 1870, 1880, and 1886. **France:** Val R. Lorwin, *The French Labor Movement* (Cambridge, Massachusetts: Harvard University Press, 1954), pp. 12, 18, 23; Edward Shorter and Charles Tilly, *Strikes in France, 1830-1968* (Cambridge: Cambridge University Press, 1974), p. 371. Data are for 1870, 1881, and 1886. **Germany:** Michael Schneider, *A Brief History of the German Trade Unions* (trans. Barrie Selman, Bonn: J. H. W. Dietz Nachf., 1991), p. 383. Data are for 1869, 1880, and 1885. **Austro-Hungarian Empire:** Marcel van der Linden and Jürgen Rojahn (eds.), *The Formation of Labour Movements* (Leiden: E.J. Brill, 1990), Vol. II, p. 334. Data refer to 1871. **Spain:** Dick Geary (ed.), *Labour and Socialist Movements in Europe before 1914* (Oxford: Berg Publishing, 1989), p. 245. Data are for 1881. **Australia:** J. T. Sutcliffe, *A History of Trade Unionism in Australia* (Melbourne: Macmillan, 1967), pp. 66-7. Data are for 1879 and 1885. **New Zealand:** H. Roth, *Trade Unions in New Zealand: Past and Present.* (Wellington: A.H. and A.W. Reed, 1973), p. 167. Data are for 1885.

3. LABOR UNION MEMBERSHIP IN SELECTED COUNTRIES, c.1890-1930

SOURCES: The primary sources were: Arthur M. Ross and Paul T. Hartman, *Changing Patterns of Industrial Conflict* (New York and London: John Wiley & Sons, 1960), pp. 200-1; George S. Bain and Robert Price, *Profiles of Union Growth: A Comparative Statistical Portrait of Eight Countries* (Oxford: Basil Blackwell, 1980); Jelle Visser, *In Search of Inclusive Unionism,* Special Issue, *Bulletin of Comparative Industrial Relations,* No. 18. (Deventer, Netherlands and Boston: Kluwer Law and Taxation Publishers, 1990), p. 18; Marcel van der Linden and Jürgen Rojahn (eds.), *The Formation of Labour Movements* (Leiden: E.J. Brill, 2 vols., 1990), pp. 141, 143, 300, 334, 357, 385, 411, 517, 666; A. P. Coldrick and Philip Jones (eds.), *The International Directory of the Trade Union Movement* (London and Basingstoke: Macmillan, 1979) *passim*; W. Schevenels, *Forty-Five Years: International Federation of Trade Unions* (Brussels: Board of Trustees of the International Federation of Trade Unions, 1956), p. 63; Commonwealth of Australia, Bureau of Census and Statistics, *Labour Reports* (Melbourne/Canberra: Government Printer), 1922-32.

Other data were drawn from: Val R. Lorwin, *The French Labor Movement* (Cambridge, Massachusetts: Harvard University Press, 1954), p. 23; Edward Shorter and Charles Tilly, *Strikes in France, 1830-1968* (Cambridge: Cambridge University Press, 1974), pp. 371-72; Michael Schneider, *A Brief History of the German Trade Unions* (trans. Barrie Selman, Bonn: J. H. W. Dietz Nachf., 1991), pp. 383-86; Daniel L. Horowitz, *The Italian Labor Movement* (Cambridge, Massachusetts: Harvard University Press, 1963), pp. 44 n. 106 (1893 data), 59 n. 21, 75, 111, 125; John W. Boyle, *The Irish Labor Movement in the Nineteenth Century* (Washington, D.C.: Catholic University of America Press, 1988), pp. 125, 127; Charles McCarthy, *Trade Unions in Ireland, 1894-1960* (Dublin: Institute of Public Administration, 1977), pp. 622, 635; Leo Wolman, *The Growth of American Trade Unions, 1880-1923* (New York: National Bureau of Economic Research Inc., 1924), p. 124; Lance E. Davis and others, *American Economic Growth: An Economist's History of the United States* (New York: Harper & Row, 1972), p. 220; H. Roth, *Trade Unions in New Zealand: Past and Present* (Wellington: A. H. and A. W. Reed, 1973), pp. 167-70; New Zealand, *Official Year Books*; John P. Windmuller, *Labor Relations in the Netherlands* (New York: Cornell University Press, 1969), p. 39; Dick Geary (ed.), *Labour and Socialist*

Movements in Europe before 1914 (Oxford: Berg Publishers Ltd., 1989), pp. 245, 254; Augustus D. Webb, *The New Dictionary of Statistics* (London: George Routledge and Sons Ltd., 1911), pp. 602, 606 (data for Austria for 1892 and 1901; and for 1906 for Hungary and Switzerland); Gary K. Busch *The Political Role of International Trade Unions* (London: Macmillan, 1983), pp. 110, 124; Walter Kendall, *The Labour Movement in Europe* (London: Allen Lane, 1975), Statistical Appendix; U.S. Bureau of Labor Statistics, *Monthly Labor Review*, December 1991, p. 48; W. Galenson (ed.), *Labor in Developing Economies* (Berkeley and Los Angeles: University of California Press, 1963), pp. 216, 283; *Longman's Trade Unions of the World* (London: Longmans, 2nd ed., 1987), p. 205 (Palestine, 1920).

4. LABOR UNION MEMBERSHIP IN SELECTED COUNTRIES, 1939/40-1970

SOURCES: As for Table 3; Japan Institute of Labour, *Japanese Working Life Profile: Labour Statistics, 1992-93* (Tokyo: Japan Institute of Labour, 1992), p. 48; *Indian Labour Book*, 1973 ed., p. 55, 1990 ed., p. 73. [Official Indian figures are known to underestimate the true level of union membership.]

5. LABOR UNION MEMBERSHIP IN SELECTED COUNTRIES, 1980-1994

SOURCES: As for Table 4: U.S. Department of Labor, Bureau of Labor Statistics, *Monthly Labor Review*, December 1991, p. 48. Australian Bureau of Statistics, *Trade Union Members, Australia* (Product No. 6325.0.40.001). 1994 data have largely been drawn from the International Confederation of Free Trade Unions and official published sources.

6. MEMBERSHIP OF THE INTERNATIONAL FEDERATION OF TRADE UNIONS, 1901-1945

SOURCES: W. Schevenels, *Forty-Five Years: International Federation of Trade Unions* (Brussels: Board of Trustees of the International Federation of Trade Unions, 1956), pp. 23, 62, 423-5; Tables 1 and 2.

7. INTERNATIONAL CONFEDERATION OF FREE TRADE UNIONS: MEMBERSHIP, 1949-1995

SOURCES: John P. Windmuller, *The International Trade Union Movement* (Deventer: Kluwer, 1980), p. 62; data after 1979 were supplied by the International Confederation of Free Trade Unions.

8. INTERNATIONAL CONFEDERATION OF FREE TRADE UNIONS: MEMBERSHIP BY REGION, 1949-1995

SOURCES: As for Table 7.

9. LABOR UNION DENSITY IN SELECTED COUNTRIES, c.1890-1930

SOURCES: As for Table 3; Australian data for 1890 and 1900 calculated by the author; Peter Flora and others, *State, Economy, and Society in Western Europe, 1815-1975* (Chicago: St. James Press, 1987), Vol. II, pp. 689-753 contains a valuable nonagricultural employees series which was used to calculate union density for some countries.

Note: (1) density refers to the number of labor union members as percentage of employees; (2) boundary changes affect the statistics (e.g., for Austria). Some of the data refer to nonagricultural employees only.

10. LABOR UNION DENSITY IN SELECTED COUNTRIES, 1950- 1990

SOURCES: As for Table 3; J. Visser, "Trends in Trade Union Membership," *OECD Employment Outlook*, July 1991, p. 140; Anthony Ferner and Richard Hyman (eds.). *Industrial Relations in the New Europe* (Oxford: Basil Blackwell, 1992), p. 285 (Austria), p.330 (Netherlands).

Note: density refers to the number of labor union members as percentage of employees.

11. WOMEN IN LABOR UNIONS IN SELECTED COUNTRIES, 1892-1994

SOURCES: George S. Bain and Robert Price, *Profiles of Union Growth: A Comparative Statistical Portrait of Eight Countries* (Oxford: Basil Blackwell, 1980), pp. 37-8, 102, 115, 123-24; United Kingdom Employment Department, *Employment Gazette*, January 1983, p. 26, January 1992, p. 188, May 1995, p. 192; Michael Schneider, *A Brief History of the German Trade Unions* (Bonn: J.H.W. Dietz Nachf., 1991), pp. 82, 184, 384-85, 387; *Statistiches Jahrbuch 1995 für die Bundesrepublik Deutschland*, p. 741; Australian Bureau of Statistics, *Trade Union Statistics, Australia* (Catalogue No. 6323.0) [1980 data]; Australian Bureau of Statistics, *Trade Union Members, Australia* (Catalogue No. 6325.0) [1990 data] *Trade Union Members, Australia* (Product No. 6325.0.40.001), p.19 [1994 data]; Leo Wolman, *The Growth of American Trade Unions, 1880-1923* (New York: National Bureau of Economic Research, 1924), pp. 98-9; James J. Kenneally, *Women and American Trade Unions* (St. Albans, Vermont: Eden Press Women's Publications Inc., 1978), p. 218; *Statistical Abstract of the United States* [data for 1954-78]; U.S. Bureau of Labor Statistics, *Employment and Earnings*, January 1991, p. 229, January 1996, p. 210; *Japan Statistical Yearbook*, 1961, p. 351; Ministry of Labour, Japan, *Year Book of Labour Statistics*, 1991, p. 320.

12. WHITE-COLLAR MEMBERSHIP OF LABOR UNIONS IN SELECTED COUNTRIES, 1892-1994

SOURCES: As for Table 11; Robert Price and George S. Bain, "Union Growth in Britain: Retrospect and Prospect," *British Journal of Industrial Relations*, Vol. XXI, No. 1 (1983), p. 51; Jürgen Kocka, *White-Collar Workers in America, 1890-1940* (London and Beverley Hills: Sage Publications, 1980, p. 234; U.S. Bureau of Labor Statistics, *Employment and Earnings*, January 1996, p. 212.

13. DISTRIBUTION OF LABOR UNION MEMBERS BY SELECTED INDUSTRY GROUPS BY PERCENTAGE, 1900-1990

SOURCES: **Australia**: Commonwealth Bureau of Census and Statistics, *Labour and Industrial Branch Report* (Melbourne: Government Printer), 1912-22; Commonwealth Bureau of Census and Statistics/Australian Bureau of Statistics, *Labour Report*

(Melbourne/Canberra: Government Printer), 1923-73; Australian Bureau of Statistics, *Trade Union Members, Australia* (Catalogue No. 6325.0), 1982, 1990. **New Zealand:** Appendix to the Journals of the House of Representatives H.11 [for pre-1924 data); *New Zealand Official Year-Book* [for data up to 1980]; Raymond Harbridge and Kevin Hince, "Unions and Union Membership in New Zealand," *New Zealand Journal of Industrial Relations*, Vol. 18, No. 3, December 1993, p. 358. **United Kingdom:** George S. Bain and Robert Price, *Profiles of Union Growth: A Comparative Statistical Portrait of Eight Countries* (Oxford: Basil Blackwell, 1980), pp. 43-78; Department of Labour, *Employment Gazette*, January 1983, p. 27, April 1992, p.189. **USA:** U.S. Department of Commerce, *Historical Statistics of the United States* (Washington, D.C.: U.S. Government Printing Office, 1975), Part 1, p. 178; George S. Bain and Robert Price, *Profiles of Union Growth: A Comparative Statistical Portrait of Eight Countries* (Oxford: Basil Blackwell, 1980), pp. 94-5; Department of Labor, Bureau of Labor Statistics, *Handbook of Labor Statistics 1975-Reference Edition* (Washington D.C.: U.S. Government Printing Office, 1975), pp. 383, 385; Department of Labor, Bureau of Labor Statistics, *Employment and Earnings*, January 1985, p. 209, January 1990, p. 231.

Note: The data used to construct this table were drawn from two different types of sources: data provided by unions for the period up to 1970 for Australia and the United States, up to 1980 for New Zealand, and up to 1990 for the United Kingdom, and data from household surveys for the remaining years. Consequently, the comparability within the table might be affected to some degree.

14. PERCENTAGE DISTRIBUTION OF UNION MEMBERS BY AGE: AUSTRALIA AND USA, 1982/83, 1990, AND 1995

SOURCES: Australian Bureau of Statistics, *Trade Union Members, Australia,* issues for March to May 1982, August 1990 (Catalogue No. 6235.0); Australian Bureau of Statistics, *Weekly Earnings of Employees (Distribution) Australia, August 1995* (Product No. 6310.0.40.001), pp. 33; U.S. Department of Labor, Bureau of Labor Statistics, *Employment and Earnings*, January 1985, p. 210, January 1991, p. 228, January 1996, p. 210.

15.   MEDIAN WEEKLY EARNINGS OF UNION MEMBERS, AUSTRALIA AND USA, 1982/83-1995

SOURCES: Australian Bureau of Statistics, *Trade Union Members, Australia* (Catalogue No. 6235.0), 1982-90.   The data for 1982 were unpublished and were taken from Table 6 of microfiche from the survey. The 1995 data are my calcuations from grouped income data from Australian Bureau of Statistics, *Weekly Earnings of Employees (Distribution) Australia, August 1995* (Product No. 6310.0.40.001), pp. 31-3;   U.S. Department of Labor, Bureau of Labor Statistics, *Employment and Earnings* (January issue from 1985 onwards).

Note: the data for 1982/83 refer to March to May 1982 for Australia and all of 1983 for the United States.

16.   LABOR UNION MEMBERS AS A PERCENTAGE OF ALL EMPLOYEES BY AGE AND SEX: AUSTRALIA, UK, AND USA, 1993

SOURCES: Australian Bureau of Statistics, *Working Arrangements, Australia*, August 1993 (Catalogue No. 6342.0), p. 23 and unpublished data (Table 1, p. 53); U.K. Labour Department, *Employment Gazette*, June 1994, pp. 191-96, February 1994, pp. S10-S11 [data refer to September to November 1993]; U.S. Department of Labor, Bureau of Labor Statistics, *Employment and Earnings*, January 1996, pp. 210, 212 [data refer to the whole of 1993].

17.   LABOR UNION MEMBERS BY SEX, INDUSTRY AND OTHER FEATURES: AUSTRALIA, UK, AND USA, 1995

SOURCES: Australian Bureau of Statistics, *Trade Union Members, Australia*, August 1994 (Product No. 6325.0.40.001), p. 1; Australian Bureau of Statistics, *Weekly Earnings of Employees (Distribution) Australia* (Product No. 6310.0.40.001), pp. 31-3;   U.K. *Labour Market Trends*, May 1996, pp. 216- 221 [data refer to September to November 1995]; U.S. Department of Labor, Bureau of Labor Statistics, *Employment and Earnings*, January 1996, pp. 210,212 [data refer to the whole of 1995].

Note: These data refer to employees in work only and were obtained from households conducted as a part of regular labor force surveys.

18. LABOR UNION MEMBERS BY PUBLIC/PRIVATE SECTOR AND OCCUPATIONAL GROUPS: AUSTRALIA, UK AND USA, 1994-95

SOURCES: As for Table 15.

BIBLIOGRAPHY

Introduction

Labor unions have always attracted interest from different disciplines, each offering its own insights; as well as historians, labor unions are regularly studied by economists, political scientists, sociologists, and lawyers. By showing the diversity of the field, the bibliography is designed to encourage greater cross-fertilization of ideas and techniques. In this regard, I hope it might be of use to specialists as well as beginners.

As the literature on this subject is vast, the bibliography is restricted mainly to scholarly books with their own bibliographies. I have given preference to works published since 1970; earlier works are listed where they have become sources in their own right or where they have attained the status of classics in the field or simply because there was no obvious later work. Because the study of organized labor is often controversial, the inclusion of a work in the bibliography does not necessarily imply my recommendation; it is simply to note its importance and possible interest to the reader.

The bibliography contains a comprehensive listing of international comparative studies of industrial relations because these works, both new and old, are convenient starting points for investigating countries as well as being useful sources of information on organized labor. Although they typically stress contemporary developments, they usually contain a summary of past historical developments.

Given that this dictionary is part of a series about religions, philosophies, and movements, it is also important not to overlook the more general guides to reference material. Of special importance is Alan Day and Joan M. Harvey (eds.), *Walford's Guide to Reference Material Volume 2: Social and Historical Sciences, Philosophy and Religion* (London: The Library Association, 5th ed., 1990).

Current information and references can be found in the journals which are listed in section A.6 of the bibliography and in works such as National Labor Relations Board, *New Books and Current Labor Articles* (Washington, D.C.). In addition, since the late 1980s the U.S. Department of Labor has published a series on all the major countries in the world called *Foreign Labor Trends*. Based on information supplied by American embassies, these publications contain a profile of the current state of labor in each country plus supporting statistics and are usually updated after several years. They are an especially valuable source for Third World countries where timely information is often hard to obtain.

The study of organized labor

For anyone just beginning to study organized labor, the best place to start is by gaining a general appreciation of economic history, specifically the Industrial Revolution and the economic, social, and intellectual ferment it created. I particularly recommend the six volumes of *The Fontana Economic History of Europe* edited by Carlo M. Cipolla (Glasgow: Collins/Fontana Books, 1972-76), Fernand Braudel's trilogy *Civilization and Capitalism:15th-18th Centuries* (London: Fontana Press, 1981, 1982, 1984), Sidney Pollard's *Peaceful Conquest: The Industrialization of Europe, 1760-1970* (Oxford: Oxford University Press, 1981), and Eric J. Hobsbawm's *Industry and Empire: An Economic History of Britain since 1750* (London: Weidenfeld and Nicholson, 1968). Hobsbawm has also written a stimulating trilogy from a Marxist point of view: *The Age of Revolution, 1789-1848* (New York: Mentor, 1962), *The Age of Capital, 1848-1875* (New York: Mentor, 1975), and *The Age of Empire, 1875-1914* (New York: Pantheon Books, 1987). For the United States, see Robert Heilbroner and Aaron Singer, *The Economic Transformation of America: 1600 to the Present.* Fort Worth, Texas: Harcourt Brace & Company, 3rd ed., 1994. Although not a history book along the lines of the previous works, I also recommend Lance E. Davis and others' *American Economic Growth: An Economist's History of the United States* (New York: Harper & Row, 1972) for the stimulating questions it raises about the process of economic development. More generally, for economic history in the twentieth century, the five-volume *Pelican History of the World Economy in the Twentieth Century* under the general editorship of Wolfram Fischer published between 1977 and 1986 is also recommended.

For the social and economic ferment of nineteenth century Europe, two good introductions from different points of view are given in the opening chapters of Philip Taylor, *The Distant Magnet: European Emigration to the U.S.A.* (New York: Harper Torchbooks, 1971) and in Dick Geary, *European Labour Protest, 1848-1939* (London: Methuen, 1984, first published in 1981). Although not about organized labor as such, John Carey, *The Intellectuals and the Masses, 1800-1939: Pride and Prejudice among the Literary Intelligentsia* (London: Faber, 1992) gives a valuable, if chilling, alternative perspective on one level of response to population growth and the rise of the modern working class. On social class, Arthur Marwick, *Class: Image and Reality in Britain, France and the USA since 1930* (Glasgow: Fontana/Collins, 1980) provides interesting reading. Works like these are important for helping to place the study of organized labor in a wider historical perspective, a perspective which can all too easily become lost in the forest of specialist studies.

For economic thought, Robert L. Heilbroner's *The Worldly Philosophers* (New York: Touchstone, 6th ed., 1986) is a masterly introduction to the world of economic ideas written with a wit and humor seldom found in such works. For economic issues generally, the major reference work is John Eastwell, Murray Milgate, and Peter Newman (eds.), *The New Palgrave: A Dictionary of Economics* (London and Basingstoke: Macmillan, 1987) which consists of four volumes and has bibliographies after each entry; the entries on arbitration, collective bargaining, strikes and trade unions are of particular interest. Also worth noting as a background reference work is Carl Heyel (ed.), *The Encyclopedia of Management* (New York: Van Nostrand Reinhold Company, 3rd ed., 1982).

Although organized labor has never lacked students since Adam Smith's famous reference to it in the *Wealth of Nations* (1776) as "combinations," they mainly attracted attention from economists and lawyers or from political theorists such as Karl Marx. By 1920 pioneers like Sidney and Beatrice Webb in Britain and John R. Commons and Selig Perlman in the United States established organized labor as an academically respectable field of study. Under their influence, organized labor tended to be studied from the viewpoint of its institutions; this was a "top down" approach with a strong emphasis on leaders.

Modern labor history dates from about 1960 with the works of American scholars like Irving Bernstein and David Brody and Eric Hobsbawm and E. P. Thompson in Britain. The publication of E. P. Thompson's *The Making of the English Working Class* (London: Victor Gollancz, 1963) was an inspirational milestone in labor history and a foundation work of modern social history.

What united the British and American works was their concern with the social and political setting of employees and to show the diversity of the experiences of particular groups. Over the past 30 years the output of social histories has been huge, although their quality has often been variable.

At this point, a word of warning is needed for the beginner. The study of organized labor is intimately bound up with the study of the Industrial Revolution whose effects have been hotly disputed by generations of participants and scholars. The older optimistic view of the Industrial Revolution, which E. P. Thompson rightly attacked, was that it represented general material progress. He was able to show that for many groups in the labor force conditions deteriorated.

Like any revolution, the Industrial Revolution had its good and bad sides but all too often only the bad is presented. Many of the sources are fiercely polemical and the secondary works are often similarly influenced. Studies often focus on the negative aspects of industrialization, on what went wrong rather than on what succeeded. It has often been more appealing to write about dramatic, noble failures, or the distressed condition of particular groups of workers than the slow, if duller process of general material improvement. Consider, for instance, the general absence of modern scholarly works about the cooperative movement compared to the abundance of books on the left wing of labor.

The debate about the Industrial Revolution continues to the present though in different forms. This is particularly evident in the attitudes of the various disciplines. The works of many of the economic writers, for example, tend to take a far more positive view of the Industrial Revolution than those of social historians. For these reasons, it is vital to keep an open mind about the subject and to be mindful of the political ideologies which often still color much of the writing about organized labor.

Finding out about organized labor

After gaining a broad appreciation of the Industrial Revolution, the following works provide a sound introduction to the study of labor unions. W. E. J. McCarthy (ed.), *Trade Unions: Selected Readings* (Harmondsworth: Penguin, 2nd ed., 1985) contains a valuable selection of important readings, some of which are hard to locate in their original form. Although written from a British and left-wing standpoint, Robin Blackburn and Alexander Cockburn (eds.), *The Incompatibles: Trade Union Militancy and the Consensus* (Harmondsworth: Penguin, 1967) is still stimulating. The political side of labor is approached in an interesting way by Walter Korpi in his *The Democratic Class Struggle* (London: Routledge Kegan Paul, 1983). There is an excellent up-to-date view of the topic by Jelle Visser, " Trade Unions from a Comparative Perspective" in Joris Van Ruysseveldt and others (eds.), *Comparative Industrial & Employment Relations* (London: Sage Publications, 1995), pp. 37-67.

For critical labor union functions and collective bargaining, see Allan Flanders (ed.), *Collective Bargaining: Selected Readings* (Harmondsworth: Penguin, 1969), and H. Katz and T. Kochan, *An Introduction to Collective Bargaining and Industrial Relations* (New York: McGraw-Hill, 1992). For labor economics, a useful introductory text is Lloyd G. Reynolds and others, *Labor Economics and Labor Relations* (Englewood Cliffs, New Jersey: Prentice-Hall, 9th ed., 1986).

There are numerous ways of approaching the many topics within the study of organized labor. For American studies, there are excellent bibliographical essays in Foster R. Dulles and Melvyn Dubofsky, *Labor in America: A History* (Arlington Heights, Illinois: Harlan Davidson, Inc., 4th ed., 1984), Bruce Laurie's *Artisans into Workers: Labor in Nineteenth-Century America* (New York: Hill and Wang, 1989), and Robert H. Zieger's *American Workers, American Unions, 1920-1985* (Baltimore and London: Johns Hopkins University Press, 1986). For British works, there are bibliographic guides in Henry Pelling's *A History of British Trade Unionism* (London: Macmillan, 5th ed., 1992) and Dick Geary's *European Labour Protest, 1848-1939* (London: Methuen, 1984).

Students of American and British labor are blessed with comprehensive and high-quality bibliographies which were published in the early 1980s, particularly those by Maurice F. Neufeld for the United States and Arthur Marsh for Britain. These can be readily supplemented by recourse to book reviews and book notices in journals like *Labor History*, the *Monthly Labor Review*, and the *British Journal of Industrial Relations*. *Labor History*, for instance, has published an annual bibliography of labor journal articles and other scholarly work since 1965.

The *Journal of Economic Literature* (Pittsburgh) contains a useful annotated listing of new books. For sheer convenience as well as breadth, there is an outstanding bibliography organized by country in Marcel van der Linden and Jürgen Rojahn (eds.), *The Formation of Labour Movements, 1870-1914: An International Perspective* (Leiden: E.J. Brill, 1990), Vol. II, pp. 701-81.

Another important bibliographical source is the International Labour Office's monthly publication *International Labour Documentation*, which has been issued since 1965. This covers all topics pertaining to labor and is international in coverage. The 195,000 records it contains can be accessed by computer (for a fee) on-line as LABORDOC.

Specific topics

Because the study of organized labor is often about the details of work, it is essential to gain some familiarity with industrial archaeology, which is concerned with the study of the physical remains and processes of the Industrial Revolution. As well as being important for its own sake, industrial archaeology gives many insights into the organization and conditions of work and living in past times. There is an excellent encyclopedia devoted to this subject, Barrie Trinder (ed.), *The Blackwell Encyclopedia of Industrial Archaeology* (Oxford: Basil Blackwell, 1992), which is international in scope and contains an excellent bibliography. In addition, Shire Publications Ltd., a British publisher, specialized in this field and their Shire Album series of over 100 booklets written by experts cover topics from chain making to woodworking tools. Several of these are listed in the bibliography.

Since the late 1970s, students of organized labor have some excellent labor-saving reference works at their disposal. There are historical directories of labor unions for Britain and the United States. The British series compiled by Arthur Marsh and Victoria Ryan consists of four volumes, *Historical Directory of Trade Unions* (Westmead: Gower Press, 1980, 1984, 1987, 1994). This remarkable series covers about 6,000 unions and a fifth volume is promised.

American unions are well covered by Gary M. Fink (ed.), *Labor Unions* (Westport, Connecticut: Greenwood Press, 1977), which has entries on over 200 U.S. unions, each entry with its own bibliography. The work also contains national union affiliation details, a chronology, union genealogies, union executive lists, membership statistics, and a glossary.

No comparable work is currently available for Australia, but in 1982 Michael Quinlan and Margaret Gardner at the School of Industrial Relations, Griffith University, Queensland, began to prepare a computer data base covering Australian unions and labor disputes between 1825 and 1925. By 1994 this data base contained reasonably full entries on 1,506 unions which operated between 1825 and 1900.

One of the most welcome developments of the past twenty years has been the appearance of biographical dictionaries of labor leaders. The labor movement is often ignored in many national biographical dictionaries, and it is often hard to find even the most elementary background information about its leaders let alone its rank-and-file. For Britain, the leading work is the nine volumes edited by Joyce Bellamy and John Saville, *Dictionary of Labour Biography* (London: Macmillan, 1972-93). For the United States, there is a one-volume work edited by Gary M. Fink, *Biographical Dictionary of American Labor* (Westport: Greenwood Press, rev. ed., 1985); first published in 1974 this work has entries on about 750 individuals.

A Biographical Register of the Australian Labour Movement, 1788-1975 is being prepared by Andrew Moore and John Shields at the University of Western Sydney; it is expected to cover 2,000 individuals.

With the exception of Britain, all these efforts seem small compared to what is now available for French labor. Jean Maitron (ed.), *Dictionnaire Biographique du Mouvement Ouvrier Français* (Paris: Les Editions Ouvriers, 1964-93) consists of 43 volumes and covers the period from 1789 to 1939. It includes leaders as well as rank-and-file members of the labor movement. Jean Maitron is also general editor of another series, *Dictionnaire Biographique du Mouvement Ouvrier International*, which consists of dictionaries for Austria, China and Japan (two volumes) and Germany. Section A.2 lists labor biographical dictionaries.

As might be expected, the greatest number of studies of organized labor concern Britain, the United States, and Western Europe. Henry Pelling's *A History of British Trade Unionism* (London: Macmillan, 5th ed., 1992) remains the best known survey work. W. Hamish Fraser, *Trade Unions and Society: The Struggle for Acceptance, 1850-1880* (London: George Allen & Unwin, 1974) covers the period well and the more recent work by Keith Laybourn, *A History of British Trade Unionism, c.1770-1990* (Wolfeboro Falls, New Hampshire: Allan Sutton, 1992), is a good guide to the academic debates of recent years. Hugh A. Clegg's *A History of British Trade Unions since 1889* (Oxford: Oxford University Press, 1964, 1985, 1994) is the standard scholarly work; the first volume was written with Alan Fox and A. F. Thompson. Although often heavy going, its three volumes now cover the period up to 1951. It is invaluable as a reference work.

For the United States, good comprehensive single-volume surveys are available in Foster Rhea Dulles and Melvy Dubofsky's *Labor in America* (Arlington Heights, Illinois: Harlan Davidson Inc., 4th ed., 1984) and Ronald L. Filippelli's *Labor in the USA: A History* (New York: Knopf, 1984). For Germany, John A. Moses, *Trade Unionism in Germany from Bismark to Hitler, 1869 to 1933* (London: George Prior Publishers, 1982, 2 vols.) provides a valuable survey with translations of some key documents. Moses's history can be profitably supplemented with the more recent work by Michael Schneider, *A Brief History of the German Trade Unions* (trans. Barrie Selman, Bonn: J.H.W. Dietz Nachf., 1991), which covers the whole period up to the present and is good for biographical details and statistics.

C. R. Dobson's *Masters and Journeymen: A Prehistory of Industrial Relations, 1717-1800* (London: Croom Helm, 1980) is a short but valuable work largely devoted to labor disputes in the eighteenth century. It is a reminder that labor unions and labor disputes were evident *before* the Industrial Revolution and, therefore, may presumably still be in existence in the often predicted post-industrial world.

For the ideas that have influenced organized labor and its general development, see Sima Lieberman, *Labor Movements and Labor Thought: Spain, France, Germany and the United States* (New York: Praeger, 1986). Michael Poole's *Theories of Trade Unionism* (London: Routledge & Kegan Paul, rev. ed., 1984) offers a sociological approach to labor unions.

Because of the variable coverage they give to organized labor, the bibliography does not include a separate section on histories of particular industries, although this is not to say they are unimportant; on the contrary, they must be investigated by serious students. That said, an exception needs to be made for John Hathcher and others' *The History of the British Coal Industry* (Oxford: Clarendon Press, 1984-93) a five-volume work on an industry which played a central role in British organized labor up to the 1950s.

Structure of the bibliography

The bibliography is in five parts. The first part lists reference works as well as journals; the second part is devoted to the attempts of labor to form international bodies and studies of labor which cross national boundaries; the third part contains a selection of works which deal with one country; the fourth part addresses features of organized labor; and the fifth part places organized labor in its social, political and economic environment, not an easy task because many titles actually fit into several categories. I have done this to remind students that the issues and trends discussed often have an international aspect. Finally, readers should note that the boundaries used are necessarily arbitrary.

A. Research guides, sources, and journals

A.1   Bibliographies and finding aids
A.2   Directories and reference works
A.3   Biographical dictionaries
A.4   Statistics
A.5   Sources
A.6   Selected classic labor studies
A.7   Journals

B. International studies

B.1   International unionism
B.2   International comparative studies

C. National studies

C.1   Histories of peak national organizations of unions
C.2   Histories of organized labor in individual countries
C.2.1   Africa
C.2.2   British Isles
C.2.3   Middle East and Asia
C.2.4   Europe
C.2.5   Latin America and the Caribbean
C.2.6   North America
C.2.7   Oceania
C.3   Industrial relations in particular countries

D. Features of labor unions

D.1   Histories of particular unions
D.2   Unions in particular industries or occupations
D.3   Ideas and movements
D.4   Biographies of labor leaders
D.5   Women's labor and labor unions
D.6   Democracy in labor unions
D.7   Industrial democracy
D.8   Inter-union relations
D.9   Labor disputes

E. Labor and its environment

E.1   The experience and study of work
E.2   Industrial archaeology
E.3   Unions and politics
E.4   Employers
E.5   Social histories and immigration
E.6   Labor and race
E.7   Labor sociology
E.8   Labor and the law
E.9   Labor and the media
E.10   Labor and the economic environment
E.11   The crisis of labor since 1980

A. RESEARCH GUIDES, SOURCES, AND JOURNALS

A.1 Bibliographies and finding aids

ABC-Clio Information Services. *Labor in America: A Historical Bibliography.* Santa Barbara, California: ABC-Clio, 1985. [Annotated bibliography of journal articles only.]

Allen, V. L. *International Bibliography of Trade Unionism.* London: Merlin Maspero, 1968.

Allison, Peter B. *Labor, Worklife and Industrial Relations: Sources of Information.* New York: Haworth Press, 1984.

Bain, George S., and Bennett, John (eds.). *Bibliography of British Industrial Relations, 1971-1979.* Cambridge: Cambridge University Press, 1985.

Bain, George S., and Woolven, Gillian B. (eds.) *Bibliography of British Industrial Relations.* Cambridge: Cambridge University Press, 1979. [Contains 15,000 works covering the period from 1880 to 1970.]

Bennett, John and Fawcett, Julian (eds.). *Industrial Relations: An International and Comparative Bibliography.* London and New York: Mansell Publishing Limited, 1985.

Bishoff, Ros; Mitchell, Richard; and Steer, Andrea (eds.). *Australian Labour Law: A Selected Bibliography.* Melbourne: Labour Studies Programme, University of Melbourne, 1985.

Burnett, John; Vincent, David; and Mayall, David (eds.). *The Autobiography of the Working Class: A Critical and Annotated Bibliography.* Brighton, Sussex, England: The Harvester Press/New York: New York University Press, 1984, 1987. 2 vols. [Covers the period from 1790 to 1945.]

Campbell, Anne and others (eds.). *Industrial Relations: A Select Annotated Bibliography.* London: Commonwealth Secretariat, c.1978.

Chan, Ming K. (ed.). *Historiography of the Chinese Labor Movement, 1895-1949: A Critical Survey and Bibliography of Selected Chinese Source Materials at the Hoover Institution.* Stanford, California: Hoover Institution Press, 1981.

Chester, A. E. *Aspects of Australian Industrial Relations: A Select Bibliography.* Adelaide: South Australian Institute of Technology, 1980.

Fox, M. J. and Howard, P. C. *Labor Relations and Collective Bargaining: A Bibliographical Guide to Doctoral Research.* Metuchen, New Jersey: Scarecrow Press, 1983.

Gibbney, H. J. (compiler). *Labor in Print: A Guide to the People who Created a Labor Press in Australia between 1850 and 1939.* Canberra: History Department, Research School of Social Sciences, Australian National University, 1975. [Lists 488 labor newspapers and publications.]

Harrison, Royden; Woolven, Gillian; and Duncan, Robert (eds.). *The Warwick Guide to British Labour Periodicals, 1790-1970: A Check List.* Atlantic Highlands, New Jersey: Harvester Press, 1977. [Lists 4,125 periodicals.]

Harzig, Christiane, and Hoerder, Dirk (eds.). *The Immigrant Labor Press in North America, 1840s-1970s: An Annotated Bibliography.* New York: Greenwood Press, 1987.

Hill, John. *Strikes in Australia: A Select Bibliography.* Canberra: Canberra College of Advanced Education Library, 1983.

Houkes, John M. *Industrial Relations Theses and Dissertations, 1949-1969: A Cumulative Bibliography.* Ann Arbor, Michigan: Xerox University Microfilms, 1973.

Huls, Mary E. (ed.). *United States Government Documents on Women, 1800-1900: A Comprehensive Bibliography. Vol. II: Labor.* Westport, Connecticut: Greenwood Publishing Group, 1993.

International Labour Office. *Annotated Bibliography on Child Labour.* Geneva: International Labour Office, 1986.

_____. *International Labour Documentation.* Geneva: International Labour Office, 1965 to date.

_____. *Women Workers: An Annotated Bibliography, 1983-94.* Geneva: International Labour Office, 1995.

Jadeja, Raj. *Parties to the Award: A Guide to the Pedigrees and Archival Resources of Federally Registered Trade Unions, Employers' Associations and Their Peak Councils in Australia.* Canberra: Noel Butlin Archives Centre, Research School of Social Sciences, Australian National University, 1994. [An extremely important research tool which includes a historical introduction and a comprehensive bilbliography.]

Jones, Gregory P. *A Guide to Sources of Information on Australian Industrial Relations.* Sydney: Pergamon Press, 1988.

Maley, Barry and others (eds.). *Industrial Democracy and Worker Participation.* Sydney: Department of Organizational Behaviour, University of New South Wales, 1979. [An annotated bibliography consisting of 560 works in English covering Australia and other countries covering the period from 1960-76.]

March, Arthur. *Employees Relations Bibliography & Abstracts.* Oxford: Employees Relations Bibliography and Abstracts, 1985. [A major bibliography with a concentration on British material.]

Marsh, Arthur (ed.). *Employee Relations Bibliography & Abstract Journal.* Oxford: Employee Relations Bibliography and Abstracts, 1989 to date. [Issued four times a year, this work supplements the same editor's 1985 *Employees Relations Bibliography & Abstracts.*]

Martens, G. R. (ed.). *African Trade Unionism: A Bibliography with a Guide to Trade Union Organizations and Publications.* Boston, Massachusetts: G.K. Hall, 1977. [Contains 946 references with over half in English.]

McBrearty, James (ed.). *American Labor History and Comparative Labor Movements: A Selected Bibliography.* Tucson, Arizona: University of Arizona Press, 1973.

Neufeld, Maurice F.; Leab, Daniel J.; and Swanson, Dorothy (eds.). *American Working Class History: A Representative Bibliography.* New York: R.R. Bowker Company, 1983. [A major work with about 7,200 entries including doctoral theses.]

Pettman, Barrie O. (ed.). *Industrial Democracy: A Selected Bibliography.* Bradford, West Yorkshire: MCB Publications, 1978.

_____. *Strikes: A Selected Bibliography.* Bradford, England: MCB Books, 1976. [Contains 1,230 references to books, reports, articles, and theses published between 1950-75 and covers thirty-two countries.]

Roth, Herbert O. (ed.). *New Zealand Trade Unions: A Bibliography.* Wellington: Oxford University Press, 2nd ed., 1977.

Shimakoa, H. R. *Selected Bibliographies on Labor and Industrial Relations in Australia, India, Japan, New Zealand and the Philippines.* Honolulu: University of Hawaii Industrial Relations Center, 1961.

Smart, John (ed.). *Records of the Department of Labour.* Ottawa: National Archives of Canada, 1988.

Smethurst, John B. (ed.). *A Bibliography of Co-operative Societies' Histories.* Manchester: Co-operative Union Ltd., n.d. [A comprehensive bibliography of British histories published in about 1971.]

Smith, Harold (ed.). *The British Labour Movement to 1970: A Bibliography.* London: Mansell, 1981. [Contains 3,838 references.]

Sri Lanka. Ministry of Labour. *Bibliography of Labour Relations.* Colombo, Sri Lanka: Ministry of Labour, 1981. 2 vols.

University of the Philippines, Asian Labor Education Center, Research Section. *An Annotated Bibliography on Philippine Labor.* Quezon City: National Book Store, 1979.

Vaisey, G. Douglas (ed.). *The Labour Companion: A Bibliography of Canadian Labour History Based on Materials Printed from 1950 to 1975.* Halifax, Nova Scotia: Committee on Canadian Labour History, 1980.

Vocino, Michael C. and Cameron, Lucille W. (eds.). *Labor and Industrial Relations Journals and Serials: An Analytical Guide.* New York: Greenwood Press, 1989.

Walsh, Kenneth. *Industrial Disputes: Methods and Measurement in the European Community.* Luxembourg, Office for the Official Publications of the European Communities: Eurostat, 1982.

Whitaker, Marian, and Miles, Ian (eds.). *Bibliography of Information Technology: An Annotated Critical Bibliography of English Language Sources since 1980.* London: Edward Elgar (Gower), 1989.

Zappala, Jon. *Workplace Industrial Relations in Australia: An Annotated and Selected Bibliography.* Sydney: Centre for Industrial Relations Research, University of Sydney and Business Council of Australia, 1988.

A.2 Directories and reference works

Arrowsmith, J. D. *Canada's Trade Unions: An Information Manual.* Kingston, Ontario: Queen's University Industrial Relations Centre Press, 1992.

Blanpain, Roger (ed.). *International Encyclopaedia for Labour Law and Industrial Relations.* Deventer, Netherlands: Kluwer, 1977 to date. 10 vols. [This work is in loose-leaf form and regularly updated.]

Bottomore, Tom (ed.). *A Dictionary of Marxist Thought.* Oxford: Blackwell Publications, 2nd ed., 1991. [First published in 1983, this comprehensive work has references at the end of entries.]

Buhle, Mari Jo; Buhle, Paul; and Georgakas, Dan (eds.). *Encyclopedia of the American Left.* New York and London: Garland Publishing, Inc., 1990. [An outstanding reference work, thorough, comprehensive, cross-referenced, references after entries, and an index.]

Campbell, Joan (ed.). *European Labor Unions*. Westport, Connecticut: Greenwood Press, 1993. [A major work dealing with both Eastern and Western Europe; it includes an appendix giving chronologies for the countries studied.]

Coldrick, A. P. and Jones, Philip. *The International Directory of the Trade Union Movement*. London and Basingstoke: Macmillan, 1979.

European Communities. *Glossary of Labour and the Trade Union Movement*. Luxembourg: European Communities, 1984. [English, French, Spanish, German, Italian, Dutch, Greek, Danish, Swedish, and Norwegian.]

Filippelli, Ronald L. (ed.). *Labor Conflict in the United States: An Encyclopedia*. New York and London: Garland Publishing, Inc., 1990.

Fink, Gary M. (ed.). *Labor Unions*. Westport, Connecticut: Greenwood Press, 1977. [A historical directory of over 200 U.S. unions. Each entry has a bibliography. The work also contains national union affiliation details, a chronology, union genealogies, union executive lists, membership statistics, and a glossary.]

Garlock, Jonathan. *Guide to the Local Assemblies of the Knights of Labor*. Westport, Connecticut: Greenwood Press, 1982.

Gifford, Courtney D. (ed.). *Directory of U.S. Labor Organizations, 1988-89 Edition*. Washington D.C.: Bureau of National Affairs, 4th ed., 1988. [First published 1982; other editions 1984, 1986.]

Greenfield, Gerald M., and Maram, Sheldon, M. (eds.). *Latin American Labor Organizations*. Westport, Connecticut: Greenwood Press, 1987.

Harbridge, Raymond, and Hince, Kevin. *A Sourcebook of New Zealand Trade Unions and Employee Organisations*. Wellington: Industrial Relations Centre, Victoria University of Wellington, 1994.

Huntley, Pat. *Australia's Super Unions*. Northbridge, New South Wales: Huntley Publications Pty. Ltd., 1993. [A loose-leaf subscription work which supersedes the author's *Australian Trade Union Monitor*.]

Industrial Relations Center, University of Hawaii. *Robert's Dictionary of Industrial Relations.* Washington, D.C.: Bureau of National Affairs/University of Hawaii Industrial Relations Center, 4th ed., 1994.

Information Australia. *Industrial Relations Index: A Guide to Unions, Employer Groups and the Industrial Relations Industry.* Melbourne: Information Australia, 1985 to date.

International Labour Office. *Encyclopaedia of Occupational Health and Safety.* Geneva: International Labour Office, 3rd ed., 1983. [First published 1930.]

Jones, J., and Morris, M. (eds.). *A-Z of Trade Unionism and Industrial Relations.* London: Heinemann, 1982.

Kittner, Michael (ed.). *Gewerkschafts Jahrbuch 1991.* Cologne: Bund-Verlag GmbH, 1991. [This German work included a chronology for 1990.]

Lecher, W. (ed.). *Trade Unions in the European Union: A Handbook.* London: Lawrence and Wishart, 1994.

Marsh, Arthur. *Concise Encyclopedia of Industrial Relations.* Westmead: Gower Press, 1979. [An excellent work with internal references and a separate bibliography.]

_____. *Trade Union Handbook.* Aldershot, England: Gower, 5th ed., 1991. [An excellent, historically informed guide to British organized labor in the early 1990s.]

Marsh, Arthur and Ryan, Victoria (eds.). *Historical Directory of Trade Unions.* Westmead, England: Gower Press, 1980, 1984, 1987 and 1994 (with John B. Smethurst, Scolar Press, Aldershot). 4 vols. [A 5th vol. is planned.]

Mikhov, Nanko. *World Trade Union Movement.* Sofia, Bulgaria: George Dimitrov Research Institute for Trade Union Studies, 1983.

Paradis, Adrian A. *The Labor Reference Book.* Philadelphia: Chilton Book Company, 1972. [A dictionary about American labor with a bibliography; it is still useful as a work for first resort.]

Rifkin, Bernard, and Rifkin, Susan (eds.). *American Labor Sourcebook.* New York: McGraw-Hill Book Company, 1979. [Although mainly about labor in the late 1970s, this excellent work includes a detailed chronology and glossary of terms.]

Russell, Spomer C., and Nixon, J. M. *American Directory of Organized Labor: Unions, Locals, Agreements, and Employers.*   Detroit, Michigan: Gale Research Company, 1992.

Schneider, Dorothy and Schneider, Carl J. (eds.).   *The ABC-CLIO Companion to Women in the Workplace.* Santa Barbara, California: ABC-Clio, 1993.

Sutcliffe, Paul, and Callus, Ron. *Glossary of Australian Industrial Relations Terms.* Sydney: Australian Centre for Industrial Relations Research and Teaching, University of Sydney, and Australian Centre in Strategic Management, Queensland University of Technology, 1994.

Trinder, Barrie (ed.). *The Blackwell Encyclopedia of Industrial Archaeology.* Oxford: Basil Blackwell, 1992. [A major reference work with international coverage and a large bibliography.]

Upham, Martin (ed.). *Trade Unions and Employers' Organizations of the World.* London: Longman, 1993. [A major reference work issued in loose-leaf form concentrating on the current scene but with some historical material.]

_____. *Trade Unions of the World, 1992-93.* Harlow, Essex: Longman Current Affairs, 3rd ed., 1991. [First published 1987.]

Yerbury, Di, and Karlsson, Maria. *The CCH Macquarie Dictionary of Employment and Industrial Relations.* Sydney: CCH Australia and Macquarie Library Pty. Ltd., 1992.

A.3 Biographical dictionaries

Andreucci, Franco, and Tommasco, Detti (eds.). *Il movimento operaio italiano; Dizionario biografico, 1853-1943.* Rome: Riuniti, 1975-78. 5 vols.

Bellamy, Joyce, and Saville, John. *Dictionary of Labour Biography.* London: Macmillan, 1972-93. 9 vols.

Bianco, L., and Chevrier, V. *Dictionnaire Biographique du Mouvement Ouvrier International: La Chine.* Paris: Editions Ouvrières, 1985. [An important reference work on the Chinese labor movement.]

Bourdet, Y. and others (eds.). *Dictionnaire Biographique du Mouvement Ouvrier International: Autriche.* Paris: Editions Ouvrières, 1982.

Droz, Jacques (ed.). *Dictionnaire Biographique du Mouvement Ouvrier International: L'Allemagne.* Paris: Editions Ouvrières, 1990. [Covers the German labor mouvement up to the 1930s.]

Fink, Gary M. (ed.). *Biographical Dictionary of American Labor.* Westport, Connecticut: Greenwood Press, rev. ed., 1985. [Contains entries on about 750 individuals. First published 1974.]

Knox, William (ed.). *Scottish Labour Leaders, 1918-39: A Biographical Dictionary.* Edinburgh: Mainstream Publishing, 1984.

Lane, A. Thomas (ed.). *Biographical Dictionary of European Labor Leaders.* Westport, Connecticut: Greenwood Press, 1995. 2 vols.

Maitron, Jean (ed.). *Dictionnaire Biographique du Mouvement Ouvrier Français.* Paris: Les Editions Ouvrières, 1964-93. 43 vols. [Covers the period from 1789 to 1939.]

Moore, Andrew and Shields, John (eds.). *A Biographical Register of the Australian Labour Movement, 1788-1975.* [In preparation.]

Shiota, S. (ed.). *Dictionnaire Biographique du Mouvement Ouvrier International: Japon.* Paris: Editions Ouvrières, 1982. 2 vols.

A.4 Statistics

Australian Bureau of Statistics, *A Guide to Labour Statistics*. Canberra: Australian Bureau of Statistics, 1986. [ABS Catalogue No. 6102.0.]

Bain, G. S., and Price, R. *Profiles of Union Growth: A Comparative Statistical Portrait of Eight Countries*. Oxford: Basil Blackwell, 1980. [The countries were Britain, United States, Australia, Canada, Germany, Sweden, Denmark, and Norway.]

Bairoch, P. and others. *The Working Population and Its Structure*. Brussels: Free University of Brussels, 1968. [Contains census data on the industry structure of the labor force from the last half of the nineteenth century to the present for every country.]

Bean, R. (ed.). *International Labour Statistics: A Handbook, Guide, and Recent Trends*. London and New York: Routledge, 1989. [Includes data on labor union membership as well as labor disputes.]

Conk, Margo. *The United States Census and Labor Force Change: A History of Occupational Statistics, 1870-1940*. Ann Arbor, Michigan: UMI Research Press, 1980.

Flora, Peter; Kraus, Franz; and Pfenning, Winfried. *State, Economy, and Society in Western Europe, 1815-1975: A Data Handbook*. Chicago: St. James Press, 1983, 1987. 2 vols. [Chapter 10, pp. 679-753 of Vol. II contains valuable annual time series on the labor force and labor disputes.]

International Labour Office. *Sources and Methods: Labour Statistics, Volume 7, Strikes and Lockouts*. Geneva: International Labour Office, 1993. [Explains the collection methods used for collecting labor dispute data for each ILO member as well as giving the titles of national publications.]

_____. *Year Book of Labour Statistics*. Geneva: International Labour Office, 1935-36 to date. [From 1927 published as Vol. II of the ILO *Year Book*, this is the principal international source of labor force data; it includes statistics on labor disputes, hours worked, unemployment, occupational health and safety, consumer prices indices, household income and expenditure surveys, but not labor unions.]

_____. *Year Book of Labour Statistics:Retrospective Edition on Population Censuses, 1945-1989.* Geneva: International Labour Office, 1990.

Lacey, Michael and Fumer, Mary (eds.). *The State and Social Investigation in Britain and the United States.* Cambridge: Cambridge University Press, 1993.

Organisation for Economic Co-operation and Development. *Historical Statistics 1960-1990.* Paris: OECD, 1992.

Plowman, D. H. *Australian Trade Union Statistics.* Sydney: Industrial Relations Research Centre, University of New South Wales, 2nd ed., 1981.

Rawson, D. W. and Wrightson, Sue. *Australian Unions 1984.* Sydney: Croom Helm Australia, 1985. [First published 1970.]

Routh, Guy. *Occupation and Pay in Great Britain, 1906-79.* London: Macmillan, 2nd ed., 1980. [First published 1965.]

United States Department of Labor, Bureau of Labor Statistics. *Employment and Earnings.* Washington: Department of Labor, Bureau of Labor Statistics, 1969 to date.

Visser, Jelle. *European Trade Unionism in Figures, 1913-1985.* Deventer, Netherlands, and Boston: Kluwer, 1989.

_____. *In Search of Inclusive Unionism.* Special Issue, *Bulletin of Comparative Industrial Relations*, No.18. Deventer, Netherlands, and Boston: Kluwer Law and Taxation Publishers, 1990.

Walsh, Kenneth. *Trade Union Membership: Methods and Measurement in the European Community.* Brussels: EUROSTAT, 1985.

A.5 Sources

Auerbach, Jerold S. (ed.). *American Labor: The Twentieth Century.* Indianapolis and New York: Bobbs-Merrill Company Inc., 1969. [This is still a useful documentary collection.]

Baxandall, Rosalyn and others (eds.). *America's Working Women: A Documentary History-1600 to the Present.* New York: Random House, 1976.

Blewett, Mary H. (ed.). *We Will Rise in Our Might: Working Women's Voices from Nineteenth-Century New England.* Ithaca, New York: Cornell University Press, 1991.

Callus, Ron; Morehead, Alison; Cully, Mark; and Buchanan, John. *Industrial Relations at Work: The Australian Workplace Industrial Relations Survey*, Australian Government Publishing Service, Canberra, 1991. [This important survey was conducted in 1989-90 and a second survey was held in 1995.]

Cole, G. D. H. and Filson, A .W. *British Working Class Movements: Select Documents, 1789-1875.* London: Macmillan, 1951. [A major collection of documents which was reprinted in 1965 and again in 1967.]

Commons, John R. and others (eds.). *A Documentary History of American Industrial Society.* New York: Russell and Russell, 1910-11. 10 vols.

Daniel, W. W. and Millward, Neil. *Workplace Industrial Relations in Britain.* London: Heinemann, 1983.

Foner, Philip S., and Shapiro, Herbert (eds.). *Northern Labor and Antislavery: A Documentary History.* Westport, Connecticut: Greenwood Press, 1994.

Gorman, John. *To Build Jerusalem: A Photographic Remembrance of British Working Class Life, 1875-1950.* London: Scorpion Publishing Ltd., 1980.

Hagan, Jim (ed.). *Australian Trade Unionism in Documents.* Melbourne: Longman Cheshire, 1986.

Hurley, F. Jack. *Industry and the Photographic Image: 153 Great Prints from 1850 to the Present.* New York: Dover Publications in association with George Eastman House, 1980.

International Labor Office. *Legislative Series.* Geneva: International Labor Office, 1919-89; continued as *Labour Law Documents,* 1990 to date.

_____. *World Labour Report 2.* Geneva: International Labor Office, 1985. [Included a report on organized labor.]

McKinlay, Brian (ed.). *Australian Labor History in Documents.* Burwood, Victoria: Collins Dove, 1990. 3 vols. [A revised version of a work originally published in 1979.]

Millward, Neil, and Stevens, Mark. *British Workplace Industrial Relations.* Aldershot, England: Gower, 1986.

Millward, Neil and others. *Workplace Industrial Relations in Transition.* Aldershot, England: Dartmouth, 1992.

Rock, Howard B. (ed.). *The New York Artisan, 1789-1825: A Documentary History.* Albany: State University of New York Press, 1989.

Traugott, Mark (ed.). *The French Worker: Autobiographies from the Early Industrial Era.* Berkeley and Oxford: University of California Press, 1993. [English translation.]

Troy, Leo and Sheflin, Neil. *Union Sourcebook - Membership, Structure, Finance, Directory.* West Orange, New Jersey: Industrial Relations Data and Information Services, 1985.

Ward, J. T. and Fraser, W. Hamish. *Workers and Employers: Documents on Trade Unions and Industrial Relations in Britain since the Eighteenth Century.* London and Basingstoke: Macmillan, 1980.

A.6 Selected classic labor studies

Bell, Lady Florence. *At the Works: A Study of a Manufacturing Town.* London: Virago Press, 1985. [Reproduction of the first edition published by Edward Arnold, London, in 1907; it was a study of Middlesborough, Yorkshire.]

Coghlan, Timothy A. *Labour and Industry in Australia from the First Settlement in 1788 to the Establishment of the Commonwealth in 1901.* Oxford: Oxford University Press, 1918. 4 vols. [Reissued by Macmillan, Melbourne, in 1968.]

Commons, John R. and others. *History of Labor in the United States.* New York: Macmillan, 1918-35. 4 vols.

Coombes, B. L. *These Poor Hands: The Autobiography of a Miner Working in South Wales.* London: Victor Gollancz, 1939.

Engels, Frederick. *The Condition of the Working Class in England.* London: Panther Books, 1969.

Fynes, Richard. *The Miners of Northumberland and Durham: A History of their Social and Political Progress.* Sunderland, England: Thos. Summerbell, 1963. [First published 1873.]

Mayhew, Henry. *London Labour and the London Poor.* New York: Dover Publications, 1968, 4 vols. [Reproduction of the edition of 1861-62.]

Orwell, George. *The Road to Wigan Pier.* Harmondsworth, England: Penguin Books, 1962, reprinted many times thereafter. [First published 1937.]

Paris, Le Comte de. *The Trade Unions of England.* Trans. Nassau J. Senior. London: Smith, Elder and Company, 1869.

Roberts, Peter. *Anthracite Coal Communities: A Study of the Demography, the Social, Educational and Moral Life of the Anthracite Regions.* New York: Macmillan, 1904.

Thompson, E. P. and Yeo, Eileen (eds.). *The Unknown Mayhew:Selections from the Morning Chronicle, 1849-50.* London: Merlin Press, 1971.

Tressell, Robert [pen-name of Robert Noonan]. *The Ragged Trousered Philanthropists.* London: Panther Books, 1965. [A novel set in the building trade in Hastings, England, in about 1906. It was originally published in an incomplete and misleading form by his daughter in 1914 and a full version based on the complete manuscript was not published until 1955]

Webb, Sidney, and Webb, Beatrice. *History of Trade Unionism.* London: Longmans, Green, rev. ed. 1907. [First published 1894.]

_____. *Trade Union Democracy.* London: Longmans, Green, 1898. 2 vols.

Wilkinson, Ellen. *The Town That Was Murdered: The Life-Story of Jarrow.* London: Victor Gollancz, 1939.

Wilson, John. *A History of the Durham Miners' Association, 1870-1904.* Durham: J.H. Veitch & Sons, 1907.

A.7 Journals

Asian Labour Update (Kowloon), 1980 to date.

British Journal of Industrial Relations (London School of Economics), 1963 to date.

Bulletin of Comparative Labour Relations (Deventer), 1968 to date.

Conditions of Work Digest (International Labor Office,Geneva), 1986 to date.

Economic and Industrial Democracy (Industrial Relations Services, London), 1980 to date.

Employee Relations (Bradford), 1978 to date.

European Industrial Relations Review (London), 1974 to date.

European Journal of Industrial Relations (London), 1995 to date.

Free Labour World (International Confederation of Free Trade Unions, Brussels), 1968 to date.

Government Employee Relations Report (Bureau of National Affairs, Washington D.C), 1952 to date. [A detailed indexed, weekly report on federal, state, and local government industrial relations in the United States.]

Historical Abstracts (New York), 1955 to date.

Historical Studies in Industrial Relations (Keele), 1996 to date.

IDS European Report (Income Data Services, London), 1984 to date.

Indian Journal of Industrial Relations (New Delhi), 1965 to date.

Industrial and Labor Relations Review (Ithaca, New York), 1946 to date.

Industrial Law Journal (London/Oxford), 1971 to date.

Industrial Relations (Berkeley), 1961 to date.

Industrial Relations Journal (Oxford), 1970 to date.

Industrial Relations Review and Report (Industrial Relations Services, London), 1975 to date.

International Journal of Comparative Labour Law and Industrial Relations (Deventer), 1977 to date.

International Journal of Human Resource Management (London), 1990 to date.

International Labor and Working Class History (Los Angeles), 1976 to date.

International Labour Review (International Labour Office, Geneva), 1923 to date.

International Review of Social History (Assen, Netherlands), 1956 to date.

Japan Labor Bulletin (Tokyo), 1961 to date.

Japanese Unionism Information (Australia-Japan Exchange Centre, University of New South Wales), 1991 to date.

Journal of Communist Studies (London), 1985 to date.

Journal of Economic Literature (Pittsburgh), 1962 to date. [Particularly useful for its annotated lists of new books which cover labor and economic history topics.]

Journal of Industrial Relations (Sydney), 1959 to date.

Journal of Labor Economics (Chicago), 1983 to date.

Journal of Labour Research (Fairfax), 1980 to date.

Journal of Management Studies (Oxford), 1964 to date.

Journal of Social History (Berkeley, California), 1967 to date.

Labor Developments Abroad (U.S. Department of Labor, Bureau of Labor Statistics), 1956-1972. [A useful compendium of international labor events and developments for this period.]

Labor History (New York), 1960 to date.

Labor Law Journal (Chicago), 1949 to date.

Labor Studies Journal (Rutgers University, New Jersey), 1975 to date.

Labour & Industry (Brisbane/Geelong), 1987 to date.

Labour and Society (Geneva), 1977 to date.

Labour Market Trends [present title: the original title was *The Labour Gazette*] (Department of Employment; formerly the Department of Labour, London), 1893 to date.

Labour/Le Travail (Halifax), 1976 to date.

Labour, Capital and Society (Montreal), 1979 to date.

Labour History (Canberra/ Sydney), 1962 to date.

Labour Research (London), 1980 to date.

Labour: Review of Labour Economics and Industrial Relations (Rome), 1987 to date.

Monthly Labor Review (U.S. Bureau of Labor Statistics, Washington D.C.), 1915 to date.

New Zealand Journal of Industrial Relations (Dunedin), 1976 to date.

Policy Studies (London), 1979 to date.

Socialist Register (London), 1964 to date.

Transfer (Brussels), 1995 to date.

Work, Employment and Society (Durham, England), 1987 to date.

B. INTERNATIONAL STUDIES

B.1 International unionism

Alcock, Antony. *History of the International Labour Organisation.* London: Macmillan, 1971.

Barnouin, Barbara. *The European Labor Movement and European Integration.* London and Wolfeboro, New Hampshire: Frances Pinter (Publishers), 1986.

Bendiner, Barton. *International Labour Affairs: The World Trade Unions and the Multinational Companies.* Oxford: Oxford University Press, 1987.

Busch, Gary K. *Political Currents in the International Trade Movement.* London: The Economist Intelligence Unit, 1980. 2 vols.

_____. *The Political Role of International Trade Unions.* London: Macmillan, 1983.

Ghebali, Victor-Yves. *The International Labour Organisation: A Case Study on the Evolution of U.N. Specialised Agencies.* Dordrecht, Boston, and London: Kluwer Academic Publishers, 1989.

Holthoon, F. van, and Linden, Marcel van der (eds.). *Internationalism in the Labour Movement, 1830-1940.* Leiden: E.J. Brill, 1990.

Horne, John N. *Labour at War: France and Britain, 1914-1918.* Oxford: Clarendon Press, 1991.

International Confederation of Free Trade Unions. *Annual Survey of Violations of Trade Union Rights.* Brussels: International Confederation of Free Trade Unions, 1984 to date.

_____. *The Challenge of Change: Report to the 14th ICFTU World Congress on the Tasks Ahead for the International Free Trade Union Movement.* Brussels: International Confederation of Free Trade Unions, 1988.

International Labour Office. *World Labour Report.* Geneva: International Labour Office, 1984 to date. [*Reports* 2 and 6 contain chapters on the state of labor unions in the world.]

Linden, Marcel van der, and Rojahn, Jürgen (eds.). *The Formation of Labour Movements: An International Perspective, 1870-1914.* Leiden: E.J. Brill, 1990. 2 vols.

MacShane, Denis. *International Labour and the Origins of the Cold War.* Oxford: Clarendon Press, 1992.

Milner, Susan. *The Dilemmas of Internationalism: French Syndicalism and the International Labor Movement, 1900-1914.* New York: Berg Publishers Ltd., 1990.

Newton, Douglas J. *British Labour, European Socialism and the Struggle for Peace, 1889-1914.* Oxford: Clarendon Press, 1985.

Prochaska, Alice. *History of the General Federation of Trade Unions.* London: Allen & Unwin, 1982. [A useful work on this neglected body which represented British labor internationally before 1914.]

Schevenels, Walther. *Forty-Five Years: International Federation of Trade Unions.* Brussels: Board of Trustees of the International Federation of Trade Unions, 1956. [An important source work written by a leading participant.]

Teague, Paul, and Gahl, John. *Industrial Relations and European Integration.* London: Lawrence & Wishart, 1992.

Thorpe, W. *The Workers Themselves: Revolutionary Syndicalism and International Labour.* Dordrecht, Netherlands: Kluwer, 1990.

Wallerstein, I. (ed.). *Labor in the World Social Structure.* London: Sage Publications, 1983.

Windmuller, J. P. *The International Trade Union Movement.* Deventer: Kluwer, 1980.

World Federation of Trade Unions. *The World Federation of Trade Unions, 1945-1985.* Prague: World Federation of Trade Unions, 1985.

B.2 International comparative studies

Adams, R. (ed.). *Comparative Industrial Relations: Contemporary Research and Theory.* London: Harper Collins, 1991.

Adams, R.A. (ed.). *Industrial Relations Under Liberal Democracy: North America in Comparative Perspective.* Columbia, South Carolina: University of South Carolina Press, 1995.

Ananaba, Wogu. *The Trade Union Movement in Africa: Promise and Performance.* London: Hurst, 1979.

Baglioni, Guido, and Crouch, C. (eds.) *European Industrial Relations: The Challenge of Flexibility.* London: Sage, 1990.

Ballot, M. and others. *Labor-Management Relations in a Changing Environment.* New York: John Wiley, 1992.

Bamber, Greg J., and Lansbury, Russell D. (eds.). *International and Comparative Industrial Relations: A Study of Industrialised Market Economies.* Sydney: Allen & Unwin, 1993.

Barbash, Jack, and Barbash, Kate (eds.). *Theories and Concepts in Comparative Industrial Relations.* Columbia, South Carolina: University of South Carolina Press, 1989.

Bean, R. *Comparative Industrial Relations: An Introduction to Cross-National Perspectives.* London: Croom Helm, 1985.

Beyme, Klaus von. *Challenge to Power: Trade Unions and Industrial Relations in Capitalist Countries.* London: Sage, 1980.

Boyd, Rosalind E.; Cohen, Robert; and Gutkind, Peter C. (eds.). *International Labour and the Third World: The Making of a New Working Class.* Aldershot, England: Aveburg, 1987. [Contains an extensive bibliography.]

Brandell, I. (ed.). *Workers in Third World Industrialization.* London: Macmillan, 1991.

Córdova, Efren (ed.). *Industrial Relations in Latin America.* New York: Praeger, 1984.

Crouch, Colin. *Industrial Relations and the European State Traditions.* Oxford: Clarendon Press, 1992.

Damachi, Ukandi G.; Seibel, H. Dieter; and Trachtman, Lester (eds.). *Industrial Relations in Africa.* New York: St. Martin's Press, 1979.

Dore, Ronald. *British Factory-Japanese Factory: The Origins of National Diversity in Industrial Relations.* London: Allen & Unwin, 1974.

Dunlop, John, and Galenson, Walter (eds.). *Labor in the Twentieth Century.* New York: Academic Press, 1978.

Ferner, Anthony and Hyman, Richard (eds.). *Industrial Relations in the New Europe.* Oxford: Basil Blackwell, 1992.

_____. *New Frontiers in European Industrial Relations.* Cambridge, Massachusetts: Blackwell Publishers, 1994.

Frenkel, Stephen (ed.). *Organized Labor in the Asia-Pacific Region: A Comparative Study of Trade Unionism in Nine Countries.* Ithaca, New York: ILR Press, 1993. [Studies Australia, China, Malaysia, New Zealand, Hong Kong, Singapore, South Korea. and Taiwan.]

Frenkel, Stephen and Harrod, Jeffrey (eds.). *Industrialization & Labor Relations: Contemporary Research in Seven Countries.* Ithaca, New York: ILR Press, 1995. [A study of South Korea, Malaysia, Hong Kong, Singapore, South Africa, Thailand and Taiwan.]

Galenson, Walter (ed.). *Comparative Labor Movements.* New York: Prentice-Hall, 1952.

_____. *Labor and Economic Growth in Five Asian Countries: South Korea, Malaysia, Taiwan and the Philippines.* New York: Praeger, 1992.

Geary, Dick (ed.). *Labour and Socialist Movements in Europe before 1914.* Oxford: Berg Publishing Ltd., 1989. [Deals with the United Kingdom, France, Germany, Russia, Italy, and Spain.]

Hanson, Charles; Jackson, Sheila; and Miller, Douglas. *The Closed Shop: A Comparative Study in Public Policy and Trade Union Security in Britain, the USA and West Germany.* New York: St. Martin's Press, 1982.

Martin, Ross M. *Trade Unionism: Purposes and Forms.* Oxford: Clarendon Press, 1989. [Concentrates on the political aspects of trade unions; it also contains a comprehensive and well-organized bibliography.]

Maurice, M.; Sellier, F.; and Silvestre, J. *The Social Foundations of Industrial Power: A Comparison of France and Germany.* Cambridge, Massachusetts: M.I.T. Press, 1986.

Mommsen, Wolfgang, J. ; and Husung, Hans-Gerhard (eds.). *The Development of Trade Unionism in Great Britain and Germany, 1880-1914.* London: George Allen and Unwin, 1986.

Peetz, David; Preston, Alison; and Docherty, Jim (eds.). *Workplace Bargaining in the International Context: First Report of the Workplace Bargaining Research Project.* Canberra: Department of Industrial Relations, 1993. [Studies Australia, Germany, Sweden, Britain, Japan, Canada, United States, and New Zealand.]

Poole, Michael. *Industrial Relations: Origins and Patterns of National Diversity.* London, Boston, and Henley: Routledge & Kegan Paul, 1986.

_____. *Theories of Trade Unionism.* London: Routledge & Kegan Paul, rev. ed., 1984. [A sociological approach to labor unions.]

Pravada, A., and Ruble, B.A. (eds.). *Trade Unions in Communist States.* London: Allen & Unwin, 1987.

Rothman, M. and others (eds.). *Industrial Relations Around the World: Labor Relations for Multinational Companies.* Berlin: De Gruyter, 1992.

Sisson, K. *The Management of Collective Bargaining: An International Comparison.* Oxford: Basil Blackwell, 1987.

Smith, E. Owen (ed.). *Trade Unions in the Developed Economies.* London: Croom Helm, 1981.

Southall, Roger (ed.). *Trade Unions and the New Industrialisation of the Third World.* London: University of Ottawa Press, 1988.

Sturmthal, Adolf F. *Left of Center: European Labor since World War II.* Urbana: University of Illinois Press, 1983.

Thirkell, John and others (eds.). *Labour Relations and Political Change in Eastern Europe: A Comparative Perspective.* London: UCL Press, 1995.

Valenzuela, J. Samuel, and Goodwin, Jeffrey. *Labor Movements under Authoritarian Regimes.* Cambridge, Massachusetts: Center for European Studies, Harvard University, 1983.

Wilkinson, Barry. *Labour and Industry in the Asia-Pacific: Lessons for the Newly Industrialized Countries.* New York and Berlin: Walter de Gruyter, 1994.

C. NATIONAL STUDIES

C.1 Histories of peak national organizations of unions

Andrews, Gregg. *Shoulder to Shoulder? The American Federation of Labor, the United States and the Mexican Revolution, 1910-1924.* Berkeley, California: University of California Press, 1991.

Clark, Jon; Hartmann, H.; Lau, C.; and Winchester, D. *Trade Unions, National Politics and Economic Management: A Comparative Study of the TUC and the DGB.* London: Anglo-German Foundation for the Study of Industrial Society, 1980.

Dorfman, Gerald A. *British Trade Unionism against the Trades Union Congress.* Stanford, California: Hoover Institution Press, 1983.

Draper, Alan. *A Rope of Sand: The AFL-CIO Committee on Political Education.* New York: Praeger, 1988.

Godson, Roy. *American Labor and European Politics: The AFL as a Transnational Force.* New York: Crane, Russak and Company Inc., 1976.

Hagan, Jim. *The History of the A.C.T.U.* Melbourne: Longman Cheshire, 1981.

Kaufman, Stuart B. *Samuel Gompers and the Origins of the American Federation of Labor, 1848-1896.* Westport, Connecticut: Greenwood Press, 1973.

Kwavnick, David. *Organized Labour and Press Politics: The Canadian Labour Congress, 1956-68.* Montreal: McGill-Queen's University Press, 1972.

Levenstein, Nelson. *Communism, Anti-Communism and the CIO.* Westport, Connecticut: Greenwood Press, 1981.

Lichtenstein, Nelson N. *Labor's War at Home: The CIO in World War II.* New York: Cambridge University Press, 1982.

Martin, Ross M. *TUC: The Growth of a Pressure Group, 1868-1976.* Oxford: Oxford University Press, 1980.

Nicholson, Marjorie. *The TUC Overseas: The Roots of Policy.* London: Allen & Unwin, 1986.

Prochaska, Alice. *History of the General Federation of Trade Unions.* London: Allen & Unwin, 1982.

Radosh, Ronald. *American Labor and United States Foreign Policy.* New York: Random House, 1969. [Mainly a study of the American Federation of Labor.]

Tuckett, Angela. *The Scottish Trade Union Congress: The First 80 Years, 1897-1977.* Edinburgh: Mainstream Publishing, 1986.

C.2 Histories of organized labor in individual countries

C.2.1 Africa

Asante, S. *The Democratization Process and the Trade Unions in Africa.* Brussels: Worldsolidarity, 1993.

Du Toit, M. A. *South African Trade Unions.* Johannesburg: McGraw-Hill, 1976.

Hirson, B. *Yours for the Union: Class and Community Struggles in South Africa, 1930-1947.* London: Zed Books Ltd., 1989.

Luckhardt, Ken, and Wall, B. *Organise or Starve! A History of the South African Congress of Trade Unions.* London: Lawrence and Wishart, 1980.

Odigie, S. A. *State Intervention in Industrial Relations in Nigeria, 1861-1989.* Benin City: [privately printed], 1993.

Otobo, D. *Foreign Interests and Nigerian Trade Unions.* Ibadan: Heinemann Educational, 1986.

C.2.2 British Isles

Boyle, John W. *The Irish Labor Movement in the Nineteenth Century.* Washington, D.C.: Catholic University of America Press, 1988.

Brown, Henry Phelps. *The Origins of Trade Union Power.* Oxford: Oxford University Press, 1986. [Although mainly about Britain, this work contains chapters on the United States, Canada, and Australia.]

Clegg, Hugh A. *A History of British Trade Unions since 1889: Volume II, 1911-1933.* Oxford: Oxford University Press, 1985.

_____. *A History of British Trade Unions since 1889: Volume III, 1934-1951.* Oxford: Oxford University Press, 1994.

Clegg, Hugh A.; Fox, Alan; and Thompson, A. F. *A History of British Trade Unions since 1889: Volume I, 1889-1910.* Oxford: Oxford University Press, 1964.

Coates, Ken, and Topham, Tony. *Trade Unions in Britain.* Nottingham, England: Spokesman, 1980. [A comprehensive profile of British organized labor in the late 1970s.]

Dobson, C.R. *Masters and Journeymen: A Prehistory of Industrial Relations, 1717-1800.* London: Croom Helm, 1980.

Fraser, W. Hamish. *Trade Unions and Society: The Struggle for Acceptance, 1850-1880.* London: George Allen & Unwin, 1974.

Laybourn, Keith *History of British Trade Unionism, c. 1770-1990.* Wolfeboro Falls, New Hampshire: Allan Sutton, 1992.

Leeson, R.A. *Travelling Brothers: The Six Centuries' Road from Craft Fellowship to Trade Unionism.* London: George Allen & Unwin, 1979.

McCarthy, C. *Trade Unions in Ireland, 1894-1960.* Dublin: Institute of Public Administration, 1977.

Pelling, Henry. *A History of British Trade Unionism.* Houndmills, Basingstoke: Macmillan, 5th ed., 1992. [First published in 1963, this is still the main single volume survey work on the UK. It includes an annotated bibliography and statistical appendix.]

Price, Richard. *Labour in British History: An Interpretative History.* London: Routledge, 1990. [First published by Croom Helm in 1986.]

C.2.3 Middle East and Asia

Chalmers, Norma. *Industrial Relations in Japan: The Peripheral Workforce.* London: Routledge, 1989.

Chen, P. K. *The Labour Movement in China.* Hong Kong: Swindon Books, 1985.

Choi, Jang J. *Labor and the Authoritarian State: Labor Unions in South Korean Manufacturing Industries, 1961-1980.* Seoul: Korea University Press, 1989.

Ingleson, John. *In Search of Justice: Workers and Unions in Colonial Java, 1908-1926.* Singapore: Oxford University Press, 1986.

Khan, B. A. *Trade Unionism and Industrial Relations in Pakistan.* Karachi: Royal Book Company, 1980.

Ladjevardi, Habib. *Labor Unions and Autocracy in Iran.* New York: Syracuse University Press, 1985.

Lee, Lai To. *Trade Unions in China, 1949 to the Present: The Organization and Leadership of the All-China Federation of Trade Unions.* Singapore: Singapore University Press, 1986.

Matsuzaki, H. *Japanese Business Unionism: The Historical Development of a Unique Labour Movement.* Sydney: University of New South Wales, 1992.

Mehta, B. L. *The Trade Union Movement in India.* New Delhi: Kanishka Publishing House, 1991.

Okochi K.; Karsh, B.; and Levine, S. (eds.). *Workers and Employers in Japan.* New York and Tokyo: Princeton University Press and University of Tokyo Press, 1974.

Ramachandran, Selvakumaran and Arjunan, Kris. *Trade Unionism in the Malaysian Plantation Industry.* Sydney: University of New South Wales Studies in Human Resource Management and Industrial Relations in Asia, No. 2, 1993.

Shalev, Michael. *Labour and the Political Economy in Israel.* New York: Oxford University Press, 1992.

Stenson, M. R. *Industrial Conflict in Malaya.* London: Oxford University Press, 1970.

Tedjasukmana, I. *The Political Character of the Indonesian Trade Union Movement.* Ithaca: Cornell University Press, 1959.

Verma, Pramod, and Mookherjee, S. *Trade Unions in India.* New Delhi: Oxford and IBA Publishing, 1982.

Woodiwiss, Anthony. *Law, Labour and Society in Japan: From Repression to Reluctant Recognition.* London: Routledge, 1991.

C.2.4 Europe

Agóes, Sándor. *The Troubled Origins of the Italian Catholic Labor Movement, 1878-1914.* Detroit: Wayne State University Press, 1988.

Barkan, J. *Visions of Emancipation: The Italian Workers' Movement since 1945.* New York: Praeger, 1984.

Berghahn, V. R. and Karsten, D. *Industrial Relations in West Germany.* Oxford: Berg, 1987.

Bridgford, Jeff. *The Politics of French Trade Unionism.* Leicester: Leicester University Press, 1991.

European Trade Union Institute. *Information Booklets on the Trade Union Movement: Great Britain, Sweden, Greece, Germany, Italy,*

Austria, Spain and Belgium. Brussels, 1982-87. [A handy and reliable source of up-to-date information.]

Golden, Miriam. *Labor Divided: Austerity and Working-Class Politics in Contemporary Italy.* Ithaca: Cornell University Press, 1988.

Horowitz, Daniel L. *The Italian Labor Movement.* Cambridge, Massachussetts: Harvard University Press, 1963.

Jecchinis, C. *Trade Unionism in Greece.* Chicago: Roosevelt, 1967.

Katzenstein, Peter J. *Corporatism and Change: Austria, Switzerland and the Politics of Industry.* Ithaca: Cornell University Press, 1984.

_____(ed.). *Industry and Politics in West Germany.* Ithaca: Cornell University Press, 1989.

Kauppinen, T. and others. *Labour Relations in Finland.* Helsinki: Ministry of Labour, 1990.

Kesselman, M. (ed.). *The French Workers' Movement: Economic Crisis and Political Change.* London: Allen & Unwin, 1984.

Lange, P.; Ross, G.; and Vannicelli, M. (eds.). *Unions, Change and Crisis: French and Italian Union Strategy and the Political Economy, 1945-1980.* London: Allen & Unwin, 1982.

Lewis, Jill. *Fascism and the Working Class in Austria, 1918-1934: The Failure of Labour in the First Republic.* New York/Oxford: Berg, 1991.

Lipski, Jan J. *KOR: A History of the Workers' Defense Committee in Poland, 1976-1981.* Berkeley: University of California Press, 1985.

Lorwin, Val R. *The French Labor Movement.* Cambridge, Massachusetts: Harvard University Press, 1954.

Macgraw, Roger. *A History of the French Working Class. Vol. I: The Age of the Artisan Revolutionary, 1815-1871; Vol. II: Workers and the Bourgeois Republic.* Oxford and Cambridge, Massachusetts: Blackwell Publishers, 1992.

Markovits, Andrei S. *The Politics of the West German Trade Unions: Strategies of Class and Interest Representation in Growth and Crisis.* Cambridge: Cambridge University Press, 1986. [An impressive study of the post-1945 period; it contains chapters on *IG Metall* and three other major unions as well as a glossary of German terms.]

Moses, John A. *Trade Unionism in Germany from Bismark to Hitler, 1869 to 1933.* London: George Prior Publishers, 1982. 2 vols. [A good survey work with translations of key documents.]

Sassoon, D. *Contemporary Italy: Politics, Economy and Society since 1945.* London: Longman, 1986.

Schneider, Michael. *A Brief History of the German Trade Unions.* Trans. Barrie Selman. Bonn: J.H.W. Dietz Nachf., 1991. [First published in German in 1989, this is an excellent and detailed survey with statistics, a German bibliography, and a list of abbreviations.]

Shkliarevsky, Gennady. *Labor in the Russian Revolution: Factory Committees and Trade Unions, 1917-1918.* New York: St. Martin's Press, 1993.

Spourdalakis, M. *The Rise of the Greek Socialist Party.* London: Routledge, 1988.

Stefancic, D. R. *Robotnik: A Short History of the Struggle for Worker Self-Management and Free Trade Unions in Poland, 1944-1981.* New York: Columbia University Press, 1992.

Thelen, Kathleen A. *Union of Parts: Labor Politics in Postwar Germany.* Ithaca, New York: Cornell University Press, 1992.

Wrigley, Chris (ed.). *Challenges of Labour: Central and Western Europe, 1917-1920.* New York and London: Routledge, 1993.

C.2.5 Latin America and the Caribbean

Decker, David R. *The Political, Economic, and Labor Climate of Argentina.* Philadelphia: University of Pennsylvania Press, 1983.

Epstein, Edward C. *Labor Autonomy and the State in Latin America.* Boston: Unwin Hyman, 1989.

Erickson, K.P. *The Brazilian Corporative State and Working Class Politics.* Berkeley: University of California Press, 1977.

French, John D. *The Brazilian Workers' ABC: Class Conflict and Alliances in Modern São Paulo.* Chapel Hill, North Carolina: University of North Carolina Press, 1992.

Greenfield, Gerald M., and Maram, Sheldon L. *Latin American Labor Organizations.* New York: Greenwood Press, 1987.

La Botz , Dan. *The Crisis of Mexican Labor.* New York: Praeger Publications, 1988.

Lewis, A. *Labour in the West Indies.* London: New Beacon, 1977.

Look Lai, Walton. *Indentured Labour, Caribbean Sugar: Chinese and Indian Migrants to the British West Indies, 1838-1918.* Baltimore and London: Johns Hopkins Studies in Atlantic History and Culture, Johns Hopkins University Press, 1993.

Middlebrook, K.J. *Unions, Workers and the State in Mexico.* San Diego, California: University of California Press, 1991.

Ramdin, Ron. *From Chattel Slave to Wage Earner: A History of Trade Unionism in Trinidad and Tobago.* London: Martin Brian & O'Keefe, 1982.

Rodney, Walter. *A History of Guyanese Working People, 1881-1905.* Baltimore and London: Johns Hopkins University Press, 1981.

C.2.6 North America

Brody, David. *Workers in Industrial America: Essays on the Twentieth Century Struggle.* New York: Oxford University Press, 1980.

Derber, Milton and others. *Labor in Illinois: The Affluent Years, 1945-80.* Urbana: University of Illinois Press, 1989.

Dulles, Foster R., and Dubofsky, Melvyn. *Labor in America: A History.* Arlington Heights, Illinois: Harlan Davidson Inc., 4th ed., 1984.

Filippelli, Ronald L. *Labor in the USA: A History.* New York: Knopf, 1984.

Foner, Philip S. *History of the Labor Movement in the United States.* New York: International Publishers: 1947-92. 10 vols. [A general history from a traditional Marxist perspective.]

Forsey, Eugene. *Trade Unions in Canada, 1812-1902.* Toronto: University of Toronto Press, 1982. [A careful and detailed work.]

Kochan, T.; Katz, H.; and McKerzie, R. *The Transformation of American Industrial Relations.* New York: Basic Books, 1986.

Montgomery, David. *The Fall of the House of Labor: The Workplace, the State and American Labor Activism, 1860-1987.* Cambridge: Cambridge University Press, 1987.

Zieger, Robert H. *American Workers, American Unions, 1920-1985.* Baltimore and London: Johns Hopkins University Press, 1986. [Contains a particularly useful bibliographical essay.]

C.2.7 Oceania

Ford, Bill, and Plowman, David (eds.). *Australian Unions: An Relations Perspective.* Melbourne: Macmillan, 1983.

Hess, Michael. *Unions under Economic Development: Private Sector Unions in Papua New Guinea.* Melbourne: Oxford University Press, 1992.

Martin, Ross M. *Trade Unions in Australia.* Harmondsworth: Penguin, 2nd ed., 1980. [A useful short survey but without a bibliography.]

Roth, H. *Trade Unions in New Zealand: Past and Present.* Wellington: A.H. and A.W. Reed, 1973.

Sutcliffe, J. T. *A History of Trade Unionism in Australia.* Melbourne: Macmillan, 1967. [First published 1921.]

C.3 Industrial relations in particular countries

Anderson, J.; Gunderson, M.; and Ponak, A. (eds.). *Union-Management Relations in Canada*. Don Mills, Ontario: Addison-Wesley, 2nd ed., 1989.

Brown, William (ed.). *The Changing Contours of British Industrial Relations*. Oxford: Blackwell, 1981. [Contains valuable survey findings.]

Chaykowski, R., and Verma, A. (eds.). *Industrial Relations in Canadian Industry*. Toronto: Dryden, 1992.

Deeks, John; Parker, Jane; and Ryan, Rose. *Labour and Employment Relations in New Zealand*. Auckland: Longman Paul, 1994. [Second edition of a text first published as *Labour Relations in New Zealand* in 1989.]

Deery, Stephen, and Plowman, David. *Australian Industrial Relations*. Sydney: McGraw Hill, Sydney, 3rd ed., 1991.

Kessler, Sid, and Bayliss, Fred. *Contemporary British Industrial Relations*. Basingstoke: Macmillan, 1992.

Lipsky, D., and Donn, C. (eds.). *Collective Bargaining in American Industry*. Lexington, Massachusetts: Lexington Books, 1987.

Murphy, T.; Hillery, B.; and Kelly, A. (eds.). *Industrial Relations in Ireland: Contemporary Issues and Developments*. Dublin: University College, Dublin, 1989.

Wrigley, Chris (ed.). *A History of British Industrial Relations, Vol. I 1875-1914; Vol. II: 1914-1939*. Brighton, Sussex: Harvester Press, 1982, 1987.

D. FEATURES OF LABOR UNIONS

D.1 Histories of particular unions

Bagwell, P. S. *The Railwaymen: The History of the National Union of Railwaymen*. London: Allen & Unwin, 1963, 1982. 2 vols.

Bray, Mark, and Rimmer, Malcolm. *Delivering the Goods: A History of the Transport Workers' Union in New South Wales 1886-1986.* Sydney: Allen & Unwin, 1987.

Buckley, K. D. *The Amalgamated Engineers in Australia 1852 - 1920.* Canberra: Australian National University, 1970.

Clinton, Allen. *Post Office Workers: A Trade Union and Social History.* London: Allen & Unwin, 1984.

_____. *The Trade Union Rank and File: Trades Councils in Britain, 1900-1940.* Manchester: Manchester University Press, 1977.

Coates, Ken, and Topham, Tony. *The History of the Transport and General Workers' Union.* Oxford: Basil Blackwell, 1991. [Published as one volume in two parts.]

Croucher, Richard. *Engineers at War.* London: Merlin Press, 1982. [A study of the British engineering unions during World War II.]

Freeman, Joshua B. *In Transit: The Transport Workers' Union in New York City, 1933-1966.* New York: Oxford University Press, 1989.

Galenson, Walter. *The United Brotherhood of Carpenters.* Cambridge, Massachusetts: Harvard University Press, 1983.

Gennard, John. *A History of the National Graphical Association.* London: Unwin Hyman, 1990. [A history of a powerful British craft union.]

Halpern, Martin. *UAW Politics in the Cold War Era.* New York: State University of New York, 1988. [Deals with the United Auto Workers.]

Moldea, Dan E. *The Hoffa Wars: Teamsters, Rebels, Politicians, and the Mob.* New York and London: Paddington Press, 1978.

Murray, Robert, and White, Kate. *The Ironworkers: A History of the Federated Ironworkers' Association of Australia.* Sydney: Hale and Iremonger, 1982.

Schatz, Ronald. *The Electrical Workers: A History of Labor at General Electric and Westinghouse, 1923-1960.* Urbana and Chicago: University of Illinois Press, 1983.

Sheridan, Tom. *Mindful Militants: The Amalgamated Engineering Union in Australia, 1921-72.* Cambridge: Cambridge University Press, 1975.

Tyler, Gus. *Look of the Union Label: A History of the International Ladies' Garment Workers Union.* Armonk, New York: M.E. Sharpe, Inc., 1995.

Wellman, David. *The Union Makes Us Strong: Radical Unionism on the San Francisco Waterfront.* Cambridge: Cambridge University Press, 1995.

Yates, C. A. B.*From Plant to Politics: The Autoworkers' Union in Postwar Canada.* Philadelphia, Pennsylvania: Temple University Press, 1993.

Zieger, Robert H. *Rebuilding the Pulp and Paper Workers' Union, 1933-1941.* Knoxville, Tennessee: University of Tennessee Press, 1984.

D.2 Unions in particular industries or occupations

Aaron, B.; Najita, J.; and Stern, J. *Public-Sector Bargaining.* Washington, D.C.: Bureau of National Affairs, 2nd ed., 1988.

Bain, George S. *The Growth of White-Collar Unionism.* London, Oxford, and New York: Oxford University Press, 1970.

Brody, David. *Steelworkers in America: The Nonunion Era.* Cambridge, Massachusetts: Harvard University Press, 1960.

Daniel, Cletus E. *Bitter Harvest: A History of California Farmworkers, 1870-1941.* Ithaca, New York: Cornell University Press, 1981.

Derickson, Alan. *Workers' Health, Workers' Democracy: The Western Miners' Struggle, 1891-1925.* Ithaca, New York: Cornell University Press, 1988.

Docherty, C. *Steel and Steelworkers: The Sons of Vulcan.* London: Heinemann Educational Books, 1983. [A British study.]

Edwards, C., and Heery, E. *Management Control and Union Power: A Study of Labour Relations in Coal-mining.* Oxford: Clarendon Press, 1989.

Ellem, Bradon. *In Women's Hands: A History of Clothing Trades Unionism in Australia.* Sydney: University of New South Wales Press, 1989.

Feldman, G. D., and Tenfelde, K. (eds.). *Workers, Owners and Politics in Coal Mining: An International Comparison of Industrial Relations.* New York: Berg, 1990.

Freeman, Richard B., and Ichniowksi, Casey. *When Public Sector Workers Unionize.* Chicago: University of Chicago Press, 1988.

Griffin, Gerard. *White-Collar Militancy: The Australian Banking and Insurance Unions.* Sydney: Croom Helm, 1985.

Hatcher, John; Flinn, Michael W.; Church, Roy; Supple, Barry; and Ashworth, William. *The History of the British Coal Industry.* Oxford: Clarendon Press, 1984-93. 5 vols.

Hearn, Mark and Knowles, Harry. *One Big Union: A History of the Australian Workers Union.* Melbourne: Cambridge University Press, 1996.

Jowitt, J. A., and McIvor, A.J. (eds.). *Employers and Labour in the English Textile Industries, 1850-1939.* New York: Routledge, Chapman & Hall, 1988.

Kazin, Michael. *Barons of Labor: The San Francisco Building Trades and Union Power in the Progressive Era.* Urbana: University of Illinois Press, 1987.

Kimeldorf, Howard. *Reds or Rackets? The Making of Radical and Conservative Unions on the Waterfront.* Berkeley: University of California Press, 1988.

Langemann, Ellen C. (ed.). *Nursing History: New Perspectives, New Possibilities.* New York: Teachers College Press, 1983.

Lawn, Martin (ed.). *The Politics of Teacher Unionism: International Perspectives.* London: Croom Helm, 1985.

Levitan, Sar A., and Noden, Alexandra B. *Working for the Sovereign: Employee Relations in the Federal Government.* Baltimore and London: Johns Hopkins University Press, 1983.

Licht, Walter. *Working for the Railroad: The Organization of Work in the Nineteenth Century.* Princeton: Princeton University Press, 1983.

McKelvey, Jean T. (ed.). *Cleared for Takeoff: Airline Labor Relations Since Deregulation.* New York: ILR Press, 1988.

Murphy, Marjorie. *Blackboard Unions: The AFT and the NEA, 1900-1980.* Ithaca, New York: Cornell University Press, 1990.

Myers, F. *European Coal Mining Unions.* Berkeley: University of California Press, 1961.

Peterson, Joyce S. *American Automobile Workers, 1900-1933.* Albany, New York: SUNY Press, 1987.

Schact, John N. *The Making of Telephone Unionism, 1920-1947.* New Brunswick, New Jersey: Rutgers University Press, 1985.

Smith, David F. *White-Collar Unionism in New Zealand.* Wellington: New Zealand Institute of Industrial Relations Research, 1987.

Stomquist, Shelton. *A Generation of Boomers: The Pattern of Railroad Labor Conflict in Nineteenth Century America.* Champaign, Illinois: University of Illinois Press, 1987.

Sturmthal, Adolf (ed.). *White Collar Trade Unions.* Urbana: University of Illinois Press, 1967.

Vinchniac, Judith E. *The Management of Labor: The British and French Iron and Steel Trade Industries, 1860-1918.*

D.3 Ideas and movements

Abell, Aaron I. (ed.). *American Catholic Thought on Social Questions.* New York: Bobbs-Merrill, 1968.

Buhle, Paul. *Marxism in the United States: Remapping the History of the American Left.* London: Verso, 1987.

Cole, G. D .H. *A History of Socialist Thought.* New York: St. Martin's Press, 1953-60. 5 vols. [This important work covers the period from the French Revolution to 1939.]

Derber, Milton. *The American Idea of Industrial Democracy, 1865-1965.* Urbana: University of Illinois, 1970.

Dubofsky, Melvyn. *We Shall Be All: A History of the Industrial Workers of the World.* Urbana and Chicago: University of Illinois Press, 2nd ed., 1988.

Farrell, Frank. *International Socialism and Australian Labour: The Left in Australia, 1919-1939.* Sydney: Hale & Iremonger, 1981.

Fogarty, Michael P.*Christian Democracy in Western Europe, 1820-1953.* London: Routledge, 1957.

George, G. S. *The History of Management Thought.* Englewood-Cliffs, New Jersey: Prentice Hall, 2nd ed., 1972.

Holton, Bob. *British Syndicalism, 1910-14: Myths and Realities.* London: Pluto Press, 1976.

Kernig, C. D. (ed.). *Marxism, Communism and Western Society: A Comparative Encyclopaedia.* Vol.VIII. New York: Herder and Herder, 1973.

Lichtheim, George. *A Short History of Socialism.* London: Weidenfeld & Nicolson, 1970.

Lieberman, Sima. *Labor Movements and Labor Thought : Spain, France, Germany and the United States.* New York: Praeger, 1986.

Linden, Marcel van der, and Thorpe, Wayne (eds.). *Revolutionary Syndicalism: An International Perspective*. Aldershot, England: Scolar Press, 1990.

Marshall, Peter. *Demanding the Impossible: A History of Anarchism*. London: HarperCollins, 1992.

Olssen, Erik. *The Red Feds: Revolutionary Industrial Unionism and the New Zealand Federation of Labour, 1908-14*. Auckland: Oxford University Press, 1988.

Ridley, F. F. *Revolutionary Syndicalism in France: The Direct Action of its Time*. Cambridge: Cambridge University Press, 1970.

Roberts, David D. *The Syndicalist Tradition and Italian Fascism*. Chapel Hill: University of North Carolina Press, 1979.

Seaton, Douglas P. *Catholics and Radicals: The Association of Catholic Trade Unionists and the Labor Movement, from Depression to Cold War*. Lewisburg, Pennsylvania: Bucknell University Press, 1981.

Wilson, Edmund. *To the Finland Station: A Study in the Writing and Acting of History*. London: Macmillan London Ltd., rev. ed., 1972. [First published 1940 and still a classic account of the history of the intellectual left up to 1917.]

D.4 Biographies of labor leaders (See also A.2)

Barnard, John. *Walter Reuther and the Rise of the Auto Workers*. Boston, Massachusetts: Little, Brown & Company, 1983.

Carlson, Peter. *Roughneck: The Life and Times of Big Bill Haywood*. New York: Norton, 1983.

Clark, Paul and others. *Forging a Union of Steel: Philip Murray, SWOC, & the United Steelworkers*. Ithaca, New York: Cornell ILR Press, 1987.

Dickmyer, Elizabeth R. *Reuther: A Daughter Strikes*. Southfield, Michigan: Spelman Publishers Division, 1989.

Dubofsky, Melvyn, and Tine, Warren Van. *John L. Lewis: A Biography.* New York: Quadrange/New York Times Book Company, 1977.

————. (eds.). *Labor Leaders in America.* Urbana: University of Illinois Press, 1986.

Fraser, Steven. *Labor Will Rule: Sidney Hillman and the Rise of American Labor.* New York: The Free Press, 1991.

Kirby, R. G. and Musson, A. E. *The Voice of the People: John Doherty, 1798-1854.* Manchester: Manchester University Press, 1975.

Morgan, Kenneth O. *Labour People: Hardie to Kinnock.* Oxford and New York: Oxford University Press, 2nd ed., 1992. [First published 1987.] [Contains a useful bibliography.]

Prothero, I. *Artisans and Politics in Nineteenth Century London: John Gast and His Times.* Folkestone: Dawson, 1979.

Reid, Fred*Keir Hardie: The Making of a Socialist.* London: Croom Helm, 1978.

Rickard, John. *H.B. Higgins: The Rebel as Judge.* Sydney: Allen & Unwin, 1985.

Robinson, Archie. *George Meany and His Times: A Biography.* New York: Simon & Schuster, 1981.

Salvatore, Nick. *Eugene V. Debs: Citizen and Socialist.* Urbana: University of Illinois Press, 1982.

Sloane, Arthur A. *Hoffa.* Cambridge, Massachusetts and London: MIT Press, 1991.

Tsuzuki, Chushichi. *Tom Mann, 1856-1941: The Challenge of Labour.* Oxford: Clarendon Press, 1991.

Wright, W. W. *G. D. H. Cole and Socialist Democracy.* New York: Oxford University Press, 1979.

Ziegler, Robert H. *John L. Lewis, Labor Leader.* Boston, Massachusetts: Twayne, 1988.

D.5 Women's labor and labor unions

Blewett, Mary H. *Men, Women, and Work: Class, Gender and Protest in the New England Shoe Industry, 1780-1910.* Urbana, Illinois: University of Illinois Press, 1988.

Briskin, Linda and McDermott, Patricia (eds.). *Women Challenging Unions: Feminism, Democracy and Militancy.* Toronto: University of Toronto Press, 1994.

Cook, Alice and others (eds.). *Women and Trade Unions in Eleven Industrialized Countries.* Philadelphia: Temple University Press, 1984.

Cunnison, S. and Stageman, J. *Feminizing the Unions: Challenging the Culture of Masculinity.* Aldershot, England: Avebury, 1995.

Drake, Barbara. *Women in Trade Unions.* London: Virago Press, 1984. [A classic study first published in 1920.]

Dye, Nancy S. *As Equals and as Sisters: Feminism, Unionism, and the Women's Trade Union League of New York.* Columbia, Missouri: University of Missouri Press, 1980.

Foner, Philip S. *Women and the American Labor Movement from Colonial Times to the Eve of World War I.* New York: The Free Press, 1979.

_____. *Women and the American Labor Movement from World War I to the Present.* New York: The Free Press, 1980.

Gabin, Nancy F. *Feminism in the Labor Movement: Women and the United Auto Workers, 1935-1975.* Ithaca, New York: Cornell University Press, 1990.

Gronman, Carol, and Norton, Mary B. (eds.). *"To Toil the Livelong Day": America's Women at Work, 1780-1980.* Ithaca, New York: Cornell University Press, 1987.

Groote, Gertjan de and Schrover, Marlon (eds.). *Women Workers and Technological Change in the Nineteenth and Twentieth Centuries*. London: Taylor and Francis, 1995.

Kenneally, James J. *Women and American Trade Unions*. St. Albans, Vermont: Eden Press Women's Publications Inc., 1978.

Kennedy, Susan E. *If All We Did Was to Weep at Home: A History of White Working-Class Women in America*. Bloomington: Indiana University Press, 1979.

Kessler-Harris, Alice. *Out to Work: A History of Wage-Earning Women in the United States*. New York: Oxford University Press, 1982.

Lawrence, Elizabeth. *Gender and Trade Unions*. Bristol, Pennsylvania: Taylor and Francis, 1994.

Lindsey, Charles, and Duffin, Lorna (eds.). *Women and Work in Pre-industrial England*. London: Croom Helm, 1985.

Norwood, Stephen H. *Labor's Flaming Youth: Telephone Operators and Workers' Militancy, 1878-1923*. Urbana, Illinois: University of Illinois Press, 1990.

Ruiz, Vicki L. *Cannery Women/Cannery Lives: Mexican Women, Unionization and the Californian Food Processing Industry, 1930-1950*. Albuquerque: University of New Mexico Press, 1987.

Soldon, Norbert C. *Women in British Trade Unions, 1874-1976*. Totowa, New Jersey: Rowman and Littlefield, 1979.

_____. (ed.). *The World of Women's Trade Unionism: Comparative Historical Essays*. Westport, Connecticut: Greenwood Press, 1985.

Summerfield, Penny. *Women Workers in the Second World War: Production and Patriarchy in Conflict*. London and Dover, New Hampshire: Croom Helm, 1984.

Ward, Kathryn (ed.). *Women Workers and Global Restructuring*. Ithaca, New York: ILR Press, Cornell University, 1990.

D.6 Democracy in labor unions

Blanpain, Roger (ed.). *Trade Union Democracy and Industrial Relations.* Special Issue, *Bulletin of Comparative Industrial Relations,* No. 17. Deventer, Netherlands and Boston: Kluwer Law and Taxation Publishers, 1988.

Botz, Dan la. *Rank and File Rebellion: Teamsters for a Democratic Union.* London: Verso, 1990.

Clark, Paul F. *The Miners' Fight for Democracy: Arnold Miller and the Reform of the United Mine Workers.* Ithaca, New York: New York State School of Industrial and Labor Relations, Cornell University, 1981.

Davis, Edward M. *Democracy in Australian Trade Unions: A Comparative Study of Six Unions.* Sydney: Allen & Unwin, 1987.

Dickenson, Mary. *Democracy in Trade Unions: Studies in Membership Participation and Control.* St. Lucia: University of Queensland Press, 1982.

Elias, Patrick, and Wing, Keith. *Trade Union Democracy, Members' Rights and the Law.* London and New York: Mansell Publishing Limited, 1987.

Fosh, Patricia, and Heery, Edmund. *Trade Unions and Their Members: Studies in Union Democracy and Organisation.* London: Macmillan, 1990.

Gould, William. *Black Workers in White Unions: Job Discrimination in the United States.* Ithaca, New York: Cornell University Press, 1977. [An important study which deals with the period from 1964 to 1973.]

McLauglin, Doris B., and Shoomaker, Anita L. *The Landrum-Griffin Act and Union Democracy.* Ann Arbor, Michigan: University of Michigan Press, 1979.

Nyden, Philip W. *Steelworkers' Rank-and-File: The Political Economy of a Union Reform Movement.* New York: Praeger, 1984.

Undy, R., and Martin, R. *Ballots and Trade Union Democracy.* Oxford: Basil Blackwell, 1984.

D.7 Industrial democracy

Dickman, Howard. *Industrial Democracy in America.* La Salle, Illinois: Open Court, 1987.

European Trade Union Institute. *Workers' Representation and Rights in the Workplace in Western Europe.* Brussels: European Trade Union Institute, 1990.

Industrial Democracy in Europe. International Research Group. *Industrial Democracy in Europe Revisited.* Oxford and New York: Oxford University Press, 1993.

Lammers, Cornelius J., and Széll, György (eds.). *International Handbook of Participation in Organizations: Vol. I-Organizational Democracy: Taking Stock.* Oxford: Oxford University Press, 1988.

Lichtenstein, Nelson, and Howell, John H. (eds.). *Industrial Democracy in America: The Ambiguous Promise.* New York: Woodrow Wilson Center Press and Cambridge University Press, 1993.

Russell, R., and Rus V. (eds.). *International Handbook of Participation in Organizations for the Study of Organizational Democracy, Co-operation and Self-Management: Vol. II-Ownership and Participation.* Oxford: Oxford University Press, 1991.

D.8 Inter-union relations

Elgar, J., and Simpson, R. *The TUC's Bridlington Principles and Inter-Union Competition.* London: London School of Economics, The Centre for Economic Performance, Discussion Paper No. 160, 1993.

Waddington, Jeremy. *The Politics of Bargaining: The Merger Process and British Trade Union Structural Development, 1892-1987.* London: Mansell, 1995.

D.9 Labor disputes

Cohn, Samuel. *When Strikes Make Sense-and Why: Lessons from the Third Republic of French Coal Miners.* New York: Plenum Books, 1993.

Batstone, Eric, Boraston, Ian and Frankel, Stephen. *The Social Organization of Strikes.* Oxford: Basil Blackwell, 1978.

Dobson, C. R. *Masters and Journeymen: A Prehistory of Industrial Relations, 1717-1800.* London: Croom Helm, 1980. [Much of this work deals with labor disputes.]

Edwards, P. K. *Strikes in the United States, 1881-1974.* Oxford: Basil Blackwell, 1981.

Filippelli, Ronald L. (ed.). *Labor Conflict in the United States: An Encyclopedia.* New York and London: Garland Publishing, Inc., 1990.

Fisher, Malcolm. *Measurement of Labour Disputes and Their Economic Effects.* Paris: Organisation for Economic Co-operation and Development, 1973.

Franzosi, Roberto. *The Puzzle of Strikes: Class and State Strategies in Postwar Italy.* Cambridge: Cambridge University Press, 1995.

Haimson, L. H., and Tilley, C. (eds.). *Strikes, Wars and Revolutions in an International Perspective.* Cambridge: Cambridge University Press, 1989.

Hanami, Tadashi, and Blanpain, Roger (eds.). *Industrial Conflict Resolution in Market Economies: A Study of Australia, the Federal Republic of Germany, Italy, Japan and the USA.* Deventer, Netherlands: Kluwer Law and Taxation Publishers, 1984.

Hyman, Richard. *Strikes.* Aylesbury: Fontana, 3rd ed., 1984. [First published 1972.]

Ingham, Geoffrey K. *Strikes and Industrial Conflict: Britain and Scandinavia.* London: Macmillan, 1974.

Iremonger, John and others (eds.). *Strikes: Studies in Twentieth Century Australian Social History.* Sydney: Angus and Robertson and the Australian Society for the Study of Labour History, 1973.

Jackson, Michael P. *Strikes.* New York: St. Martin's Press, 1987. [An excellent study of strike trends in Britain, United States, and Australia.]

Lane, Tony, and Roberts, Kenneth. *Strike at Pilkingtons.* London: Collins/Fontana, 1971. [A rare work: a readable and interesting account of a major strike while it was in progress.]

Loewenberg, J.J. and others. *Compulsory Arbitration: An International Comparison.* Lexington, Massachusetts: D.C. Heath, 1976.

Metcalf, David and Milner, Simon (eds.). *New Perspectives on Industrial Disputes.* London and New York: LSE/Routledge, 1993.

Rachleff, Peter. *Hard-Pressed in the Heartland: The Hormel Strike and the Future of the American Labor Movement.* Boston: South End Press, 1993.

Reddy, Y. R. K. *Trends, Patterns and Impact of Strikes: The Indian Case.* New Delhi, India: Society for Policy Analysis and Development, 1990.

Ross, Arthur M., and Hartman, Paul T. *Changing Patterns of Industrial Conflict.* New York and London: John Wiley & Sons, Inc., 1960. [The pioneering international study of the topic.]

Shorter, Edward; and Tilly, Charles. *Strikes in France, 1830-1968.* Cambridge: Cambridge University Press, 1974. [A major pioneering work based largely on an analysis of 36,000 individual disputes from 1890 to 1935.]

Tilly, Charles, Tilly, Louise and Tilly, Richard. *The Rebellious Century.* Harvard: Cambridge University Press, 1975.

Walsh, Kenneth. *Strikes in Europe and the United States: Management and Incidence.* London: Frances Pinter, 1983.

Waters, Malcolm. *Strikes in Australia: A Sociological Analysis of Industrial Conflict.* Sydney: George Allen & Unwin, 1982.

Winterton, Jonathan, and Winterton, R. *Coal, Crisis and Conflict: The 1984-5 Miners' Strike in Yorkshire.* Manchester: Manchester University Press, 1989.

Zetka, James R. Jnr. *Militancy, Market Dynamics and Workplace Authority: The Struggle Over Labor Process Outcomes in the U.S. Automobile Industry, 1946 to 1973.* Albany, New York: State University of New York Press, 1995.

E. LABOR AND ITS ENVIRONMENT

E.1 The experience and study of work

Argyle, Michael. *The Social Psychology of Work.* Harmondsworth: Penguin, 1974. [First published 1972.]

Boris, Eileen. *Home to Work: Motherhood and the Politics of Industrial Housework in the United States.* New York: Cambridge University Press, 1994.

Braverman, Harry. *Labor and Monopoly Capital: The Degradation of Work in the Twentieth Century.* New York: Monthly Review Press, 1974.

Burnett, John (ed.). *Useful Toil: Autobiographies of Working People from the 1820s to the 1920s.* London: Allen Lane, 1974.

Chinoy, E. *Automobile Workers and the American Dream.* Urbana: University of Illinois Press, 2nd ed., 1992.

Cross, Gary. *A Quest for Time: The Reduction of Work in Britain and France, 1840-1940.* Berkeley: University of California Press, 1989.

Brody, David. *In Labor's Cause: Main Themes on the History of the American Worker.* New York and Oxford: Oxford University Press, 1993.

Derickson, Alan. *Workers' Health, Workers' Democracy: The Western Miners' Struggle, 1891-1925.* Ithaca, New York: Cornell University Press, 1989.

Doeringer, P. B., and Piore, M. J. *Internal Labor Markets and Manpower Analysis.* Lexington, Massachusetts: D.C. Heath, 1971.

Edwards, R. *Contested Terrain: The Transformation of the Workplace in the Twentieth Century.* London: Heinemann, 1979.

Fraser, Ronald (ed.). *Work: Twenty Personal Accounts.* Harmondsworth: Penguin, 1968, 1969. 2 vols.

Gordon, D. M.; Edwards, R.; and Reich, M. *Segmented Work, Divided Workers: The Historical Transformation of Labor in the United States.* Cambridge: Cambridge University Press, 1982.

Grint, Keith. *The Sociology of Work: An Introduction.* Oxford and Cambridge: Basil Blackwell and Polity Press, 1991.

Harrison, Royden, and Zeitlin, Jonathan (eds.). *Divisions of Labour: Skilled Workers and Technological Change in 19th Century Britain.* Urbana: University of Illinois Press, 1985.

International Labour Office. *Encyclopaedia of Occupational Health and Safety.* Geneva: International Labour Office, 3rd ed., 1983. [First published 1930.]

Jacoby, S. M. *Employing Bureaucracy: Managers, Unions and the Transformation of Work in American Industry, 1900-1945.* New York: Columbia University Press, 1985.

Joyce, Patrick (ed.). *The Historical Meanings of Work.* Cambridge: Cambridge University Press, 1987.

Kamata, Satoshi. *Japan in the Passing Lane: An Insider's Account of Life in a Japanese Auto Factory.* New York: Pantheon, 1982.

Lincoln, J. R. and Kalleberg, A. L. *Culture, Control and Commitment: A Study of Work Organization and Work Attitudes in the United States and Japan.* Cambridge: Cambridge University Press, 1990.

Montgomery, David. *Workers' Control in America: Studies in the History of Work, Technology, and Labor Struggles.* Cambridge: Cambridge University Press, 1979.

Pahl, R. E. (ed.). *On Work: Historical, Comparative and Theoretical Perspectives.* Oxford: Basil Blackwell, 1988.

Roediger, David R., and Foner, Philip S. *Our Own Time: A History of American Labor and the Working Day.* New York: Verso Paper, 1989.

Rule, J. *The Experience of Labour in Eighteenth Century England.* London: Croom Helm, 1981.

Shaiken, Harley. *Work Transformed.* New York: Holt, Rinehart and Winston, 1984.

Shields, John (ed.). *All Our Labours: Oral Histories of Working Life in Twentieth Century Sydney.* Sydney: University of New South Wales, 1992.

Strom, Sharon H. *Beyond the Typewriter: Gender, Class and the Origins of Modern American Office Work, 1900-1930.* Chicago: University of Illinois, 1992.

Terkel, Studs. *Working.* New York: Pantheon Books, 1972. [Also available in paperback by Avon.]

Whipp, Richard. *Patterns of Labour: Work and Social Change in the Pottery Industry.* London: Routledge Chapman and Hall, 1990.

E.2 Industrial archaeology

Atkinson, Frank. *The Great Northern Coalfield, 1700-1900.* Newcastle upon Tyne: Frank Graham, 3rd ed., 1979.

Fogg, Charles. *Chains and Chainmaking.* Aylesbury, Buckinghamshire: Shire Publications Ltd., 1981.

Gale, W. K. V. *Ironworking.* Aylesbury, Buckinghamshire: Shire Publications Ltd., 1981.

Gorman, John. *Images of Labour: Selected Memorabilia from the National Museum of Labour History.* London: Scorpion Publishing Ltd., 1985.

Griffin, A. R. *The Collier.* Aylesbury, Buckinghamshire: Shire Publications Ltd., 1982.

Hudson, Nenneth. *Industrial Archaeology: A New Introduction.* London: J. Baker, 3rd ed., 1976.

Raistrick, Arthur. *Industrial Archaeology: A Historical Survey.* London and New York: Eyre Methuen, 1972.

Trinder, Barrie (ed.). *The Blackwell Encyclopedia of Industrial Archaeology.* Oxford: Basil Blackwell, 1992.

E.3 Unions and politics

Alba, Victor. *Politics and the Labor Movement in Latin America.* Stanford: Stanford University Press, 1968.

Carsten, F. L. *The German Workers and the Nazis.* Aldershot, England: Scolar Press, 1995.

Chatterji, Rakhahari. *Unions, Politics and the State: A Study of Indian Labour Politics.* New Delhi: South Asian Publishers, 1980.

Conner, Valerie J. *The National War Labor Board: Stability, Social Justice and the Voluntary State in World War I.* Chapel Hill: University of North Carolina Press, 1983.

Davidson, Roger. *Whitehall and the Labour Problem in Late-Victorian and Edwardian Britain.* London: Croom Helm, 1985.

Davis, Mike. *Prisoners of the American Dream: Politics and Economy in the History of the U.S. Working Class.* London: Verso, 1986.

Draper, Alan. *A Rope of Sand: The AFL-CIO Committee on Political Education, 1955-1967.* New York: Praeger, 1989.

Filippelli, Ronald L. *American Labor and Postwar Italy, 1943-1953: A Study of Cold War Politics*. Stanford: Stanford University Press, 1989.

Fink, Leon. *Workingmen's Democracy: The Knights of Labor and American Politics*. Urbana: University of Illinois Press, 1983.

Form, William. *Segmented Labor, Fractured Politics: Labor Politics in American Life*. New York and London: Plenum Press, 1995.

Fulcher, James. *Labour Movements, Employers and the State: Conflict and Co-operation in Britain and Sweden*. Oxford: Clarendon Press, 1991.

Gall, Gilbert. *The Politics of Right to Work: The Labor Federations as Special Interests, 1943-1979*. Westport, Connecticut: Greenwood Press, 1988.

Haydu, Jeffrey. *Between Craft and Class: Skilled Workers and Factory Politics in the US and Britain, 1890-1922*. Berkeley: University of California Press, 1988.

Katzenstein, Peter J. *Corporatist and Change: Austria, Switzerland and the Politics of Industry*. Ithaca: Cornell University Press, 1984.

Kirchner, Emil J. *Trade Unions as Pressure Group in the European Community*. Farnborough, England: Saxon House, 1977.

Korpi, Walter. *The Democratic Class Struggle*. London: Routledge Kegan Paul, 1983.

Marks, Gary. *Unions in Politics: Britain, Germany, and the United States in the Nineteenth and Early Twentieth Centuries*. Princeton: Princeton University Press, 1989.

McMullin, Ross. *The Light on the Hill: The Australian Labor Party, 1891-1991*. Melbourne: Oxford University Press, 1991.

Mink, Gwendolyn. *Old Labor and New Labor in American Political Development: Union, Party and State, 1875-1920*. Ithaca, New York: 1986.

Minkun, Lewis. *The Contentious Alliance: Trade Unions and the Labour Party.* New York: Columbia University Press, 1993. [A study of the British Labour Party and organized labor.]

Montgomery, David. *The Fall of the House of Labor: The Workplace, the State, and American Radicalism, 1865-1925.* New York: Cambridge University Press, 1987.

Murray, Robert. *The Split: Australian Labor in the Fifties.* Melbourne: Cheshire, 1970. [Reprinted by Hale & Iremonger, Sydney, in 1984.]

Pelling, Henry. *A Short History of the Labour Party.* London: Macmillian, 8th ed., 1985. [First published 1961.]

Pimlott, Ben, and Cook, Chris. (eds.). *Trade Unions in British Politics: The First 250 Years.* New York and London: Longman, 2nd ed., 1991 [First published 1982.]

Rehmus, Charles M. and others (eds.). *Labor and American Politics: A Book of Readings.* Ann Arbor, Michigan: University of Michigan Press, 1978. [A useful compilation.]

Roxborough, Ian. *Unions and Politics in Mexico: The Case of the Automobile Industry.* Cambridge: Cambridge University Press, 1984.

Singleton, Gwynnoth. *The Accord and the Australian Labour Movement.* Melbourne: Melbourne University Press, 1990.

Taylor, R. *The Trade Union Question in British Politics: Government and Unions since 1945.* Oxford: Blackwell, 1994.

Tolliday, S., and Zeitlin, J. (eds.). *Shopfloor Bargaining and the State.* Cambridge: Cambridge University Press, 1985.

Wilentz, Sean. *Chants Democratic: New York City and the Rise of the Working Class, 1788-1850.* New York: Oxford University Press, 1984.

E.4 Employers

Chubb, B. *FIE: Federation of Irish Employers, 1942-1992.* Dublin: Gill and MacMillan, 1992.

Cohen, Isaac. *American Management and British Labor: A Comparative Study of the Cotton Spinning Industry.* Westport, Connecticut: Greenwood Press, 1990.

Gillespie, Richard. *Manufacturing Knowledge: A History of the Hawthorne Experiments.* New York: Cambridge University Press, 1991.

Gospel, H. F., and Littler, C.R. (eds.). *Managerial Strategies and Industrial Relations.* London: Heinemann, 1983.

Harris, Howell J. *The Right to Manage: Industrial Relations Politics of American Business in the 1940s.* Madison, Wisconsin: University of Wisconsin Press, 1982.

Hattam, Victoria C. *Labor Visions and State Power: The Origins of Business Unionism in the United States.* Princeton: Princeton University Press, 1993.

Jacoby, S. (ed.). *Masters to Managers: Historical and Comparative Perspectives on American Employers.* New York: Columbia University Press, 1991.

Jowitt, J. A. and McIvor, A. J. (eds.). *Employers and Labour in the English Textile Industries, 1850-1939.* London: Routledge, Chapnon & Hall, 1988.

Myer, Stephen. *The Five Dollar Day: Labor Management and Social Control in the Ford Motor Company, 1908-1921.* Albany: New York: State University of New York Press, 1981.

Tolliday, S., and Zeitlin, J. (eds.). *The Power to Manage? Employers and Industrial Relations in Comparative-Historical Perspective.* London and New York: Routledge, 1991.

Windmuller, J.P., and Gladstone, A. (eds.). *Employer Associations and Industrial Relations: A Comparative Study.* New York: Oxford University Press, 1984.

Wright, Christopher. *The Management of Labour: A History of Australian Employers.* Melbourne: Oxford Unversity Press, 1995.

E.5 Social histories and immigration

Atkinson, Frank. *North-East England: People at Work, 1860-1960.* Ashbourne, Derbyshire: Moorland Publishing, 1980. [Contains a comprehensive collection of photographs.]

Babson, Steve. *Building the Union: Skilled Workers and Anglo-Gaelic Immigrants in the Rise of the UAW.* New Brunswick, New Jersey and London: Rutgers University, 1991.

_____. *Working Detroit: The Making of a Union Town.* Detroit: Wayne State University Press, 1984.

Bahl, Vinay. *The Making of the Indian Working Class.* New Delhi: Sage, 1995.

Berlanstein, Lenard R. *Rethinking Labor History: Essays on Discourse and Class Analysis.* Champaign, Illinois: University of Illinois Press, 1993.

Bernstein, Irving. *The Lean Years-A Study of the American Worker, 1920-33.* Boston: Houghton Mifflin, 1960.

_____. *The Turbulent Years: A History of the American Worker, 1933-1941.* Boston: Houghton Mifflin, 1969.

Bodnar, John. *Workers' World: Kinship, Community, and Protest in an Industrial Society, 1900-1940.* Baltimore: Johns Hopkins University Press, 1982.

Brody, David. *Workers in Industrial America: Essays on the Twentieth Century Struggle.* New York: Oxford University Press, 1980.

Cantor, Milton (ed.). *American Working-Class Culture: Explorations in American Labor and Social History.* Westport, Connecticut: Greenwood Press, 1979.

Cherwinski, W., and Kealey, G. (eds.). *Lectures in Canadian Labour and Working-Class History.* St. Johns, Newfoundland: Committee on Canadian Labour History, St. Johns, 1985.

Crew, David. *Town in the Ruhr: A Social History of Bochum, 1860-1914.* New York: Columbia University Press, 1979.

Docherty, James C. *Newcastle: The Making of an Australian City.* Sydney: Hale & Iremonger, 1983.

Drummond, Diane K. *Crewe: Railway Town, Company and People, 1840-1914.* Aldershot, England: Scolar Press, 1995.

Dublin, Thomas. *Women at Work: The Transformation of Work and Community in Lowell, Massachusetts, 1826-1860.* New York: Columbia University Press, 1979.

Emberson-Bain, 'Atu. *Labour and Gold in Fiji.* Melbourne: Cambridge University Press, 1994.

Faue, Elizabeth. *Community of Suffering & Struggle: Women, Men and the Labor Movement in Minneapolis, 1915-1945.* Chapel Hill: University of North Carolina Press, 1991.

Frisch, Michael, and Walkowitz, Daniel J. (eds.). *Working-Class America: Essays on Labor, Community and American Society.* Urbana: University of Illinois Press, 1983.

Fry, Eric (ed.). *Common Cause: Essays in Australian and New Zealand Labour History.* Wellington and Sydney: Allen & Unwin/Port Nicholson Press, 1986.

Gardner, James B., and Adams, George R. (eds.). *Ordinary People and Everyday Life: Perspectives on the New Social History.* Nashville, Tennessee: American Association for State and Local History, 1983.

Gerstle, Gary. *Working-Class Americanism: The Politics of Labor in a Textile City, 1914-60.* New York: Cambridge University Press, 1989.

Gorman, John. *Banner Bright: An Illustrated History of the British Trade Union Movement.* London: Allen Lane, 1974.

Guerin-Gonzales, Camile, and Strikwerda, Carl (eds.). *The Politics of Immigrant Workers: Labor Activism and Migration in the World Economy since 1830.* New York and London: Holmes and Meier, 1993.

Gutkind, P.; Cohen, R.; and Copans, J. (eds.). *African Labor History.* London: Sage, 1978.

Gutman, Herbert G. *Work, Culture, and Society in Industrializing America; Essays in American Working-Class and Social History.* Oxford: Blackwell, 1977.

Hoerder, Dirk (ed.). *"Struggle a Hard Battle": Essays on Working-Class Immigrants.* De Kalb, Illinois: North Illinois University Press, 1986.

Kealey, G., and Patmore, G. (eds.). *Canadian and Australian Labour History: Towards a Comparative Perspective.* Brisbane: Australian Society for the Study of Labour History, 1990.

Kleinberg, S. J. *The Shadow of the Mills; Working-Class Families in Pittsburgh, 1870-1907.* Pittsburgh: University of Pittsburgh Press, 1989.

Kornblum, William. *Blue-Collar Community.* Chicago: University of Chicago Press, 1974. [Deals with American steelworkers.]

Krause, Paul. *The Battle for Homestead, 1880-1892: Politics, Culture, and Steel.* Pittsburgh and London: Pittsburgh University Press, 1992.

Laslett, John H. M. *Nature's Noblemen: The Fortunes of the Independent Collier in Scotland and the American Midwest, 1855-1889.* Los Angeles: UCLA Institute of Industrial Relations Monograph and Research Series No. 34, 1983.

Lever-Tracy, Constance. *A Divided Working Class: Ethnic Segregation and Industrial Conflict in Australia.* London and New York: Routledge & Kegan Paul, 1988.

Lichtenstein, Nelson, and Myer, Stephen (eds.). *On the Line: Essays in the History of Auto Work.* Champaign: University of Illinois Press, 1989.

Lummis, Trevor. *The Labour Aristocracy, 1850-1914.* Aldershot, England: Scolar Press, 1994.

McCord, Norman. *North East England: An Economic and Social History.* London: Batsford Academic, 1979.

Mohl, Raymond A., and Betten, Neil. *Steel City. Urban and Ethnic Patterns in Gary, Indiana, 1906-1950.* New York and London: Holmes and Meier, 1986.

Moody, J. Carroll, and Kessler-Harris, Alice (eds.). *Perspectives on American Labor History: The Problems of Synthesis.* De Kalb: Northern Illinois Press, 1989.

Norris, P.; Townsend, A. R.; and Dewdney, J. C. *Demographic and Social Change in the Durham Coalfield.* Working Papers 23, 24, 25. Durham: University of Durham, Department of Geography, Census Research Unit, 1983 and 1984. [An impressive study of 65,000 records of individuals from the population censuses of 1851, 1861, 1871 and 1881 covering occupational change, birthplace, and migration.]

Oestreicher, Robert L. *Solidarity and Fragmentation: Working People and Class Consciousness in Detroit, 1875-1900.* Urbana: University of Illinois Press, 1986.

Prude, Jonathan. *The Coming of Industrial Order: Town and Factory Life in Rural Massachusetts, 1800-1860.* New York: Cambridge University Press, 1983.

Rorabaugh, W. J. *The Craft Apprentice: From Franklin to the Machine Age in America.* New York: Oxford University Press, 1986.

Saunders, Kay (ed.). *Indentured Labour in the British Empire, 1834-1920.* London: Croom Helm, 1984.

Schultz, Ronald. *The Republic of Labor: Philadelphia Artisans and the Politics of Class, 1720-1830.* New York: Oxford University Press, 1993.

Shergold, Peter R. *Working-Class Life: The "American Standard" in Comparative Perspective, 1899-1913.* Pittsburgh: Pittsburgh University Press, 1982. [An important, and all too rare, study of comparative working-class living standards in Pittsburgh, Pennsylvania, and Birmingham, England.]

Stearns, Peter. *Lives of Labour: Work in a Maturing Industrial Society.* London: Croom Helm, 1975.

Thompson, E. P. *The Making of the English Working Class.* London: Victor Gollancz, 1963. [Better known from the Penguin edition of 1968; the 1986 reprint contains an updated postscript.]

Zippay, Allison. *From Middle Income to Poor: Downward Mobility among Displaced Steelworkers.* New York: Praeger, 1991.

E.6 Labor and race

Draper, Alan. *Conflict of Interests: Organized Labor and the Civil Rights Movement in the South, 1954-1968.* Ithaca, New York: ILR Press, 1994.

Harris, William H. *The Harder We Run: Black Workers since the Civil War.* New York: Oxford University Press, 1982.

Honey, Michael K. *Southern Labor and Black Civil Rights: Organizing Memphis Workers.* Urbana: University of Illinois Press, 1993.

Kent, Ronald C. and others (eds.). *Culture, Gender, Race, and U.S. Labor Relations.* Westport, Connecticut and London: Greenwood Press, 1993.

Rachleff, Peter S. *Black Labor in the South: Richmond, Virginia, 1865-1890.* Philadelphia: Temple University Press, 1984.

Ramdin, Ron. *The Making of the Black Working Class in Britain.* Aldershot, England: Gower, 1987.

Roediger, David R. *The Wages of Whiteness: Race and the Making of the American Working Class.* London and New York: Verso, 1991.

Saxton, Alexander. *The Indispensable Enemy; Labor and the Anti-Chinese Movement in California.* Berkeley: University of California Press, 1971.

E.7 Labor sociology

Halle, David. *America's Working Man: Work, Home, and Politics among Blue-Collar Property Owners.* London and Chicago: University of Chicago Press, 1984.

Marwick, Arthur. *Class: Image and Reality in Britain, France and the USA since 1930.* Glasgow: Fontana/Collins, 1980.

Reiner, Robert. *The Blue-Coated Worker: A Sociological Study of Police Unionism.* Cambridge: Cambridge University Press, 1978.

Willis, Paul E. *Learning to Labour: How Working Class Kids Get Working Class Jobs.* Guildford, England: Gower, 1978.

Zweig, Ferdynand. *The British Worker.* Harmondsworth, England: Penguin, 1952.

_____. *The Worker in an Affluent Society: Family Life and Industry.* London: Heinemann, 1962.

E.8 Labor and the law

Aaron, Benjamin, and Wedderburn, K. W. (eds.). *Industrial Conflict: A Comparative Legal Survey.* New York: Crane, Russak, 1972.

Atleson, J. *Values and Assumptions in American Labor Law.* Amherst, Massachusetts: University of Massachusetts Press, 1983.

Bennett, Laura. *Making Labour Law in Australia: Industrial Relations, Politics and Law.* Sydney: The Law Book Company Limited, 1994.

Betten, Lammy. *International Labor Law: Selected Issues.* Deventer, Netherlands and Boston: Kluwer, 1993.

Blanpain, Roger. *Labour Law and Industrial Relations of the European Community.* Deventer, Netherlands: Kluwer Law and Taxation Publishers, 1991.

_____. *Labour Law and Industrial Relations of the European Union: Maastricht and Beyond, from a Community to a Union.* Deventer, Netherlands: Kluwer Law and Taxation Publishers, 1992.

Blanpain, R. and Engels, C. (eds.). *Comparative Labour Law and Industrial Relations in Industrialized Market Economies.* Deventer, Netherlands and Boston: Kluwer Law and Taxation Publishers, 5th ed., 1993.

CCH Canada Ltd. *Canadian Master Labour Guide: A Guide to Canadian Labour Law.* Don Mills, Ontario: CCH Canada, 8th ed., 1993.

Creighton, Breen, and Stewart, Andrew. *Labour Law: An Introduction.* Sydney: The Federation Press, 2nd ed., 1994. [First published 1989. This is an introduction to Australian labor law.]

Deery, Stephen J., and Mitchell, J. (eds.). *Labour Law and Industrial Relations in Asia: Eight Country Studies.* Melbourne: Longman Cheshire, 1993. [The countries covered are: Hong Kong, Malaysia, Singapore, South Korea, Japan, the Philippines, Thailand, and Taiwan.]

England, J., and Rear, J. *Industrial Relations and Law in Hong Kong.* Hong Kong: Oxford University Press, 1981.

Ewing, K. D. *Trade Unions, the Labour Party and the Law: A Study of the Trade Union Act 1913.* Edinburgh: Edinburgh University Press, 1982.

Forbath, W. E. *Law and the Shaping of the American Labor Movement.* Cambridge, Massachusetts: Harvard University Press, 1991.

Hanson, Charles. *The Closed Shop: A Comparative Study of Public Policy and Trade Union Security in Britain, the USA and West Germany.* London: Gower, 1982.

Hepple, Bob (ed.). *The Making of Labour Law in Europe: A Comparative Study of Nine Countries up to 1945.* London: Mansell Publishing Limited, 1986.

Hill, Herbert. *Black Labor and the American Legal System* Vol. I: *Race, Work and the Law*. Washington, D.C.: Bureau of National Affairs, 1977.

Kahn-Freund, Otto and others. *Labour Law and Politics in the Weimar Republic.* Oxford: Basil Blackwell, 1981.

International Labour Office. *Freedom of Association: Digest of Decisions and Principles of the Freedom of Association Committee of the Governing Body of the ILO.* Geneva: International Labour Office, 3rd ed., 1985. [First published 1972.]

_____. *Freedom of Association and Collective Bargaining.* Geneva: International Labour Office, 1994.

Linnick, Stuart and others. *The Developing Labor Law.* Washington, D.C.: Bureau of National Affairs, 2nd ed., 3rd supplement, 1988.

Sugeno, Kazuo. *Japanese Labor Law.* Seattle: University of Washington Press, 1992.

Tomlins, Christopher L. *Law, Labor and Ideology in the Early American Republic.* New York: Cambridge University Press, 1993. [Covers the period from 1790 to 1850.]

_____. *The State and the Unions: Labor Relations, Law, and the Organized Labor Movement in America, 1880-1960.* New York: Cambridge University Press, 1985.

E.9 Labor and the media

Jones, Stephen G. *The British Labour Movement and Film, 1918-1939.* London: Routledge & Kegan Paul, 1988.

Puette, W. J. *Through Jaundiced Eyes: How the Media View Organized Labor.* Ithaca, New York: ILR Press, 1992. [Covers the period from 1930 to 1991 and includes film and television as well as the press.]

E.10 Labor and the economic environment

Bain, George S., and Elsheikh, Farouk. *Union Growth and the Business Cycle: An Econometric Analysis.* Oxford: Basil Blackwell, 1976. [This work examines various theories used to explain union growthusing historical data from eight countries.]

Bluestone, B., and Harrison, B. *The Great U-Turn: Corporate Restructuring and the Polarizing of America.* New York: Basic Books, 1985.

Booth, A. L. *The Economics of the Trade Union.* Cambridge: Cambridge University Press, 1995.

Brown, E. H. Phelps, and Browne, Margaret H. *A Century of Pay: The Course of Pay and Production in France, Germany, Sweden, the United Kingdom, and the United States of America, 1860-1960.* New York: St. Martin's Press, 1968.

Brunetta, R., and Dell'Aringa, C. (eds.). *Labour Relations and Economic Performance.* London: Macmillan, 1990.

Bruno, Michael, and Sachs, Jeffrey D. *The Economics of Worldwide Stagflation.* Cambridge, Massachusetts: Harvard University Press, 1985.

Clarke, Thomas (ed.). *International Privatisation: Strategies and Practices.* Berlin: Walter de Gruyter, 1994.

Ehrenberg, R. G., and Smith, R. S. *Modern Labour Economics: Theory and Public Policy.* Glenview, Illinois: Scott Foresman, 3rd ed., 1988.

Fallick, J. and Elliott, R. (eds.). *Incomes Policies, Inflation and Relative Pay.* London: Allen & Unwin, 1981.

Flanagan, R. J.; Soskice, D. W.; and Ulman, L. *Unionism, Economic Stabilisation and Incomes Policies: European Experience.* Washington, D.C.: The Brookings Institute, 1983.

Handy, L .J. *Wages Policy in the British Coalmining Industry: A Study of National Wage Bargaining.* Cambridge: Cambridge University Press, 1981.

Hirsch, Barry T. *Labor Unions and the Economic Performance of Firms*. Kalamazoo, Michigan: W.E. Upjohn Institute, 1991.

Hirsch, Barry T., and Addison, John T. *The Economic Analysis of Unions: New Approaches and Evidence*. Boston: Allen & Unwin, 1986.

Hyman, R., and Streeck, W. *New Technology and Industrial Relations*. Oxford: Basil Blackwell, 1988.

Kaufman, Bruce E. *The Economics of Labor Markets and Labor Relations*. Chicago: The Dryden Press, 2nd ed., 1989.

Kleinknecht, A.; Mandel, E.; and Wallerstein, I. (eds.). *New Findings in Long Wave Research*. London: Macmillan, 1992.

Lane, Christel, *Management and Labour in Europe*. Aldershot, England: Edward Elgar, 1989.

Lewis, H. G. *Union Relative Wage Effects: A Survey*. Chicago: University of Chicago Press, 1986.

Lindberg, Leon N., and Maier, Charles S. (eds.). *The Politics of Inflation and Economic Stagnation*. Washington, D.C.: The Brookings Institute, 1985.

Marshall, Ray. *Unheard Voices: Labor and Economic Policy in a Competitive World*. New York: Basic Books, 1987.

Mishels, Lawrence, and Voos, Paula (eds.). *Unions and Economic Competitiveness*. Armonk, New York: M.E. Sharpe, 1992.

Piore, Michael J., and Sabel, Charles F. *The Second Industrial Divide*. New York: Basic Books, 1984.

Reynolds, Lloyd G. and others. *Labor Economics and Labor Relations*. Englewood Cliffs, New Jersey: Prentice-Hall, 9th ed., 1986. [A useful introductory text.]

Schott, Kerry. *Policy, Power and Order: The Persistence of Economic Problems in Capitalist Societies*. New Haven, Connecticut: Yale University Press, 1984.

Sengenberger, Werner and Campbell, Duncan (eds.). *International Labour Standards and Economic Interdependence.* Geneva: International Institute for Labour Studies, 1994.

Villa, Paola. *The Structuring of Labour Markets: An Analysis of the Italian Construction and Steel Industries.* Oxford: Oxford University Press, 1987. [Contains an important introduction to the study of labor market structures.]

Weinberg, Paul. *European Labor and Multinationals.* New York: Praeger, 1978.

E.10 The crisis of labor since 1980

Beaumont, P. B. *The Decline of Trade Union Organisation.* London: Croom Helm, 1987.

Brierley, William (ed.). *Trade Unions and the Economic Crisis of the 1980s.* London: Gower, 1987.

Clark, G. L. *Unions and Communities Under Siege: American Communities and the Crisis of Organized Labor.* Cambridge: Cambridge University Press, 1989.

Coates, D. *The Crisis of Labour: Industrial Relations and the State in Contemporary Britain.* Oxford: Philip Allan, 1989.

Craver, C. B. *Can Unions Survive? The Rejuvenation of the American Labor Movement.* New York: New York University Press, 1993.

Crouch, C. and Traxler, F. *Organized Industrial Relations in Europe: What Future?* Aldershot, England: Avebury, 1995.

Evatt Foundation. *Unions 2001: A Blueprint for Trade Union Activism.* Sydney: Evatt Foundation, 1995. [Deals with Australian unions.]

Galenson, Walter. *Trade Union Growth and Decline: An International Study.* Westport, Connecticut: Praeger, 1994.

Goldfield, Michael. *The Decline of Organized Labor in the United States.* Chicago: University of Chicago Press, 1985.

Gourevitch, P.; Martin, A.; Ross, G.; Bornstein, S.; Markovits, A.; and Allen, C. *Unions and Economic Crisis: Britain, West Germany and Sweden.* London: George Allen & Unwin, 1984.

Grant, John. *Blood Brothers: The Division and Decline of British Trade Unions.* London: Weidenfeld & Nicholson, 1992.

Hoerr, John P. *And the Wolf Finally Came: The Decline of the American Steel Industry.* Pittsburgh: University of Pittsburgh Press, 1988.

Juris, H.; Thompson, M.; and Daniels, W. (eds.). *Industrial Relations in a Decade of Change.* Madison, Wisconsin: Industrial Relations Research Association Series, 1985.

Kochan, T. (ed.) *Challenges and Choices Facing American Unions.* Cambridge, Massachusetts: MIT Press, 1985.

Lash, Scott, and Urry, J. *The End of Organized Capitalism.* Madison, Wisconsin: Wisconsin University Press, 1987.

Lipset, Seymour M. (ed.). *Unions in Transition: Entering the Second Century.* San Francisco: Institute for Contemporary Studies, 1986.

Moody, Kim. *An Injury to All: The Decline of American Unionism.* London and New York: Verso, 1988.

Perrucci, C. and others (eds.). *Plant Closings: International Context and Social Costs.* New York: Walter de Gruyter, 1988.

Regini, Marino (ed.). *The Future of Labour Movements.* London: Sage Publications, 1992.

Smith, Chris and others (eds.). *The New Workplace and Trade Unionism.* New York: Routledge, 1995. [A British study.]

Strauss, George and others (eds.). *The State of the Unions.* Madison, Wisconsin: Industrial Relations Research Association Series, 1991.

Turner, L. *Democracy at Work: Changing World Markets and the Future of Labor Unions.* Ithaca, New York: Cornell University Press, 1991.

Weil, David. *Turning the Tide: Strategic Planning for Labor Unions.* New York: Lexington Books, 1994.

Willman, Paul; Morris, Tim; and Aston, Beverly. *Union Business: Trade Union Organisation and Financial Reform in the Thatcher Years.* Cambridge: Cambridge University Press, 1993.

ABOUT THE AUTHOR

JAMES C. DOCHERTY was born in Gosford, New South Wales, in 1949 and is a graduate of the University of Newcastle (B.A.) and the Australian National University (M.A., Ph.D.). Before joining the Australian Bureau of Statistics in 1978, he worked as a research assistant with the Australian Dictionary of Biography at the Australian National University. Since 1984 he has been employed mainly as a researcher by the federal Department of Industrial Relations. In January 1990 he became an Honorary Research Associate with the National Centre for Australian Studies at Monash University. His publications include: *Selected Social Statistics of New South Wales, 1861-1976* (1982); *Newcastle: The Making of an Australian City* (1983); "English Settlement in Newcastle and the Hunter Valley" in James Jupp (ed.), *The Australian People: An Encyclopedia of the Nation, Its People and Their Origins* (1988); and *Historical Dictionary of Australia* (1992). He was an editorial consultant and contributor to *Australians: Historical Statistics* (1987), contributed the entries on Australian history, politics, industrial relations, and institutions in David Crystal (ed.), *The Cambridge Encyclopedia* (1990), and was an editor and contributor to *Workplace Bargaining in the International Context* (1993).

357